European Practice Library

EC
ELECTRICITY LAW

By

Leigh Hancher, MA, LLB, PhD
Professor of Economic Law,
Erasmus University, Rotterdam.

Chancery Law Publishing
A Division of John Wiley & Sons Ltd,
London, New York, Chichester, Brisbane, Toronto, Singapore

Published in the United Kingdom by
Chancery Law Publishing Ltd
22 Eastcastle Street
London W1N 7PA

Published in North America by
John Wiley & Sons, Inc
7222 Commerce Center Drive
Colorado Springs, CO 80919
USA

First reprinted 1993

Typeset by The Setting Studio
Newcastle upon Tyne

Printed in Great Britain by
Ipswich Book Company Ltd.

ISBN 0471 93646 4

A copy of the CIP entry for this book is available from the British Library.

The moral right of the author has been asserted.

To Hans

Contents

CONTENTS

Foreword

This is a very timely monograph. This year sees a sustained effort to complete the Community's internal market. Professor Hancher looks at progress so far in liberalising electricity supply and shows that, while much has been achieved, there is still a long way to go.

By a combination of legislation and application of Treaty rules in specific cases, the Community institutions are setting about the task of bringing internal market principles to bear in energy markets, which are of course of enormous significance for the rest of industry. Under phase two of the current policy, a small number of large electricity users will be freed from some of the shackles of monopoly. There will be some effect on prices, but a further effort will be needed to open up markets and competition policy will play its part in that process.

Even in the countries where governments have shaken up monopolistic structures, the results so far are uneven. Further and irreversible changes are needed before electricity prices and supply are determined by market conditions. Incumbent monopolies tend to regard change with apprehension and electricity is no different from other industries in this respect. The Commission's task is to bring about change in a way which provides for open trade and competition, while preserving security and public service.

The co-operation of the various parties concerned is essential. The scope for individual action under the Community's competition rules is considerable and the Commission is open to representations from all sides on how competition is actually developing in electricity markets. Competition policy's impetus to industrial change has proved effective in other sectors and it will play a full part in electricity liberalisation. Professor Hancher's book is an important guide to this process.

Sir Leon Brittan QC

Preface

This book has been written at a time when the application of Community law to the utilities sector is developing at a rapid pace. After 30 years of relative immunity from the reach of competition law, the European electricity supply industry is now being compelled to adjust to the fact that the internal market for electricity is fast becoming a reality.

This work provides a guide to the application of European law to the electricity sector. Although as yet, there are relatively few Court cases or Commission decisions dealing expressly with this sector, there is certainly a growing body of law relating to the utilities sector. This book attempts to extrapolate a number of general principles from the case law and from Commission decisions, and to apply these principles to the electricity sector.

The first chapter traces the development of Community policy towards the industry. Chapters 2-5 deal with the general principles of Community law. They are intended primarily as an introduction for those with little familiarity with European law. Each chapter draws on examples from the electricity sector in order to explain the application of the general principles on free movement, competition and state aids to this particular sector.

The second part of the book deals specifically with what might be termed "European electricity law". Chapters 6-8 examine the application of Community law to concrete issues in the generation, transmission, distribution and pricing of electricity. Chapter 9 examines the complexities of the environmental dimension of electricity generation, while Chapter 10 discusses the increasingly important subject of public procurement.

The reader who is searching for an analysis of the compatibility of any particular national electricity regulatory system with the principles of Community law must, I am afraid, look beyond the pages of this book. This work deals exclusively with European law, and does not venture to examine any particular national regime in its light. It is of course to be hoped that it will nonetheless serve as a useful guide to those who embark on the latter task.

I would like to acknowledge the helpful insights into Community competition law provided by John Ferry at Le Boeuf Lamb Leiby and MacRae in Brussels.

Leigh Hancher
Rotterdam
February 1992

Tables

TREATIES, CONVENTIONS AND PROTOCOLS

EC REGULATIONS

EC DIRECTIVES, DECISIONS, RECOMMENDATIONS

PROPOSED EC DIRECTIVES

Chapter 1
EC Electricity Policy: Forging a Framework

1. Introduction

This chapter aims to outline the evolution of the European Commission's **1.1** policies towards the European electricity sector over the last five years. The main policy documents relating to the sector are examined, with the aim of highlighting the policy goals which the Community institutions intend to realise through the application of the primary rules of Community law (*i.e.* the relevant articles of the Treaties of Paris and Rome) and, where applicable, by the adoption of secondary legislation.

The following section sketches out the various measures relating to the electricity sector which the Community had adopted prior to the publication of its Working Document on the Internal Energy Market in May 1988 (see section 3 below). Section 3 outlines the priorities for the electricity sector set down by the Commission in its 1988 Working Document, and briefly examines the legal instruments which the Commission has selected as best suited to achieve those objectives. Section 4 traces the progress that has been made towards the completion of the internal market for electricity since the publication of the Working Document. The final section outlines the most recent policy initiatives.

2. Background

Prior to the adoption of the internal energy market, discussed in section 3, **1.2** below, Community involvement in the electricity sector had been minimal. The main focus of Community attention after the oil crises of 1973–74 and 1978 had been on security of supply, with special attention to security of oil supplies. Electricity featured only indirectly in the Community's various policy documents. Secondary legislation, including Directives, Decisions and Recommendations etc dealt in the main with security-related matters.

(i) Emergency stocks

Directive 75/339/EEC (OJ 1975 L153/35), for example, obliged Member **1.3** States to take all appropriate measures to oblige electricity producers to maintain, permanently, a minimum level of stocks of fossil fuel at their

3

thermal power stations sufficient to ensure at all times the continuation of electricity supplies for a period of at least 30 days.

(ii) Restrictions on fuel use

1.4   Directive 75/404/EEC (OJ 1975 L178/24) required that the conclusion of new contracts for the supply of natural gas to power stations, the extension of contracts on expiry and the construction of new power stations using natural gas were to be subject to prior authorization by the authorities of the Member States responsible for the power station concerned. This Directive has now been annulled.

Directive 75/405/EEC also stipulated that the construction of new power stations which will use fuel oils exclusively or mainly, as well as the conversion of existing power stations to burn such fuels exclusively or mainly must be subject to approval by the competent authorities (OJ 1975 L178/26).

(iii) Information

(a) Notification of investments

1.5   Since 1972 Member States have been required to furnish the EC Commission with information on certain major investments in the natural gas, petroleum and electricity sectors. In the case of electricity, the investment projects concerned are;
(a) conventional thermal power stations (generators with a unit capacity of 200mw or more);[1]
(b) hydro-electric power stations (with a capacity of 50mw or more); and
(c) overhead transmission lines if they have been designed for a voltage of 345kv or more, and underground and submarine transmission cables if they have been designed for a voltage of 100kv or more and constitute essential links in national or international interconnecting networks.

Notification is to cover projects on which work is scheduled to start within three years from 1 January of the year in question. The notification must also indicate the volume of capacities in commission or under construction or which are scheduled to be taken out of commission within three years.

To enable the Member States to comply with their obligations the undertakings concerned must submit details of such investment projects before 15 January of each year. Commission Regulation (EEC) 3025/77 (OJ 1977 L358/12) lays down additional requirements as to the form of notification to be made to the Commission.

(b) Mutual exchange of information on siting of plants

1.6   An EC Council Resolution of 1978 (OJ 1978 C286/1) stresses the need for mutual exchange of information on matters relating to the siting

---

[1] Nuclear Power stations are notifiable under Arts 40– 42 of the Euratom Treaty.

of power stations at Community level. Resolutions are of course, non-binding.

(c) Pricing and tariffs

In 1982 the Council adopted a non-binding recommendation on energy **1.7** prices and tariffs (Council Rec 81/924). This Recommendation sets out various broad principles which should govern the design of electricity tariff structures in the Member States. It is discussed further in Chapter 7, and is reproduced at Appendix 1.

(d) Freedom of establishment and freedom to provide electricity services

As part of its general programme to abolish restrictions on freedom of **1.8** establishment and on the freedom to provide services in the Community, the Council adopted EC Directive 66/162/EEC (JO 1966 L42/584). This Directive applies to electricity generation, transmission and distribution (Art 2(1)(2)(a)), albeit with numerous restrictions.[2-3] So far as the transmission of electricity is concerned, the Directive applies only to the abolition of restrictions on freedom of establishment. In other words it does not require abolition of restrictions on freedom to provide transmission services.

It should be noted that the electricity sector, in common with the energy sector in general was excluded from the scope of the various Council Directives on the award of public works and public supply contracts, and the Directive 71/304/EEC on the abolition of restrictions to provide services in respect of public works contracts (JO 1971 L185/1). These Directives are further discussed in the context of public procurement and the electricity sector (Chap 10).

3. The Internal Energy Market –
1988 Working Document

(i) The Commission's priorities

The first comprehensive discussion of the European electricity sector is to **1.9** be found in the Commission's Working Document on the Internal Energy Market, published in May 1988. This Document deals with the general issues involved in realising a single market for energy. It endorses the Commission's commitment to a more competition-orientated approach to energy market integration, based on the application of the general principles of Community law. The Document contains several annexes

---

[2-3] See especially Art 3(b) and preamble, second recital.

which firstly examine the degree of market integration in each energy sector, secondly list the potential obstacles to the creation of a more open market and thirdly outline the Commission's priorities. Annex IV of the Document deals with the electricity sector. Electricity production, transmission and distribution are discussed separately.

In the case of *production,* the Commission stresses that:

> "the concept of an open internal market in electricity production implies the production of electricity on an economically competitive basis, subject only to the protection of the environment and the requirements of the Community energy policy".

The obstacles to the realization of this goal fall into several categories.

1.10   (a) Differences of fiscal and financial treatment of producer utilities and differing criteria of access to capital markets and state aids which result in distortions in overall production costs. The financial situation of utilities is further influenced by the treatment of asset valuation and depreciation policy and conditions of access to capital markets, for which rules vary between the Member States. These differences are inevitably reflected in the pre-tax prices of electricity and thus distort competition.

(b) Differences in the consent procedures for the authorization of new construction, particularly site authorization, which result in differences between utilities in their ability to manage properly their investment programmes, which have consequences for overall product costs.

(c) Differences in the costs of fuels for electricity production. Statutory and de facto restrictions on the fuels which electricity producers may have access to as well as certain requirements to use specified quantities high-cost indigenous fuels produce differences in pre-tax electricity prices.

(d) Differences between Member States concerning standards of environmental protection and other security measures, affect, differentially, the costs of electricity production. "An open internal market would imply some degree of harmonization of such requirements".

1.11   The obstacles to a more open market for electricity *transmission* are divided into two categories: organizational and technical. Although internal high-voltage system interconnection within national boundaries is highly developed, trade between these grids is managed largely on a co-operative as opposed to a competitive basis. The national grid networks and the international interconnectors are themselves operated by concessionary monopolies, many of which are publicly owned. The Commission opines that it is "an issue for consideration as to whether a change in the operational as distinct from the ownership system would be conducive to further opening of the internal market".

1.12   The Commission also notes that it intends to consider the arguments for and against the use of the interconnection systems on a "common carriage" basis, although it recognises that "the arguments put forward by electricity producers concerning the technical problems of management and security of supply are very powerful and are borne out by experience in other countries." In particular it recognises that there are certain technical requirements for the operational management of transmissions to reduce the inevitable power losses to a practical minimum. Finally, it recognises that several Member States, including Ireland and Greece are not directly connected to any of the major international networks.[4]

At the distribution level, the Commission considers that:

"to be consistent with the principle of an open market, distributors should charge prices which, inter alia accurately reflect the cost of the most economic electricity supplies available to them".

The conditions under which private industrial auto-producers and private producers using renewable energy sources may dispose of their surplus energy, however, vary significantly between the Member States.

Distribution utilities throughout the Community in turn enjoy a statutory or de facto monopoly to deliver electricity to certain classes of consumer. Although this situation was unlikely to change for low and medium **1.13** consumers the Commission believed that "there is an argument for a degree of harmonization of the behavioural patterns of distributors towards consumers, in terms of the technical conditions of supply and pricing and tariff structure practices". While the latter was already the subject of a Council Recommendation[5], the issue of a more regulatory approach fell to be considered, "for example by limiting the duration of exclusive contracts".

For *large consumers,* the issue of contractual rights to transport electricity through distribution and transmission networks was briefly considered. The technical and economic problems which this might cause for the existing public supply utilities were noted as matters which merited further study but were not further discussed.

Finally, the Commission discusses a number of specific issues relating to **1.14** the transfer and sale of electricity. These included firstly, the wide variations in the taxation of electricity. These result not only from differences in the rate of value-added tax but also other specific taxes levied in the different Member States. The Commission concluded that: "the magnitude of these variations is sufficient to induce distortions of competition, unrelated to the economies of electricity production or transport." Secondly the problem of the general lack of transparency in the prices charged to large customers, in the prices at which electricity is transferred between systems and in the prices paid by producers for fuels is highlighted.

In conclusion the "potential problem" areas which were identified for

---

[4] Finance for the extension of these networks is currently provided through the REGEN initiative.
[5] 81/924/EEC.

priority consideration were as follows:

1.15   19. Fiscal treatment and access to the financial market
– Differential fiscal impositions on electricity prices and the modalities of such impositions.
– Differing financial treatment of and requirements for electricity utilities.
20. Standards and administrative constraints
– Lack of harmonization of technical requirements for electricity supply to consumers.
– Differing standards for environmental protection and security requirements for electricity production plant.
– Differing requirements for the authorization of the construction of power plants.
21. Monopolies and exclusive rights
– Monopolies of electricity distribution to consumers.
– Exclusive rights of the use of distribution and interconnecting transmission systems, particularly insofar as this affects consumers' ability to obtain supplies from sources other than their allotted distributor.
– Lack of liberal access to fuel supplies by electricity producers. .
22. Prices and costs of electricity
– Lack of harmonization of pricing and tariff structure practices.
– Lack of transparency of electricity prices to large consumers, electricity production costs, prices for electricity transfer between systems and fuel prices for electricity production.
– General consideration of the role of transparency in an open internal market.
23. Infrastructure
– Lack of high-tension electricity interconnection of Ireland and Greece with other Member States.
– The existing limitation of the operational aspects of the high-voltage interconnection system (see also para 17 above) insofar as they affect aspects of the common carrier concept and the economics of electricity supply to consumers.
– Operational aspects of the high-voltage system affecting the producers' requirements for peaking and reserve capacities.

(ii) Legal implications of the Working Document

1.16   It is evident that different strategies and different legal instruments are required to deal with these various priorities. The issues listed in paragraphs 19, 20 and 22 are primarily matters for harmonization via the adoption of secondary legislation.[6] In 1990 the Council adopted Council Directive 90/377/EEC on price transparency (OJ 1990 L185/6, see Appendix 3),

---

[6] As the completion of the internal electricity market falls within the objectives listed in Art 8A, harmonization measures can be adopted under Art 100A EEC in so far as the relevant subject matters falls within the province of the EEC Treaty (see further Chap 2). Art 100A provides that "the Council shall, acting by a qualified majority on a proposal from the Commission in cooperation with the European Parliament and after consulting the Economic and Social Committee, adopt the measures necessary for the approximation of the provisions laid down by law, regulation or administrative action in Member States which have as their object the establishment and functioning of the internal market."

but the Commission has yet to reach the stage of producing proposals on issues covered in the remaining paragraphs. (The Council Directives on transit through natural gas grids and through high-voltage electricity grids are discussed in detail in Chap 6 and Appendix 5.)

Paragraph 21 deals with matters which concern the application of the basic principles of Community law. The various monopoly and exclusive rights enjoyed by electricity suppliers are singled out, as are the restrictions on free access to fuel supplies by electricity producers.

It is interesting to note the absence of any detailed discussion on statutory **1.17** and other forms of restrictions on imports and exports in this Annex. Nor are the potential problems caused by the public status of many firms and the availability of state subsidization for their activities examined. As to the first issue, paragraphs 55-61 of the main text of the Working Document sketch out some of the main problems involved.

The relevant text reads as follows: **1.18**

B. State monopolies of a commercial character

55. Two considerations should govern reflections in this respect:

(1) In accordance with the particular characteristics of the energy sector, there has been a large recourse to such national monopolies (with very diverse characteristics) in several fields such as petroleum, gas and electricity.

(2) Such monopolies are subject to the rules of the Treaty and more particularly Article 37, which provides that when the transition period has ended no discrimination regarding the conditions under which goods are produced and marketed may exist between nationals of Member States.

56. In the annexes the different types of existing monopolies are explained in detail as well as the potential obstacles that they can present to a better integration of the Community energy market.

This is a fundamental area as much for its diversity and judicial complexity as also for the potential effect that each important change could bring about in the Community's energy structure.

57. The Commission considers therefore that this is a priority area. It considers also that for the reasons detailed above a definitive solution merits a more careful examination.

58. For the moment the Commission proposes in this regard the following orientations:

60. Exclusive rights to import and export other products

Member States have reserved for themselves or delegated to public or private enterprises exclusive rights for the importing or exporting of other energy products. This is particularly the case in the gas and electricity fields.

The Commission should examine in what manner these measures are compatible with the provisions of Article 37 and the actions it may be suitable to take in this respect.

61. Exclusive rights of transport and distribution

For certain energy products such as electricity and gas for example, the States or the regional entities give exclusive right of transport and distribution to public and private enterprises.

It is appropriate to make an inventory and to examine in what sense these exclusive rights prevent or make more difficult exchanges between Member States. It is accordingly appropriate to examine if such a situation is compatible with the rules of the Treaty and more particularly with Articles 30 and 37.

More specifically in the transport domain and in regard to the distribution of electricity and gas (even if these two sectors have characteristics which set them apart) two essential economic problems seem to dominate:
– how to encourage the free transit of natural gas and electricity inside the Community while having a high level of security of supply and having the conditions of transport on an economic basis? This would permit a transport or distribution company to have direct access to a resource;
– under what possible conditions direct access to a resource might be extended to a large industrial consumer.

Both these two options imply that third parties could have the possibility to have access, on payment of a reasonable tariff, to existing transport networks (i.e. "common carriage" common transport for third parties).

1.19   It is understood that the work on the compilation of the inventory referred to in paragraph 61 has now been completed by Directorate-General IV, responsible for Competition, and that the Commission is now in the processing of examining the compatibility of the various national regulations with Articles 30 and 37 EEC. In March 1991 it announced that it would be commencing procedures against those nine Member States which maintained statutory restrictions in force.[7] DG IV is also preparing a programme of action to tackle the privileged financial relations between governments and state-sector companies. These issues are discussed more fully in Chapters 2, 4 and 5.

4. Progress towards the Single Market

1.20   It is clear that creation of an internal market for electricity is a complex matter both politically and legally. Two factors emerge clearly from the Working Document.

First, its main objective is to outline the obstacles to the creation of a single market and the opening up of national markets for energy. It does not seek to change the objectives of Community energy policy as previously spelled out in various Council Resolutions and Commission Communications. While it would be over-stating the case to speak of a coherent energy policy at Community level, there has been a consistent

[7] Agence Europe 22 March 1991.

concern at least since the first oil crisis of 1973-74, to achieve a number of objectives.

These include the reduction of dependence on imported sources of **1.21** energy, through the assurance of adequate, stable and secure supplies of energy, particularly using indigenous or renewable sources, and maximum transparency and uniformity in approach in the field of pricing. In addition the Community has committed itself to striking an adequate balance between energy and environmental objectives.[8] The Working Document would therefore appear to be placing the emphasis on a pro-competition or "market-oriented" approach to achieving these objectives.

Second, to achieve the dual objectives of opening up the energy market while supporting the general objectives of energy policy, the Commission has very few policy instruments at its disposal. As paragraphs 55 *et seq* above make clear, the key instruments available to the Commission without recourse to secondary legislation, are the powers contained in the chapters of the EEC Treaty on the removal of quantitative restrictions on trade between Member States, and on competition.

A problematic aspect facing the Commission in 1988 was that these **1.22** powers had rarely been applied to the energy sector, or indeed to any of the utility sectors such as water, transport or telecommunications. These industries share many but not all of the features of the electricity market: a concentration of state ownership and monopoly organization, long lead times for new investments. In addition they are charged with public service functions.

Efforts to liberalise these utility sectors, and particularly the telecommunications sector, have undoubtedly served as a source of inspiration in the energy field. More importantly for our purposes, the drive to remove obstacles to the creation of an internal telecommunications market by 1992 has yielded up some highly significant legal precedents.

In the course of 1991 the Court of Justice handed down a series of **1.23** judgments applying the EC competition rules to public service monopolies. These cases are discussed in detail in later chapters, and in particular in Chapter 4. It is important to note here, however, that they have now resolved a number of issues over which there had been a substantial legal debate (see also Chap 10). The recent clarification of its legal powers has undoubtedly strengthened Commission resolve to tackle the energy sector.

Certainly, the "locomotive effect" that the liberalization of electricity markets can play in stimulating competition on primary fuel markets has never been lost sight of at Community level. Electricity has remained at the focus of a number of recent Community initiatives related to the Internal Energy Market initiative.

In a document published in November 1989 entitled "Energy and the **1.24** Environment",[9] the Commission considered various scenarios for the

---

[8] The current objectives of Community energy policy are contained in the Council Resolution of September 1986 (OJ 1986 C241/1).
[9] COM (89) 369 final, Brussels, November 1990.

growth of demand for electricity in the Community, all of which point to the urgent need to reduce SO_2, CO_2 and NO_x emissions. In its Communication on the internal energy market in November 1988 the Council of Energy Ministers of the Community reiterated as one of the Community's basic energy objectives for the period 1986-95:

> "that the achievement of a satisfactory balance between energy and the environment – in accordance with the Single Act – must constitute a major goal of the Community's work". [10]

This objective is reiterated in the recitals to Directive 90/547/EEC on transit through high-voltage grids.[11] Chapter 9 of this book examines the subject of electricity and the environment.

1.25   More recently, in a document entitled "Security of Supply, the Internal Energy Market and Energy Policy", published in mid-1990[12] the Commission has singled out electricity for further special treatment. This communication, which was drawn up prior to Iraq's invasion of Kuwait, proclaims that security of supply must be the central pillar of Community energy policy, and that the realization of the internal energy market calls for the development of new concepts in this respect.

It considers two options: national security measures must either be replaced by Community norms or should be incorporated in a Community framework, and finally favours the latter "strategy of convergence". It suggests that this framework could be established in two stages.

1.26   First, the Community intends to compile an inventory of national "security" measures – in particular state aids and fiscal incentives. Their compatibility with Community objectives will then be checked in the context of the diverse national energy situations, in order to determine which particular energy markets warranted protection, and by what means.

The second stage is expressed in terms of goals, as opposed to the means to achieve them: it would seek to exploit more fully the "existing interdependence and complementarity in the Community". Implicit in this statement is surely a transfer of sovereignty to the Community institutions on energy decision-making. It is therefore hardly surprising that there is no attempt to spell out the second-stage instruments. In May 1990 the Council refused to endorse a Commission proposal on the notification of planned energy investments to it (see below). Yet it is precisely Community powers over planning and investment which will be needed if interdependence and complementarity are to become meaningful concepts.

Alongside this "two-stage" approach, the document envisages a separate strategy for the least-integrated of Community energy markets – the electricity market. It proposes an immediate freeze on long-term energy subsidies and supply agreements at present levels. The proportion of national electricity markets which can be earmarked for national

---

[10] Quoted in *Energy in Europe,* "Major Themes in Energy", Special Issue, September 1989, 25.
[11] Appendix 5.
[12] Currently available as SEC (90) 1248, Brussels, September 1990.

companies will then be restricted by a Community-wide quota expressed in percentage terms, to be progressively reduced and eventually abolished by the year 2000.

The Commission's determination to apply this strategy was made clear in **1.27** a speech by Sir Leon Brittan in London on 18 April 1991.[13] Sir Leon offered "a clear vision of where it wished to go."

> "Time is short, because energy cannot lag behind progress towards the completion of the rest of the internal market and the end of 1992 is barely 20 months away.
>
> I want to see open competition in electricity and gas within two fundamental constraints: the need to provide security of supply and the related public service obligation of universal, uninterrupted provision.
>
> Within those two fundamental constraints our objectives can be clearly stated: consumers should have a choice of suppliers, prices should be set by competition, suppliers should be able to deliver their production through someone else's network, state subsidies should be transparent and limited and there should be no barriers to trade between the Community's Member States.
>
> On the issue of security of supply our Member States generally have chosen to protect about 20% of electricity production by reserving it in various ways to domestic primary energy sources. We will move to a Community security of supply system as the internal market takes hold and indeed the opening up of markets within the Community will contribute to overall security of supply for one and all. What we say for the time being though, is that Member States should protect no more than 20% of electricity production on security of supply grounds. This figure should come down to 15% as soon as possible to reflect the Community's progress...
>
> The public service obligations of companies operating in the energy sector vary from country to country, but a common commitment to safe, uninterrupted supply is discernible throughout the Community. There is absolutely no reason why a competitive regime, accompanied by the necessary regulation imposing certain indispensable constraints should not satisfy these requirements."

5. Recent developments

(i) Towards the internal market for electricity

It is within this emerging policy framework that the application of **1.28** Community law to the electricity sector must be understood. The Commission appears determined to use the instruments available to it under the competition rules, to achieve an open market for electricity as well as other forms of energy.

Nevertheless a common thread runs through each of the various

---

[13] "Competition in the European Community's Electricity and Gas Markets", The Institution of Civil Engineers, London.

policy documents, resolutions and speeches discussed in this chapter. The application of the competition rules must be subject to two fundamental constraints: security of energy supply and the need to ensure universal, uninterrupted provision to all consumers – the public service obligation.

1.29   The Commission has moved now towards quantifying the permissible level of protection of indigenous energy sources for use in electricity generation: no more than 20% of electricity production may be secured at present, and this is to be progressively reduced. It is of course the Court of Justice, and not the Commission, which will ultimately decide whether this approach is in conformity with Community law.

The most important outstanding issue remains the reconciliation of the public service obligation to a fully competitive regime for electricity supply. In his speech in London, Sir Leon merely hinted at "certain indispensable constraints" which would have to be recognised. He did not spell these out.

In the summer of 1991, however, the services of the Commission began preparing various draft proposals dealing with the public service obligation, and giving it something of a "Community content".

1.30   In late September 1991, in a speech to the VGB Congress in Berlin, the Commissioner responsible for energy, Mr Cardoso e Cunha, offered further indications of the Commission's intended approach.[14]

> "First steps towards an Energy Internal Market have already been undertaken by the adoption of the Council Directives on Transit and Price Transparency. Yet, the situation in the electricity and gas sectors are still characterised by a number of obstacles which have to be removed in order to create a truly integrated market where the three basic conditions must be met:
> – the free movement of products;
> – improved security of supply;
> – improved competitiveness.
> A true Internal Market demands not only the first and second conditions. All three must be observed.
> For these reasons, my services are preparing a whole package of integration measures and I would like to briefly present to you the most important ones.
> Firstly, we are considering the removal of special and exclusive rights. This includes the abolition of export/import and production monopolies, as well as those related to the construction of transmission lines. These proposals are justified not only because these monopolies are incompatible with the EEC Treaty, but also because they are an obstacle towards increased competition. It is in particular on the level of power generation that the arrival of new players, including auto-producers are necessary to ensure a more diversified offer.
> Secondly, the administrative separation of the production, transmission and distribution activities is unavoidable. This does not mean that the existing structures of the electricity industry are to be modified, but the ''unbundling' will imply that, within the companies, separated divisions for the three stages have to be created and each of them will keep its own accounts. This measure

---

[14] IP (91) 854.

is necessary, on the one hand, to avoid cross-subsidization between the different sectors and, on the other hand, to allow competition in the production and distribution areas.

Thirdly, the idea of Open Access should be introduced to give the consumer the possibility of choosing, directly or indirectly, the best supplier. In fact, Open Access means that any consumer may negotiate an electricity or gas supply contract with different producers in the Community. The grid operator (or operators), if capacity exists, cannot refuse to carry the contracted electricity from the generator to the customer on the basis of published rules and tariffs. Of course, the grid operator cannot be held liable in case of primary non-delivery, but shall use its best endeavours to keep the transmission/distribution network stable. In the past, this was considered a formidable task, eventually impossible to accomplish. It still is a critical condition, but today's technology allows it to be done. In fact it is being done now.

I firmly believe that only the combination of these three measures, namely removal of monopolies, unbundling and access to networks, is the right way to achieve the desired integration of the energy market. However, in order to guarantee the necessary flexibility, the introduction of these measures has to take place in a phased manner allowing

– the highest possible degree of harmonized conditions in a competitive environment;

– the highest security of supply; and

– the improved stability and safety of transmission networks.

Nobody should therefore interpret Community measures as ignoring the general interest. Quite the contrary.... It is not the first time that a broader Community approach interferes with the stability of established operators. But it is our collective responsibility to evolve with the times and to avoid the decline and shocks which are the fruits of rigidity."

These recurrent themes – the reconciliation of the goals competition **1.31** and security of supply – and the scope and content of public service obligations under Community law – will be returned to and developed in the following chapters.

(ii) The Commission's Proposal for a Council Directive concerning common rules for the internal market in electricity

At the end of December 1991, following detailed discussion within the **1.32** Commission services, and in the light of an initial appraisal of its proposals by the Energy Council in the previous month, the Directorate-General for Energy began work on a revised set of proposals on "Completing the internal market for electricity and gas". These proposals were endorsed by the Commission on 23 January 1992.

In its memorandum accompanying the proposals for two Directives, on **1.33** common rules for the electricity and for the gas market, respectively, the Commission has set out four general principles which inform the present proposals (COM (91)548, 21 February 1992 p7).

"The first of these principles is the need for a gradual approach. The internal market for electricity and natural gas should take shape over a period of time sufficiently long to enable the industry to adjust in a flexible and ordered manner to its new environment. This implies a step-by-step approach, with the Commission laying down a minimum level of liberalization to be achieved at each stage while at the same time allowing each Member State discretion to opt for greater liberalization of the domestic market.

However the idea of a gradual approach is not enough unless accompanied by a clear vision of the objectives pursued. Uncertainty for investors must be avoided. The electricity and gas industries are capital intensive, and lead times for planning and construction are relatively long, as is the time needed to show a return on investments in technical and economic terms. Economic operators must have some point of reference for the future in order to decide on investment programmes. It is therefore up to the Community to pinpoint now its long-term objectives for the liberalization of the market.

The second principle is that of subsidiarity. The Community must not impose rigid mechanisms, but rather should define a framework enabling Member States to opt for the system best suited to their natural resources, the state of their industry and their energy policies.

As its third principle, the Community must also avoid the trap of excessive regulation. The sectors in question are characterised by monopoly situations which call for a substantial degree of regulation, notably in the form of price controls. Moves towards greater liberalization will undoubtedly make it necessary to introduce new regulation, although these will replace rather than supplement the existing ones. But the Community must take care not to go beyond what is strictly necessary in order to achieve the aims of liberalization and, as in the case of transit for example, to leave scope for commercial negotiation between undertakings concerned.

On the institutional front, the Commission has opted for an approach based on Articles 52(2), 66 and 100A, since this provides for a political dialogue with the Council and the European Parliament under these cooperation procedure, and also enables the consultations with other interested parties to be pursued. However the Commission reserves the right to make use of all the powers conferred on it by the Treaty as and when appropriate."

1.34   The implementation of the Commission's plans is to take place over three stages. The first stage, which comprised the implementation of the Directive on transit and the Directive on price transparency (see Chaps 6 and 7 respectively) is now completed. The second stage will begin with the adoption of the proposed common rules, which is scheduled for January 1993. In this stage the Commission hopes to introduce a limited degree of third party access for certain large users and for distribution companies. The proposal also provides for the introduction of more competition in generation and the construction of transmission and distribution lines, as well as for the "unbundling" of vertically-integrated electricity supply companies (this concept is discussed in more detail in Chap 4).

Stage three will involve the total liberalization of the electricity market.Its introduction will be conditional on progress achieved in stage two, but the Commission has indicated that this last stage could be implemented in 1996.

The principle of subsidiarity will play an important role in stage two. The **1.35** Commission interprets this concept to mean that the Member States should retain substantial flexibility in applying the common rules at national level. In particular the proposed Directive provides that:

> "Member States will retain powers to regulate electricity prices for all end-users not eligible for TPA.
>
> Member States will remain free to determine the extent and nature of distribution companies' rights and their public service obligations.
>
> Member States will also be free to lay down detailed criteria, of varying stringency, for the granting of licenses to build power stations and transmission and distribution lines.
>
> Finally, Member States will be free to choose how they implement the directive, in particular whether to set up a regulatory authority or to rely on competition legislation."

The individual articles set out in the proposed Directive are discussed in detail in the later chapters of this book.

6. Conclusion

The Commission has now made considerable progress in developing its **1.36** plans to create an internal market for electricity. At the time of writing, however, these plans remain tentative proposals. In section 5(ii) above it was noted that pending their adoption, the Commission reserves the right to make full use of all the powers conferred upon it by the Treaty. Furthermore, in applying the common rules set out in the new proposals the Member States themselves will, irrespective of the operation of the principle of subsidiarity, remain subject to the Treaty rules on free movement and competition.

The application of these basic principles of Community law to the electricity sector raises a number of problems. In particular the goals of liberalization and competition must be reconciled with the aims of securing supply and guaranteeing the integrity of integrated electricity networks. The problems which this process must inevitably raise are developed in the following chapters of this book.

6. Conclusion

Chapter 2
Electricity and the Three Treaties: General Principles of Community Law and Free Movement

1. Introduction

Electricity is an intermediate or an end product, and not a primary fuel; **2.1** the fuels used for its generation may be subject to one of the three Treaties creating the European Communities. Coal[1] is subject to the rules set out in the Treaty of Paris creating the European Coal and Steel Community (ECSC), while nuclear generated electricity is partially subject to the other Treaty of Rome, creating the European Atomic Energy Community (Euratom) in so far as it is generated from materials subject to that Treaty (as defined in Art 197).

In this and the following three chapters, the principal articles of the three Treaties which are of relevance to electricity generation, transmission and distribution are discussed. This chapter deals with the general principles governing free movement of goods. Chapter 3 examines the competition rules and their application, Chapter 4 the relevant Community law principles on public enterprises and monopolies while in Chapter 5 the rules on state aids are discussed.

It is not intended to provide a detailed, comprehensive analysis of each **2.2** of the three Treaties. The aim of these chapters is to introduce the reader to the general principles of Community law which are of relevance to a specific and complex sector. Part I of this chapter highlights certain fundamental differences between the respective objectives of the Treaties, and their style and scope, which are of relevance to the development of EC electricity law. Part II deals in greater detail with the principle of free movement of goods under the EEC Treaty. Part III is devoted to a short analysis of a special provision included in the EEC Treaty's chapter on free movement of goods – Article 37, which governs state trading monopolies.

---

[1] As defined by Annex I to the ECSC Treaty.

Part I

2. Brief comparison of the three Treaties

(i) The three Treaties

2.3   There are significant differences in the underlying philosophies of these different Treaties. These are reflected in their different structures, their aims and objectives, and in the legal instruments provided for their realization. The EEC Treaty is a *traité-cadre* – or framework Treaty – whereas the other two are *traités-lois*. The EEC Treaty is an instrument of *general* economic integration; the ECSC and Euratom Treaties are instruments of *sectoral* integration.

2.4   These differences become evident in the degree of specificity used to define the various instruments provided to achieve each Treaty's main goals and objectives. The EEC Treaty rules are for the most part expressed in terms of general principles which may be supplemented by secondary legislation. The other two Treaties provide for detailed rules governing such matters as research, investment, health and safety, and in the case of the ECSC Treaty, cartel and state aid regulation, which do not always require further implementing legislation.[2]

2.5   The potential application of the EEC, ECSC and Euratom Treaties to various phases and types of electricity production may give rise to problems, given the differences between the three Treaties. As the ECSC Treaty is due to expire in 2001, the coal and steel will in all probability be assimilated into the general EEC regime, following the expiry of a transitional period.[3]

   In the meantime the Court has been prepared to apply similar techniques of interpretation to the EEC and the ECSC Treaties where it deems the relevant provisions to share a "common inspiration",[4] but it has refused to transpose certain powers available under only one of the Treaties to the other.[5] The Euratom Treaty is unlimited in duration.

(ii) The inter-relationship between the three Treaties

2.6   The legal relationship between the three Treaties is dealt with in Article 232 EEC. Article 232(1) provides that the EEC Treaty shall not affect the provisions of the ECSC Treaty. Article 232(2) states that it shall not derogate from the rules establishing the Euratom Treaty.

   The Court of Justice has held that regulation of matters in the ECSC is exclusive. In Case 188/80 *France, Italy and the United Kingdom* v *Commission*

---

[2] Chapters III and VII Euratom, on health and safety and on safeguards, respectively, are an exception.

[3] *Agence Europe*, no 5483, 1 May 1991, p7. See also *Memorandum of the ECSC Consultative Committee on the future of the ECSC Treaty* (OJ 1990, C302/3).

[4] Case 13/60 *Geitling* [1962] ECR 83.

[5] In Case 6/72 *Continental Can* [1975] ECR 495, the Court refused to draw a comparison between merger control provisions under Art 66 ECSC and Arts 85 and 86 EEC.

[1982] ECR 2545 the Court held that Commission Directive 80/723/EEC on financial transparency could not be applied to undertakings in the coal sector as the ECSC contains rules governing this matter. It is therefore important to determine whether a particular matter is governed by the ECSC Treaty.

Where certain issues are not dealt with in the sectoral Treaties, they may **2.7** be legislated for under the relevant provisions of the EEC Treaty. Thus for example, the ECSC Treaty does not deal with issues such as free movement of services or freedom of establishment. Hence, the new Council Directive 90/513/EEC on procurement rules for the utilities sector,[6] was adopted on the basis of Article 100A EEC and covers all three energy sectors.

The Euratom Treaty, unlike the ECSC Treaty, makes no special provision **2.8** for competition or state aids, so that these matters fall within the ambit of the relevant articles of the EEC Treaty.

Before turning to a more detailed analysis of the relevant substantive law, a number of observations on the institutional aspects of the three Treaties are in order.

(iii) The Three Treaties and the Single European Act

The Single European Act of 1987 amends all three Treaties, but its **2.9** impact on the Euratom and ECSC Treaties is much more limited. Articles 4 to 5 and Articles 26 to 29 of the Act supplement, respectively the provisions of the ECSC and Euratom Treaty. These articles provide, *inter alia,* that the new Court of First Instance has competence to hear and determine certain classes of action. The amendments to the Treaty of Rome establishing the EEC are of far more wide-reaching significance, and it is important to bear in mind that they are confined to that Treaty.

The amendments to the Treaty of Rome which are of direct relevance **2.10** to electricity policy objectives are Article 100A, which allows legislation to be adopted by qualified majority in co-operation with the European Parliament for the purposes of achieving the internal market by 1992; Article 149 which defines the co-operation procedure; Articles 130A-E on economic and social cohesion, Articles 130F-Q on research and technological development and Articles 130R-T on the environment. In addition Articles 8A-C on the nature of the internal market, the measures to be taken for its achievement and the timetable set out therein, have an obvious bearing on the completion of a single electricity market.

One result of these various amendments has been to generate **2.11** some confusion over the proper basis for Commission legislative proposals. The choice of legal basis has a number of consequences, firstly for the role of the European Parliament; secondly for the voting procedure

---

[6] OJ1990 L297/1. See further, Chap 10.

to be followed in Council; and thirdly for the objective and nature of the adopted measures, and the possibility of derogations from them.[7]

2.12   The new voting and co-operation procedures only apply to some but not all articles of the EEC Treaty. They do not apply to the Euratom or ECSC Treaties. It will therefore usually be in the interests of the Commission and the Parliament to advocate Article 100A EEC as the preferred legal basis for electricity-related legislation. Since the introduction of the Single European Act, a number of controversies have arisen over the legal basis question, some of which have reached the Court of Justice.

These cases have involved disputes over whether Article 100A should be preferred over other articles of the EEC Treaty, and in particular with the articles on environment.[8] These cases will be examined in detail in Chapter 9 on Electricity and Environmental Policy.

2.13   Controversies have also arisen over which *Treaty* should be used as a legal basis. In the wake of the accident at the nuclear installation at Chernobyl in 1986, the Council adopted a Regulation on the maximum permitted levels of radioactive contamination of foodstuffs (OJ 1987 L371/11). The European Parliament had consistently demanded stricter control levels, but as the proposal was based on Article 31 Euratom[9], its role was restricted to one of consultation. It therefore rejected the proposal outright, but since rejection is deemed to constitute delivery of an Opinion, the Council was able to adopt the measures. Subsequently the Parliament brought an action against the Council based on the infringement of essential procedural requirements.[10]

The complex issues of the Parliament's *locus standi* to bring such an action were considered by the Court of Justice, in 1990.[11] In October 1991 the Court ruled on the substantive issues raised by the case. Parliament had contended that Article 31 Euratom constituted a narrow legal basis for measures directly related to the protection of the public in connection with the operation of nuclear plants and handling of nuclear fuel, whereas this Regulation concerned the movement of goods.[12] The Court rejected this interpretation of Article 31 Euratom (see further Chap 9, para 9.40).

(iv) **The concept of the common market**

2.14   The ECSC Treaty provides for a common market, involving the abolition of customs duties, quantitative restrictions on trade, the removal of

---

[7] See generally, Bradley, "The European Court and the legal basis of Community legislation", (1988) EL Rev 379. See also (1991) 16 EL Rev 175.

[8] Case C-300/89 *Commission* v *Council* (titanium oxide), judgment of 11 June 1991, not yet reported; Case 62/88 *Greece* v *Council* [1990] ECR 1527.

[9] This article which is to be found in Chapter III of the Euratom Treaty on Health and Safety allows the Commission to work out "basic standards" for the protection of health of workers and the general public against the dangers of ionizing radiations. The proposals must be adopted by the Council, acting by a qualified majority.

[10] Case 70/88 *Parliament* v *Council,* OJ 1988 C90/6.

[11] Case 70/88 *Parliament* v *Council* [1990] ECR 2041.

[12] For a detailed rejection of this argument, see J Grunwald, "Tchernobyl et les communautés européennes: aspects juridiques", (1987) 308 RMC 396-408 at 404.

discrimination in prices, prohibition of state subsides and removal of restrictive practices leading to collusive market sharing. It also endows the Commission as the executive organ under the ECSC Treaty, with extensive interventionist powers to deal with situations of over-supply and of scarcity in coal and steel. The enumeration of detailed objectives in Article 2 illustrates that the ECSC Treaty aims at a high degree of market integration.

The Treaty does *not* establish a true customs union, with a common **2.15** external tariff and unified customs procedures, however. Commercial policy matters are primarily reserved to the Member States (Art 71).[13] This in effect means that Member States retain some discretion in fixing import quotas for, and duties payable on coal originating in non-EC countries.[14]

Article 72 ECSC allows the Member States themselves to determine tariffs within certain limits. The Member States did however, reach an agreement on 19 November 1957 as to a harmonised, but not common ECSC tariff to be applied from 10 February 1958.[15]

Article 74 however allows the Commission to take protective measures in **2.16** certain circumstances. Recent ECSC Decisions have declared that the Community provisions to ensure the uniform application of the Common Customs Tariff shall apply to the products falling within the province of the ECSC Treaty. [16]

Nevertheless there are indications from the case law that the ECSC is not a true customs union with regard to goods imported from third countries. Unlike Articles 9 and 10 EEC the ECSC Treaty contains no provision *expressly* stating that products originating in third countries and in free circulation in a Member State benefit from the prohibition on customs duties and charges having equivalent effect in trade between Member States. Article 4(a) ECSC does contain such a basic prohibition, however.

In Cases 9 & 12/60 *Vloeberghs* the Court held that ECSC products originating in non-Member States and released into free circulation in a Member State do benefit from internal free movement, a principle recognised by the former High Authority in May 1955.[17] However, in the context of the *Vloeberghs case*, which concerned an action for damages against the former High Authority for wrongful omission to ensure the free movement of goods originating in third countries, the Court was cautious in applying the principle.[18]

In Case 36/83 *Mabanaft* v *HZA* [1984] ECR 2497, however, the Court **2.17** went so far as to uphold a differential tariff applying to imports into Germany. The question at issue related to the validity of a Recommendation

---

[13] Cases 9 and 16/60 *Vloeberghs* [1961] ECR 197.
[14] They would also appear to retain considerable discretion in the administration of export and import licences for trade with third countries under the Art 73(1). Cases 6 & 9/60 *Vloeberghs*.
[15] ECSC Sixth General Report, p 82.
[16] Dec 86/98/ECSC, OJ 1986 L81/29.
[17] See [1961] ECR 197, at 215.
[18] For a fuller discussion of the nature of the principle of free movement of goods in the ECSC Treaty, both in comparison with Art 10 EEC and in the context of the GATT principles, see the Opinion of Advocate General Roemer, in Cases 9 & 12/60, *loc cit* at 231-232.

of the former High Authority from 1959 allowing Germany to impose customs duties on coal imports originating from third countries. In this particular instance the coal was in free circulation in the Netherlands and had subsequently been imported into Germany.

2.18 The Court repeated the principle laid down in *Vloeberghs,* and described the ECSC as "more akin in its structure to the principle of a customs union" than a mere free-trade area. But the Court emphasised that Article 4(a) only prohibited import duties and other restrictions "as provided in this Treaty". Article 74(3) authorises the Commission, if coal or steel products as defined in the Treaty are "imported into the territory of one or more Member States in relatively increased quantities and under such conditions that these imports cause or threaten to cause serious injury to production within the common market of like or directly competing products" to make recommendations to the Member States. The Court found that such conditions had continued to prevail in Germany, so that the Recommendation was still valid.

2.19 It should however be observed that in *Mabanaft* the Court rejected the German Government's more restrictive interpretation of Article 71 ECSC, which the latter alleged gave a Member State not only the powers to pursue an independent commercial policy but could unilaterally levy customs duties on imports from goods originating in third countries, but in free circulation in a Member State.

Usher has summarised the Court's view of the ECSC Treaty as follows:

> "The ECSC is sufficiently akin to a customs union for its Member States not to be able unilaterally to impose customs duties on goods in free circulation in other Member States, but it is not sufficiently a customs union for its institutions to be prohibited from authorising Member States to impose such customs duties."[19]

Although the Commission has recently annulled its Recommendation allowing Germany to levy customs duties on imported, non-EC coal[20] it has allowed Spain to impose similar restrictions.[21]

Thus the Member States continue to be able to exercise powers to restrict the entry of cheap coal imported from third countries to protect their domestic industry.

2.20 In the *Euratom Treaty* the concept of the common market is a subsidiary one. In achieving its task of promoting the development of the nuclear industry, the Community was given a number of interventionist powers. In particular, to ensure that all users of nuclear energy would receive a regular and equitable supply of ores and fuels, a centralised European Supply Agency was created (Chap VI). This body was to be given exclusive rights of importation and a right of first option to purchase from producers inside the Community.

---

[19] Usher, "The Single Market and goods imported from third countries", (1986) *Yearbook of European Law* 159-182 at 163.
[20] OJ 1990 L346/18.
[21] OJ 1990 L346/20.

This regime has never worked in the manner intended for it by the Treaty framers. The Agency's import monopoly was relaxed for small quantities of ores and source materials (but not fissile materials) (Reg 17, OJ Spec ed 1965-66, 297). **2.21**

A "supervised exception" applies if the Agency is unable, within a reasonable period, to fulfil an order for supplies or is able only to fulfil it at an excessive price (Art 66).

In practice transactions concerning all three categories of materials are concluded directly between producers and consumers, although the Agency must approve these contracts.[22] **2.22**

Chapter VIII provides for a special system of ownership for "special fissile materials", as defined in Article 197. Article 86 vests property in these materials – whether produced or imported – in the Community, although Member States, persons or undertakings have the unlimited right of use and consumption of these same materials. **2.23**

The EEC Treaty's objectives, as enumerated in Article 3 are fundamentally different. The emphasis is on market integration and the general mechanisms for the creation of a single European market are more fully and clearly stated than in the ECSC Treaty. Interventionist powers are confined largely to the co-ordination of short-term economic policies (Art 103(4)). **2.24**

The concept of the *common market* in the EEC Treaty is one in which all goods, persons, services and capital can move freely. The ECSC and Euratom contain no equivalent provisions on free movement of services and capital.

Electricity, and indeed energy in general, is not dealt with explicitly in the Treaty of Rome of 1957 which created the European Economic Community. It may therefore be supposed that electricity, natural gas, petroleum and crude oil and alternative energy sources are, for the purposes of the rules on free movement and competition, to be treated in the same way as any other product subject to the Treaty rules. **2.25**

The question of whether the supply of "electricity" is in fact to be considered as the supply of a good, and covered by Articles 30-37, or the supply of a service subject to Articles 59-66 EEC, has yet to be finally decided by the European Court.

In Case 6/64 *Costa* v *Enel* [1964] ECR 585 the Court appeared to assume that electricity was a good for the purposes of Article 37, although it did not directly address this question. Council Directive 85/374/EEC on product liability also treats electricity as a good for the purposes of the provisions of that Directive (OJ 1985 L210/29). Electricity is also defined as a good in the Brussels Nomenclature (Heading 27.17).

---

[22] For the Rules of the Euratom Supply Agency see OJ 1975 L193/37.

Part II

3. Doctrine of measures having equivalent effect to quantitative restrictions and free movement of goods

2.26 The elimination of quantitative restrictions on imports and exports, and measures having equivalent effect (Arts 30-37 EEC) is central to the achievement of the common market.

The terms "measures having an equivalent effect to a quantitative restriction" on imports (Art 30) or exports (Art 34) have been interpreted widely by the European Court of Justice, to cover not only national legislation, regulatory instruments and administrative practices, but also policies which are not expressed in formal documents.

2.27 Thus, for example, in Case 174/84 *Bulk Oil AG* v *Sun International* [1986] ECR 539 the Court held that the British Government's unofficial policy of restricting oil exportation to Israel was a "measure having equivalent effect to a restriction on exports" for the purposes of Article 34 EEC. All such measures restricting *imports* are prohibited where their effect is to put national products at an advantage.

In Case 8/74 *Dassonville* [1974] ECR 837, a case involving imports of whisky into Belgium, the Court adopted a very wide definition of the phrase "measure having equivalent effect to a quantitative restriction on trade". It stated that:

> "All trading rules enacted by Member States which are capable of hindering, directly or indirectly, actually or potentially, intra-Community trade are to be considered as measures having an effect equivalent to quantitative restrictions."

This interpretation of Article 30 was confirmed in Case 120/78 *Cassis de Dijon* [1979] ECR 649, but here the national rules at issue applied not only to imports but to domestic products also.

(i) Article 30 and private parties

2.28 Article 30, although not expressly addressed to Member States, is usually taken as intended to apply to State or public measures.[23] Measures adopted by professional bodies have been held to fall within the prohibition where they have been performing an act of public authority duly delegated to them.[24] The acts of public or state-owned companies will not usually be caught by Article 30, although the state legislation creating them or reserving certain tasks exclusively to them, might well be.[25] This matter is dealt with further in Chapters 4, 6 and 7.

---

[23] Case 311/85 *VVR* [1987] ECR 3801; Case 65/86 *Bayer Chemical Company* v *Sollhofer* [1988] ECR 5249.

[24] Case 249/81 *Commission* v *Ireland* [1982] ECR 4005 at 4032; Cases 266 & 267/87 *R* v *Royal Pharmaceutical Society of Great Britain, ex parte the Association of Pharmaceutical Importers et al* [1989] ECR 1295.

[25] Case C-202/88 *France* v *Commission*, judgment of 19 March 1991, not yet reported.

(ii) **Free movement of goods and energy**

The Court's wide interpretation of the concept of a "measure having   **2.29** equivalent effect", together with its doctrine of "indistinctly applicable measures" have not been without relevance to the energy sector, although this jurisprudence has never been directly applied to the electricity sector: [1974] ECR 837.

In Case 231/83 *Cullet* v *Leclerc* [1985] ECR 315, for example, the Court interpreted Article 30 to extend to national minimum price regulations for petrol where these prices were fixed at a level which operated to put imported products at a disadvantage vis-a-vis domestic products. In *Leclerc* minimum prices were fixed on the basis of national ex-refinery products, thus depriving imported products of any competitive advantage.[26]

(a) *The non-fossil fuel quota*

Prior to the enactment in the United Kingdom, of the Electricity Act 1989,   **2.30** a complaint was submitted to the European Commission by the Council for the Protection of Rural England (CPRE) alleging, *inter alia,* that the non fossil fuel quota (NNFQ), as provided for in what is now section 32 of the Act, restricted the freedom of the distribution companies to purchase from the most efficient sources of energy. It was therefore a restriction on free movement in the Community.

In its decision, the Commission dealt only with the state aid implications of the non-fossil fuel levy, and not the quota itself. It was prepared to authorise the levy on the grounds that it was designed to keep existing plant in operation, thereby contributing to supply security, and that it placed the burden of costs on the electricity consumer as opposed to the taxpayer.[27]

(iii) **Exports**

As for *exports* the Court has been less strict; it will usually require evidence   **2.31** of intent to discriminate.[28] It should be noted that in its jurisprudence, the Court appears to have drawn a distinction between: (a) restrictions on production and (b) restrictions on sale.[29]

(a) *Production*

In Case 15/79 *Groenveld* v *Produktschap voor Vee en Vlees* [1979] ECR 3409 the   **2.32** Court held that Article 34:

"concerns national measures which have as their specific object or effect the

---

[26] The Court has generally not looked favourable on quota arrangements reserving a particular share of the market to national producers. See for example, its ruling in Case C-347/88 *Commisson* v *Greece* [1990] ECR 4747. See further Chap 7.

[27] Commission press release, IP(90) 267. See also, Commission of the EC, 20th Report on Competition Policy, 1991, at pt 258.

[28] See further Case 174/84, *loc cit.*

[29] See further Oliver, p 100.

restriction of patterns of exports and thereby the establishment of a difference between the domestic trade of a member State and its export trade in such a way as to provide a particular advantage for national production or for the domestic market of the State in question at the expense of the production or of the trade of other member States."

2.33   This formula has been repeated in Case 155/80 *Oebel* [1981] ECR 1993 and in Case 238/82 *Duphar* [1984] ECR 523. In the former case, the Court appears to have reduced the test for a measure to constitute a measure of equivalent effect under Article 34 to two cumulative conditions:

– the measure must have as its specific object or effect the restriction of patterns of export; and

– it must discriminate in favour of goods intended for the domestic market against exports so as to favour national production.

Oliver has argued that these two tests should not be seen as cumulative, but that the better interpretation would seem to be that the second limb is a gloss on the first, and should be seen merely as example of such a measure.[30]

(b) Sale

2.34   It has been argued that the *Cassis de Dijon* principle should be applied *mutatis mutandis* to restrictions on export sales.[31] In Case 173/83 *Commission v France* [1985] ECR 491 the Court ruled on the legality of export licences without referring to the *Groenveld* formula in its judgment.[32]

In Case 302/88 *Hennen Olie* (judgment of 10 December 1990) the Court was asked to examine the effects of a charge levied on certain oil products and paid to ICOVA, a state-sponsored organization responsible for the management of emergency oil stocks. The relevant Dutch legislation had required undertakings marketing oil in the Netherlands to stock a certain proportion of the oil sold on the Dutch market.[33] Any oil exported was not taken into account when calculating the level of the reserves required. The legislation also provided that companies could entrust the third party, ICOVA, to hold stocks on their behalf. ICOVA in turn charged firms affiliated to it storage costs which could be passed on to their customers.

2.35   Hennen Olie argued that as a result of this system dealers who bought from affiliates and exported it were less competitive on export markets than affiliates who were not burdened with any part of the storage obligation. The system was in fact substantially altered in 1987, but Hennen Olie argued that prior to that date, it had suffered from the fact that it had to pay ICOVA's charges indirectly through the price it paid to ICOVA's affiliates for oil.

The Court ruled that while the system resulted in a difference in

---

[30] At p 102.
[31] Gormley, p 110; Oliver, p 103. See also A G Capotorti in *Groenveld* and in *Oebel*.
[32] *Cf* the judgment of the three-judge Chamber of the Court in Case 172/82 *Syndicat national des fabricants raffineurs d'huile* v *Inter Huiles*, [1983] ECR 561.
[33] As required under Dir 68/414/EEC, JO 1968 L308/14, as amended.

treatment between two categories of exports, this did not in itself amount to a breach of Article 34. Undertakings could decide freely whether to become members of ICOVA or not.

(iv) Permissible restrictions on free movement

Member States continue to retain a limited scope to impose restrictions on trade if these can be justified, either under Article 36, in the case of restrictions which apply only to imports/exports, or under what has become known as the "rule of reason" in the case of restrictions which are equally applicable to domestic and imported goods alike. [34]

2.36

(a) Security of supply

The principle justification advanced for restrictions on the free movement of electricity is that these are required in order to guarantee security of supply. Two possible applications of the term "security of supply" should be distinguished.

2.37

On the one hand, it can be used to refer to those measures enacted to secure or guarantee access to certain fuels for the continued generation of electricity. On the other hand, the term can be interpreted to mean security in the sense of continuity of service to consumers.

The first application of the term is of obvious relevance to state-imposed restrictions, both direct and indirect, on the types of fuels used in electricity generation. The second relates primarily to the organization of electricity supply, and to any restrictions, direct or indirect, on who may import, export, market or otherwise supply electricity via the public supply networks.

Short and long-term measures

The first type of measures may in turn be classified into either of two categories. Firstly, there are measures designed to guarantee supply security in emergency or short-term crisis situations.

2.38

In accordance with Council Directive 75/339/EEC (OJ 1975 L153/35), operators of thermal power stations are obliged to maintain a minimum level of emergency fossil fuel stocks sufficient to ensure at all times the continuation of electricity supplies for a period of at least 30 days.

Secondly, there are measures designed to guarantee longer-term production security in terms of a stable and reliable source of supply of generating fuels. These may include the obligation to supply a specified proportion of electricity from a particular fuel source, as in the case of the United Kingdom, for example, where the regional supply companies are under an obligation to purchase a fixed quota of nuclear-generated electricity.

2.39

Certain other forms of restrictions may also be justifiable, however, on

---

[34] Case 8/74 *Dassonville, loc cit.*

environmental grounds (Case 302/86 *Commission* v *Denmark* [1988] ECR 4607, discussed below).

(b) Article 36

2.40   Article 36, first sentence, permits limited derogations from the rules on free movement where restrictions are necessary to guarantee, *inter alia* public security, and where the means used are proportionate to the ends sought. The Court has consistently maintained that Article 36 must be strictly interpreted and that the list of exemptions is *exhaustive* (Case 7/68 *Commission* v *Italy* [1968] ECR 423 at 431). It has also insisted that Article 36 deals with non-economic justifications (Case 7/61 *Commission* v *Italy* [1961] ECR 317 at 329).

The Court has also repeatedly ruled that Article 36 cannot be used to justify measures which are not essential for the achievement of legitimate, non-economic objectives. This is the principle of proportionality: if the legitimate objective could be effectively achieved by means less restrictive to trade then the measures under review will not be upheld.

(c) Greek petroleum case

2.41   A good example of the application of this rule to the energy sector is to be found in the recent Case C-347/88 *Commission* v *Greece*. In accordance with the relevant Greek legislation distributors were obliged to submit annual supply programmes for governmental approval, and to conform to a regime of quotas. The Commission had contended that these requirements were contrary to Article 30. The Court rejected the Greek Government's claims that these latter restrictions were necessary to maintain public security and to ensure a sufficient supply of petroleum products at all times.

Recalling its judgment in Case 72/83 *Campus,* (see below) it replied that only measures necessary to guarantee a minimum supply could potentially benefit from exemption, and even then they must be justifiable and proportionate to the ends sought. A simple system of *notification* of supply plans could, in the Court's view guarantee that the Greek government would have the necessary information to arrange for an adequate level of supply from its two public refineries in the event of an emergency.

(d) Campus Oil case

2.42   The Court interpreted the meaning of the term "public security" in Case 72/83 *Campus Oil* [1984] ECR 2727 to cover measures necessary to ensure sufficient supplies of oil products to guarantee the continued functioning of certain essential public services. It is for the Member State to demonstrate that the rules are necessary to give effective protection to the interests referred to in Article 36, and that they are in conformity with the proportionality rule.

Given the fundamental importance of the Campus ruling to the electricity sector, it is worthwhile to set out the facts and the relevant parts of the judgment in full.

The case arose by way of a reference from the Irish courts on the legality **2.43** of an Order made by the Irish Minister for Industry and Energy. The Order requires any person who imports any of the various petroleum products to which it applies to purchase a certain proportion (approximately 35%) of their requirements from the Irish state-owned refinery, INPC at a price to be determined by the Minister, taking into account the costs incurred by the INPC.

The Irish Government sought to justify this measure on the grounds that it was necessary to keep refining capacity in operation in Ireland, a country almost totally dependent on oil imports.

The Court had no difficulty in classifying the Order as a measure having **2.44** equivalent effect to a quantitative restriction on imports (para 20). It then looked to whether it could be justified under Article 36. It began by underlining that: "petroleum products, because of their exceptional importance as an energy source in the modern economy, are of fundamental importance for a country's existence since not only its economy, but above all its institutions, its essential public services and even the survival of its inhabitants depend upon them" (para 34).

It went on to consider its jurisprudence restricting Article 36 to matters of a non-economic nature. It ruled that:

> "A Member State cannot be allowed to avoid the effects of measures provided for in the Treaty by pleading the economic difficulties caused by the elimination of barriers to intra-Community trade. However, in the light of the seriousness of the consequences that an interruption in supplies of petroleum products may have for a country's existence, the aim of ensuring a minimum supply of petroleum products at all times is to be regarded as transcending purely economic considerations and thus as capable of constituting an objective covered by the concept of public security".[35]

It also rejected the Commission's contentions that national rules of the **2.45** type laid down by the 1982 Order were not justified under Article 36 because the Community had adopted the necessary rules to ensure supplies of petroleum products in the event of a crisis. It found that this system did not give the Member State concerned an "unconditional assurance that supplies will in any event be maintained at a level to meet its minimum needs" (para 31).

Finally, it examined the question of proportionality. It is of particular **2.46** interest here to note that the case concerned the supply of an intermediate fuel – petroleum products. The Court admitted that if a crisis were to occur, it would in all probability lead to a severe reduction or interruption in crude oil deliveries. The Commission and the plaintiffs had argued that in these circumstances it was very unlikely

---

[35] Advocate General Slynn, at p 2764 has adopted an essentially similar definition of the term "public security", which in his view covered measures "vital to the stability and cohesion of the life of the modern State". He went on to add that the measures at issue might also be capable of falling within the concept of "public policy".

that a refinery could ensure supplies of petroleum products. Once again the Court rejected the Commission's line of argument. It reasoned that:

> "the fact of having a refining capacity on its territory enables the State concerned to enter into long-term contracts with the oil producing countries for the supply of crude oil to its refinery which offer a better guarantee of supplies in the event of a crisis.... Furthermore the existence of a national refinery constitutes an additional guarantee against the risk of an interruption in deliveries of refined products to which a State with no refining capacity of its own is exposed" (paras 39 and 40).[36]

2.47   However, as regards the quantities of petroleum which the oil companies were to be obliged to purchase, these were "in no case to exceed the minimum supply requirements of the state concerned without which public security, as defined above, and in particular the operation of its essential public services ... would be affected" (para 47).

(e) Greek petroleum monopoly

2.48   In Case C-347/88 *Commission* v *Greece* the Court ruled that the Greek Government could not rely upon the public security exemption to justify marketing restrictions on distributors of petroleum products when the government had not produced any evidence to support its claim that the relaxation of the restrictions would prevent its national refineries from remaining active. Furthermore, restrictions could only be justified if they were limited to the minimum requirements necessary to keep certain public services functioning. It was for the Greek Government to demonstrate this necessity.[37]

Article 36, second sentence, imposes a further restriction on Member States. Even where a measure capable of hindering imports and exports can be justified in principle under the first sentence, it must not constitute a means of arbitrary discrimination or a disguised restriction on trade between Member States.

(f) Observations

2.49   On the basis of *Campus* it may be concluded that the existence of a Council Directive obliging certain, but not all generators to hold emergency stocks of oil products at their power stations, would not necessarily exclude the continued scope for Member States to take *short-term* measures to guarantee electricity supply security.

It may also be concluded that Member States may seek to rely upon Article 36 to justify measures relating to the production of intermediate fuels if this would enhance the security of access to basic fuels. Nevertheless the judgment must be seen in context. Ireland is almost totally dependent

---

[36] Advocate General Slynn was of the opinion that public security ends could be guaranteed by less restrictive means, such as the keeping of stocks (at 2768).

[37] Judgment of 13 December 1990, not yet reported, especially at paras 43, 44 and 60.

upon imports, and petroleum products cannot be substituted by other fuels in all circumstances. Electricity is, of course, of a different order.[38]

(v) **The rule of reason, energy efficiency and environmental protection**

The "rule of reason" in Article 30, sometimes referred to by the Court as the "mandatory requirements" is the product of the Court's own jurisprudence.   **2.50**

National measures which apply to domestic and imported products alike[39], but which operate in practice to protect domestic production may also be justified if they are necessary to satisfy certain *mandatory requirements* relating *inter alia,* to the protection of public health, the promotion of fair trading, consumer protection and the defence of the consumer (Case 120/78 *Rewe* [1979] ECR 649).

In Case 18/88 *RTT* v *GB-Inno,* Advocate General Darmon recognised that national measures enacted with the aim of protecting the security and integrity of telecommunications networks could be deemed a "mandatory requirement".[40] Indeed this had been recognised by the Commission itself. In its judgment of 13 December 1991 the Court endorsed this view, but went on to hold that the reservation of the right to approve and connect telephone equipment to a national monopoly was contrary to Article 30, if the legislation did not provide for the possibility of an appeal to an independent body against the decisions of the monopoly.

Measures justifiable under the rule of reason test must be reasonable and are subject to the proportionality test. In Case 302/86 *Commission* v *Denmark,* the so-called "Danish Beer Bottles" case [1988] ECR 4607, the Court ruled that the protection of the environment is a mandatory requirement of Community law which may limit the application of Article 30 EEC. It therefore ruled that a national compulsory system for the return and re-use of used drink containers was a legitimate measure for the defence of the environment. A requirement that only containers which have been approved by a national environmental protection agency was disproportionate to that aim.   **2.51**

To draw an analogy with the electricity sector, a national rule that all coal-fired generating plant should be fitted with certain pollution control devices would probably be justified under this approach, but a requirement that these devices had to be approved by a national standards authority or by a monopolist generator, would contravene Article 30 (Case 45/85   **2.52**

---

[38] It is interesting to note that in Cases 351 & 360/85 *Charleroi* v *Commission* [1987] ECR 3549 the Court ruled that the Commission could not justify a special exemption from Community rules on steel quotas and subsidies or the basis that these were necessary to ensure the survival of the only steel plant operating in Denmark.

[39] Oliver, at p 103, has opined that as long as the Court takes the view that the rule of reason is only open to equally applicable measures yet continues to propound its discrimination test under Art 34 EEC for such measures it is difficult to see how the rule of reason can be used in relation to measures capable of hindering exports.

[40] Paras 13, 14 and 15 of his Opinion of 15 March 1989.

Dundalk [1988] ECR 4929; Case 18/88 *RTT* v *GB Inno*).

2.53   Measures falling within the scope of the rule of reason test must not constitute a means of arbitrary discrimination or a disguised restriction on trade.[41] Although the category of measures which might be deemed "mandatory requirements" is an open one, it is unlikely that the Court would accept any restrictions adopted other than for non-economic ends.

(a) Observations

2.54   It is submitted that measures to promote the efficient use of energy could be deemed "mandatory requirements", so long as they do not result in an arbitrary restriction on trade or are a disguised restriction on trade.[42] In a number of Member States the penetration of electricity for certain uses is discouraged or even forbidden in the interests of efficient energy use.

Where, however, it was obvious that electricity was excluded only as a means to give preference to the use of indigenous fuels, such as natural gas which is also more environmentally benign, then this would be a breach of Article 30.

2.55   It must be stressed that the rule of reason is essentially a device devised by the Court as a compromise between the potentially far-reaching effects of Article 30 and the need to recognise the legitimate interests of the Member States in regulating their economies. Thus "the rule of reason" is essentially a temporary acceptance of state regulation of the interest or value concerned pending Community regulation which will replace the need (and thus the justification) for national measures.[43]

(vi) **ECSC and Euratom Treaties**

2.56   There is no general prohibition on measures having equivalent effect to restrictions on trade in the ECSC Treaty, although its Article 4(b) prohibits discrimination between producers, purchasers and consumers.[44]

Chapter IX of the Euratom Treaty, which establishes the nuclear common market, only applies to ores and special fissile materials listed in Annex IV to the Treaty. This Chapter contains no general prohibition on measures having equivalent effect.

---

[41] Case 8/74 *Dassonville* [1974] ECR 837 at 852.

[42] In Case 240/83 *ADBHU* [1983] ECR 531, Advocate General Lenz (at 536) recognized the conservation of energy supplies as a justifiable restriction of free trade, although the Court only made reference to environmental protection. In the related Case 172/82 *Fabricants raffineurs d'huile de graissage* v *Inter Huiles* [1983] ECR 561, it was held that the goals of ensuring efficient energy use could be achieved by less restrictive means than the conferral of an exclusive right of export on French firms.

[43] Kapteyn and Verloren van Themaat, *Introduction to the Law of the European Communities*, 368.

[44] Art 4(a) only covers import and export duties, or charges having equivalent effect and quantitative restrictions on the movement of products. There is no equivalent to Art 30 EEC. The principle of non-discrimination in Art 4(b) falls short of the more comprehensive "Dassonville formula" Case 8/74, *loc cit.*

Part III

4. State trading monopolies and Article 37

As the Working Document of 1988 indicates, Article 37 is of particular **2.57** relevance to the electricity sector. It is a complex provision which has become notorious for its "obscure clarity".

Some commentators have argued that its position in the Treaty is misplaced; the original intention of the drafters had been to include it in the chapter on competition. Given the fundamental importance of the article to electricity sector, it is useful to recall the purpose envisaged for it. This was dealt with at some length by Advocate General Gand in *Albatros* [1965] ECR 29.

He reasoned that such monopolies can employ a wider range of restrictive measures than quotas, and thus that the mechanisms of the previous articles in Chapter 2 were ill-adapted to realising the Treaty's aims in relation to them.

Article 37(1) provides that:

"Member states shall progressively adjust any State monopolies of a commercial **2.58** character so as to ensure that when the transitional period has ended no discrimination regarding the conditions under which goods are procured and marketed exists between nationals of Member States."

In Case 59/75 *Manghera* [1976] ECR 91 the Court ruled that this provision became directly effective at the end of the "transitional period".[45] Article 37(2) provides that:

"Member States shall refrain from introducing any new measure which is **2.59** contrary to the principles laid down in paragraph 1 or which restrict the scope of the Articles dealing with the abolition of customs duties and quantitative restrictions between Member States."

This provision became directly effective on the entry into force of the Treaty.[46]

(i) Scope of Article 37

It is important to determine the scope of this complex provision in relation **2.60** to the electricity sector.

First, the provision applies to trading monopolies and not monopolies of production. Production monopolies fall under the provisions of Articles 59,

---

[45] That is as of 1968 for the original six Member States. By virtue of Art 44 of the first Act of Accession, Demark, Ireland and the UK were obliged to adjust their state monopolies by 31 December 1977. Greece was obliged to adjust its state monopolies by 31 December 1985 by virtue of Art 40 of the Act of Accession of Greece (OJ 1979 L291/1). Spain and Portugal have also been required to adjust their respective state monopolies by the end of 1991 (Arts 48 and 208 of the Act of Accession of Spain and Portugal, OJ 1985 L302/1).
[46] Case 6/64 *Costa* v *Enel* [1964] ECR 585.

85, 86 and 90.[47] Service monopolies must, in principle, be dealt with under Articles 59, 86 and 90.[48] If one considers that electricity transmission and distribution involve the provision of various services to ensure the delivery of a good, then it is important to ascertain the applicability of Article 37.

2.61   Second, it is limited to *goods* and does not cover monopolies providing services. This can be deduced from its position in the chapter of the Treaty which deals with goods. Until recently it was an open question whether in the field of service monopolies the principle laid down in Case 59/75 *Manghera, i.e.* that exclusive import rights are incompatible with the EEC Treaty also applied to services monopolies. In 1988 the Commission adopted Directive 88/301/EEC liberalising not only the marketing but also the servicing of telecommunications equipment, citing Articles 37 and 90 as the legal basis (OJ 1988 L131/73). The French Government challenged the Commission's powers to adopt this Directive on procedural as well as substantive grounds.

2.62   In the subsequent Case C-202/88 *France* v *Commission*[49] the Court upheld the Commission's contention that exclusive rights to connect, bring into service and maintain terminal equipment to be abolished if private enterprises were to be able to compete fully with state enterprises.[50] It made no reference to the goods/services distinction.

2.63   In Case C-260/89 *ERT* v *Dimotiki*[51] the Court dealt expressly with the compatibility of certain exclusive rights to emit radio sound and television images which were conferred on the ERT – the Greek State radio and television undertaking. It held that a television monopoly, being a service monopoly is not as such incompatible with the free movement of goods.

Nevertheless, the movement of all material connected with that service is subject to the rules concerning free movement of goods. Exclusive television rights and the granting of a supporting exclusive import right are not as such contrary to Article 30 (and therefore Art 37). This would be different if and when discrimination between national and imported products would result.[52]

2.64   There would appear to be an important divergence of approach between Case C-202/88 and Case C-260/89. In the first case the Court treated telecommunications terminal equipment as a good, and applied the *Dassonville* test to exclusive rights to market and service them. Hence the Court ruled that any measure which may restrict trade, directly or indirectly, actually or potentially, is in breach of Article 30. In the second

---

[47] In Case C-347/88 *Commission* v *Greece* the Commission chose not to challenge a provision in a Greek petroleum law conferring a monoploy to refine crude oil on national refiners and so the Court declined to rule on the legality of the production monopoly. In the subsequent case of *ERT* v *Dimotiki*, however, theCourt made it clear that a law creating monopoly over broadcoasting fell within the scope of Articles 86 and 90(1), see Chap 4.

[48] Case 155/73 *Sacchi.*

[49] Judgment of 19 March 1991, not yet reported.

[50] At paras 40-44.

[51] Judgment of 18 June 1991, not yet reported.

[52] This is essentially the position adopted by the Court in Case 352/85 *Bond van Adverteerders* v *Netherlands State* [1988] ECR 2085, and in Case 271/81 *Mialocq*[1983] ECR 2507.

case, however, the Court considered the monopoly as a service. To fall within the prohibitions contained in Article 30, it would have to be established that the rules in question discriminated against imported products. This issue will be dealt with in greater detail in the chapter on transit.

Article 37 does not apply to trade with third countries. In Case 91/78　**2.65** *Hansen* v *HZA Flensburg (Hansen II)* the Court deduced this from the position of Article 37. It concluded that:

> "the provisions of that Article cannot be applied to products imported from third countries since the arrangements for the importation of such products are subject not to the provisions governing the internal market but to those relating to commercial policy."

It is generally assumed, however, that Article 37 *does* apply to goods originating in third countries but in free circulation in the Community.[53]

(ii) Definition of the term "state monopoly"

Article 37(1) second paragraph, provides a wide definition of this term:　　**2.66**

> "the provisions of this Article shall apply to any body through which a Member State, in law or in fact, either directly or indirectly supervises, determines or appreciably influences imports or exports between Member states. These provisions shall apply likewise to monopolies delegated by the State to others."

In Case 30/87 *Bodson* [1988] ECR 2479 the Court confirmed that Article 37 extended to local authorities such as communes. However, the Court went on to hold that where the communes had granted an exclusive concession to a group of private undertakings and that group was therefore able to influence trade, no state monopoly existed.

The Court reasoned that the position of the group was not then　**2.67** attributable to any act of the public authorities.[54] Hence the particular situation had to be dealt with under Articles 85, 86 and 90.

The reasoning of the Court in Case 30/87 may have influenced the Commission's decision not to include the German electricity sector in its recent initiative on national electricity monopolies (see below).

Article 37 applies also to monopolies delegated to a private enterprise or　**2.68** a group of enterprises. The resultant monopoly could take the form of an institution, but would probably also apply to a system of licensing where the right to import and market products is restricted to a limited or closed class of persons.

An import licensing system does not in itself constitute a state monopoly.[55] In Case 118/86 *Openbaar Ministerie* v *Nertsvoederfabriek* [1987] ECR 3883 the Court held that a Dutch law which required the processing of poultry offal

---

[53]F Woodridge. "Some recent decisions concerning Article 37 *Legal Issues of European Integration* (1979), 105.
[54] This judgment has been criticised: J Shaw, (1989) 14 ELRev 421.
[55] Case 161/82 *Commission* v *France* (artificial insemination) [1983] ECR 2979.

into useful products but only by licensed persons, did not fall within the scope of Article 37.[56]

(iii) Meaning of "adjustment"

Exclusive import/export rights

2.69   Article 37(1) only requires Member States to "adjust" their national monopolies. It does not require their total abolition. The meaning of "adjustment" has been the scope of much debate. Since the Court's ruling in Case 59/75 *Manghera* it has been clear that exclusive rights to import goods are contrary to Article 30. The Court's recent judgment in Case C-202/88 *France* v *Commission,* has confirmed this.

2.70   The Commission is now applying this jurisprudence to the electricity sector. It has issued a series of letters to nine Member States, announcing that it intends to commence enforcement proceedings against them on the basis of Article 169.[57] The Member States have been asked to withdraw the absolute or exclusive rights to import and export, which they have conferred on particular undertakings.

(iv) Related exclusive rights

2.71   The question of whether other types of exclusive rights, including marketing rights, connection rights and exclusive rights to provide other forms of "ancillary services" are also contrary to Community law cannot be readily answered in the abstract.

    In Case 59/75 Advocate General Warner argued that exclusive marketing rights should be abolished because the abolition of a monopoly's exclusive import right would be hollow if that monopoly's exclusive right to market goods was maintained.

    Although the Court did not rule on this point in Case 59/75, in Case C-202/88 *France* v *Commission* it held that exclusive rights to market telecommunications equipment were contrary to Article 30.

    It further ruled that monopoly or exclusive rights to provide related services, including connection to a network, repair and maintenance and after sales services were contrary to Articles 3(f) and 30 EEC.

2.72   Similarly, in Case C-347/88 *Commission* v *Greece* the Court held that exclusive rights to market petroleum products reserved to the state monopoly were contrary to both Articles 30 and 37.

    This jurisprudence will be returned to in the following chapters on state firms and on transit.

(v) Relationship between Articles 37 and 36

2.73   It remains an open question as to whether the exceptions to the rules on free movement contained in Article 36 are also applicable to Article 37.

---

[56] Or, indeed, Article 30.

[57] The Commission's powers under this article are discussed in more detail in Chap 10.

Unfortunately, and although presented with a clear opportunity to do so, the Court declined to rule on this point in its recent ruling in Case C-347/88 – the Greek petroleum products case – the Greek Government had reserved to its state oil refineries the exclusive right, *inter alia,* to import petroleum products. Advocate General Tesauro was of the opinion that as these exclusive rights clearly were in breach of Article 37, there was no need for the Court to go on to examine whether they were also in breach of Article 30 or to consider the application of Article 36 (para 19).

The Court did not address this point directly. The Greek Government **2.74** argued that Article 30 had not been breached as the rules applied equally to imported finished products or products domestically refined from imported crude. The Court dealt with the potential application of Article 36 to Article 30 alone. It rejected the Greek Government's contentions on the grounds that the measures guaranteed an outlet for domestic refinery production irrespective of whether the original crude oil was imported or not. It did not deal with the potential applicability of Article 36 to Article 37, nor did it consider whether such restrictions could be justified under the rule of reason.

A possible interpretation of Case C-347/88 is to view it as confirmation **2.75** that the Court now views Article 37 as nothing more than a specific application of the rules on free movement to the organisation of a state monopoly. Hence the rules constituting such monopolies may be judged under either set of provisions, and the Article 36 exception or the rule of reason applied.[58]

If this interpretation is correct, it may be possible for Member States to seek to rely upon it to justify exclusive import and export rights, in defence to the Commission's enforcement proceedings, discussed above.

5. Conclusion

The principles of free movement of goods and services which are **2.76** fundamental under the EEC Treaty, are of potentially wide application, as the Court's jurisprudence has made repeatedly clear.

As electricity has not been given any special status under the EEC Treaty, one must begin from the assumption that these principles apply to activities in this sector in full. That said, it must be recalled that the scope of exceptions to the rules on free movement as discussed above – security in two senses and continuity of supply – also require further concrete elaboration in the context of this particular sector. The environmental

---

[58] This would seem to be confirmed by the court's judgement in Case C-202/88 *France* v *Commission, loc cit,* where the Court disposed of the issues before it entirely under Art 30, even although the Directive in question had been based on, *inter alia* Art 37. The Court has now adopted a similar approach in Case 18/88 *RTT* v *GB-INNO* (13 December 1991) where it disposed of the case on the basis of Arts 30 and 86, even though the Commission had argued that a breach of Art 37 was involved.

aspects of electricity use and supply add further complications to the straightforward elimination of all barriers to trade.

Although Article 37 EEC has been singled out by Commission as a key article for the electricity sector, the jurisprudence on it has been especially confused. While the Court of Justice has offered some clarification of its scope, it has been reluctant to offer any general principles on its application, and has preferred to confine its judgments to the facts of the case before it. It is therefore advisable to examine Article 37 in conjunction with concrete issues, a task which is taken up in Chapters 4 and 6.

CONTENTS OF CHAPTER 3

Chapter 3
Competition Rules

1. Introduction

The institution of a system ensuring that competition in the common **3.1** market is not distorted is a principal aim of the EEC Treaty (Art 3(f)). In the ECSC Treaty certain forms of anti-competitive practices are recognised as incompatible with the functioning of a common market for coal and steel. In accordance with Article 5 ECSC, the Community is charged with the duty of "ensuring the establishment, maintenance and observance of normal competitive conditions". The Euratom Treaty makes no special provision for competition.

This chapter begins with an examination of the basic principles of competition law in the EEC and ECSC Treaties, and explores their applicability to undertakings in the electricity sector. The impact of the competition rules to the relations between Member States and undertakings is the subject of Chapter 4.

(i) EEC Treaty competition rules

Articles 85 and 86 EEC are addressed to undertakings. Article 85 prohibits **3.2** restrictive practices and agreements while Article 86 prohibits the abuse of a dominant position. In Case 45/85 *Verband der Sachversichere EV v Commission (Fire Insurance)* [1987] ECR 405 confirmed that these rules apply to all sectors with the exception of those that are subject to a special Regulation, such as agriculture and road, rail, sea and air transport.

The Court expressly added that Article 85(3) allows the characteristics of the sector in question to be taken into account without it being necessary to resort to a Regulation under Article 88(2) EEC.

Both in origin and in their practical application, Articles 85 and 86 are **3.3** primarily a complement to the provisions of the EEC Treaty on free movement of goods. Article 30 *et seq* apply to public acts, while Articles 85 and 86 apply to undertakings.[1] Member States, however, are obliged under Articles 3(f) and 5 EEC to take all appropriate measures to ensure the fulfilment of the aims of the treaty and to abstain from any measures which might jeopardise their attainment.

Thus in Case 13/77 *INNO v ATAB* [1977] ECR 2115 the Court ruled that:

"while it is true that Article 86 is directed at undertakings, nonetheless it is also true that the Treaty imposes a duty on Member States not to adopt or maintain

---

[1] Cases 56 & 58/64 *Consten* v *Grundig* [1966] ECR 299 at 342.

in force any measure which could deprive that provision of its effectiveness. Likewise, Member States may not enact measures enabling private undertakings to escape from the constraints imposed by Articles 85 to 94 of the Treaty."

3.4   As the Court's subsequent jurisprudence has made abundantly clear, Articles 85 and 86 may be applicable to the legislative and regulatory acts of Member States. This developing body of jurisprudence is of particular relevance to the electricity sector because there are many occasions where governments utilise the industry – whether public or private – as an instrument of intervention in the economy. It is examined in full in the next chapter.

2. Competition rules for undertakings: Articles 85 and 86

(i) General principles

3.5   As Articles 85 and 86 are the subject of numerous specialised commentaries, it is not proposed to discuss their general application in great detail here. The purpose of this section is rather to examine several basic principles and establish their potential relevance to the electricity sector. The application of these principles to specific issues relating to prices and tariffs, transit and long-term contractual arrangements are the subject of separate chapters.

(a) "Inter-state" element

3.6   Article 85(1) prohibits as incompatible with the common market:

> "all agreements between undertakings, decisions by associations of undertakings and concerted practices which may affect trade between Member States and which have as their object or effect the prevention, restriction, or distortion of competition within the common market".

Article 86 provides that:

> "Any abuse by one or more undertakings of a dominant position within the common market or in a substantial part of it shall be prohibited as incompatible with the common market in so far as it may affect trade between Member States."

A general problem which must be addressed is whether certain arrangements or practices do in fact lead to restrictions in inter-state trade, given the generally low level of trade in electricity between the Member States at present.

3.7   The relevant test for *Article 85* – formulated by the Court in Case 56/65 *Société Technique Minière* [1965] ECR 249 – is that:

"it must be possible to foresee with a sufficient degree of probability on the basis of a set of objective factors of law or of fact that the arrangement in question may have an influence, direct or indirect, actual or potential, on the pattern of trade between Member States".

In other words trade flows must have been diverted from the pattern they would normally have followed in a single, integrated market (see most recently Case 27/87 *Erauw – Jacquery* v *La Hesbignonne* [1988] ECR 1919).

Further, it is clear from the Court's judgment in Case 193/83 *Windsurfing International* v *Commission* [1986] ECR 611, paras 95-97 that in determining whether an agreement has an *effect* on inter-state trade, one must examine the agreement as a whole, so that it is irrelevant that individual restrictions might not infringe Article 85(1).

An example of an *indirect restriction* on trade from the Court's earlier **3.8** jurisprudence which may be of particular relevance to electricity markets is its ruling in Case 123/83 *BNIC* v *Clair* [1985] ECR 402. Thus where a product covered by an agreement is not itself exported to another Member State, but a product derived from it is, then restrictions on competition in trade in the intermediate product could be capable of affecting intra-Community trade, even if there is no trade in that intermediate product, where the product constitutes the raw material for another product marketed elsewhere in the Community.

This example of an indirect restriction might be applicable to restrictions on import/export of electricity by or to large users, such as chemical or aluminium producers for whom electricity is a significant "raw material" in the sense that it constitutes a major proportion of their production costs.

Further, the Court has ruled that certain agreements which contain **3.9** indirect restrictions relating to the sales of domestic products within a single state may affect trade indirectly, for example, by making it harder for imports to penetrate the market, especially where the agreement extends over the whole national territory.

Thus an agreement which "by its very nature has the effect of reinforcing the compartmentalization of markets on a national basis, thereby holding up the inter-penetration which the Treaty is designed to bring about and protecting domestic production" could be contrary to Article 85.[2]

In its more recent jurisprudence the Court has increasingly condemned practices or behaviour on the sole ground that it artificially changes the structure of competition.[3]

In examining the potential effects of restrictions on trade, the Court **3.10** has also recognised that changing market conditions must be taken into account. In Case 107/82 *AEG* v *Commission* [1983] ECR 3201 the Court held that:

---

[2] Case 8/72 *Cementhandelaren* v *Commission* [1972] ECR 977 at 991; See also Case 246/86 *Belasco* v *Commission* [1989] ECR 2181.
[3] See Case 311/85 *Vlaamse Reisbureaus* [1987] ECR 3801, and most recently Case T-51/89 *Tetra Pak* [1991] 4 CMLR 333 at para 22.

"the mere fact that at a certain time traders applying for admission to a distribution network... are not engaged in intra-Community trade cannot suffice to exclude the possibility that restrictions on their freedom of action may impede intra-Community trade, since the situation may change from one year to another in terms of alterations in the conditions or composition of the market both in the common market as a whole and individual national markets".

3.11 For *Article 86* the Court has focused not so much on the consequences of abusive behaviour on the pattern of imports and exports, but on the impact of that behaviour on the structure of competition within the common market. The monopoly in question must enjoy "a dominant position within the common market or in a substantial part of it".

3.12 Article 86 applies to buyers and to sellers. In its Decision on the complaint initiated by the National Association of Licensed Opencast Operators (NALOO), of 23 May 1991, discussed below, the Commission held that as the two major generators, National Power and Power Gen are the only purchasers of coal for electricity generation "they are therefore jointly dominant as buyers of this coal in England and Wales" (para 55).

3.13 The test of "substantial part" is a relative one which is not limited to the geographical extent of the market in question, but depends on the economic importance of the market[4]. Neither the importance of the market or the product can be assessed on purely quantitative criteria alone.[5] It is therefore a matter of fact to be established on a case by case basis, although the Court has given some guidance on the criteria to be applied. For the electricity sector the following findings would appear relevant.

  (i)   A statutory monopoly within the territory of a single Member State has been found to satisfy the "substantial part" test.[6]

  (ii) The size of the market share held by an undertaking or group of undertakings which is shielded from any competition at all as a result of an exclusive concession; or

  (iii) The influence of that monopolistic situation with regard to supplies of goods and services not covered by the exclusive concession; or

  (iv) The financial resources of the group/undertaking.[7]

3.14 In reviewing the Commission's interpretation of the meaning of the term "effect on inter-state trade", the Court has adopted an equally wide approach to the phrase. It is of interest to note, however, that in Case 733/74 *Groupement des Fabricants de Papiers Peints de Belgique* v *Commission* [1975] ECR 1491 that the Court did overturn the Commission's finding that a national system of collective resale price maintenance affected inter-

---

[4] Cases 40-48, 50, 54-56, 111, 113 & 114/73 *Suiker Unie* [1975] ECR 1663.

[5] Case 77/77 *BP* v *Commission* [1978] ECR 1511. See most recently, Case T-69/89 *RTE* v *Commission*, judgment of 11 July 1991, where the Court of First Instance rejected RTE's contention that the market for information on TV programmes in the minor frontier region of another Member State was of marginal significance to inter-state trade (at para 77).

[6] Case 41/83 *Italy* v *Commission* [1985] ECR 873; Case 311/84 *CBEM* v *CCT* [1985] ECR 3261; Case C-41/90 *Höfner*, judgment of 23 April 1991; Case C-260/89 *ERT* v *Dimotiki*, judgment of 18 June 1991.

[7] Case 30/87 *Bodson* [1988] ECR 2479.

state trade, since the case was a relatively one and the Commission had not explained in sufficient detail the precise way in which inter-state trade would be affected. This precedent may not be without relevance to the electricity sector, where restrictions relating to electricity may have complicated repercussions on primary fuel markets.

(ii) **The de minimis rule**

3.15 Agreements or practices will fall outside the scope of Articles 85 and 86 if they do not affect trade to an *appreciable* extent. It will be a matter of fact and degree in each case.

The Court has given some guidance in earlier cases. For example, the weakness on the market of the parties to an agreement may be such that it is of insufficient importance to be caught under Article 85(1). However where the parties to the agreement are large undertakings the Commission has in the past disregarded arguments based on the small volume of goods covered by the agreement in question, especially in oligopolistic markets (see, for example, its Decision in Fisher Price, OJ 1988 L49/19).

Conduct which is wholly confined to a single Member State and has no perceptible repercussions outside that territory probably cannot affect trade between Member States.[8]

This jurisprudence may be of some relevance to the application of competition rules to the complaints of discriminatory treatment from auto-generators in individual Member States where the latter's production is small and the potential for import and export minimal. It will, however, be a question of fact and degree in each case.[9]

3.16 The Court has applied similar reasoning – requiring an appreciable effect on trade between Member States – in its decisions on Article 86.

In Case 30/87 *Bodson* (at 2513) the Court took the view that the activities of a group covering one third of the population in France constituted a substantial part of the common market, but left it for the national court to determine whether there was an effect on inter-state trade.

3.17 In its initial assessment of the various agreements concluded between Scottish Power and Scottish Hydro-Electric the Commission appeared implicitly to have applied the *de minimis* rule (OJ 1990 C191/10). In its recent, final Decision on the Scottish Nuclear Agreement, however, it has ruled that:

> "because of the interdependence between the networks on the one hand between Scotland and England and on the other hand between England and France, and also because of the proposed development of these inter-connections, the agreement is likely to affect trade between Member States."(OJ 1991 L178/31 at paras 30 and 31)

---

[8] Case 22/78 *Hugin* [1979] ECR 1869; see however Cases C-260/89 *ERT* and C-41/90 *Höfner.*
[9] The Commission's Notice of 3 September 1986 on notification of agreements of minor importance gives further guidance on the nature of the goods and the availability of substitutes, the aggregate turnover of the parties etc.

The Commission has, however, taken the view that the proposed "Renewables Contracts" in England and Wales are subject to this rule (Case IV 33.470, OJ 1990 C191/13).

(iii) Article 85(1): substance

3.18　Article 85 prohibits agreements between *independent* undertakings. It is not concerned with agreements between undertakings belonging to the same group of companies, and having the status of parent company and subsidiary if the undertakings form an economic unit within which the subsidiary has no real freedom to determine its course of action on the market, and if the agreements are concerned merely with the internal allocation of tasks as between the undertakings (Case 30/87 *Bodson* [1988] ECR 2479).

The question of whether an agreement between electricity producers and generators constituted nothing more than the centralization and allocation of tasks to a single body and thus fell outside the scope of Article 85, was considered by the Commission in its Decision in the *IJsselcentrale* case (Commission Dec 91/50/EEC, OJ 1990 L28/32).

This Decision concerned Article 21 of a Co-operation Agreement between the Dutch organization, SEP, which has responsibility for, *inter alia*, planning electricity supply and generation in the Netherlands, and the various generating companies (see p33 of the Decision). The generating companies are in fact the shareholders of the SEP as well as parties to the Agreement, and the SEP is a joint subsidiary which acts as a vehicle for co-operation between them.

3.19　SEP argued that the participating electricity generating companies together form an economic unit, because they are components in "one indivisible public electricity supply system". The real function of the article of the Co-operation Agreement at issue was therefore to secure the allocation of tasks between the generators, with certain tasks being centralised and allocated to the SEP.[10] SEP therefore contended that there can be no question of competition between the parties and that Article 85 did not apply.

The Commission declared that it could not accept this reasoning:

> "To begin with, the four participants do not belong to a single group of companies. They are separate legal persons and are not controlled by a single person, natural or legal. Each generating company determines its own conduct independently. It is hard to see how else there could be differences between the prices different generators charge for power....
> The fact that the generators all form part of one indivisible system of public supply changes nothing here. The distributors likewise form part of the same system, but there is no reason to suppose that they form an economic unity with the generators on that ground alone.

---

[10] SEP invoked the Court's judgment in Case 170/83 *Hydrotherm* [1984] ECR 2999.

Finally it cannot be said that SEP itself forms an economic unit with one or more of the generating companies. SEP is a joint venture controlled by its parent companies together"(para 24, p40).

The agreement may take a number of forms. The concept of a *concerted* **3.20** *practice* in Article 85(1) has been defined by the Court as "a form of co-ordination between undertakings which, without having reached the stage where an agreement properly so called has been concluded, knowingly substitutes practical co-operation between them for the risks of competition".[11]

(iv) External effect

The fact that one of the undertakings to an agreement is established in a **3.21** third country does not prevent the applicability of Article 85 if the agreement has effects within the territory of the common market.[12]

Agreements between non-Community undertakings may also fall within the ambit of Article 85(1) if they lead to a restriction of competition within the Community which is capable of having adverse effects on trade between the Member States. In Cases 89/85, 104/85, 114/85, 116-17/85 & 125-29/85 *"Wood Pulp"* [1988] ECR 5193 the Court held that the Treaty of Rome does not prevent the application of the competition rules to undertakings situated outside the Community so long as the restrictive agreement is implemented within the Community and has the object or direct effect of restriction competition within the common market. An agreement will be implemented within the EC when it concerns the price, quantity or quality of a product sold to a buyer in the EC.[13]

(v) Agreements which restrict competition

Obviously Article 85(1) will only apply to cases where there is some **3.22** competition to be restricted. In the electricity sector it may be important to establish whether and to what extent the absence of competition is a result of government intervention.

In Cases 40-48/73 *Suiker Unie,* the Court of Justice held that measures taken to regulate the market for sugar in Italy, fundamentally restricted the scope for competition between sugar producers.[14] The Commission's finding of an infringement was therefore quashed. Where, however, despite public intervention, some room remains for competitive pressures to influence the decisions of market participants, further restrictions of

---

[11] Case 48/69 *ICI* v *Commission* [1972] ECR 619; see most recently, the Commission's Decision 91/297/EEC *Soda-ash, ICI, Solvay,* OJ 1991 L152/1.
[12] Case 22/71 *Beguelin* v *SAGL Import Export* [1971] ECR 949; Case 48/69 *ICI* v *Commission, loc cit.*
[13] Lange and Sandage, "The Wood Pulp Decision" (1989) 26 CMLRev, 137 at 155. See also the Commission's recent decision in *ANSAC,* OJ 1991 L 152/94.
[14] The Court has not accepted in its subsequent case law, however, as defence that competition is de facto excluded in highly regulated markets. See the cases discussed *infra.*

competition which result from the behaviour of the undertakings themselves will fall foul of Article 85(1).[15]

3.23   In Case 123/83 *BNIC* v *Clair* the Court considered an agreement fixing prices concluded within the framework and in accordance with the procedures of a public law body which only had private law effects after having been declared binding by a Minister, as falling under Article 85(1) (see further Chap 7 – Prices and Tariffs).

In Case 30/87 *Bodson,* however, the Court held that Article 85 did not apply to a system of concession or licensing arrangements between French licensing authorities acting in their capacity as public authorities and undertakings entrusted with the provision of a public service. Although it is now well-established in the case law of the Court that Article 85 and 86 apply to state undertakings,[16] the Court appeared to draw a distinction between the exercise of public law powers, in which a Member State would not be regarded as an undertaking and the conduct of commercial activities, where it would.

To the extent that government measures leave enterprises room to compete on the market they have to do so.[17] Indeed the Commission has contended that in such circumstances the anti-competitive effects of private arrangements are all the more significant.[18]

(vi) **Horizontal and vertical agreements**

3.24   Article 85 applies to agreements between undertakings operating at the same level in the process of production and distribution (horizontal agreements) and to agreements between undertakings operating at different levels (vertical agreements).[19] The Co-operation Agreement between the SEP and the electricity generators in the Netherlands has been considered by the Commission to amount to a horizontal and a vertical restriction on competition. Article 21 of this Agreement prohibited the importation and exportation of electricity by undertakings other than SEP. It had "horizontal effects" because it prohibited generators from exporting or importing and it had "vertical effects" because it required generators to impose the same ban on distributors in their supply agreements.[20]

The Commission's Decisions, as confirmed by the case law of the Court of Justice show that multilateral horizontal agreements in which prices, restrictions of production and/or market sharing are provided for, will rarely escape the prohibition of Article 85(1).[21]

---

[15] Art 86 will also apply – see Case C-41/90 *Höfner.*
[16] *BRT* v *SABAM op cit.*
[17] Cases 240-242, 261, 262, 268 & 269/82 *Stichting Sigarettenindustrie* [1985] ECR 3860; Case 13/77 *INNO* v *ATAB, loc cit.*
[18] Cases 209-215 & 218/78 *Van Landewyck* v *Commission (FEDETAB)* [1980] ECR 3125 at 3261.
[19] Cases 56 and 58/64 *Consten and Grundig loc cit.*
[20] Para 25 at pp40-41 of Commission Dec 91/50, *loc cit.*
[21] See further Kapteyn and Verloren van Themaat – *Introduction to the Law of the European Communities,* 540-541 and the relevant case law cited at nn 319 and 322.

(a) Prohibited agreements

Examples of agreements likely to restrict competition are given in Article   **3.25**
85(1): These are agreements which:

"(a) directly or indirectly fix purchase or selling prices or any other trading
conditions;
(b) limit or control production, markets, technical development, or investment:
(c) share markets or sources of supply;
(d) apply dissimilar conditions to equivalent transactions with other trading
parties, thereby placing them at a competitive disadvantage;
(e) make the conclusion of contracts subject to acceptance by other parties of
supplementary obligations which, by their nature or according to commercial
usage, have no connection with the subject of such contracts."

This list is by no means exhaustive. In essence it covers the classic forms
of cartels which will almost always automatically result in a restriction of
competition for third parties.

Kapteyn and Verloren van Themaat offer some useful general guidelines   **3.26**
on agreements other than those specified in Article 85(1)(a) to (d), where
a restriction on competition may be involved. Two requirements must be
met:

"In the first place, the agreement will have to restrict the free market behaviour
or market policy of one or more of the parties on one point or another. In the
second place, either an intended effect on third parties or an actual effect on
the position of third parties (competitors, suppliers, or buyers) will have to be
established. In the case of horizontal agreements an intended effect on third
parties will generally follow simply from the market position... In the case of
bilateral vertical agreements (exclusive dealing agreements, resale price
maintenance, long term selling contracts) on the other hand, as a rule a more
detailed examination of the market position of the parties involved, the specific
characteristics of the product, and the alternatives for competitors and
suppliers will have to take place." (*Ibid* at 513)

In its recent decisions in Case C-277/88 *Sandoz* [1990] ECR 45 and Case   **3.27**
C-279/87 *Tipp-ex* [1990] ECR 261 the Court has upheld the Commission's
condemnation of what appeared at first sight to be essentially a matter of
unilateral action.[22]

(vii) **Permissible co-operation**

(a) Article 85(1)

Certain forms of co-operation between undertakings have been considered   **3.28**
by the Commission and the Court not to amount to a restriction on
competition within the meaning of Article 85(1). There are a number of
Notices in effect.[23] In 1968 the Commission published a Notice on

---

[22] This Court had developed this doctrine earlier in Cases 25 & 26/84 *Ford Werke* v *Commission*
[1985] ECR 2725.
[23] See further Jones *et al, Competition Law Handbook* (1991) 2nd ed.

Co-operation Agreements setting out the considerations by which it would be guided in considering whether particular agreements did not fall within the provisions of Article 85(1).[24] The Commission has recently published two further Notices regarding restraints ancillary to concentrations (OJ 1990 C203/5) and regarding concentration and co-operation operations (OJ 1990 C203/6).

It is generally agreed that these Notices offer little more than useful guidance to parties to a potential agreement. In particular, the Commission has construed the scope of the 1968 Notice very narrowly, and a number of its decisions, subsequently endorsed by the Court indicate that it is unsafe for firms to rely upon a strict interpretation of its provisions.[25]

(b) Article 85(3)

3.29   Article 85(3) allows for Article 85(1) to be declared inapplicable if the agreement:

> "contributes to improving the production or distribution of goods or to promoting technical or economic progress,while allowing consumers a fair share of the resulting benefit, and which does not:
> (a) impose on the undertakings concerned restrictions which are not indispensable to the attainment of these objectives:
> (b) afford such undertakings the possibility of eliminating competition in respect of a substantial part of the products in question."

3.30   These are usually referred to as the two positive and two negative requirements. For the first positive requirement – *i.e.* the contribution of the agreement to the improvement of production etc – it is necessary to demonstrate that the agreement will lead to distinct *objective* advantages, such as reductions in the cost of purchase, processing, sale and transport. It is not enough that the agreement confers *subjective* advantages on the parties (Cases 56 & 58/64 *Consten, loc cit*).

The second positive requirement can be satisfied if reductions in cost and improvement in quality can be demonstrated and the resulting benefits are passed on to consumers.[26]

3.31   Even where an agreement fulfills the positive requirements, it must also overcome the negative conditions. The first of these is an application of the proportionality rule: it must be established that any restriction on competition is a condition *sine qua non* for the realization of the improvements sought. It is not merely a question of showing that the positive effects outweigh the negative effects of the agreement.[27]

In its Decision on the agreement between the Dutch electricity producers and the SEP (the *IJsselcentrale* Decision) the Commission held that:

---

[24] Notice of 29 July 1968, JO 1968, C75/3. For the current version see OJ 1986 C231/2.
[25] See further Whish – *Competition Law*, 239, Bellamy and Child – *Common Market Law of Competition*, 101.
[26] The term "consumers" is usually taken to be wide enough to extend to users. See, for example, *Re ACEC/Berliet,* JO 1968 L201/7.
[27] See further, Bellamy and Child, 142-152.

"... the absolute effect which SEP has given to the import and export ban in Article 21 is not indispensable to the attainment of the objectives of the Co-operation Agreement. The third test of Article 85(3) is in any event not satisfied." (para 53 at p 45)

3.32 The second negative condition is a guarantee that the other three conditions will be met. It is unlikely that the condition can be met where the cartel in question dominates the relevant product or geographical market. Suppliers and buyers should have an alternative. Potential competition from other parties may suffice, but there must be a real short term possibility of competition. The Commission's assessment of the effect of the coal supply agreements between the British Coal Corporation and the two electricity generators in England and Wales offers a useful example of the application of the principles involved here (see below).

3.33 Where the Commission is of the opinion that the Agreement does not come within the scope of Article 85(1) it can grant negative clearance in accordance with Article 2 of Regulation 17. Alternatively, it may grant an individual exemption to an agreement which satisfies the criteria of Article 85(3).

If it intends to consider either course of action, it is required by Article 19(3) of Regulation 17 to publish in the *Official Journal* a summary of the relevant application and invite all interested parties to submit their observations. It will usually indicate whether or not it intends to adopt a favourable position. The final decision must also be published (Reg 17, Art 21).

Exemption is only granted for a fixed period and may be subject to conditions (Reg 17, Art 8).

(viii) Application of Article 85 to the electricity sector

3.34 In recent years the Commission has taken a more active interest in the workings of the electricity sector.

In 1990 the Commission published three Notices pursuant to Article 19(3) of Regulation 17 relating to the electricity sector. These concerned: the reorganization of the electricity industry in England and Wales (OJ 1990 C191/9) and the reorganization of the electricity industry in Scotland (OJ 1990 C245/9). Earlier in 1990 it also issued a Notice relating to the so-called "Jahrehundert contract" relating to the supply of German coal to electricity producers (OJ 1990 C159/7).

In January 1991 it adopted Decision 50/91/EEC on the *IJsselcentrale* case, which has already been referred to. In April 1991 the final Decision 91/329/EEC on the Scottish Nuclear Agreement was published (OJ 1991 L178/31). As this latter Decision is definitive, subject of course to any appeal to the Court, and as it deals with the application of Article 85(1) and (3) in more precise detail than the earlier Notices, it will be analysed first. Some of the themes emerging from the August 1990 Notices are examined in Chapter 8, which deals with long-term contracts.

(a) Scottish Nuclear Agreement

3.35 In the course of reorganising the Scottish electricity industry, the UK Government has created two separate independent and competing vertically-integrated electricity utilities – Scottish Power and Scottish Hydro-Electric. The non-nuclear generating assets of the former state-owned Scottish electricity boards have been redistributed between these two new companies.

In addition a series of long-term contractual arrangements have been set in place to create rights and obligations between the two utilities in relation to certain of the generating assets and transmission systems of each, effectively replacing ownership of these assets with long-term contractual entitlement the duration of which corresponds to the currently expected lifetime of the power stations concerned. Responsibility for the operation of the Scottish nuclear stations has been transferred to the publicly owned Scottish Nuclear Ltd. The latter sells all its output under contract to Scottish Power and Hydro-Electric. Under the terms of the "Nuclear Energy Agreement", the two companies are obliged to purchase all Scottish Nuclear's output on a take or pay basis. The agreement also contains provisions for the calculation of the prices to be paid by Scottish Power and Hydro-Electric.

3.36 The Commission has decided that the Nuclear Energy Agreement is an agreement between undertakings within the meaning of Article 85(1). It restricts competition in three ways:
– Scottish Nuclear is constrained to sell only to the two Scottish companies.
– Scottish power and Hydro-Electric are restricted, through the operation of the quota system, in their choice of suppliers. Scottish Power purchases 74.9% and Hydro-Electric 25.1%. Since they may not deviate from the quotas, they are unable to gain any competitive advantage one over the other.
– The price at which nuclear electricity is purchased is fixed and identical for the two companies.

3.37 The Decision then considers whether the Agreement meets the necessary conditions for exemption under Article 85(3).

As to the first two positive tests, the Commission reasons firstly, that production will be improved because it allows the long-term planning that is required for reliable production ensuring security of supply and an independent energy market. Further it allows stations to function at their full capacity, thus offsetting high investment costs and allowing for the realization of economies of scale. It then goes on to add, somewhat perplexingly, that the agreement will also allow *overcapacity* in the Scottish nuclear industry to be eliminated.

3.38 Secondly, consumers will benefit from the introduction of competition into a system that was hitherto monopolistic.

The two negative tests were also deemed to have been satisfied. The Commission required the lifetime of the agreement to be reduced from 30 to 15 years. This period was sufficient to provide the stability and guarantee necessary for long-term planning by the two private companies, and is sufficient to allow Scottish Nuclear to become fully profitable and competitive. Although nuclear represents some 44% of electricity generated in Scotland, the Commission did not view the agreement as eliminating competition from the market for electricity generation, with the exception of nuclear.

(b) Jahrhundertvertrag Notice

In its Notice on the German *Jahrhundertvertrag* (Case No IV/33.151, OJ **3.39**
1990 C159/7) the Commission considered the legality of an agreement concluded between the Association of the German Public Electricity Supply Industry and the General Association of the German Coalmining Industry concerning the sale of fixed quotas of German coal to the public electricity supply industry. The Commission took the view that as the agreement was designed to share markets it fell within Article 85(1).

Although the agreement was concluded between German coal mines and German electricity producers, the Commission found that:

> "Trade between Member States is affected since, to the extent that the electricity supply companies are obliged to use German coal for the generation of electricity, the use of other primary sources of energy such as heavy fuel oil, natural gas or nuclear energy is excluded; however, the use of coal from other Member States does not in principle seem to be excluded.... It should be noted in this context that intra-Community trade in coal is of little or no significance. Trade between Member States is also affected since, to the extent that the electricity supply companies are obliged to use German coal for electricity generating, the import of electricity from other Member States is excluded."

It went on to find, however, that the agreement between the coal **3.40**
and electricity producers "seems to justify exemption under Article 85(3) under certain conditions." Consumers could benefit because the agreements contributed to improving the generating and distribution of electricity and since they served to safeguard electricity supplies. It was not however evident to the Commission that these arrangements satisfied the proportionality test. It therefore proposed to grant a limited authorization of the agreement until 31 March 1991, subject to the condition that the quotas did not exceed their present levels. This temporary authorization has now been extended (Case IV/33.152, OJ 1991 C116/6).

This Notice is of interest for two reasons. Firstly, the Commission was prepared to assess the effect of the agreement on inter-state trade in primary fuels as well as in electricity. Secondly, it considered that the positive conditions in Article 85(3) could be interpreted to cover contractual arrangements designed to safeguard electricity supply and improve generation and distribution. The fact that the agreements resulted in consumers paying more for their electricity was not considered.

(c) IJsselcentrale Decision

3.41 This Decision originated in a complaint from a distribution company which wished to import electricity into the Netherlands. The complaint was formally made in 1988, a year prior to the enactment of a new Electricity Act in the Netherlands. The entry into force of this law made the legal situation more confused, as in accordance with that law, only large customers and not distributors, have express rights to import and transport electricity. The law was however, silent on the question of exports.

The interaction of the new law and the earlier agreement between the SEP and the electricity producers – the OVS – was extremely complex, and although the Commission reviewed and discussed several of its consequences in its Decision, it chose to confine its ruling to the residual effects of the OVS on imports by large customers and exports of electricity surplus to public requirements by distributors, large customers and auto-generators.

3.42 The Commission went on to find that the agreement fell within the scope of Article 85(1), and that, as it had not been notified, it could not be considered for exemption under Article 85(3). The Commission also expressed the view, that even if it had been notified, it would have in all probability not qualified for exemption. It then considered SEP's defence based on Article 90(2) (see 3.91 below, and further, Chap 4, for a detailed discussion of this article) to the effect that it would not be able to perform its public function in guaranteeing security of supply if it lost control over imports and exports. The Commission did not accept this argument, at least in so far as imports destined for, and exports from non-public supply were concerned.

(d) Observations

3.43 It emerges from these Notices and the Decision on the Scottish Nuclear Agreement that the Commission is prepared to consider various forms of agreements as capable of exemption under Article 85(3) if they improve security of supply, viewed as beneficial to consumers, and if they improve electricity production and distribution. Emphasis has been placed largely on the first two positive tests in Article 85(3).

In the agreements concluded in the context of the British privatization exercise, the Commission has been prepared to accept the argument that they provide a certain amount of stability in the transitional period from state ownership to full competition.

3.44 Nevertheless the Commission was not prepared to accept the argument advanced by the Dutch electricity industry that an agreement which amounted to an *absolute* ban on imports and exports could be exempted under Article 85(3) (Dec 91/50/EEC). In the Notice on the Jahrhundertvertrag, it also indicated that security of supply might be secured in ways which had less restrictive effects on trade than the German quota system.

It will of course be for the Court to determine whether the Commission has been correct in its interpretation of Article 85(3) as covering supply security.

(e) Exemptions for specialization and research and development agreements

Exemption on the basis of Article 85(3) has also been granted to **3.45** agreements in the electricity sector which enable parties to specialise in particular areas of production or which provide for collaboration in research and development prior to industrial exploitation. In a specialization agreement, competing or potentially competing manu-facturers each agree to cease production of certain products and to specialise in the production of other products. It is common for each party to agree in addition to obtain from the other the products which have has agreed not to produce himself.[28] Many specialization agreements also have significant R & D aspects.

Specialization agreements and R & D agreements are dealt with under separate block exemptions, and even where individual cases do not fall within the conditions of the block exemption, the Commission generally takes a favourable approach to co-operation agreements.[29]

In *Carbon Gas Technologie* (OJ 1983 L376/17) the major Community **3.46** suppliers agreed to collaborate via a joint subsidiary in a development programme to produce a coal gasification process. The purpose of the development was to construct a demonstration plant at a likely cost of some DM 400-500 million. All the parties except one agreed not to compete with the joint subsidiary, the parties were expressly prohibited from conducting independent research, and further, they agreed not to compete with the joint subsidiary for five years after withdrawing from the project.

The Commission held that Article 85(1) applied in that at least some of **3.47** the parties could achieve the object of the co-operation independently, but granted an individual exemption under Article 85(3) on the basis that the agreement would save both time and money in the development of an important new process. The non-competition clauses were seen as indispensable ancillary restrictions on competition.

The Commission has also tended to adopt a favourable attitude to R & D **3.48** co-operation agreements in the nuclear engineering industry. Exemptions have been granted in the following decisions; *Re KEWA* (OJ 1976 L15/5); *GEC/Weir* (OJ 1977 L327/26) and *Re Amersham International* (OJ 1982 L314/34).

In *Re United Processors* the Commission exempted a series of agreements between KEWA, British Nuclear Fuels Limited and the French Commissariat at l'Energie Atomique, establishing a joint company, United Reprocessors GmbH to market oxide fuels reprocessing services and the arrangement of associated transport services. KEWA agreed to refrain from investment in oxide fuel reprocessing plant and BNFL and the CEA also

---

[28] See in general, Bellamy and Child, Chap 5.
[29] See *e.g.* the Commission's Decision in *KSB-Goulds-Lowara-ITT,* OJ 1990 L19/25.

agreed not to raise their annual capacity for reprocessing oxide fuels above an agreed quantity. The agreement also provided for the fixing of prices for oxide fuels reprocessing services.

The Commission ruled that this agreement restricted competition within the meaning of Article 85(1) but that it could be exempted under Article 85(3) as it fulfilled the two positive and negative conditions. The agreements allowed the development of a completely new industry to the point where effective conditions of competition could be created.

In its Decision in *GEC/Weir* the Commission granted an individual exemption on the basis of Article 85(3) to a production joint venture. Although the case did not involve the formation of a joint company, but instead a network of contractual arrangements for the joint development, production and sale by the parties of sodium circulators, and the allocation of development and production work between the parties. The sodium circulator is for use in pumping and circulating sodium coolant in high pressure reactors.[30]

3.49   In this particular case the Commission indicated that it was prepared to exempt this type of joint venture even although it recognised that there were considerable restrictions on competition involved, because it recognised *inter alia* the urgency to achieve safe performance in nuclear reactors.[31]

Similarly in its Decision in *Amersham Butler,* the Commission accepted that although the foundation of a joint venture between Buchler GmbH and Amersham International and the conclusion of an exclusive distributorship agreement between the joint venture and the Radiochemical Centre with the object of establishing a joint venture for the manufacture and marketing of radioactive materials and products. Although the agreements would have an appreciable restriction on competition, they also contributed to improving the production and distribution of the goods in question, particularly since they enabled the parties to comply with stringent national and international safety requirements as regards transport and storage of radioactive products.

(f) Related agreements in the energy sector

3.50   **The IEA agreement (Dec 83/671/EEC, OJ 1984 L376/30)**
The International Energy Programme (IEP) which was concluded under the auspices of the International Energy Agency in Paris (IEA) in 1974 provides, inter alia for the co-operation of oil companies with one another and with the IEA in the framework of the IEP and in the operation of an emergency oil allocation system. The EC Commission considered that this co-operation could amount to a concerted practice, and issued a decision on the matter. The allocation system involves three types of activities:

---

[30] For a fuller analysis, see Bellamy and Child, at 236-237.
[31] See *Seventh Report on Competition Policy* (1978) pt 155.

(a) in response to an emergency, companies may voluntarily and independently of any requests by the IEA, rearrange their own supply arrangements;

(b) in response to requests by the agency reporting companies will voluntarily rearrange supplies;

(c) if additional actions are required, the participating countries can establish what further action is required.

The Commission took the view that although these arrangements could **3.51** have appreciable restrictions on competition, they also contributed to improving distribution of goods and to promoting economic progress. It granted an exemption for a period of 10 years. The exemption was made subject to the obligation that the Commission be notified at the earliest possible moment by the oil companies to which the decision is addressed of certain information, as specified in Article 3, and subject to the obligation that the Commission is to have access for its representatives to any consultations between the oil companies as provided for in the IEP, as well as access to all related documentation.

3. **Abuse of a dominant position – Article 86**

Article 86 EEC provides that:

"Any abuse by one or more undertakings of a dominant position within the **3.52** common market or in a substantial part of it shall be prohibited as incompatible with the common market in so far as it may affect trade between Member States. Such abuse may, in particular, consist in:

(a) directly or indirectly imposing unfair purchase or selling prices or unfair trading conditions;

(b) limiting production, markets or technical development to the prejudice of consumers;

(c) applying dissimilar conditions to equivalent transactions with other trading parties, thereby placing them at a competitive disadvantage;

(d) making the conclusion of contracts subject to acceptance by the other parties of supplementary obligations which, by their nature or according to commercial usage have no connection with the subject of such contracts."

This list of abuses is not exhaustive: Article 86 is intended to capture a **3.53** wide variety of exploitative as well as discriminatory behaviour. The prohibition only applies first, when a firm occupies a dominant position, and second where it abuses that position to the detriment of inter-state trade.[32] It is not the intention here to provide an exhaustive account of Article 86, but rather to sketch out the key aspects which are of potential relevance to the electricity sector.

---

[32] For the application of the inter-state trade test to Art 86, see above at 3.5.

(i) **Dominant position**

3.54   To establish whether a firm is dominant, it is necessary to establish that the firm exercises a dominant position on (i) the relevant product market and (ii) the geographical market.[33]

It should always be borne in mind that Article 86 is not only concerned with conduct *in* the market on which the company is dominant: conduct may also be abusive if it has the effect of strengthening the dominant position which this company may enjoy on a separate market (see most recently, Case 62/86 *Akzo* v *Commission,* judgment of June 1991).

The relevant product market

3.55   Although the Court has never laid down a definitive test of what constitutes the relevant product market, it has placed considerable emphasis on the concept of "interchangeability" or "substitutability". If goods or services can be regarded as interchangeable, they are within the same product market.

In establishing whether a firm generating electricity is in a dominant position it may be arguable that the relevant market is that for all fuels and not necessarily that for electricity alone. It is submitted that much will depend on the context and on the structure of supply and demand. In Case 322/81 *Michelin* the Court ruled that if one looked at the structure of supply and demand and could determine that the product in question was purchased and used in particular circumstances then it was legitimate to distinguish it as a falling within a separate market.

In the case of electricity it is submitted that it is necessary to distinguish demand and supply "upstream and downstream".

Downstream

3.56   *Supply.* Electricity in contrast to other fuels, is used for lighting. The case may be different in the cases of fuels used for heating or propulsion.
Demand. Ordinary domestic consumers are unlikely to be able to switch fuels easily, while very large consumers may indeed be in a position to do so. It may therefore be necessary to distinguish between domestic and non-tariff markets.[34]

Upstream

3.57   Suppliers of fuel for electricity generation may also be considered to be dominant purchasers of a particular fuel if no other fuel offers adequate

---

[33] In numerous cases it will also be necessary to establish the temporal quality of the market, as competitive conditions vary according to the season, for example. It is submitted that this aspect will be of limited relevance to the market for electricity production and distribution. It may however be of more direct relevance to transmission activities if one accepts that demand for electricity is higher at particular times of the year, so that there is limited excess capacity in a transmission system.
[34] A product having different functions may give rise to sub-markets based on each of these different functions – Case 85/76 *Hoffman La Roche* v *Commission* [1979 ECR 461 at 515-517.

substitutability.[35] In its Decision on the complaint submitted by NALOO in relation to certain practices of the British Coal Corporation, the Commission appears to have examined the position of the BCC on the market for coal used for electricity generation. It did not consider other fuels to offer adequate substitutability.

> "Coal can be replaced as a fuel for power stations by oil to the extent that there is oil-fired capacity that is not fully utilized at present. However, the price of heavy fuel oil is extremely volatile.
>
> Existing port facilities could perhaps handle an additional 10-15 million tonnes of imports of steam coal (*i.e.* coal suitable for use in electricity generating stations or for industrial steam raising) a year. Higher levels of imports would require substantial investment in ports and infrastructure and could not be achieved within the time period of the coal supply contracts.
>
> Any significant increase in the purchase of steam coal on the international market would be likely to increase the price as the world trade in steam coal is only about 200 million tonnes a year.
>
> In the short to medium term BCC will remain the most important supplier of fuel to the generating companies in England and Wales. Part of the fuel requirements of the electricity supply industry in England and Wales cannot be met by sources other than BCC."(paras 24-27)

In its Decision on Scottish Nuclear (Dec 91/329/EEC), however, the **3.58** Commission considered the relevant product market to be that of the production, supply and distribution of electricity.

In certain situations the relevant market may be defined by statute. Thus for example in Case 226/84 *BL* v *Commission*[36] the relevant legislation provided that only BL could provide type-approval for certificates, as required by the relevant Department, in respect of BL cars.

(b) The geographical market

In Case 27/76 *United Brands* v *Commission* [1978] ECR 207 the Court ruled **3.59** that the opportunities for competition must be considered:

> "with reference to a clearly defined geographic area in which [the product] is marketed and where the conditions are sufficiently homogenous for the effect of the economic power of the undertaking to be able to be evaluated".

In other words, the geographical market " ...is an area where the objective conditions of competition applying to the product in question must be the same for all traders".[37]

Where country-wide statutory monopolies exist, there is usually no **3.60** difficulty in determining the geographical market.[38] Where monopolies

---

[35] Where the product is a raw material it does not usually make any difference if its derivatives are substitutable by other end products, if the immediate purchasers of the raw material are dependent on its physical and technical properties – Cases 6 & 7/73 *Instituto Chemiotherapico Italian and Commercial Solvents Corporation* v *Commission* [1974] ECR 223 at 249-250.

[36] See also Case 26/75 *General Motors* v *Commission* [1975] ECR 1367.

[37] Case 247/86 *Alsatel* v *Novasam* [1988] ECR 5987 at para 14.

[38] See most recently, Case C-41/89 *Höfner;* Case C-260/89 *ERT.*

are restricted by statute to a particular region, however, it would be necessary to go on to show that the regional company was capable of exercising power over the wider national market.[39]

3.61   A firm which had a statutory monopoly on its domestic market, and then proceeded to export into another Member State, would probably not be seen as occupying a dominant position on the latter market, but would be competing with the domestic suppliers, as well as with other firms exporting into that market.

The situation might be different, however, where the undertaking abused its monopoly on the home market to wipe out competition in a geographically adjacent market.[40] The concept of a dominant position is also dependent on the abuse in question. Hence it has been contended that even an undertaking with a dominant position outside the Community but with only a small market share within the Community could fall foul of Article 86.[41]

(ii) Market power

3.62   Where monopoly is conferred by statute, as is often the case in the electricity sector, then there will be few problems involved in establishing whether or not an undertaking has sufficient power over a market to fall within the scope of Article 86.

In the absence of a total statutory monopoly, the Commission and the Court look at market shares, although this is not in itself a conclusive factor in establishing dominance.[42] The Court and the Commission will also look at the share of the nearest rival,[43] and other factors indicating dominance. This latter concept includes a variety of barriers to entry, such as legal barriers to entry into a market resulting from government controls or planning regulations; superior technology, access to capital, and the ability to behave independently of competitors and consumers.

(iii) Substantial part of the market

3.63   The Court has consistently held that a statutory monopoly on a national market will satisfy the "substantial part of the common market" test, the territory of each Member State being considered as a substantial part of that market.[44]

---

[39] Case 247/86 *Alsatel* v *Novasam* [1988] ECR 5987; parts of a Member State can, in certain circumstances, constitute a "substantial part of the common market for the purposes of Article 86" – Cases 40-48 etc/73 *Suiker Unie, loc cit;* Case 30/87 *Bodson, loc cit,* Case C-179/90 *Merci Converzionale Porto di Genova* v *Siderurgica Gabrielli* (10 December 1991).

[40] See Case T-69/89 *RTE* v *Commission, loc cit,* where the Irish company RTE was held to have abused its statutory monopoly rights under Irish copyright law to prevent a competing company from satisfying consumer demands in the neighbouring market of Northern Ireland.

[41] Kapteyn and Verloren van Themaat, 556; *cf* Van Gerven, pt 297.

[42] Case 22/76 *United Brands* [1978] ECR 207.

[43] Case 322/81 *Michelin, loc cit.*

[44] Case C-41/89 *Höfner, loc cit;* Case C-260/89 ERT, *loc cit.*

(iv) Abuse

3.64 The concept of the abuse may be interpreted with reference to the non-exhaustive list of examples given in the article itself, but it must also be related to the objectives of the establishment of a common market and the introduction of a system of undistorted competition under Articles 2 and 3 EEC.

This means that the prohibition is not only intended to protect competitors, suppliers and buyers from discriminatory conduct on the part of dominant undertakings, but that it also extends to exploitative conduct on the part of such undertakings. The prohibition does not only cover market behaviour but it also extends to activities which could change the structure of competition on the market.[45]

This wider concept of the purpose and scope of Article 86 is of particular relevance to the electricity sector where certain activities such as transmission and distribution may constitute a natural monopoly irrespective of whether a particular firm enjoys a statutory monopoly. Although it is not an abuse in itself to hold a dominant position on a particular market, certain consequences and obligations may flow from it.

3.65 In the first place firms may not only be obliged to refrain from certain types of conduct, but may also have a positive duty towards those which are in a position of economic dependence. This proposition finds support in the Court's ruling in *Michelin* where the Court stated that a firm in a dominant position "has a special responsibility not to allow its conduct to impair undistorted competition on the common market."

3.66 This positive obligation was reaffirmed in the recent Case T-69/89 *RTE* v *Commission* where the Court held that a monopolist had positive duties towards a competitor which was economically dependent on it, so that the refusal of RTE to provide to a competitor information over which it held a legitimate monopoly of reproduction under national copyright law amounted to an abuse.

Furthermore, conduct which would be essentially unobjectionable on competitive or dispersed markets, such as for example, predatory pricing, takes on a different significance in highly concentrated markets.[46]

3.67 In the second place, where an undertaking holding a dominant position on one market uses that dominance to extend its activities into an adjacent market or a sub-market, thus altering the structure of competition in the common market, this too may be caught by Article 86.

Thus in Case 311/84 *CBEM* v *Compagnie Luxembourgeoise de Télédiffusion SA et al* [1985] ECR 3261 the Court ruled that where a company which enjoyed a broadcasting monopoly extended its activities to the

---

[45] Case 6/72 *Continental Can* [1973] ECR 215.

[46] See *e.g.* the Commission's reasoning in recital 13 of Commission Dir 88/301/EEC on competition in telecommunications terminal equipment (OJ 1988 L 131/73) discussed further in Chap 4. See also Case 62/86 *Akzo v Commission, loc cit* and Commission Dec 91/299/EEC, *Solvay* (OJ 1990 L152/21).

related but separate market of telemarketing, this amounted to an abuse contrary to Article 86.[47]

3.68 It is evident that in applying this interpretation of the concept of abuse the Commission, or where relevant, the injured third party, will seek to draw the relevant product market narrowly and to argue that the firm enjoying a dominant position on that market is effectively attempting to extend or reinforce its market power on a related sub-market. It is therefore in the interests of the defendant undertaking to seek to draw the relevant product as widely as possible.[48]

It is interesting in this respect to note that in its Decision 91/50, *IJsselcentrale,* the Commission implied that, albeit with reference to Article 85, that while the SEP's Co-operation Agreement denying the right of third parties to use its interconnections amounted to an import monopoly, its "complete refusal to make power lines available to others... could constitute a separate infringement of Article 85" (para 29). It did not pursue this matter further, however.

3.69 Hence the Commission, and indeed the Court have yet to rule on whether electricity production, interconnection, transmission and distribution are to be considered as separate markets or sub-markets for the purposes of applying Article 86.

The Commission has now applied the "adjacent market" line of reasoning in several decisions condemning statutory monopolies over postal services which had attempted to extend their monopoly power into related sub-markets such as courier and express postal services.[49] Commission Directive 90/388/EEC on telecommunication services also follows a similar line of reasoning.[50]

3.70 The Court has recently also condemned as contrary to Articles 86 and 90(1) the conferral of a statutory monopoly over the retransmission of imported radio and television broadcasts on a state undertaking which has a monopoly over the broadcasting of nationally produced programmes (Case C- 260/89 *ERT* v *Dimotiki, loc cit;* see also Case 18/88 *RTT* v *GB Inno, loc cit*). This jurisprudence, which has recently been applied to national legislation creating statutory monopolies, is of considerable potential significance for the electricity sector. It is considered in more detail in the following chapters.

---

[47] This case would appear to amount to a reversal of the Court's ruling in the earlier Case 155/73 *Sacchi* [1974] ECR 409, where it held that an extension of the monopoly's activities would not amount to an abuse.

[48] Case T-69/89 *RTE* v *Commission* etc provide a useful illustration. The broadcasting companies argued that the relevant product market for information on TV programme schedules should include all types of publications, whether these appeared in as daily or as weekly guides. The Commission's finding that daily papers and weekly guides were separate products was confirmed by the Court of Justice.

[49] The Spanish and Dutch PTT Decisions are discussed in Chap 4.

[50] See also the Commission's guidelines on the application of the competition rules to the telecommunications sector, June 1990, for a detailed discussion of the application of this interpretation of Art 86.

(v) **Joint dominance**

Article 86 refers to abuses "by one or more undertakings" of a dominant **3.71** position. Although the Commission has been inclined to interpret this phrase to cover dominance by several independent companies on an oligopolistic market, the Court has so far been reluctant to endorse this approach.[51] The Commission has not abandoned its efforts to use Article 86 in oligopolistic situations, however, and in 1986 it announced that it had completed a study of the concept.[52] Two essential features of dominance were identified:

(a) the presence of a small number of firms no one of which enjoyed a dominant position; and

(b) a high degree of interdependence among the decisions of the enterprises.

In these circumstances the Commission believes that tacit collusion arises **3.72** from either awareness of interdependence or the probability of unfavourable consequences following an unfavourable decision and that this could be deduced from the commercial conduct of the firms over a period of time.[53]

It has applied this reasoning in its Decision in *Italian Flat Glass* (OJ 1989 L33/44) which is now under appeal: Case 75/89 *SIV* v *Commission*.

The Court's ruling on the question of shared dominance may have significance for the enforcement of competition on oligopolistic markets, as for example in Germany, where no single electricity production and transmission company is dominant throughout the national territory, but where in fact a small number of very large undertakings control the major part of the market.

(vi) **Mergers and acquisitions**

Pursuant to Regulation (EEC) 4064/89, certain types of "concentrations", **3.73** as defined in Article 3(1) must be notified to the Commission for prior approval. Only those concentrations with a "Community dimension" as defined in Article 1(2) need be notified. Thus a concentration within the meaning of Article 3(1) where:

(a) the aggregate world-wide turnover of all the undertakings concerned is more than 5 billion ECU; and

(b) the aggregate Community-wide turnover of each of at least two of the undertakings concerned is more than 250 million ECU must be notified.

A concentration will not have a Community dimension, if each of the undertakings concerned achieves more than two-thirds of its aggregate Community-wide turnover within one and the same Member State.

---

[51] *Hoffman La Roche* v *Commission, loc cit.*

[52] *Sixteenth Competition Report,* 1986, 230, para 331.

[53] The advantage of this approach being that the Commission would not have to furnish hard evidence of parallel conduct as required by the Court for proof of a concerted action under Art 85; see *ICI.*

As this complex legislation is now the subject of detailed commentaries and articles, only two points of potential relevance to the electricity sector shall be highlighted here.

(a) Position of public enterprises

3.74   Recital 12 of the Regulation states that:

> "Whereas the arrangements to be introduced for the control of concentrations should, without prejudice to Article 90(2) of the Treaty, respect the principle of non-discrimination between the public and private sectors; whereas, in the public sector, calculation of the turnover of an undertaking concerned in a concentration needs, therefore, to take account of the undertakings making up an economic unit with an independent power of decision, irrespective of the way in which their capital is held or of the rules of administrative supervision applicable to them."

3.75   ### (b) Protection of legitimate interests by Member States

Article 21(3) empowers Member States:

> "to take appropriate measures to protect legitimate interests other than those taken into consideration by this Regulation and compatible with the general principles and other provisions of Community law."

Public security, along with plurality of the media, are expressly stated to be legitimate interests. In the case of any other public interest, a decision must first be obtained from the Commission before the measures are put into effect.

3.76   In the Commission's view these powers are limited in nature, and do not confer any new rights, but merely confirm the powers at present reserved to Member States to intervene in certain aspects of concentrations coming within their jurisdictions. It does not imply any power to authorise concentrations which the Commission may have prohibited under the Regulation. (See further the Commission's interpretative statement on Article 21 [1990] 4 CMLR 314).

4. ECSC rules on competition

3.77   It has already been mentioned in the introduction to this chapter that the competition rules under the ECSC Treaty, although similar in some respect to Articles 85 and 86 EEC, diverge in a number of important respects. This section first examines the basic rules and then goes on to discuss their recent application by the Commission in a decision concerning the British Coal Corporation and the two major generators in England and Wales – hereafter the "NALOO Decision".

3.78   Article 4(d) ECSC provides that restrictive practices which tend towards the sharing or exploiting of markets are incompatible with the common market for steel and coal. Articles 65 and 66 contain highly detailed rules for undertakings on agreements and concentrations in the coal and steel sector.

Article 65 provides that:

3.79

"1. All agreements between undertakings, decisions by associations of undertakings and concerted practices tending directly or indirectly to prevent, restrict or distort normal competition within the common market shall be prohibited, and in particular those tending:
(a) to fix or determine prices;
(b) to restrict or control production, technical development or investment;
(c) to share markets, products, customers or sources of supply."

In accordance with Article 65(2) the High Authority shall authorise certain categories of agreement under certain conditions (as specified in Art 65(2)(a)-(c), and has a discretion to authorise other forms of agreement.

Article 66 provides:

"Any transaction shall require prior authorization of the High Authority, subject to the provisions of paragraph 3 of this Article, if it has in itself the direct or indirect effect of bringing about ... a concentration between undertakings."

Article 66(2) requires the High Authority to grant authorization for certain types of transactions, under certain conditions.

3.80

Article 66(7) provides that:

"If the High Authority finds that public or private undertakings which, in law or in fact hold or acquire in the market for one of the products within its jurisdiction, a dominant position shielding them against effective competition in a substantial part of the common market are using that position for purposes contrary to the objectives of this Treaty, it shall make to them such recommendations as may be appropriate to prevent the position from being so used."

Prior to examining the application of these rules, a number of points should be made. First, for the purposes of the ECSC Treaty Article 80 defines undertakings as any undertaking engaged in production in the coal or the steel industry (see Cases 9 & 12/60 *Vloeberghs*).

3.81

Article 66, however, which regulates concentrations, is applicable if only one of the undertakings is a producer or wholesaler dealer or middleman for coal or steel.

Second, unlike the rules on competition for undertakings in the EEC Treaty, there is no requirement in the ECSC Treaty that agreements should affect intra-Community trade. This is an important distinction between the two sets of rules.

Third, while the direct effectiveness of Articles 85 and 86 is now beyond doubt, the Court had never expressly held that Articles 65 and 66 ECSC are directly effective.

3.82

Fourth, the Court has interpreted Articles 65 and 66 ECSC to cover situations of joint dominance in oligopolistic markets.[54]

3.83   Fifth, Article 66 requires that all mergers and concentrations must be approved by the Commission unless they are of minor importance. In this respect it differs from the EEC Treaty, which contains no express rules on mergers. The EC Council has now adopted a Regulation requiring advance notification of mergers and take-overs which fall within the scope of the EEC competition rules (Reg 4064/89, OJ 1989 L395/1), but this system does not apply to the coal and steel sectors which remain subject to Article 66.[55]

3.84   Authorization under Article 66(2) is conditional on, *inter alia,* whether the concentration in question does not give rise to the power to determine prices, control or restrict production or distribution, or prevent the maintenance of effective competition in a substantial part of the market for the products concerned.[56] The concentration must not give the power to evade the rules of competition, in particular by the creation of an artificially privileged position involving a substantial advantage in access to supplies or markets. It must be stressed, however, that Article 66 may also be applicable where a concentration between a coal undertaking and a third party, such as an electricity generator, is involved.[57]

(i) **NALOO Decision**

3.85   The complaint by NALOO, concerned, *inter alia,* the three year supply contracts concluded between British Coal and the two major generators in England and Wales. These contracts, for the supply of steam coal to power stations, came into force on 1 April 1990. They provide, *inter alia,* for the British Coal Corporation (BCC) to sell and National Power (NP) and PowerGen (PG) to buy 70 million tonnes of coal in each of the first two years and 65 million tonnes in the third year. The contracts expire on 31 March 1993. In addition the contracts fixed a basis price, and included escalation and de-escalation formulae to take account of movements in the retail price index and in the sterling/$ exchange rate.

3.86   BCC is a wholly state-owned corporation which is the beneficial owner of

---

[54] Case 13/60 *Geitling* v *High Authority* [1962] ECR 83 and Case 66/63 *Netherlands* v *High Authority* [1964] ECR 533.

[55] See further, Hayden, "The demise of the ECSC Treaty: some competition law implications", (1991) 4 Eur Competition Law Rev 160-166.

[56] In a recent decision the Commission authorised the so-called *Huttenvertrage* – a collective set of agreements under which Ruhrkohle supplies most of the German steel works with solid fuel – on the ground that it contributed to the rationalization of the coal sector and therefore could be justified under Art 65(2)ECSC (OJ 1989 L 101/21).

[57] Art 66(1) ECSC was applied in the Commission's decision concerning a merger between EBV and Ruhrkohle. Under the takeover agreement Ruhrkohle was to take over a contract between Arbed and the EBV for the total supply of blast furnace coke to Arbed's works in Luxembourg. The Commission ruled that the contract restricted competition in that it commits the parties to the exclusive supply and purchase of Arbed's requirements of blast furnace coke. The agreement was authorised under Art 66(2) – only such a contract could ensure that Arbed's requirements were met. *Re Concentration between EBV and Ruhrkohle* (OJ 1989 L14/37).

all the UK coal reserves. It has the power to license private production of coal and is authorised under the Coal Act 1946 to charge royalties for its production. NP and PG are public limited companies all of whose shares were held by the UK authorities until they were partially privatised (60%) in March 1991. Between them they operate all the coal and oil-fired electricity generating stations in England and Wales. Electricity generation in the UK consumes the equivalent of about 123 million tonnes of coal a year. Three sources of very low marginal cost production, hydro generation and nuclear generation and electricity imports from France account for 29.4 million tonnes of coal equivalent, leaving 93.3 million tonnes of coal equivalent for oil and coal. In 1989 BCC supplied 81% of this requirement.

NALOO and others complained to the Commission that BCC had abused **3.87** its position as a dominant supplier of electricity generating coal, within the meaning of Article 66(7) ECSC, to secure favourable terms for itself, particularly in terms of volume and price, which had a detrimental effect on its competitors. It was further alleged by all the complainants that the generating companies are jointly dominant, in that they are the only purchasers of electricity generating coal, and that these companies abused their dominant position contrary to Article 86 of the EEC Treaty by discriminating against the members of the complainant associations in comparison with BCC, by refusing to purchase coal in sufficient quantity and by offering prices that were unjustifiably lower than those paid to BCC.

The Commission held that:

"An agreement by which a dominant supplier obtains the right to provide   **3.88** some 94% of the requirements of the two largest customers, forecloses the market and can be justified only in the most exceptional circumstances" (para 78).

Unfortunately it did not go on to specify whether there were any such attenuating circumstances applicable in this particular case.[58] However, further on in its Decision (para 81) the Commission states that it:

"considers that the complaints made under, *inter alia*, Article 85 were justified in so far as they concerned the situation after 1 April 1990 when the coal supply contracts entered into operation."

Having ruled that NP and PG were jointly dominant purchasers on the   **3.89** UK market for electricity generating coal, the Commission also specified their obligations towards the private licensed operators under Articles 66(7) ECSC and 86 EEC.[59] Hence they could only refuse to contract with the latter, for example:

---

[58] Instead it merely indicated that the compatibility of the supply agreements with the competition rules of the EEC were being examined under separate procedures, the agreements having been notified to the Commission in early 1990.
[59] The Commission also makes specific reference to Art 63 ECSC – see below.

"– if the cost of transporting that mine's coal to the power station, ... is above the cost of transporting coal from another small mine, providing that this does not cause the generating company's total purchases to fall below the overall quantity which it has undertaken to buy.
– for quality reasons, as far as new contracts are concerned if objective, technically justified, non-discriminatory quality standards are applied to all suppliers including BCC. The generating companies will also be expected to fulfil their obligations under existing contracts." (para 66).[60]

5. Some procedural aspects of Articles 85 and 86

(i) Introduction

3.90 The procedural aspects of EC competition law are complex, and as they are the subject of several comprehensive studies, they need not be dealt with in any detail here.[61] This section deals only with the principal aspects of the procedure under Regulation 17 – which concerns the EEC Treaty rules. The application of the ECSC provisions is secured through separate rules.[62]

The EEC notification procedure is singled out, both because of the advantages it may confer and because of its impact on the legal position of the parties before the national courts.

(ii) Exemptions

3.91 The power to grant exemption in respect of individual agreements is reserved by Article 9 of Regulation 17 to the Commission, to the exclusion of the national competition authorities. This Regulation is of general application to all sectors, with the exception of the transport sectors.

Parties to an agreement may make a formal application using Form A/B for either a negative clearance or an exemption.

Article 4(1) of Regulation 17 lays down the general principle that until agreements have been notified to the Commission they cannot be the subject of a decision in application of Article 85(3). Even where an agreement would self-evidently satisfy the conditions laid down in Article 85(3) it cannot be exempted, unless it falls into one of three categories.

3.92 Certain types of agreement are excused notification because they pose no serious threat to competition and are considered particularly likely to qualify for exemption.

Article 4(2) contains a list of these types of agreements.

Article 4(2) has been strictly construed by the Commission. To a large extent it has been superseded by the block exemption Regulations,

---

[60] The Commission's Decision is now subject to appeal, registered as Case T-57/91.
[61] See Kerse, *Antitrust Procedure* (1989).
[62] See High Authority Dec 1-65.

considered below. It is to the parties advantage, in terms of legal security, to try to bring their agreements under one or other of the relevant block exemptions.[63]

In relation to agreements which fall within the block exemption **3.93** Regulations prior notification is not necessary. There are currently no Regulations applying the block exemption procedure to the electricity sector, but the terms of the various Regulations may be of relevance to particular types of agreements within the sector.

In addition to the special block exemptions for particular sectors[64], a number of "horizontal" block exemptions apply to:
– exclusive distribution agreements;
– exclusive purchasing agreements;
– research and development agreements;
– specialization agreements;
– know-how licences;
– franchise agreements.

Finally, it may be possible for an agreement to be exempted on the basis **3.94** of Article 90(2) even where it has not been notified.

In the *IJsselcentrale* Decision, the Commission could not consider exemption under Article 85(3) because the agreement in question had never been notified. It found that the Co-operation Agreement continued to infringe Article 85 in various respects, but went on to consider whether it could be justified under the exemption provided in Article 90(2).

Article 90(2) states that undertakings:

"entrusted with the operation of services of general economic interest are to **3.95** be subject to the rules contained in the Treaty, in so far as the application of such rules does not obstruct the performance, in law or in fact, of the particular tasks assigned to them."

This provision is discussed in greater detail in Chapter 4, but here it is worth noting that the Commission considered that to fall within the exemption an agreement would have to fulfill several cumulative tests.

First, it must be demonstrated that the undertakings in question have **3.96** been entrusted with the operation of a service of general economic interest. An obligation to ensure the reliable and efficient operation of the national electricity supply at costs which are as low as possible and in a socially responsible fashion, in the Commission's view fell within the definition of a service of general economic interest (paras 40-41).

Second, the undertakings must have been entrusted with this task by an act of public law. In *IJsselcentrale* the grant of concessions by the relevant Minister amounted to an act of public authority.[65] Third, it must be shown that the application of the competition rules results in an

---

[63] Kerse, *Antitrust Procedure* 1989.
[64] These include motor vehicles (Reg 123/85, OJ 1985 L15/5); Sea Transport (Reg 4260/88, OJ 1988 L376/1); Liner Conferences (Reg 4056/86, OJ 1986 L378/14); Air Transport (Reg 3975/75, 3976/87, Reg 2671/88, Reg 2672/88, Reg 2673/88 and Reg 4261/88).
[65] See also Case 66/86 *Saeed*.

obstruction of the tasks so assigned. The substance of this test is discussed in Chapter 4.

In *IJsselcentrale* the Commission formed the view that this last test was not satisfied at least for "non-public supply". Despite non-notification the Commission adopted a decision under Article 3 of Regulation 17:

> "finding that an infringement has been committed in the past, in order to clarify the legal position, and to require the undertakings concerned to bring such infringement to an end, to the extent that it still continues." (para 55).

(iii) Consequences of notification

3.97   Where the activity takes place under an agreement which has been notified, the parties are protected by Article 15(5) against the imposition of fines.[66]

3.98   Kapteyn and Verloren van Themaat (at 523) offer a useful summary of the additional legal effects of the notification procedure.

> "1. Agreements subject to notification which have not been notified are prohibited by law and are void – the so-called *Bosch* doctrine.[67]
> 2. 'Old agreements' subject to notification i.e. those existing upon the entry into force of Regulation 17 and notified by the dates specified in Article 5(1)[68], are fully effective as long as the Commission has not taken a decision under Article 85(3) and Regulation 17 (Article 15(6)).
> 3. In the case of standard agreements with identical content the notification of one agreement also has the legal effects attached to notification with regard to the other agreements.
> 4. In relation to all 'new' agreements (i.e. those concluded after the entry into force of Regulation 17) falling within Article 85 it must now be accepted that litigants may plead before their national courts that they are void: there is no need to wait for a decision of the Commission."

3.99   Kapteyn and Verloren van Themaat suggest that the national court may well wish to suspend the proceedings "in order to allow the parties to obtain the Commission's standpoint, unless it establishes either that the agreement does not have any perceptible effect on competition or between trade between Member States or that their is no doubt that the agreement is incompatible with Article 85."[69]

> "5. The Court has recognized that a determination of nullity of all 'new' cartels by a national court has retroactive effect.
> 6. The case-law of the Court in conjunction with the system of the Treaty and

---

[66] The Commission may put an end to immunity by informing the parties that following a preliminary investigation, it has formed the view that Art 85(1) applies to the agreement and exemption under Art 85(3) is not justified – Art 15(6).

[67] Case 13/61 *Bosch* [1962] ECR 45.

[68] 1 February 1963 for bilateral agreements, otherwise 1 November 1962. For the new Member States, see Art 25 of Reg 17/62, as amended, and Bellamy and Child, *op cit*, 478 *et seq*.

[69] Quoting the Court's judgment in Case 48/72 *Brasserie de Haecht* [1973] ECR 77 at 87.

Regulation 17 leads to the conclusion that neither the notification as such nor the initiation of proceedings under Articles 2, 3 and 6 of Regulation 17 terminates the competence of the national court in any civil disputes about a notified agreement.[70]

(iv) Competition rules and national courts

Articles 85 and 86 EEC have been held to be directly effective[71] but this principle is in fact qualified in two ways. **3.100**

First, Articles 85(1) and 86 are only directly effective within the framework of any implementing measures adopted under Article 87, including Regulation 17.[72] Second, the Court has adopted the "doctrine of provisional validity" as a compromise between Article 85(2) which provides that prohibited agreements are automatically void, and the power to grant retrospective validation in Article 7 of Regulation 17.

Articles 85 and 86 may be invoked in proceedings before national courts as a form of so-called "Euro-defence" *i.e.* as a challenge to the validity of transactions of which the enforcement is being sought. **3.101**

The Court has held Article 85(2) to be directly effective, but the sense of the provision must be kept in mind – only agreements which are caught by Article 85(1) and not capable of exemption under Article 85(3) are void. Only the Commission can grant this exemption (Reg 17, Art 9(1)). The national court may rule that the agreement does not fall under Article 85(1) or alternatively it may rule that the agreement was a notifiable one, but has not been duly notified.

The situation is different where the agreement has been notified, or if it is an "old" agreement which is non-notifiable. It is in this context that the doctrine of provisional validity becomes relevant. **3.102**

In Cases 48/72 *Brasserie de Haecht* v *Wilkin (no 2)* [1973] ECR 77 the Court held that:

> "In the case of old agreements: the general principle of contractual certainty requires, particularly when the agreement has been notified in accordance with the provisions of Regulation no 17, that the Court may only declare it to be automatically void after the Commission has taken a decision by virtue of that Regulation.
>
> In the case of new agreements, as the Regulation assumes that so long as the Commission has not taken a decision the agreement can only be implemented at the parties' own risk, it follows that notifications in accordance with Article 4(1) of Regulation 17 do not have suspensive effect." (*Ibid* at 86-87).

---

[70] See for example, the so-called "Perfumes" cases, Cases 253/78 & 1-3/79 *Procureur de la République et al* v *B Giry and Guerlain SA et al* [1980] ECR 2327.

[71] Case 127/73 *BRT* v *SABAM* [1974] ECR 62.

[72] For a discussion of the special Regulations affecting the transport sector see Greaves, "Transport Law of the European Community", 1991.

(a) Power to apply Article 86

3.103   Even where an agreement has been exempted by the Commission under Article 85(3) a national court may still be entitled to condemn it, or certain aspects of it, under Article 86. In Case 66/88 *Saeed* the Court confirmed that national courts may apply Article 86 to tariff agreements between airlines.

In Case T-51/89 *Tetra Pak* [1990] ECR 312 (at para 39) the Court of First Instance ruled that "the grant of an exemption under Article 85(3) cannot be such as to render inapplicable the prohibition set out in Article 86."

(v) **Severance**

3.104   In Case 56/55 *STM* [1966] ECR 235, the Court of Justice declared that the automatic nullity provision of Article 85(2) only applied to those parts of agreements affected by the prohibition, or "to the agreement as a whole if it appears that those parts are not severable from the agreement itself."

It is a question of national law, however, as to whether once the offending clauses have been severed, the agreement remains in tact.

(vi) **Mergers and takeovers**

3.105   As the new Merger Regulation (EEC) 4064/89 disapplies Regulation 17, concentrations not within the Regulation fall to be considered, where relevant, by the competent national competition authorities.

(vii) **Remedies**

3.106   Similarly, the availability of remedies for the enforcement of Articles 85 and 86 are also questions of national law.[73]

(viii) **Commission's power to obtain information**

3.107   In Case T-39/90R *SEP* v *Commission* (Order of the President of 21 November 1990, [1990] ECR 649), the SEP requested the President of the Court of First Instance to suspend a Commission decision based on Article 11(5) of Regulation 17, ordering SEP to supply information on a gas purchasing contract concluded with the Norwegian company, Statoil. SEP had refused to transmit this information pursuant to the Commission's initial request, because it feared that the Dutch authorities would use the contract for other purposes. It referred in this respect to Article 10 of Regulation 17 which obliges the Commission to supply national authorities with copies of the most important documents in a competition case.

3.108   SEP argued that this information was not "necessary" within the meaning of Regulation 17 and that its implementation would cause serious and

---

[73] For a short discussion, see Bellamy and Child, 455-460.

irreparable damage, as the Dutch authorities would be made aware of the purchasing conditions offered by Statoil. This in turn would undermine SEP's negotiating position during gas negotiations with the Dutch Government.

Although the President accepted that the Commission's assessment of the "necessity" of the information was subject to the control of the Court, he was not prepared to grant interim relief. He observed that the Commission's obligations under Article 10(1) are limited to the most important documents, that is those documents relevant to establishing a possible infringement of the competition rules. He further considered that these documents could only be transmitted to the competent authorities of the Member States and that those authorities are in turn bound by the confidentiality rules of Article 20 of Regulation 17. Thus the information they receive can only be used for the purpose of the pending competition case. The President went on to rule that the SEP's interest was sufficiently protected by Article 20, irrespective of the outcome of the Court's final assessment of the legality of the Commission' decision. The SEP initially intended to appeal to the Court of Justice against the President's ruling, but later withdrew the appeal (OJ 1991 C178/8). **3.109**

On 12 December 1991 the Court of First Instance gave its judgment on the main proceedings (Case T-39/90 *SEP* v *Commission*). The Court confirmed the Commission's interpretation of Article 10 of Regulation 17 and further ruled that Article 20 of that Regulation constituted sufficient protection of SEP's commercial interests. It was for the Member States, in accordance with their obligations under Article 5, EEC, to adopt the measures necessary to guarantee that commercially sensitive information would not be passed between different departments of government. (For a detailed account of this complex procedural litigation see paragraphs 10-14 of Case T-39/90.) **3.110**

Chapter 4
Relationship between Member States and their Electricity Industries

1. Introduction

State intervention in, or control over the activities of the European **4.1** electricity sector takes a number of forms. In the first place, state control may be exerted through complete or partial ownership of an undertaking. In the second place, Member States may exercise an influence over the organization of the sector, by reserving certain activities to particular firms, whether public or private. In the third place, many activities in this sector, ranging from plant siting and construction to tariff policy are subject to state approval in one form or another.

This chapter is concerned with the relationship between Member States and electricity undertakings in the first and second situations.

Although electricity companies take a variety of legal forms and are **4.2** owned and organised in different ways in the individual Member States, they may all be considered as "utilities". In other words, they invariably enjoy some form of privileged status (whether *de jure* or *de facto*) in return for carrying out tasks deemed to be in the public interest.

Many electricity utilities enjoy exclusive or monopoly rights, either to produce, transport or distribute electricity, or to perform one or more of these functions. In the majority of Member States the right to import and/or export electricity is often conferred on a single undertaking.

The activities of public enterprises as well as privileged private firms **4.3** enjoying monopoly rights pose a number of problems for the application of the Community principles on free movement and competition. Such enterprises may be deliberately used by the Member States as an instrument of economic or industrial policy. Furthermore they may be used to achieve indirectly certain goals which would be illegal if pursued by Member States themselves.

A state measure, for example, which limits the use of certain power in fuel stations may be caught by Article 30 if it puts indigenous fuels as opposed to imported products, in a more advantageous position. The state could achieve similar results by conferring an exclusive right to supply all fuels for generation on a single firm, so that in effect all fuel imports must be channelled through that enterprise.

4.4   This chapter examines the relevant Community law governing the creation, operation and maintenance of monopolies and other types of exclusive rights in the electricity sector. It focuses on the application of these rules to the legislative, regulatory and other forms of administrative measures enacted or otherwise adopted by the Member States themselves. Its primary focus is on the EEC Treaty, but the relevant articles of the Euratom and ECSC Treaties are also discussed. Part I examines the general scope of the Treaty rules. Part II analyses several recent cases of the Court of Justice and assesses how much scope Member States may retain to create and maintain monopolies. Part III examines the application of the principles developed in Part II to specific types of organizational structures in the electricity sector. Part IV deals with the application of the EEC competition rules to state regulations which may distort competition in a variety of other ways, besides conferring exclusive privileges.

Part I

2. General principles

4.5   The following general principles govern the relationship between Member States and electricity undertakings under the EEC Treaty:
(a) Member States are free to establish undertakings, to nationalise private undertakings, to grant special or exclusive rights to private or public undertakings, or to entrust them with tasks in the general public interest;
(b) Member States must not enact (or maintain) toward private or public undertakings measures contrary to the EEC Treaty;
(c) The rules of competition (Arts 85 and 86) apply without any substantial difference to all undertakings, irrespective of their private or public character and of their relationships with the public authority.

4.6   The first proposition can be derived from Article 222 of the EEC Treaty, which preserves national rules on private property[1], and Article 90(1). Article 222 states:

> "This Treaty shall in no way prejudice the rules in Member States governing the system of property ownership."

4.7   All three Treaties take a neutral position on ownership. There is therefore nothing in principle to prevent Member States from taking any part of their electricity industry into public ownership or from subsequently privatising it.

---

[1] Art 83 ECSC and Art 91 Euratom are expressed in similar but not identical terms.

3. Article 90

At the same time it is equally clear that these enterprises are subject in full **4.8**
to the Treaty's rules on free movement and competition. This follows from
Article 90(1), second sentence (see below). Article 90(2) allows only for a
limited exemption for firms entrusted with the operation of services of
general economic interest (see below).

Article 90(1) and (2) governs the application of the Treaty rules to
Member States and the enterprises on which they confer certain special
and exclusive rights.

Article 90(1) fulfills a similar role to Article 37(1) and (2), discussed in
some detail in Chapter 2. The latter applies to state trading monopolies
with exclusive import and export and related rights, whereas the former
applies to the conferral of exclusive rights on other forms of enterprise,
whether public or private.

Both Article 90(1) and Article 37 are addressed to the Member States, **4.9**
while Article 90(2) is addressed to Member States and undertakings.

Article 90(1) provides that:

> "in the case of public undertakings and undertakings to which Member States
> grant special or exclusive rights, Member States shall neither enact nor
> maintain in force any measure contrary to the rules contained in this Treaty, in
> particular to those rules provided for in Article 7 and Articles 85 to 94."

Article 90(1) EEC is a specific application and amplification of the
general principles set out in Articles 3(f) and 5 EEC that the Member States
must refrain from doing anything which would jeopardise the achievement
of the Community's tasks, and in particular the institution of a system of
undistorted competition in the common market (Case 13/77 *INNO* v *ATAB*;
Case 66/86 *Saeed*; Case C-41/90 *Höfner*; Case C-179/90 *Porto di Genova* and
Case 18/88 *RTT* v *GB-Inno*). The obligations of Member States under
Article 90(1) are considered in detail in Parts II and III of this chapter.

(i) Exemptions

Article 90(2) states that:

> "Undertakings entrusted with the operation of services of general economic **4.10**
> interest ... shall be subject to the rules contained in this Treaty, in particular to
> the rules on competition, in so far as the application of such rules does not
> obstruct the performance, in law or in fact, of the particular tasks assigned to
> them. The development of trade must not affected to such an extent as would
> be contrary to the interests of the Community."

The Commission has ruled that the electricity undertakings are entrusted **4.11**
with the operation of services of general economic interest within the
meaning of Article 90(2), first sentence (Dec 91/50/EEC, OJ 1991 L
28/32).

4.12   Article 90(2) provides for a limited exemption from *all* the relevant Treaty rules where a firm, whether public or private, would otherwise be obstructed in law or in fact from performing its public service duties.

In the context of the EEC competition rules Article 90(2) provides an additional exemption from Article 85(1), and it is the only exemption which applies to Article 86.[2] As with any provision which derogates from the basic Community rules, Article 90(2) has been strictly interpreted by the Court and by the Commission (Case C-179/90 *Porto di Genova;* Case 18/88 *RTT* v *GB-INNO*).

The potential application of the exemption to electricity monopolies is considered in detail in Part II, below.

4.13   (ii) **Article 90(2) and direct effect**

Case C-260/89 *ERT* v *Dimotiki* provides an important clarification on the procedural aspects of Article 90(2). It would now seem that national courts may directly apply the exemption in full. In its earlier case law the Court seemed to indicate that while the national courts could *deny* the application of the exemption to particular undertakings (Case 153/73 *Sacchi*), they could not apply it in their benefit (Case 10/71 *Muller* [1971] ECR 821).

In Case 66/86 *Saaed* the Court suggested that national authorities were to determine first, whether there was a government act entrusting an enterprise with the operation of a service of a general economic interest and second, whether the operation of that service would be obstructed if the competition rules were applied. It did not go on to confirm, however, that the national court could grant the exemption. In its latest ruling in Case C-260/89 *ERT,* at recital 34, the Court clearly stipulates that the national courts can in fact apply the third stage.

4.14   If the national authority is unwilling to dispose of the case, it may make a reference to the Court of Justice or alternatively stay the proceedings and ask the Commission for its opinion.

Nevertheless it is for the Commission to decide ultimately whether the granting of an exemption may adversely affect the Community. It may therefore choose to address a decision to the Member State under Article 90(3) or challenge the national authorities' decision to allow the exemption.

4.15   (iii) **Procedural aspects**

Article 90(3) states that:

> "The Commission shall ensure the application of the provisions of this Article and shall, where necessary address appropriate directives or decisions to the Member States."

Although the Commission has begun in the last five years to make more use of these powers to inject competition into a number of sectors, and in

---

[2] See further, L Hancher and PJ Slot, "Article 90", [1990] 1 ECLR 30.

particular telecommunications, transport and postal services[3], it was not initially inclined to do so for electricity or gas.

An early draft of the Electricity Transit Directive (discussed in Chap 6) made implicit reference to these powers as a possible means to introduce common carriage. The relevant provision did not, however, appear in the text of the measure which was formally adopted by the Council in October 1990.

In mid-1991 the Commission appeared to revert to its earlier position. A proposal for a Directive based on Article 90(3) which would have required Member States to remove certain exclusive rights and privileges conferred on electricity undertakings was initially considered by the Commission services as a means of removing obstacles to competition in the electricity market. Following political rather than legal objections, the Commission appears to have abandoned this strategy.

(a) Scope of Article 90(3)

Directives

The potential use of its powers under Article 90(3) in the electricity sector   **4.16**
is now more attractive for the Commission following the recent judgment in Case C-202/88 *France* v *Commission* (also referred to as "Telecoms").

The Court held that Article 90(3) enables the Commission to define in a general way the obligations which the Treaty imposes on the Member States. The Commission had not used the Directive procedure to challenge specific infringements. If this had been the case it would be obliged to use the enforcement procedures laid down in Article 169 EEC.[4]

As to the competence of the Commission to require the abolition of   **4.17**
exclusive rights, France and the other governments intervening, had claimed that only the Council could have adopted such a Directive on the basis of Article 87 or 100A. The Court dismissed these arguments. It confirmed that Article 90(3) confers a duty of surveillance on the Commission. Furthermore the fact that the Council could adopt measures either under Article 87 or Article 100A which impinge on the specific field of Article 90 does not prevent the Commission from validly exercising its powers under the article (Cases 188-190/80 *France, Italy and UK* v *Commission* [1982] ECR 2545).

It follows from this ruling that although a Directive adopted under Article 90(3) is a Directive within the meaning of Article 189, it is not a *legislative* measure. It is rather a specification by the Commission, under its duty of surveillance of the Member States' obligations. *The definition of these obligations is a matter for the Commission as guardian of the Treaties.* This does

---

[3] The Commission has now adopted three Directives on the basis of Art 90(3). Dir 80/723/EEC on financial transparency was unsuccessfully challenged in Case 188/80 *France, Italy and the United Kingdom* v *Commission* (see further, Chap 5). Its Directive on telecommunication equipment was also upheld by the court in Case 202/88. Its latest Dir 90/388/EEC on telecommunication services is presently the subject of challenge by several member states.
[4] The Commission's powers under this article are discussed in Chap 10.

not exclude however the adoption by the Council of common rules in order to give concrete expression to these obligations.[5]

Thus, if the Commission wishes to abolish exclusive rights in the electricity sector, it should probably, as guardian of the Treaty, base its proposals on Article 90(3), whereas a Council Directive based on Article 100A should elaborate the common rules necessary to realise full competition in the electricity sector.

Decisions

4.18   Recitals 17 and 18 of Case C-202/88 only deal with Directives. The scope of the Commission's powers to adopt decisions of a repressive nature under Article 90(3) remains unclear at present. It has been argued that any action against specific infringements should be based on Article 169. This argument is based in part on the fact that the procedure in Article 169 provides certain procedural safeguards which Article 90(3) does not. Further, Article 90(3) does not provide for a specific derogation to the Article 169 procedure, unlike Articles 93(2) 100A(4) and 225.

4.19   The Commission has in fact issued several Decisions to Member States to remedy specific infringements, but until recently its competence to do so has not been challenged in the Court of Justice.[6] In 1991 the Court of Justice was requested to examine this issue in Cases C-48 & 66/90 *Netherlands* v *Commission,* a case concerning an appeal by the Dutch Government against a Commission Decision requiring it to abolish certain exclusive rights conferred on the national post and telecommunications authority to provide express postal services.[7] The Advocate-General recommended that the Court should quash the contested decision. Although Advocate-General van Gerven endorsed the power of the Commission to adopt the Decision, he recommended its annulment on grounds of a number of procedural defects (Opinion of 16 October 1991).

In its judgement of 12 February 1992, the Court affirmed the Commission's powers to adopt Decisions under Article 90 (3) (see recitals 28-37), but went on to rule that the Commission had failed to respect the procedural rights of both the Dutch government and Netherlands Post Office (recitals 48-54).

4. **ECSC and Euratom Treaties and public firms**

4.20   Neither the ECSC nor the Euratom Treaty make a distinction between state and private firms. As already noted, the Euratom Treaty does not contain any specific rules on competition, so the EEC rules apply in full. Articles 65 and 66 ECSC do not draw any distinction as to the ownership of coal and

---

[5] As for example, in the field of public procurement, discussed in Chap 10.
[6] In Case 226/87 *Greece* v *Commission* [1988] ECR 3611.
[7] Case C-66/90 *Netherlands* v *Commission,* OJ 1990 C132/9.

steel undertakings, and are equally applicable to public and private firms. Article 63 ECSC provides, however, that:

> "if the High Authority finds that discrimination is being systematically practised by purchasers, in particular under provisions governing contracts entered into by bodies dependent on a public authority, it shall make the appropriate recommendations to the Governments concerned."

In its decision on a complaint from the British NALOO and other independent coal mine operators, the Commission upheld the claim that the two UK generators were systematically discriminating against the licensed coal producers in offering lower prices and less favourable conditions. As BCC, NP and PG were wholly owned by the Government of the United Kingdom at the time when the relevant coal supply contracts were signed, "these contracts fell to be examined, *inter alia,* under Article 63 ECSC" (para 49 of Dec of 23 May 1991 – see Appendix II).

Part II

5. Scope of Member State's powers to create and maintain monopolies

(i) Nationalization and privatization

Community law may affect the manner in which firms are nationalised, or privatised, especially if there is an element of state financing involved to make the deal more attractive to the market in the case of privatization.[8] It may also be of relevance to any arrangements, such as restrictions on share ownership, made in order to secure that a certain percentage of the assets of the newly privatised firm remain in the ownership of residents of the particular Member State (Art 67(1) and (2)).   **4.21**

(a) Significance of ownership

Article 90(1) and Article 222 and state-owned monopolies

It has been argued that a combination of these two articles creates "a strong presumption" as to the legality of certain exclusive rights conferred by Member States on undertakings. There is nothing in the Treaty to prevent Member States setting up public sector monopolies; it is only the subsequent exercise of those monopoly powers by the undertaking which is subject to control under the competition rules.[9]   **4.22**

It is difficult to find support for this contention either in the Treaty itself, or in the case law of the Court of Justice.

---

[8] It might be noted that in its recent opinion on the privatization of the German company, Saltzgitter, the Commission ruled that the proceeds of privatization should not be used as a state aid for environmental purposes (OJ 1990 C139/39).

[9] Advocate-General Teasuro, in Case C-202/88.

Articles 222 and 90 deal in reality with quite separate sets of issues: the grant of exclusive or special rights under Article 90(1) relates to public and private undertakings and draws no distinctions between the ownership status of such firms. Furthermore, private firms cannot rely on Article 222 to protect themselves from allegations of abusive conduct under Articles 85 and 86. The same must be true of public firms.[10]

4.23   In Case C-202/88 *Telecoms* the Court did not make any reference to Article 222, even although a number of telecommunications utilities in the Member States are in public ownership. It disposed of the case entirely under Article 30 EEC, thus confirming that in so far as the application of Article 30 is concerned, the Court is unwilling to draw any distinctions between public and private firms.[11]

(ii) **Structural barriers**

(a) General

4.24   It is clear that the mere existence of monopolies in any sector of the Treaty, whether public or private, may create problems for the full and proper application of the Treaty rules.

If a Member State reserves the monopoly of electricity production, for example, to a state-owned enterprise, there can be no right of establishment or right to provide services on the part of potential competitors. The legal monopoly constitutes an absolute barrier to entry and there is also no competition from within the Member State concerned.

The Court's judgment in Case 155/73 *Sacchi* is often cited in support of this argument:

4.25   "nothing in the Treaty prevents Member States, for considerations of public interest of a non-economic nature, from removing radio and television etc from the field of competition by conferring on one or more establishments an exclusive right to conduct them."

Hence, it is argued, Member States may only set up monopolies for reasons of public interest of a non-economic nature.[12]

4.26   A similar "structural" argument may be made in the context of Article 37. The notion of adjustment has to be assessed in the light of goal of the provision: that is to ensure that no discrimination, actual or potential, could continue to exist. This requires the exclusion of discrimination, and not just its prohibition. Emphasis is placed upon the preventative significance of the provision which in turn requires structural, as opposed to a mere behavioural modification of the monopolies to which Article 37 was directed.

---

[10] See Cases 56 & 58/64 *Consten and Grundig* v *Commission, loc cit;* Case 24/67 *Parke, Davis* v *Centraform* [1968] ECR 55. See also the Commission's Decision in *Verenigde Bloembollenveilingen Aalsmeer,* OJ 1988 L262/27.

[11] Case 182/83 *Feardon* v *Land Commission* [1984] ECR 3677, at para 7.

[12] See also Case 90/76 *Van Ameyde* v UCI [1977] ECR 1091.

(b) Existence v exercise

A significant problem which both Articles 90(1) and 37 raise is that the **4.27** extent to which Member States can continue to confer exclusive rights on undertakings is not made clear. On the one hand, Article 90(1) allows them to do so in so far as these rights are not contrary to the rules contained in the Treaty. The competition rules, and Article 86 in particular, are targeted at the abuse of a dominant or a monopoly position, and not at the mere existence of the monopoly. A direct link between the exclusive right and an abuse of the dominant position it creates must be established (Case 226/84 *British Leyland* v *Commission*).

On the other hand, Article 37(1) requires Member States to "adjust" their state monopolies: it does not require their abolition (Case 59/75 *Manghera*).

Some commentators have argued that an analogy could be drawn with the Court's jurisprudence on intellectual property rights; the *existence* of certain exclusive rights is presumed to be compatible with Community law, but their *exercise* is subject to the rules on free movement and competition.[13]

(iii) **Case law of the Court**

The debate over whether these articles relate only to the exercise of **4.28** exclusive rights, and not their mere existence has to some extent been settled by a series of important rulings handed down by the Court of Justice in 1991 – Case C-202/88 *France* v *Commission;* Case C-41/90 *Höfner* and Case C-260/89 *ERT* v *Dimotiki;* Case C-179/90 *Porto di Genova;* and Case 18/88 *RTT* v *GB-Inno*).

In all five cases the Court held that the exclusive right at issue was contrary to Community law; it did not examine the exercise of that right. The Court has been unwilling to take a doctrinal stance on the "exercise v existence" debate, however. Nor has it yet formulated any general norms indicating when the very existence of an exclusive right will be contrary to the Treaty rules.

To understand the application of Community law to Member State **4.29** measures which structure and organise national monopolies, whether public or private, it is best to examine the Court's case law on the relationship between Article 90(1) and the relevant Treaty rule which was alleged to have been breached.

(a) Articles 30 and 37

In recent years the Commission has taken the position the very existence of **4.30** certain forms of monopoly or exclusive rights in the utilities sector will create distortions to trade, contrary to Article 30 and 37 therefore be

---

[13] See, for example, the Opinion of Advocate-General Tesauro in Case C-202/88. It is respectfully submitted that a distinction should be drawn between intellectual property rights, which are usually conferred on any party able to satisfy a set of objective conditions, and the types of special and exclusive rights which fall within the province of Art 90(1) which is directed at the very situations where such objective criteria are absent.

abolished. This interpretation of the Treaty clearly emerges, for example, from the recitals of its Directive 88/301/EEC on telecommunications terminal equipment.

"3. Article 30 of the Treaty prohibits quantitative restrictions on imports from other Member States and all measures having equivalent effect. The grant of special or exclusive rights to import and market goods to one organization can, and often does, lead to restrictions on imports from other Member States.

4. Article 37 of the Treaty states that Member States shall progressively adjust any State Monopolies of a commercial character so as to ensure that when the transitional period has ended no discrimination regarding the conditions under which goods are procured and marketed exists between nationals of Member States...

5. The special or exclusive rights relating to terminal equipment enjoyed by national telecommunications monopolies are exercised in such a way as, in practice, to disadvantage equipment from other Member states, notably by preventing users from freely choosing the equipment that best suits their needs ...regardless of origin. The exercise of these rights is therefore not compatible with Article 37...

6. The provisions of installation and maintenance services is a key factor in purchasing or rental of terminal equipment. The retention of exclusive rights in this field would be tantamount to retention of exclusive marketing rights. Such rights must therefore be abolished if the abolition of exclusive import and marketing rights is to have any practical effect."

4.31   Article 2 of the Directive requires Member States to withdraw all special and exclusive rights granted to undertakings with respect to importation, marketing, connection, etc.

Article 3 provides that Member States must ensure that economic operators have the right to market, connect etc, terminal equipment.

4.32   The Commission's powers to adopt this Directive on the basis of Article 90(3) (see above) were challenged by the French Government, supported by the Belgian, Greek and Italian Governments in Case C-202/88 *France* v *Commission*. These Governments based their challenge on a number of procedural and substantive grounds. Only the latter shall be discussed here.

The French Government, supported by the intervening Governments, argued that the Commission could not adopt a Directive on the basis of Article 90(3) requiring Member States to abolish exclusive rights. Article 90(1) presupposes the legality of such rights. The Court disagreed.

4.33   The Court held that exclusive rights to import and market terminal equipment deprives economic operators or the possibility of having their products purchased directly by consumers. It recalled its broad interpretation of the scope of Article 30, as first applied in Case 8/74 *Dassonville*.[14] The related exclusive rights for connection, etc were also condemned as contrary to Article 30 and Article 3(f): there could be no guarantee that a monopoly operator could ensure these ancillary services for equipment supplied by competitors, nor that he would have any incentive to do so.

---

[14] See in general, Chap 2.

In reaching its conclusion, the Court did not refer to any presumption of **4.34** the legality of the Member States' power to grant exclusive rights. It ruled that even if Article 90(1) presupposes the existence of undertakings having exclusive or special rights, this does not mean that all special or exclusive rights are necessarily compatible with the Treaty. That depended on the nature of the rights themselves (at recital 22).

In establishing the legality issue the Court invoked a proportionality test. It took, as its point of departure, the effect of the exclusive rights on inter-state trade in the goods and services at issue. It then balanced the interests of the Member States against those of the Community and indicated that it was willing to accept the continuance of special or exclusive rights in favour of certain undertakings which could be justified on the basis of the "rule of reason".

In other words if a Member State could show, for example, that it was **4.35** necessary for consumer protection that all goods had to be sold by a particular monopoly, this could be prima facie justifiable. In Case C-202/88, Article 3 of the Directive at issue sets out the conditions under which restrictions by Member States could be justified. The French Government had not claimed that any other essential requirements should be taken into account.

The Court therefore ruled that the Commission had been right in finding that exclusive rights to import, market and to connect etc, terminal equipment were no longer compatible with Article 30. Furthermore it had also been correct to require the removal of a variety of related exclusive rights to provide connection and after-sales services. These were ruled to be incompatible with Articles 30 and 3(f).

(b) Exclusive or special rights?

In Case C-202/88 the Court annulled Article 2 of Directive 88/301/EEC in **4.36** so far as it obliged Member States to withdraw special rights. It held that the Commission had not defined the concept in the Directive, nor had it given sufficient motivation. The Court itself offered no basis on which to distinguish between the two categories of rights. It did not, however, suggest that Member States had an unlimited discretion to entrust enterprises with special rights.

Prior to Case C-202/88 special and exclusive rights had not been thought **4.37** of as two separate and distinct categories. The purpose of Article 90 is to cover all enterprises the behaviour or polices of which the Member State has a special responsibility because of the influence they can exercise over them. The legal form through which that influence is exerted is a secondary consideration (Cases 188-190/80, grounds 12 and 26).

It would seem that for enterprises to fall within the scope of Article 90(1) **4.38** that some particular activity is reserved to them. A right which is conferred upon those carrying on an economic activity which is open to anyone, who thus form part of an indefinite class is unlikely to be regarded as exclusive (Case 13/77 *GB INNO* v *ATAB*). The mere fact that an activity is subject to an open licensing system is not sufficient to bring it within the scope of Articles 37(2) and 90(1) (Case 118/86 *Openbaar Ministerie* v *Nertsvoederfabriek BV* [1987] ECR 3883).

The mode of granting the right (whether by an act under public law or by private contract, for example) is immaterial to Article 90(1). It is the potential for influence which is the key factor.

(c) Article 86

4.39　The Commission also takes the view that Article 86 may be applied to measures enacted or otherwise adopted by Member States which reserve monopolies to certain organizations. It has now adopted, on the basis of Article 90(3), several Decisions and two Directives, based on this interpretation of Article 86.

In this series of Decisions and in its two Directives the Commission has not actually challenged the national laws or other measures which have created the monopolies in question. It uses Articles 3(f), 5, 86 and 90(1) to challenge the extension of that monopoly position to an "adjacent" market (see further Chap 3).

Decisions

4.40　In its Decision on the Spanish Postal Monopoly (OJ 1990, L233/19) it states, at paragraph 10:

> "An abuse of a dominant position within the meaning of Article 86 is committed where an undertaking holding a dominant position reserves to itself or to an undertaking belonging to the same group, without any objective necessity, an ancillary activity which might be carried out by another undertaking as part of its activities on a neighbouring or separate market, with the possibility of eliminating all competition from such an undertaking."

4.41　The relevant Spanish legislation reserved to the Post Office not only the basic letter collection services, but also the new international express service for letters. This amounted to an abuse under Article 86(b), similar to that prohibited by the Court in Case 311/84 *CBEM* [1985] ECR 3261, at ground 27.

A similar line of reasoning was deployed in its Decision on the Netherlands Express Service Decision, against which the Dutch government subsequently appealed (OJ 1990 L10/47). In Cases C-48 & 66/90, the Advocate-General has confirmed the Commission's general line of reasoning even though he has recommended the annulment of the Decision on other grounds (Opinion of 16 October 1991). In its judgment of 12 February 1992 the Court disposed of the case on procedural grounds only.

4.42　**Directives**

Recital 5 of Commission Directive 90/388/EEC (OJ 1990 L192/10) on competition in telecommunication services, states that:

"The granting of special or exclusive rights to one or more undertakings to operate the network derives from the discretionary power of the State. The granting by a Member State of such rights inevitably restricts the provision of such services by other undertakings to or from other Member states."[15]

In this Directive the Commission takes the position that certain monopoly or exclusive rights may be legitimate and can be exempted under Article 90(2). These are the monopoly rights to provide voice telephony services. Where, however, a state measure extended this monopoly into an adjacent market for so-called "value added services" this could amount to an abuse because it strengthens the dominant position of the original monopoly.[16] Hence these monopoly rights in ancillary markets must be abolished in accordance with Article 2(1) of the Directive.

This Directive has been challenged on both procedural and substantive grounds by several governments.[17]

(d) Case law of the Court

The Court of Justice has recently examined the application of Article 86 to   **4.43** Member State legislation creating monopolies in two cases.

Case C-41/90 *Höfner and Elser* v *Macrotron* (judgment of 23 April 1991) concerned the statutory monopoly enjoyed by the Bundesanstalt für Arbeit (BA) to provide recruitment and placement services for executive positions in Germany. The German court which referred the case asked the Court, *inter alia,* whether, taking into account that Article 90(2) must be read in conjunction with the other Treaty provisions ... does the monopoly of recruitment constitute an abuse of a dominant position, contrary to Article 86?

The Court interpreted this question as requesting it to give a ruling on   **4.44** whether the BA's monopoly constituted a breach of Article 86, taking account of the provisions of Article 90(1) and (2).

It first examined the legality of the exclusive rights of the monopoly in relation to Article 90(1) and to the effect of Article 90(2). Although it was a public office, the BA remained subject to the rules of competition, unless in accordance with Article 90(2) it could be demonstrated that the application of those rules was incompatible with the exercise of its functions.

It concluded that the application of Article 86 did not obstruct the performance of the BA's tasks when that office was manifestly unable to satisfy market demand for its services and when it had indeed tolerated in the past competition from private agencies.

The Court also ruled that while it was true that Article 86 is addressed to   **4.45** enterprises, and must be applied within the limits of Article 90(2) to public or entrusted enterprises, it nevertheless remains the case that the Treaty

---

[15] A similar line of reasoning can be found at recitals to the earlier Dir 83/301/EEC.
[16] Commission Dir 90/388/EEC on competition in the markets for telecommunications services, contains a similar reasoning, at recitals 12-17.
[17] Registered as Cases 271, 281 & 289/90, OJ 1990 C274/20.

imposes obligations on Member States not to create or maintain in force measures depriving the competition rules of their proper effect. Article 90(1) provides that Member States shall not take or maintain in force any measure contrary to the Treaty rules. It follows that all such measures which maintain in force a legal disposition which creates a situation in which a public office will be necessarily compelled to contravene Article 86, must be incompatible with the Treaty (recital 27).

4.46   The simple fact of creating a dominant position through the grant of an exclusive right in the sense of Article 90(1) would not automatically constitute a breach of Article 86. A Member State will only be in breach of its Treaty obligations when the enterprise in question is forced by the simple exercise of its exclusive rights to abuse its dominant position (recital 29).

In this particular case the Member State had created a situation in which the statutory monopoly was manifestly unable to satisfy the demands for its services, while private competitors were forbidden from entering the market by a legal provision which rendered any contract for such services null and void.

4.47   The situation in which the holder of an exclusive right is unable to satisfy demand for the services in question is foreseen by Article 86(b). Its abusive nature was confirmed by the Court in Case 238/87 *Volvo* v *Veng* [1988] ECR 6211 and in Case 53/87 *Maxicar* v *Renault* [1988] ECR 6039.

Case C-260/89 *ERT* v *Dimotiki* (judgment of 18 June 1991) involved a reference from the Greek courts on the legality of a statutory monopoly conferred on the Greek television station, ERT, to produce and to transmit radio and television broadcasts in Greece. The same law also prohibited any other person from engaging in these types of activities.

4.48   As a point of departure the Court recalled its jurisprudence in the earlier Case 155/73 *Sacchi* to the effect that nothing in the Treaty prevents Member States from conferring exclusive rights to broadcast for non-economic reasons. At recital 12, however the Court stressed that *the methods of organization and exercise of that monopoly must not run contrary to the rules on free movement of goods and services and the competition rules* (emphasis supplied).

In its analysis of the compatibility of the monopoly with the Treaty competition rules, the Court began by repeating its reasoning in *Höfner*: Article 86 prohibits the abuse of a dominant position, and not the mere holding of such a position. It then recalled its past jurisprudence on the obligations of Member States not to deprive the competition rules of their effectiveness. In the present case the ERT enjoyed a monopoly over all broadcasting, including its own programmes and those produced elsewhere in the Community and re-transmitted in Greece.

4.49   The Court therefore ruled that Article 86 prohibits the grant of an exclusive right by a Member State to retransmit television programmes to an enterprise which has an exclusive broadcasting right, where these rights are liable to create a situation in which the enterprise is compelled to breach Article 86 by giving preferential treatment to its own programmes (recital 37).

This line of reasoning has been followed in Case 18/88 *RTT* v *GB-Inno* (13 December 1991). In this case the Court ruled that the conferral of exclusive rights to approve, connect, service and maintain all telephone equipment to an undertaking which had an exclusive right to construct and operate the national network could amount to a breach of Articles 86 and 90(1). Such rights allowed the undertaking in question, the RTT, to extend its monopoly power from the provision of network services into related markets for the provision and servicing of equipment. This in itself was in breach of Articles 86 and 90(1). It was not necessary to go on to show that the RTT had actually abused its position in those markets.

(e) Article 59

In Case C-260/89 *ERT* the Court also considered the application of Article **4.50** 59, which prohibits restrictions on the free movement of services, to statutory monopolies. It essentially endorsed the Commission's view that ERT's *accumulation of monopolies* to produce and re-transmit programmes gave the ERT ample potential to favour its own programmes, to the detriment of foreign material. It was for the national court to establish whether this accumulation of exclusive rights had in fact resulted in discrimination. It added that while Article 56 might be invoked to justify restrictions in free movement in the interests of public health, security or public order, that article could not be relied upon to justify the legislation at issue here (recital 25).

(f) Observations

In Cases C-202/88, C-41/90, C-260/89, and more recently in C-179/90 **4.51** and 18/88 the Court has now made it clear that it will be prepared to condemn state measures as leading to breaches of Articles 30, 48, 59 and 86. Although it has not yet said that all exclusive rights will *automatically* lead to such a breach it is clear that Article 90(1) does not give Member States unlimited rights to grant exclusive rights to public or other undertakings. In all of these cases the Court has looked at whether the operation or organization of the monopolies established by the various forms of exclusive rights at issue is in practice incompatible with the aims of the Common market.

(iv) Possible exemptions for Member States

Given that the Court is now prepared to strike down exclusive rights it is **4.52** important to establish to whether and to what extent exemptions are available. The Court itself provided indications of when monopolies may be justifiable:
(1) based on Article 36 (Case 72/83 *Campus*);
(2) based on the "mandatory requirements"(Case C-202/88 *Telecoms;* Case 18/88 *RTT* v *GB-Inno*);
(3) where there is a dominant position which is ancillary to or adjacent to another dominant position which is not incompatible (Case C-347/88 *Commission* v *Greece*);

(4) where there is a dominant position which is ancillary or adjacent to another dominant position and this can be justified for objective reasons (Case 18/88);

(5) based on Article 56 (Case C-260/89 *ERT*);

(6) based on Article 90(2) where the application of the Treaty rules would obstruct the performance of the special tasks entrusted to the enterprise (Case C-260/89; Case C-179/90 *Porto di Genova*).

(a) Article 90(2)

4.53 Given the potential importance of this exemption to the utility sector in general and to the electricity sector in particular, it is necessary to consider its scope and application in more detail.

To benefit from the exemption, a number of stages must be passed through:

4.54 (1) The enterprise in question must show that it has been *entrusted* with a particular task. This must be by an act of public authority, for example, through a law or regulatory act or by a concession (Case 66/86 *Saaed;* Dec 91/50/EEC *IJsselcentrale*).

4.55 (2) It must be shown that the enterprise is engaged in the performance of the tasks entrusted to it; the exemption cannot be claimed in connection with extraneous activities (Case 31/48 *Italy* v *Commission;* Case 311/83 *CBEM*; Case T-69/89 *RTE* v *Magill*).

4.56 (3) It is necessary to show that the government measure entrusting the performance of a particular task meets the proportionality tests under the relevant Treaty articles. The recent jurisprudence in Case C-202/88 *Telecoms,* Case C-41/90 *Höfner,* Case C-260/89 *ERT* Case C-179/90 *Porto di Genova* and Case 18/88 *RTT* v *GB-Inno,* discussed above, is authority for this point. In Case 18/88 the Court itself suggested other less restrictive ways in which security could be ensured.

Where the relevant government measure restricts free movement of goods, it will be incumbent upon the national government to show that it is justified under the mandatory requirements (Case C-202/88) or under one of the exemptions in Article 36 (Case 72/83 *Campus Oil*). Where a restriction on services is concerned, the Member State must prove that it is justified under Article 56 (Case *ERT*).

If the relevant provisions of the national law compel the enterprise to abuse the dominant position which has been conferred upon it, Article 90(2) is the only possible exemption to Article 86. In this type of situation the Court has considered whether the exercise of the monopoly is or is not prejudicial to consumers, within the meaning of Article 86(b). Where it has found that the monopoly fails to meet the demand for the services it provides, as in *Höfner,* or where it fails to provide a full range of services for the consumer, as in *ERT,* it has been prepared to condemn the state measures in question.

4.57 (4) It is then further necessary to show that the performance of its tasks is obstructed in law or in fact by the application of the Treaty rules. At the time of writing, the Court has never granted an exemption on these grounds. In Case 41/83 *Italy* v *Commission,* for example, the Court held that a mere decline in profits as a result of exposure to competition did not amount to obstruction. According to the Commission an undertaking would have to demonstrate that it has no other technically and economically feasible means of performing the particular task (*ANSEA-NAVEVA* OJ 1981 L167/17). In Case C-179/90 *Porto di Genova,* the Court has implied that substantial evidence that the undertaking could not fulfill the tasks required of it would have to be available to it before it would consider granting an exemption

Article 21 of the agreement – the OVS – at issue in Commission Decision 91/50/EEC, *IJsselcentrale,* prohibited imports and exports via the public network by parties other than the SEP, the company responsible for managing the high transmission grid. The Commission considered that Article 90(2) could not be used to justify a ban on *exports* surplus to the needs of public supply by distribution companies, or *imports/ exports* by large industrial consumers. It declined to give a decision on the application of Article 90(2) to imports for use in, or exports from the public supply system, however. This decision has been challenged before the Court of First Instance by the distribution companies (Case T-16/91 *Rendo* v *Commission*).

The Commission has meanwhile indicated that it is prepared to recognise that certain activities fall within the scope of Article 90(2). In its recent Directives on telecommunications equipment (88/301/EEC) and telecommunications services (90/388/EEC), the Commission has indicated that exclusive rights to provide "voice telephony services" as opposed to certain "value added services" can be reserved to public or entrusted firms. The Court did not question the reservation of the telephone network to a state enterprise in Case 18/88 *RTT* v *GB-Inno.*

(5) Finally, in accordance with the last paragraph of Article 90(2), the development of trade must not be affected to such an extent as would be contrary to the interests of the Community. This phrase appears to refer to the process of establishing the common market.[18] There is no case law on this point, but at paragraph 47 of the *IJsselcentrale* Decision, and having examined the absolute nature of the ban on imports and exports, the Commission stated:

4.58

> "In view of the foregoing, there is no need to consider the last sentence of Article 90(2). It is clear, however that obstruction of imports and exports such as that deriving from Article 21 of the OVS does affect trade to an extent contrary to the interests of the Community. In the light of the Community's efforts to achieve a single internal market in energy such obstruction ... which moreover is intended to continue for a period of 25 years, cannot be accepted."

[18] See Advocate-General Rozes in Case 78/82 *Commission* v *Italy (Tobacco Margins)* [1983] ECR 1955.

Part III

6. Monopoly and exclusive rights in the electricity sector

(i) Introduction

4.59 This section considers the application of the principles discussed above to the different types and configurations of monopoly and exclusive rights prevalent in the electricity sector. The following discussion should be understood in the context of the Commission's commitment to a gradual or staged introduction of competition into the electricity market. The Commission has now commenced Article 169 infringement proceedings against those Member States which continue to confer exclusive rights to import and export electricity on particular undertakings. In the Commission's view these rights are in breach of Article 37.

4.60 The Commission has also put forward to the Council a proposal for a Directive based on Articles 100A, 57(2) and 66 requiring the adoption of a number of common rules for the electricity market. The proposal does not deal directly with exclusive rights to produce, transmit or distribute electricity. Their removal is implicitly required to give effect to the proposed common rules.

(ii) Production monopolies

4.61 The conferral of a production monopoly on a particular firm, whether public or privately owned, raises problems under several EEC Treaty articles. These are dealt with in turn:

(a) Article 37

4.62 To date the Commission has never considered that a purely national production monopoly is contrary to Articles 30, 37 or 86 EEC.

Hence in Case C-347/88 *Commission* v *Greece,* the Commission did not challenge the legality of the provisions of the national law which conferred a monopoly of refining on the Greek state sector. It did, however, challenge the monopoly rights of these refiners to import crude oil. The Court held that, given the absence of domestic crude oil production, however, the monopoly over imports was an integral part of the refiners' production monopoly. As the Commission had declined to attack that monopoly, it could not go on to attack the crude oil import monopoly on the basis of either Articles 30 or 37 (see further Chap 2).

Where, however, the production monopoly also has absolute control over imports and exports, this could be contrary to Articles 3(f), 30 and 37 and 59 (Cases C-202/88 and C-260/89).

4.63 *(b) Article 86 – abuse of a dominant position*

Article 86, it will be recalled, is concerned with the abuse of a dominant position. The mere existence of the monopoly is not contrary to

Community law. There must be an abuse and that abuse must affect Community trade.

In Case C-260/89 *ERT* the Court rules that it would contrary to Articles 86 and 90(1) if a Member State granted special or exclusive rights to an undertaking where an accumulation of such rights were capable of leading to a situation where an enterprise not only occupied a dominant position but was compelled to abuse that position by discriminating against foreign produced programmes.

4.64 Where the production rights are *not* combined with other exclusive rights, such as exclusive rights to import or export, and/or exclusive rights to transit, it is unlikely that the production monopoly alone could be condemned under Articles 90(1) and 86, unless perhaps it could be shown that a situation similar to that condemned by the Court in *Höfner* exists – that is where the monopoly was manifestly not in a position to satisfy demand. In other words the creation and maintenance of a monopoly which prevents competition from private generators may constitute a limitation on production, in breach of Article 90(1) and Article 86(b), unless justification could be made out.

(c) Article 52 EEC – production monopolies and the right of establishment

4.65 Article 52 provides that restrictions on freedom of establishment of nationals of a Member State in the territory of another Member State shall be abolished. The right of establishment rests on the prohibition against discrimination. Nationals from another Member State should have the right to equal treatment with nationals of the host Member State. Thus, as long as it respects the equal treatment principle, in the absence of Community harmonising legislation, each Member State would appear, in principle, to be free to regulate electricity production on its national territory (Case 221/85 *Commission* v *Belgium* [1987] ECR 719; Case 6/64 *Costa* v *ENEL* at 1163).

4.66 In the recent Case C-340/89 *I Vlassopoulou* (judgment of 7 May 1991), however, the Court of Justice appears to have developed its jurisprudence on Article 52 so that certain measures, even if applied without discrimination as regards nationality, would nevertheless be condemned where those measures have the effect of impeding the exercise of the right of establishment guaranteed by Article 52.

It might therefore be argued that a national measure reserving electricity production to state-owned firms has indeed the effect of preventing nationals from other Member States from exercising the rights guaranteed to them under Article 52.

(d) Coal and nuclear production – ECSC and Euratom Treaties

4.67 The ECSC Treaty does not contain any specific rules on establishment and services, and so as a result of Article 232 EEC, Articles 52-66 of that Treaty apply.

Article 97 of the Euratom Treaty provides that:

"No restriction based on *nationality* may be applied to natural or legal persons, whether public or private, under the jurisdiction of a Member State, where they desire to *participate* in the construction of nuclear installations of a scientific or industrial nature in the Community" (emphasis added).

4.68   This provision is only aimed at discrimination based on nationality and even then is limited to persons *participating* in certain construction projects. This term can probably best be understood in the context of the Treaty itself, which aims to encourage joint undertakings to encourage the development of nuclear power (Chap V, Euratom).

The rights of companies established in another Member State and wishing to construct a nuclear facility on a fully independent basis would therefore fall to be considered under the EEC Treaty.

(e) Commission's proposals for production

4.69   Article 2 of the Commission's early draft Directive on competition in the electricity market, based on Article 90(3), required Member States to abolish all exclusive rights to construct, operate, buy or sell electricity generating plant.

Reservations about the legal basis of this proposal, with reference to the jurisprudence cited at 4.65 above, have been expressed by the Commission's legal services. The Article 90(3) proposal has now been withdrawn.

The Commission's first package of measures, published in June 1991 included a parallel proposal for a Council Directive, based on Article 100A, which contained common rules on criteria and procedures for granting production licenses. It might be questioned whether such a measure could be adopted on the basis of Article 100A alone. In the light of the Court's judgment in Case C-300/89 *Commission* v *Council* (judgment of 11 June 1991, not yet reported) where it ruled that Article 100A provided an appropriate legal basis for all harmonising measures affecting production costs, the Commission may have been justified. (This judgment is considered in more detail in Chap 10.) Its most recent proposal (Com (91) 548, 21 February 1992) for a Directive is based on Articles 100A, 57(2) and 66, however.

Article 4 of the present draft provides that:

4.70   "1. Member States shall allow undertakings established in the Community to build, operate, purchase or sell generating installations which are located on their territory and which are intended for the generation of electricity for own use or for sale subject only to criteria and procedures for authorization to be established in accordance with paragraphs 2 to 6 below.

4.71   2. Member States shall lay down the criteria which shall be met by an undertaking applying for a licence to build or operate a generating installation. The criteria shall be objective and non-discriminatory. They shall be published not later than six months after the entry into force of the Directive.
The criteria shall relate exclusively to:
– security and safety of the installation;
– environmental protection requirements;

– land use and siting;

– the technical and financial capacity of the applicant undertaking.

However, Member States may, for reasons of environmental policy or of security of supply, supplement these criteria by criteria restricting the nature of the primary energy source that may be used for the generation of electricity.

3. Member States shall lay down and publish, not later than six months after the entry into force of this Directive as provided for in Article 28, the licensing procedures to be followed by undertakings applying for a licence to build and operate generating installations.   **4.72**

The procedures shall be non-discriminatory.

The procedures may vary according to the nature of the primary energy source to be used and the technical type of generating installations. In the case of major installations, a licence may be granted for each successive phase of construction.

(4) Member States shall ensure that the criteria and procedures are applied in a manner which is non-discriminatory and that all applications are handled in a timely manner.

Any change to the criteria and procedure made during the course of an application shall be applied in a non discriminatory manner to all applicants whose applications are under consideration.

5. Member States may attach conditions and requirements to the licence provided that such conditions and requirements are non-discriminatory and are no more restrictive than is necessary to ensure that the criteria are respected.   **4.73**

6. Member States shall ensure that the reasons for any refusal to grant a licence are given to the applicant and shall establish a procedure enabling the applicant to appeal against such refusals."   **4.74**

These proposals are likely to prove controversial, especially in Member States which endow a monopoly of production on state-owned firms.

(iii) Vertically integrated monopolies

A number of Member States confer exclusive rights on a single enterprise, whether public or private, to carry out the import, export, production, transmission, and distribution of electricity. The Court's latest juris-prudence in Case C-202/88 *Telecoms,* Cases C-41/90 *Höfner,* C-260/89 *ERT* and Case18/88 casts doubts on the legality of such arrangements, and suggests that they might be attacked on two fronts.   **4.75**

(a) Article 30 and Article 37

In Case C-202/88 the Court ruled, first, that where a Member State conferred exclusive rights to market a product on a single firm this would deprive the suppression of exclusive import and export rights of their effectiveness.   **4.76**

Second, in Case C-202/88 the Court ruled that exclusive rights to provide related services, including interconnection and maintenance would have to be abolished to ensure that other economic operators could offer a full range of services in the domestic market, and to ensure that competition was undistorted.

(b) Article 86

4.77   In Case C-260/89 *ERT* the Court based its attack on the monopoly rights in question *inter alia* on Articles 90(1) and 86, and condemned the accumulation of monopolies entrusted to the Greek television monopoly. A similar line of attack could be directed at vertically-integrated electricity industries.

An alternative line of argument against vertically integrated monopolies, based on Case 311/84 *CBEM* could be that the company in question has extended its monopoly over certain activities, such as for example, the construction and maintenance of the network, to an adjacent market for supply and transport of electricity. This might amount to an abuse under Article 86(b). It would be necessary for the enterprise to show that the extension of its activities could be objectively justified (Case 18/88 *RTT* v *GB-Inno*).

A third possibility open to the Commission is to attack combined supply/transit arrangements as a tie-in, in contravention of Article 86(d).

(c) Commission's current proposals

4.78   On the basis of this case law, the Commission is now proposing that Member States remove certain exclusive rights and further "unbundle" vertically-integrated monopolies.

It is implicit in the new proposal that all exclusive rights to transit electricity must be removed. Article 5(1) requires that Member States shall grant licences to build or operate electricity transmission or distribution lines and associated equipment on their territory. The proposed draft Council Directive also stipulates that common rules must be adopted for transmission system operation. Article 8 provides that:

> "1. Member States shall designate or shall require the undertakings which own or are responsible either for transmission systems ... or for system control or dispatch to designate a system operator, which has the obligation to operate and ensure the maintenance and development of the transmission system in a given area and its interconnectors with other systems.
> 2. Member States shall lay down provisions requiring the transmission system operator to be operated separately from the generation and distribution divisions of any integrated electricity undertakings and from any generation and distribution undertakings."

4.79   Article 16(4) of the draft Council Directive contains similar provisions for the unbundling of distribution activities:

> "Member States shall designate or shall require the undertakings which own or are responsible for distribution systems (including electrical lines forming part thereof) to designate a distribution system operator, which has the obligation to operate and to ensure the maintenance and development of the distribution system in a given area and its interconnectors with other systems."

In accordance with Article 23 Member States must make the necessary arrangements for ensuring that vertically integrated electricity undertakings organise their electricity generation, transmission and distribution activities – as the case may be – in as many separate divisions as there are activities. Any state aid granted to one division may not benefit another Directive.

These "unbundled" divisions will be required to keep separate accounts (Art 24).

The proposed rules on transit are considered in more detail in Chapter 6.

(iv) Disaggregated electricity industries

Where production, transmission and distribution are entrusted to independent operators which nevertheless enjoy monopoly rights or other exclusive privileges, the Treaty rules may apply.   **4.80**

Pure production monopolies have already been considered above.

(a) Transmission

Where a single enterprise has a statutory monopoly of transmission through-out the national territory[19], the application of Articles 30 and 37 as well as Article 59 must be considered. These articles, together with possible justifications for transmission monopolies, are discussed more fully in Chapter 6.   **4.81**

(b) Distribution

Where a single enterprise enjoys a monopoly over distribution throughout the national territory this would probably amount to a measure having equivalent effect contrary to Article 30; alternatively a state-owned or controlled monopoly could be held to be contrary to Article 37.   **4.82**

A distribution monopoly may be justified on the basis of Article 30 or 36, where it could be shown, for example, that such a monopoly was necessary to ensure consumer protection or security of supply. The Court has been prepared to accept justification for marketing monopolies based on Article 36 in a number of recent cases concerning pharmacy monopolies, for example.[20] It is for the Member State to produce evidence to demonstrate (a) that a restriction is objectively justified and (b) that it is proportional to the ends sought.

On the basis of the Court's reasoning in *Höfner*, if it could be demonstrated that the distribution company was incapable of meeting demand, then the monopoly might be open to attack under Articles 90(1) and 86(b), providing of course that the "substantial part of the common market" test can be satisfied (Case C-179/90 *Porto di Genova*).   **4.83**

---

[19] For example, REDESA, in Spain.
[20] Case C-369/88 *Delattre,* judgement of 21 March 1991. Case 60/89 *Sammani* judgement of 21 March 1991.

Where a number of enterprises are entrusted with the provision of regional distribution within the national territory, Article 37 may apply (Case 30/87 *Bodson*) but not necessarily Articles 85 and 86.

Distribution monopolies may alternatively be subject to Article 59, following the Court's ruling in Case C-260/89 *ERT,* where it can be shown that the conferral of an exclusive distribution right puts imported services at a disadvantage.

(c) Commission's current proposals on distribution

Article 16(1) of the Draft Council Directive states that:

4.84   "Member States shall define the rights and the public service obligations of distribution companies and the rights and obligations of their customers.

Article 16(2) provides that they "may lay upon distribution companies an obligation to supply the customers located in a given area, with respect to the volume for which they do not exercise their right, or do not have the right to be supplied by other suppliers ...."

Articles 17-22 lay down certain conditions which will govern the activities of the distribution operator (as defined in Art 16(4)).

Thus, provided there is access to the network for eligible entities and provided any consumer may deal with another supplier by means of a direct line, Member States may continue to grant exclusive distribution concessions.

Article 7(1) requires Member States to allow any customer on their territory to purchase and to be supplied with electricity from a producer in that Member State or another Member State. These proposals are considered in more detail in Chapter 6.

Part IV

7. State intervention and "mixed situations"

4.85   It remains to consider the potential application of the competition rules to a number of other instances where the distinction between public and private conduct may not necessarily be clear.

4.86   Articles 3(f) and 5 EEC, in combination with Articles 85 and 86, have been utilised as a legal basis by the Court of Justice in order to deal with these so-called "mixed situations".[21]

In addition to the creation of state enterprises, and the conferral of special and exclusive rights on certain public or private undertakings, Slot has suggested that mixed situations[22] may also include:

---

[21] L Gyselen, "State action and the effectiveness of the EEC Treaty's competition provisions", (1989) 26 CML Rev 33-60.

[22] Slot, "The applications of Articles 3(f), 5 and 85 to 94 EEC", (1987) 12 EL Rev 179 at 179-80.

(i) State enterprises charged with regulatory powers

The British Telecom case[23] shows that such powers do not exempt the   **4.87**
enterprise from scrutiny under Articles 85 and 86.

(ii) Government regulations

These may oblige private enterprises to perform certain acts which are or   **4.88**
may be contrary to Articles 85 and 86. This was the situation in Case 229/83
LeClerc v *Au ble vért* [1985] ECR 1.

(iii) Sanctioning of agreements restricting competition between enterprises by governments

The Asjes[24] and BNIC[25] cases provide examples of the application of Article   **4.89**
85(1) to such arrangements.

(iv) Coercive government regulations

Governments may in addition to taking legislative measures, coerce   **4.90**
enterprises into acts which contravene Articles 85 and 86. Such was the case
in the cigarette industry in the Netherlands[26], and more recently in the
German labour market in *Höfner.*

(v) Permissive government regulations

Government regulations authorising private enterprises to perform certain   **4.91**
acts which are or may be contrary to Articles 85 and 86. An example of this
is provided by the *British Leyland* case (Case 226/84 [1986] ECR 323).

(vi) Governmental regulations and measures restricting competition

This category comprises a wide range of measures. The case law shows a   **4.92**
diversity of situations with a varying impact on competition.

(a) in the *Sugar* case[27] the European Court found that a complex set of
measures of the Italian Government had the effect of effectively foreclosing
the possibility for competition by the enterprises involved.

(b) In the tobacco industry, the *INNO-ATAB, Fedetab*[28] and *Stichting
Sigarettenindustrie* cases show that there was a significant restriction of
competition which nevertheless left room for competition in the industry.

---

[23] Case 41/83 *Italy* v *Commission* [1985] ECR 873.
[24] Cases 209-213/84 [1986] ECR 1425.
[25] Case 123/83 *BNIC* v *Clair* [1985] ECR 391.
[26] Cases 240-242, 261, 262, 268 & 269/82 *Stichting Sigarettenindustrie* [1985] ECR 3831.
[27] Cases 40-48, 50, 54-56, 11, 113, 114/73 *Suiker Unie and others* v *Commission* [1975] ECR 1663 at
paras 34-72.
[28] Cases 209-215 & 218/78 [1980] ECR 3125.

4.93   (c) The *Van Tiggele*[29] and *Buys*[30] cases show that government price regulation may actually be enacted to replace restrictive agreements by the industry. In these cases the government legislation was assessed under Article 30 – see further Chapter 7.

(d) The *Forest*[31] case where the power of the French Government to set production quotas was contested.

(e) Government regulation stimulating cartel agreements in the industry. In the *Meldoc*[32] decision a minimum price regulation provided the industry with an excellent opportunity "to construct their own cartel arrangements."

4.94   As Slot has pointed out: "mixed situations can also be analysed by contrasting and comparing Articles 30 and 85."[33] He stresses that it is important to bear in mind that the scope of Article 30 does not coincide entirely with Articles 85 and 86. Article 30 does not apply to trade with third countries, while Articles 85 and 86 do (Case 51/75 *EMI Records* v *CBS United Kingdom* [1976] ECR 811). Articles 85 and 86 are wider in scope than the case law on Article 34, discussed above. Article 30 does not recognise the *de minimis* principle, while Article 85 does (see Chap 3).

It should also be pointed out that the Commission has far more extensive investigatory and enforcement powers under the competition rules.[34]

4.95   The case law referred to above has resulted in the formulation of the following propositions. A Member State should not render the Treaty's competition provisions "ineffective" by "reinforcing the effects" of an agreement that violates Article 85(1) or an abuse of a dominant position under Article 86.[35] It should not facilitate or require such conduct. Hence Member States are obliged not to enact economic regulations which would deprive Articles 3(f), 5 and Articles 85 and 86 of their effectiveness or prejudice their full and uniform application.

4.96   In its judgment in Case 267/86 *Van Eycke* [1988] ECR 4769 the Court "restated" its case law as meaning:

"that a Member State fails to comply with that obligation
(a) when it requires or encourages undertakings to conclude cartels contrary to Articles 85 or reinforces the effects thereof; or
(b) when it divests its regulations of their public character by delegating to the undertakings there responsibility to take decisions concerning the parameters of competition."[36]

The Commission has not as yet instigated infringement proceedings against any Member State for breach of Articles 3(f) and 5 in conjunction with Articles 85 and 86. However, it has argued that these provisions have been infringed in a case currently before the Court of Justice

[29] Case 82/77 [1978] ECR 25.
[30] Case 5/79 [1979] ECR 3202.
[31] Case 148/85 [1985] ECR 3449.
[32] OJ 1986 L348/50.
[33] *Op cit* at 181.
[34] See in general, *Whish – Competition Law*, 351-375.
[35] See most recently, the judgement in Case 66/86 *Saeed* [1989] ECR 803.
[36] Gyselen at 36, referring to recital 16 of the Court's judgement.

concerning a German regulation on commission for insurance brokers (Case C-2/91 *Meng*).

It follows, that in addition to the situations described in Parts I and II of this chapter, in certain other circumstances, domestic legislation may be contrary to Articles 3, 5 , 85 and 86.

Whish has suggested, on the basis of the current case law, that two **4.97** requirements must be satisfied for a successful challenge to a national law or regulation on the basis of these articles.

> "First it must be clear, as Community law stands, that undertakings have entered into agreements or indulged in anti-competitive behaviour which is in breach of Articles 85 and 86 ... Secondly the legislation to which objection is taken must strengthen or encourage illegal agreements or anti-competitive behaviour". (p 342)

What is not yet clear from the Court's case law is the types of links which must exist between the "private" anti-competitive behaviour and a contested national regulations for Articles 3, 5, 85 and 86 to apply to national measures. Case C-2/91, currently before the Court, may present a useful occasion for further clarification on this point.

The impact of this line of case law will be considered further, in particular in Chapters 7 and 8.

Chapter 5
State Aids and Community Law

1. Introduction

The Community rules on state aids can have a number of consequences for **5.1** the electricity industry. They may be of relevance to the financial relationship between a state-owned enterprise and its government, where for example, the latter makes capital funds or export credits, available on favourable terms. Similarly, the rules may apply to any financial restructuring of a firm prior to privatization. The state aid provisions may be of relevance to public and private sector firms alike in assessing the legality of state funded aid for specific research and development projects or for financing environmentally-related investment. Last, but by no means least, tariffs levied by enterprises over which the state has an element of control may fall within the definition of a "state aid" for the purposes of the EEC Treaty.

The application of the state aid rules under the EEC and ECSC Treaties **5.2** to the electricity sector present a large number of practical and theoretical problems. The conceptual problems are considerable.

In the first place the application of each of the Treaties' sets of state aid rules is not mutually exclusive – an exemption for an indirect aid to an electricity producer to encourage the use of domestic coal while sanctioned under the ECSC Treaty rules, may not necessarily be immune from attack under the EEC rules. The application of the state aid rules to the "upstream activities" of the electricity industry is not yet well developed.

In the second place, as to the practicalities of implementing and **5.3** enforcing the state aid rules, the Commission is faced with the problem that in sectors such as electricity which are characterised by a high degree of public ownership, it is difficult to determine whether transfers from public funds to the industry have actually been effected.

Further problems may also arise "downstream" in the context of special tariffs to particular classes of consumer. When can an aid be said to be provided from state resources, and when is it be deemed as aid which "favours certain undertakings or the production of certain goods"? To what extent is it legitimate to cross-subsidise one category of consumers at the expense of another?

This chapter explains the operation and application of the Community **5.4** rules to the "upstream" activities of the electricity sector. Part I examines the relevant provisions of the ECSC and EEC Treaties. Part II looks at the particular problems the Commission must confront in obtaining evidence of illicit transfers from public funds.

111

The potential application of the state aid rules to "downstream" questions, including the legality of cross-subsidization is discussed in detail in Chapter 7.

Part I

2. **ECSC and EEC Treaties' approach to state aids**

5.5 State aids to undertakings are dealt with in the Treaty of Paris and the Treaty of Rome creating the EEC.[1] The approach taken by each Treaty to the legality of state aids, is quite different, however.

(i) **ECSC Treaty**

5.6 Article 4(c) ECSC places an absolute prohibition on all subsidies or aids granted by states, or special charges in any form whatsoever. There is no possibility for exemption for state aids under the ECSC regime comparable to Articles 92(2) and (3) EEC. This absolute prohibition is to be explained in part by the more limited functions of the ECSC Treaty itself and in part by the very different role envisaged in it for the Community institutions. Firstly, the Coal and Steel Treaty is restricted to two sectors of the economy which had traditionally benefitted from government support. Strict limitations on the nature of that support were considered necessary at the time of the Treaty's drafting. Secondly, the ECSC Treaty provides the Commission with many more interventionist powers to direct the affairs of the industry, and to lend financial support to those activities it considered desirable. In effect the Commission was empowered to formulate an industrial policy replacing that of the individual Member States.

5.7 In practice the Commission has never really fulfilled this role, and the Member States have retained considerable sovereignty in ordering the affairs of their respective coal and steel industries. In this context, and given the steady decline in demand for coal and steel in the last two decades, the ECSC's absolute ban proved unworkable.

Hence the Commission availed itself of Article 95 ECSC to enact a special regime for state aids to the Community coal sector.[2]

Financial aid which Member States intend to grant to the Community coal industry is currently governed by Decision 2064/86/ECSC (OJ 1986 L177/1), discussed below.

5.8 The Court of Justice has defined "aid" widely for the purposes of the ECSC Treaty, and has held that it is wider than a subsidy, which is:

"...normally defined as a payment in cash or in kind made in support of an undertaking other than the payment by the purchaser or consumer for the

---

[1] There is no provision on state aids in Euratom Treaty. Hence the EEC provisions will apply.
[2] Decisions to derogate from Art 4 ECSC based on Art 95 ECSC necessitate Council unanimity (*cf* Art 93 EEC).

112

goods or services which it produces. An aid is a very similar concept, which however, places emphasis on its purpose and seems especially devised for a particular objective which cannot normally be achieved without outside help. The concept of an aid is nevertheless wider than that of a subsidy because it embraces not only positive benefits, such as subsidies themselves, but also interventions which, in various forms, mitigate the charges which are normally included in the budget of an undertaking and which would without therefore, being subsidies in the strict sense of the word, be similar in character and have the same effect." (Case 30/59 *Steenkolenmijnen* v *HA* [1961] ECR 1 at 19)

(ii) EEC Treaty

Article 92 EEC, by way of contrast to the ECSC Treaty, permits a declaration **5.9** of incompatibility with the common market, but not a directly applicable prohibition of an aid. It is thus a far more flexible provision.

Article 92(2)(a) EEC provides that certain forms of aids, including aids having a social character, granted to individual consumers, shall be compatible with the Treaty, provided that aid is granted without discrimination related to the origin of the products concerned.

Article 92(3)EEC provides for certain forms of aid which may be compatible with the common market. Responsibility for the supervision of state aids lies with the Commission. The Court has ruled that Member States are under a duty to collaborate and assist it in its tasks (Case 102/87 *France* v *Commission* [1988] ECR 4067). This duty of "Community solidarity" must be read in conjunction with the requirements that a Member State must notify new aids or plans to alter existing aids under Article 93(3) and to provide the Commission with the necessary information to enable it to discharge its duty under Article 93(1) to keep under constant review all systems of aid existing in the Member States.

3. State aids and the electricity sector

As the ECSC Rules are more straightforward, they shall be dealt with first. **5.10**

(i) Aids to the use of coal in electricity generation

As noted the legality of aid to the coal sector is presently governed by Decision 2064/86/ECSC.

In accordance with that Decision, such aid can only be considered compatible with the proper functioning of the common market if it complies with one of the following objectives:

– improved competitiveness in the coal industry, helping to ensure a better security of supply;

– creation of new capacities as long as they are economically viable;

– solution of social and regional problems related to changes in the coal industry.

5.11   Aid must cover no more than the difference between projected average costs and projected average revenue per tonne of coal produced. It must not exceed operating losses (Art 3(1)).

Pursuant to Article 9(2) of this Decision, Member States must inform the Commission of the financial measures it intends to take each year in order to give direct and indirect support to the coal industry. Aid to promote innovation in the coal industry must also be notified pursuant to Article 9(2) and Annex 2b of the Decision.[3]

5.12   The Commission must examine this aid in conjunction with Article 67 ECSC.[4] Pursuant to Article 11(2) of the Decision the Commission must ensure that the direct aid to coal production which it approves is used exclusively for the purposes set out in Articles 3 to 6. It must therefore be informed of the amounts of payments and the manner in which they are apportioned.[5]

Other forms of aid such as compensatory payments to electricity producers who have concluded coal purchasing contracts must be notified as "other measures" pursuant to Article 9(2) and Annex 2b. This aid must also be compatible with Article 67 ECSC.

Approval of this type of aid is usually expressed to be without prejudice to its compatibility with Articles 85 and 86 EEC and Articles 65 and 66 ECSC.[6]

(a) Indirect aid

5.13   The legality of national "aid schemes" to compensate electricity producers for using more expensive national coal is yet to be determined. In its various decisions on the application of Decision 2064/86/ECSC on national measures to support the coal industry, the Commission has preferred to leave this question open.[7]

Some years ago, and before the present drive to complete the internal market, the Commission indicated that aid to compensate electricity producers for using coal may fall outside Article 92 where they gain no advantage over other producers of electricity.[8]

---

[3] See, for example, Commission Decision 91/3/ECSC on financial measures by Spain in respect of the coal industry in 1988 and 1990, OJ 1991 L5/27.

[4] Art 67 ECSC is equivalent to Art 101 EEC.

[5] In Case 183/89 *Gesamtverband des Deutschen Steunkohlen bergbaus* v *Commission,* presently before the Court, German coal producers and others are challenging Dec 89/226/ECSC of 30 March 1989 on the measures taken by the FRG to support its coal industry.

[6] The decision approving aid to the UK coal industry in 1989, includes a statement that it "applies without prejudice to the compatibility with the Treaties of arrangements or agreements governing sales of coal mined in the United Kingdom to electricity producers" (Dec 89/584/ECSC, OJ 1989 L326/33). This problem is dealt with in fuller detail in Dec 90/198/ECSC (OJ 1990 L 105/119) concerning financial support to the Spanish coal industry. The measures included compensatory payments to electricity producers using Spanish coal produced by undertakings that have negotiated contracts with the said electricty producers under a scheme to promote the use of coal in power stations. This system is financed by a compensation fund managed by Ofico – the Electricity Compensation Office.

[7] See note at 6.

Similarly, the legality of agreements between coal producers and **5.14** electricity generators requiring that the latter should purchase fixed quotas of national coal, usually at a pre-determined price, has not yet been the subject of a definitive decision from the Commission.[9] It should be noted that potentially, such agreements could either be caught by Article 85(1) EEC which prohibits restrictive agreements, or by Article 65 ECSC.

In this respect the Commission's observations on the three-year coal supply agreements between British Coal Corporation and the two major generators in the United Kingdom should be noted:[10]

"An agreement by which a dominant supplier obtains the right to provide some 94% of the requirements of the two largest customers forecloses the market and can only be justified in the most exceptional circumstances" (at para 78).

As the compatibility of the supply agreements with the EEC competition rules is still under consideration, the Commission did not go on to expand on this point, however.

4. EEC rules

(i) Definition of an aid

As already mentioned, Article 92 EEC is potentially a more flexible **5.15** provision than its ECSC counterpart. That the definition of an aid under Article 92(1) is potentially very wide is evident from the language of that article. The provision reads as follows:

"Save as otherwise provided in this Treaty, any aid granted by a Member State through state resources in any form whatsoever which distorts or threatens to distort competition by favouring certain undertakings or the production of certain goods, shall, in so far as it affects trade between Member States be incompatible with the common market."

Thus the aid can take "any form whatsoever". The Court has repeatedly **5.16** held that it is the effect not the form of the aid which is crucial: in Case 310/85 *Deufil* [1987] ECR 901 the Court held that:

"[Article 92] does not therefore distinguish between the measures of state intervention concerned by reference to their causes or their aims but defines them in relation to their effects ...The general objectives of the national rules

---

[8] Commission Fourth Annual Report on Competition Policy at pt 163-165; Seventh Annual Report on Competition Policy at pt 257.
[9] See, however, Case IV/33.151 – *Jahrhundertvertrag, loc cit,* where the Commission indicated it was prepared to give temporary approval to a cartel arrangement between German coal mining companies and electricity producers. A formal decision on the arrangements between British Coal and PowerGen and National Power has yet to be issued.
[10] Dec dated 23 May 1991, unpublished.

forming the basis of the grant in aid are not themselves sufficient to put it outside the scope of Article 92."

(a) Conditions for application of Article 92

5.17 For Article 92 to apply it is necessary that:
(i) the aid has been imposed by a public authority;
(ii) the grant results in a transfer of resources from the state or in the state receiving less resources;
(iii) the aid distorts competition by favouring certain undertakings or the production of certain goods competing with the undertakings or production of other Member States;
(iv) the products in question are traded within the Community.

Scope of the public authority

5.18 The aid in question must be granted by a Member State or through state resources. Thus Article 92 applies to central, regional and local authorities, as well as public undertakings.

In Cases 67, 68 and 76/84 *Gebroeders van der Kooy* v *Commission* [1988] ECR 219, a case involving an allegedly preferential tariff for the benefit of the Dutch horticultural industry, the Court examined the ownership and management of the Dutch gas company, Gasunie. The Dutch State not only held 50% of the shares of the company, but it also was empowered to approve its tariffs. Taken as a whole these factors demonstrated that the contested tariff was the result of action by the State, and thus fell within the meaning of an "aid" under Article 92 EEC.

State resources

5.19 The financial benefit granted to the recipient must have been brought about the state. It is not necessary that the benefit results in a direct debit to public resources.[11] In Case 290/83 *Commission* v *France* [1985] ECR 439 at 449 a payment made by a public body out of the surplus proceeds of private funds was condemned as a state aid because the payment was required by and subject to the approval of the state.[12]

5.20 In Cases 213/80 & 15/81 *Norddeutsches Vieh und Fleischkontor,* the Advocate-General suggested that the independent grant by Member States of pecuniary advantages which are not paid for by the Member State is caught by Article 92.

"Advantages which come to mind, are ... reduced rates which Member States might require private electricity companies ... to grant (without reimbursement) to certain undertakings or in respect of certain products" [1982] ECR 3583 at 3617.

Private as well as public bodies appointed to administer an aid constitute the "state" or "state resources" (Case 78/76 *Steinike* [1977] ECR 595).

---

[11] See however, Case 82/77 *Van Tiggele* [1978] ECR 25 at 52, discussed further in Chap 7.
[12] See also Case 57/86 *Greece* v *Commission* [1987] ECR 1423.

Where, however, private bodies administer aid that does not come from state resources and without any intervention of a state body, Article 92 is probably not applicable.

Financial transfers from state resources in any form are clearly **5.21** prohibited. Thus the provision of capital through share acquisitions or other forms of capital injections may be caught by Article 92 (Case 323/82 *Intermills* v *Commission* [1984] ECR 3809).

Similarly, capital injections by a state holding company to one of its subsidiaries may fall within the scope of Article 92. In Case C-305/89 *Italy* v *Commission* (judgment of 21 March 1991) the Court of Justice upheld the legality of Commission Decision 89/661, condemning capital injections by the Italian Government, via the public holding companies, IRI and Finmeccanica into the ailing firm of Alfa Romeo as an illegal state aid.

Article 92 does not apply if all undertakings within a Member State **5.22** benefit from assistance, without any distinction being made between them. General financial measures escape Article 92, but specific measures do not.[13] The Court has, however, been reluctant to allow general aid systems to escape prohibition where they result in the exclusion of a large class of producers (Cases 6 & 11/60 *Commission* v *France* [1969] ECR 523).

It is also clear that for Article 92 to apply the undertaking must have obtained an advantage or benefit which it would not have received in the normal course of business.

In *Daimler Benz* the Commission considered that state assistance for meeting the costs inherent in preparing a building site and providing connection to various utilities services did not fall within Article 92(1), since the company would contribute to those costs through local taxes (Seventeenth Report on Competition Policy (1988) pt 220).

The aid must distort competition within the Community. The Court has **5.23** consistently rejected a *de minimis* rule for state aids regulation – *i.e.* it is not necessary to demonstrate that the aid has an "appreciable effect" on competition.

> "When state financial aid strengthens the position of an undertaking compared with other undertakings competing in intra-Community trade the latter must be regarded as affected by that aid." (Case 730/79 *Philip Morris* v *Commission* [1980] ECR 2671)

This approach has been subsequently confirmed in Case 142/87 *Belgium* v *Commission* ([1990] ECR 959).

(ii) Categories of aid compatible with common market

Article 92(2) lists the categories of aid which are automatically compatible **5.24** with the common market. This type of aid is still subject to Commission

---

[13] Such measures may be justified under Art 103 as short-term conjunctural policy instruments. The Commission's Task Force on state aids is presently considering the dividing line between Arts 102 and 92.

control, however, as the latter remains under a duty to keep all systems of aid under review.

5.25   Article 92(a) exempts aid of a social character, granted to individual consumers provided that such aid is granted without discrimination related to the origin of the products concerned. Thus the Commission has considered that a German measure designed to give tax relief to individual consumers purchasing cars fitted with pollution reduction devices could be exempted under Article 92(a) but was considering whether or not it resulted in discrimination as to origin of the goods, contrary to Article 30.

Article 92(b) exempts aid to make good caused by disasters or exceptional occurrences.

5.26   The third category – aid granted to certain areas of the Federal Republic of Germany affected by the division of Germany, has acquired renewed importance as a result of the reunification of Germany.

(iii) **Aid which may be compatible with common market**

5.27   Article 92(3) covers aid which *may* be compatible with the common market, but requires formal Commission approval to determine that status. The first three categories of aid are subject to control by the Commission, whereas pursuant to Article 92(3)(d), the Council has a power of decision to exempt other categories of aid. It must do so on the basis of a qualified majority on a proposal from the Commission.

The three categories of aid subject to Commission approval are:
– regional aid (Art 92(3)(a);
– aid to promote the execution of an important project "of European interest" (Art 92(3)(b)); and
– sectoral and regional aid which does not adversely affect trading conditions to an unacceptable degree (Art 92(3)(c).

5.28   Although there is some overlap between Article 92(3)(a) and (c), it should be emphasised that the latter potentially offers more scope to the Member State seeking to justify the aid. Hence in Case 248/85 *Germany* v *Commission* [1987] ECR 4013 the Commission determined that paragraph (a) was not applicable since the region in question enjoyed favourable economic conditions when compared to the rest of the Community. Nor was paragraph (c) satisfied because unemployment in the particular areas did not vary greatly from the average in Germany as a whole.

The Court rejected this approach. It held that paragraph (c) gave the Commission power to authorise aid intended to promote economic development in areas of a Member State which are disadvantaged in relation to the national average. Paragraph (c) thus offers further possible justifications when compared to (a), and would seem to place a premium upon the value of the interpretation of "common interest" as a safeguard.

5.29   Article 93(2) confers considerable discretion upon the Commission when evaluating whether an aid scheme is compatible or not. Its decisions are subject to review by the Court of Justice. In Case 730/79 *Philip Morris*

the Court set out the criteria on which the Commission must base its decision on whether or not to exercise its powers to approve an aid. In summary, these are as follows:
– the aid must promote or further a project that is in the Community interest as a whole;
– the aid must be necessary for the achievement of this result, and if the objective could not have been obtained in its absence;
– the duration, intensity and scope of the aid must be proportional to the importance of the intended result.

(a) Specific provisions

Article 92(3)(a) regional aid

In *Philip Morris* the Court stressed that in assessing regional aid schemes, **5.30** the local standards of living and unemployment levels must be measured against a Community-wide standard. In 1988 the Commission published a notice on the application of Article 92(3)(a) and (c) to less-developed areas (OJ 1988 C212/2 and Commission Communications of March 1989 (OJ 1989 C78/5) and July 1990 (OJ 1990 C163/6). Regions covered by paragraph (a) are those suffering from abnormally low living standards or serious underemployment where the per capita gross domestic product does not exceed 75% of the Community average in purchasing power parities.

Regions falling under Article 92(3)(c) are those with more general development problems in relation to the national as well as the Community situation. The Commission applies two alternative primary tests which enable regional problems to be assessed in a Community context. The two alternative tests applied at the national level are income (measured by GNP or gross value added) and structural unemployment. Thus in a wealthy Member State, the disparities between the region and the state must be considerable to justify the aid.

Article 92(3)(b): aid to promote execution of a project of common European interest

In March 1989 the Commission issued a press release in which it detailed **5.31** its reasons for granting exemption under Article 92(3)(b) to the UK's proposed fossil fuel levy and non-fossil fuel quota system, which was to be introduced as part of the restructuring of the electricity sector in England and Wales.

The levy is intended to cover the extra cost of nuclear electricity for which the privatised electricity distribution companies will be obliged to contract with Nuclear Power. The non-fossil fuel obligation will cover 8500 MW of nuclear capacity and a smaller quantity (of about 500 MW) of electricity generated from renewables, which together will represent a total of some 17% of overall electricity demand in the United Kingdom. The rate of the levy, which the Commission authorised for a period of eight years, would initially be 10.5% but should come down to about 5.5% by 1998.

5.32   The Commission also authorised a government guarantee of some 3.38 billion ECUs to cover possible increases in the cost of storage and reprocessing of nuclear waste and the decommissioning of existing power stations.

Finally, the Commission approved the writing off of 1.9 billion ECUs of debt accumulated by the Scottish nuclear industry.

The Commission has indicated that schemes for energy saving and for diversifying energy resources may be exempt as important projects of common interest.[14]

The Commission has a wide discretion in its assessment, and not every technological advance the application of which will lead to energy efficiency, will be *per se* in the "common interest".[15]

Article 92(3)(c)): aid "to facilitate the development of certain economic activities or of certain economic areas"

Sectoral aid

5.33   Aid to traditional energy producers other than coal producers is dealt with by the usual guidelines for sectoral aid.[16]

Aid to energy intensive users is usually also dealt with under Article 92(3)(c).[17] The Commission Decision 86/60 (OJ 1986 L72/30) on aid which the Land of Rheinland-Pfalz granted to an undertaking producing primary aluminium is illustrative of its approach. This undertaking was alleged to be in difficulties following a steep rise in the electricity charges it had to pay following the expiry of its electricity supply contract in September 1982.

5.34   The Commission noted that steep rises in electricity charges are a serious problem for all aluminium producers who do not generate their own electric power, and their importance originates from the fact that electricity costs may account for more than 30% of the costs of smelting aluminium. The aid in question, although argued by the German authorities to constitute a rescue aid, was not linked to any restructuring plan which would improve the undertaking's competitiveness and secure its long-term viability. It was therefore considered as an aid for continued operation, provided to the undertaking in order to partially offset the increase in the electricity tariff.

> "[i]t cannot be considered as ''facilitating the development' of the economic activity in question within the meaning of Article 92(3)(c)."

---

[14] Commission Seventh Report on Competition Policy, at pts 250–254, 255, 256; Ninth Report on Competition Policy at pt 186; Eleventh Report on Competition Policy at pt 221 and Twelfth Report on Competition Policy at pt 161.

[15] See Cases 62 & 72/87 *Executif Regional Wallon and Glaverbel SA v Commission*

[16] See EEC Seventh Report on Competition Policy, pts 246–249; Commission Twelfth Report on Competition Policy, pt 1994.

[17] See Commission Fifteenth Report on Competition Policy, pt 182, for the Commission's general policy on aid to energy.

Consequently the aid was disallowed.

The Commission has determined, after a preliminary investigation, that a number of long-term contracts between the French electricity producer, EDF, and various energy intensive users do not contain state aid elements as long as the prices for fuel cover the average variable costs of supplying the energy under contract.

Horizontal aid schemes

Environment The Commission has used Article 92(3)(c) to elaborate a series **5.35** of guidelines on aids to the environment.[18] In assessing the compatibility of aids schemes, the Commission will examine *inter alia* the intensity of the aid and the size of the overall budget. (See further para 9.37.)

In June 1989 the Commission began Article 93(2) proceedings against **5.36** the French State in connection with a scheme introduced by the Air Quality Agency for investments in de-sulphurization plant. The aid took the form of grants of up to 50% of investment costs and its annual budget totalled FFr 90 million. The Commission considered that the intensity of the aid and the size of the budget were liable to distort competition and affect intra-Community trade, since it reduced running costs of the recipient firm which competitors in other Member States have to pay in full.[19]

In the following year the Commission investigated an unnotified Bavarian scheme to assist new technologies contributing to more efficient energy use. The annual budget was some 3.6 million ECUs, and the rate of the aid varied from 30 to 50% depending on the project. Given the small scale of the aid, which was mainly for the benefit of small and medium size businesses, the programme was exempted under Article 92(3)(c) (Twentieth Report on Competition Policy, pt 289).

The Commission also exempted a German aid scheme to encourage **5.37** district heating and the use of CHP systems (Twentieth Report on Competition Policy, 1990, pt 290).

Research and development The Commission is generally well-disposed to horizontal aids to promote research and innovation, because of the contribution that these aids can make towards achieving the goals set out in Article 2 EEC. A number of conditions must be satisfied, however. These conditions are summarised at point 218 of the Commission's Fifteenth Report on Competition Policy, and in its Communication of 1986 on its "Framework for state aids for research and development" (OJ 1986 C83/2).

---

[18] Commission, Sixteenth Report on Competition Policy, 1987, pt 259.
[19] Commission, Nineteenth Report on Competition Policy, 1990, pt 198. *Cf* the Commission's assessment of a Dutch tax incentive scheme for less-polluting cars. Art 93(2) proceedings were abandonded as the incentives only represented a small percentage of costs; they were granted irrespective of the origin of the cars, and finally there was no element of subsidy (Nineteenth Competition Report, 1990, pt 199).

5. **Procedural aspects**

5.38 Article 93 provides a set of procedural powers for the Commission to review the legality of state aids within the meaning of Article 92. For the purposes of Article 93 a distinction should be drawn between new and existing aids.

(i) **New aids**

5.39 Member States are obliged to notify new aids, that is any plans to grant or alter aid, to the Commission in sufficient time to enable the latter to submit its comments (Art 93(3)).[20] New aids should not be put into effect until the latter has given its decision.

The Commission will then conduct a preliminary investigation, and if this leads it to believe that Article 92(1)EEC applies, it will open formal procedure under Article 93(2). If, on the basis of the preliminary investigation, the Commission is of the opinion that the aid does not fall within the scope of Article 92(1) or that conditions of Article 92(3) are satisfied, it closes the procedure (Art 93(3)). The Commission gave a favourable decision on the UK's nuclear fuel levy, notified to it in accordance with these procedures (see above).

(a) Unnotified new aid

5.40 Unnotified new aid shall not, according to Article 93(3) last sentence, be put into effect until the procedures referred to in Article 93(3) or 93(2) have resulted in a final decision. In Case 173/73 *Lorenz* v *Germany* [1973] ECR 1471 the Court held that the Commission is empowered to apply the procedure of Article 93(2) to unnotified as well as notified aids. It added, however, that the Court need not fix a time limit when applying the Article 93(2) procedure to unnotified, implemented aid.

(b) Notified new aid

5.41 Following notification, the Commission has two months to submit its comments or initiate the procedure under Article 93(2).[21] These comments are subject to judicial review (Cases 166 & 220/86 *Irish Cement* [1988] ECR 6473 at 6501).

The Commission takes the view that the two month period begins to run from the time that it has received all the information necessary for its assessment of the proposed aid.[22] The Commission may also issue an interim order requiring the Member State to supply it with the necessary information (Case 301/87 *France* v *Commission* [1990] ECR 307; Case 142/87 *Belgium* v *Commission, loc cit.*

---

[20] On the Commission's views on the obligation to notify, see Communication at OJ 1983 C318/3.
[21] In Case 84/82 *Germany* v *Commission, loc cit*, the Court held that the Commission must act "with due expedition … otherwise, after the expiry of an appropriate period which the Court set at two months, the Member State concerned may implement the measures in question after giving the Commission prior notice thereof."
[22] This is the subject of some controversy, however. See further Slot (1990) 27 CML Rev 741–760.

During the two month "standstill" period Member States are prohibited   **5.42**
from implementing the proposed aid. This standstill clause lapses if the
Commission fails to submit its comments in time or to initiate the Article
93(2) procedure. The standstill continues however once the Article 93(2)
procedure is commenced. It expires only when the Commission has issued
a decision that the aid is compatible. It continues to apply if it finds that the
aid is incompatible.[23]

If the Commission decision finding compatibility is subsequently
annulled by the Court of Justice the standstill clause will probably revive
(Case 169/84 *Cofaz II* [1992] CMLR 177). If, in the alternative, the Court
annuls a decision of incompatibility, the standstill clause expires.[24]

If at the end of the preliminary investigation, the Commission approves   **5.43**
the aid, it must communicate its decision to the Member State. The aid
then becomes an "existing aid" subject to the supervision rules under
Article 93(1).

In Case 223/85 *RSV* v *Commission* [1987] ECR 4617 the Court held that
by taking 26 months after the opening of the Article 93(2) procedure to
reach a negative decision, and without justification for the delay, the aid
recipient had a legitimate expectation that the aid was lawful. The Court
did not, however, indicate a period in which the Commission must reach a
decision.

(c) Non-notified new aid

Non-notification does not automatically make such aids incompatible with   **5.44**
the common market (Case 301/87). The fact that Article 93(3) last
sentence has direct effect does not relieve the Commission of the duty to
examine the aids and test their compatibility with Article 92. The standstill
clause applies, but the two month rule does not apply in this case.

In Case 354/90 the Court ruled that a national court may apply Article
93(3) and declare an aid which was not properly notified to be illegal, even
though the Commission subsequently determines that the aid is compatible
with Article 92(3) (see below para 5.56).

The Commission has recently issued a proposal for Regulations to deal
with non-notified state aid. Its modified proposals are as follows:

"Whenever the Commission services learn of aid being granted, they will   **5.45**
immediately send a request for information to the Member State concerned
usually with a deadline of 15 working days. If at the end of the time, there has
been no reply, or no sufficient reply has been received, the Commission services
will send a detailed information request letter fixing a new deadline of 15
working days. If the legal text setting up aid is available to the competent
services, they may request additional information from the Member State

---

[23] Slot, "Procedural aspects of state aids", (1990) 27 CML Rev 741–760.
[24] See, however, the Commission's Notice C50/83 (OJ 1992 C10/3) on the consequences of the
Cofaz decision, where it indicates that it intends to re–open the Art 93(2) procedure. This seems
to suggest that, in the Commission's view, the standstill clause was not revived by the Court's
annulment of its initial decision.

concerned. In this case, the time limit for replying should not exceed 20 working days.

5.46 If the reply received after this time is sufficient, the commissioner in charge will submit a proposal to the Commission within two months. In the event of an insufficient reply or no reply at all, the commissioner in charge will propose to the Commission:

(a) initiation of the procedure under Article 93(2) giving official notice to the Member State concerned to communicate, within one month, all the information and data necessary for the examination of aid accounting with the common market;

(b) to take, if needs be and jointly, a provisional decision charging the Member State in question to immediately suspend the application of the aid system or the payment of a specific aid and to inform the Commission that the decision will be respected within 15 working days.

Should a Member State, despite the formal notice, omit to supply the requested information within the time limit, the Commissioner will propose to the Commission, within one month, that it take, within the framework of the procedure under Article 93(2) a final decision noting aid incompatibility with the Common Market on the basis of elements available to the Commission services. Should a Member State not conform to the provisional decision or the final negative decision, the Commissioner will propose that the Commission refer the case directly to the Court of Justice within one month, with appeal, if such is the case, to summary procedure."[25]

(ii) Existing aids

5.47 Article 93(1) requires the Commission to keep under constant review all existing systems of aid. It must propose to Member States any appropriate measure required by the progressive development or functioning of the common market. Such proposals are not binding, but are of legal relevance as a mandatory step in the process for initiating the contentious procedure laid down in Article 93(2). If the aid is considered prima facie incompatible, the following procedures are commenced:

– the Commission gives notice to the parties concerned to submit their comments;

– the Commission, in the light of the comments it receives, makes a finding of incompatibility or compatibility, or that the aid is being misused;

– the Commission takes a formal decision requiring the Member State to abolish the aid or alter it within a fixed period of time.

5.48 If the Member State fails to comply within the prescribed time limits, the Commission or any other interested state may refer the matter directly to the Court of Justice.

In accordance with Article 93(2)(3) a Member State may apply to the Council for a decision permitting the aid, on the ground of it being justified by "exceptional circumstances", notwithstanding its incompatibility with Article 92. If the Commission has initiated the contentious procedure, the

---

[25] *Agence Europe* no 5367, 9 November 1990, p 10.

very act of notification serves to suspend Commission proceedings until the Council "has made its attitude known". The latter has three months in which to do so, after which the Commission may proceed to give its decision.

(iii) **Supervisory review by the Court**

(a) Procedural defects

A decision of incompatibility must be properly reasoned, has prospective **5.49** effect only, and must indicate to the Member State concerned which aspects of the aid are regarded as incompatible and subject to abolition or alteration.

The Court has annulled a number of Commission Decisions for insufficient reasoning. Where, however, Member States fail to supply information to the Commission, and they then claim that the Commission's reasoning is inadequate, the Court is less sympathetic (see for example Case 102/87 *France* v *Commission* [1988] ECR 4067).

In addition the Court has annulled decisions where the Commission has **5.50** drawn incorrect findings of a fact from the evidence before it. This may amount to a manifest error of law (Case 169/84 *Cofaz II*).

The Commission may also be guilty of a manifest error of law where it has exercised its discretion in a manner contrary to the purpose of the Treaty. This may include excessive delay in reaching a decision to initiate the Article 93(2) procedures(Case 84/82 *Commission* v *Germany;* Case 223/85 *RSV*).

The Court has also indicated that in certain circumstances the **5.51** Commission must demonstrate that it has given a Member State adequate guidance as to what action would be necessary to terminate a breach of Article 92. This may be particularly important in cases where the Commission considers that a state aid element is present in a tariff structure, where it is not the type of transaction which is problematic but the level at which a price or tariff is set.

In Case 213/85 *Commission* v *Netherlands* [1988] ECR 281 which **5.52** concerned a special gas tariff available to glasshouse growers in the Netherlands, the Commission had challenged the tariff as an aid. The Dutch Government subsequently adjusted the tariff raising the ceiling from 42.5 cents per cubic meter to 45 cents. In the Commission's view this did not amount to compliance with its original decision and it initiated declaratory proceedings under Article 93(2).

The Court held that as there was no indication in the Commission's original decision as to the level of tariff which it would hold to be devoid of any aid, the Dutch Government was entitled to assume that it was giving proper effect to that decision. Any action by the Commission concerning the new level of tariff, if it believed it still to contain an aid element, would require new action.[26]

---

[26] This reasoning may explain the Commission's decision to treat the Gasunie tariff as a "new" aid – Commission Notice C50/83, *loc cit.*

(b) Locus standi

5.53 Third parties and other Member States enjoy certain procedural rights, in delimited circumstances, and may have a right under Article 173 EEC to challenge a Commission decision permitting an aid (Case 84/82 *Germany* v *Commission* [1984] ECR 1451).

This right is not open to all competitors, however. It is necessary to prove that the relevant decision has direct and individual effect. This may be inferred where the third party has been active in the Article 93(2) procedures.[27] Trade associations will not normally have a right of action (Case 282/85 *DEFI* v *Commission* [1986] ECR 2469) unless they have been directly involved, for example, as a party to the negotiations on the aid (Cases 67, 68, 70/84 *Van der Kooy*).

5.54 The Commission's decision not to open Article 93(2) proceedings when doubts remain as to the compatibility of the aid with Article 92 may be subject to appeal (Case 84/82 *Germany* v *Commission*).[28]

If on the other hand, the Commission considers that, after a preliminary examination that the aid conforms with the Treaty, it is not obliged to take a decision within the meaning of Article 189.[29]

(iv) Procedural guarantees

5.55 The Court has ruled that the Article 93(2) procedure is a contradictory one, so that the Commission is obliged to ensure the right to a fair hearing; to communicate to the Member State concerned its opinion on the observations presented by third parties and on which the Commission intends to base its decision.

In Case 301/87 it ruled that the Commission cannot base its decision on information on which the Member State has not been given an opportunity to comment. However this irregularity would only lead to annulment if it is established that, had it not been for the irregularity the outcome of the decision would have been different.

The Article 93(3) procedure does not appear to offer similar safeguards, although it is invariably accompanied by informal discussions.

(v) Direct effect

5.56 The Commission is given the task of assessing the compatibility of state aids with the common market, in accordance with the procedures set out in Article 93(3) or (2). Article 92(1) has no direct effect, unless it is implemented by acts based on Article 94 or by the particular cases envisaged in Article 93(2)

---

[27] Case 169/84 *Cofaz I* [1986] ECR 391 at 414-415; *cf* Cases 67, 68 & 70/84 *Gebroeders van der Kooy*, *loc cit.*

[28] Two actions pending before the Court also concern this point: Case 294/90 *British Aerospace* v *Commission;* and Case 313/90 *Comité International* v *Commission.*

[29] The Commission's decision not to take a decision on an alleged aid to a steel firm is presently the subject of an appeal in Case C-198/91 *Cook* v *Commission*, OJ 1991 C234/7.

Article 93(3), last sentence, is directly effective however, as it provides a clear and unequivocal prohibition on the Member State's introduction of aid schemes prior to the expiry of the Commission decision-making process (Case 78/76 *Steinike und Weinlig* [1977] ECR 595). In Case C-354/90 *Salmon Fisheries* (judgment of 21 November 1991) the Court held that a national court could give effect to Article 93(3) for an aid which was not properly notified to the Commission, even though the Commission subsequently ruled that the aid in question was not incompatible with Article 92 (1). The Commission's eventual decision could not legitimise a posteriori the illegal acts of a Member State. It follows that potential competitors who can prove that they have suffered loss during the period in which the aid scheme had been put into effect, and prior to the Commission's final decision declaring compatibility may have an action for damages in the national courts.

Furthermore, a national court may investigate whether there is a state aid element involved in deciding whether a contested measure falls under the Treaty provisions on state aids, or under another Treaty provision, such as Article 30 (Case 78/76).

(vi) Repayment and recovery

It was established some 20 years ago that where a Member State continues **5.57** to give aid contrary to a Commission decision, the latter can seek recovery (Case 70/72 *Commission* v *Germany* [1973] ECR 813). Recovery must be obtained in accordance with applicable national law (see Commission Notice, OJ 1983 C318/3).

The Court has ruled that the ensuing bankruptcy of the recipient did not absolve the grantor state from its duty to recover illegally paid aid. The only defence left open was for the Member State to plead absolute impossibility (Case 52/84 *Commission* v *Belgium*). In Case 63/87 *Commission* v *Greece* [1988] ECR 2875, the Court observed that any financial difficulties which exporters might face following abolition of the illegal aid did not constitute absolute impossibility.

Recovery of illegal aids has to be effected under national law, subject to **5.58** the proviso that the relevant national provisions should not take place in such a manner as to impair the recovery required by Community law (Case 5/89 *Commission* v *Germany* [1990]ECR 3437). The principle of legitimate expectations is only given limited recognition by the Court of Justice. As diligent economic operators, enterprises should verify whether the relevant procedures have been respected.[30] Enterprises may only rely on the principle in exceptional circumstances, while Member states cannot rely upon it at all.

---

[30] In this context, see Council Dir 90/531/EEC, discussed in full in Chap 10.

6. **Conclusion**

5.59   Three general points about the potential future application of the state aid
rules to the energy sector may be made here.[31]

Firstly, the relationship between the EEC Treaty provisions on state aid
and its prohibition of measures having equivalent effect to quantitative
restrictions is complex. Although the Court has ruled that the aids referred
to in Articles 92 and 93 do not as such fall within the field of application of
Article 30, this might not necessarily prevent a national court from finding
that a particular part of an overall scheme was contrary to Article 30.

5.60   Thus, for example, in Case 249/81 *Commission* v *Ireland* [1982] ECR 4004,
it ruled that if the object of the measure in question is to restrict imports,
the fact that it also included a permitted aid cannot preclude the operation
of Article 30. More recently, in Case C-21/88 *Pont du Nemours* the Court
held that the provisions of the Treaty relating to the free movement of
goods and state aid had a common purpose of ensuring the free movement
of goods between Member States under normal conditions of competition.
Therefore, the rules on state aid could not override the prohibition
contained in Article 30 ([1990] ECR 889 at paras 19–21).

This would seem to indicate that, despite the Commission's approval of
the UK's fossil fuel levy, the non-fossil quota could be open to challenge as
an infringement of Article 30 in the national courts.

5.61   Secondly, the relationship between indirect aids to the coal sector via
aids to the electricity sector, may be attacked under Article 92 EEC or
alternatively the relevant competition rules of the EEC and ECSC Treaties.

Finally, the legality of environmental aids which do not adhere to the
"polluter-pays" principle remains questionable, especially now that Article
130R(2) elevates this to a Treaty provision (see Chap 9, below). The
Commission has indicated that it shall reconsider this matter following the
expiry of the present Environmental Action Programme in 1992.

Part II

7. **Detection of state aids to public sector companies**

5.62   One of the principle problems of the EC's state aid regime is the absence
of enforcement legislation corresponding to that derived from Articles 85
and 86.

The adoption of Commission Directive 80/723/EEC in 1980 only went
some way to alleviate the problem, and the Commission has gone on to
adopt several Guidelines and Communications intended to improve its
access to information on the financial relations between Member States
and public sector firms.

---

[31] The control of "state aid" elements in electricity tariffs is discussed below.

(i) **Transparency Directive**

In 1980 the Commission used its powers under Article 90(3) EEC to adopt **5.63**
the so-called Transparency Directive (Commission Dir of 25 June 1980 on
transparency of financial relations between Member States and their public
undertakings, OJ 1980 L195/35, as amended, OJ 1985 L229/20). The aim
of this Directive, as amended, is "to ensure that the discipline of State aids
is also applied in an equitable manner to public enterprise" (EC Bulletin
1985, no 7/8, p 47).

This Directive is designed to enhance the Commission's surveillance
powers in the exercise of its functions under Article 90(3).

The preamble recalls the Commission's duty to ensure that Member **5.64**
States do not grant undertakings, public or private, aids incompatible with
the common market, and the need for equality of treatment of public and
private enterprises. The complexity of financial relations between Member
States and public undertakings hinders the achievement of that equality,
hence the necessity for the Directive.

(ii) **Meaning of "public undertaking"**

The Court has yet to define the concept exhaustively, but in Cases **5.65**
188–190/80 it appeared to approve the Commission's definition set out in
the Directive. According to that Directive a public undertaking is:

"...any undertaking over which the public authorities may exercise directly or
indirectly a dominant influence by virtue of their ownership of it, their financial
participation therein or the rules which govern it."

Article 2 of the Transparency Directive creates certain presumptions so
that a "dominant influence" will be said to exist where the public authorities
hold the major part of the undertaking's capital, or control the majority of
votes attached to the share issued by the undertaking or can appoint more
than half of the members of the undertaking's administrative, managerial
or supervisory body.

The Court held that this definition of a public undertaking did not
amount to an abuse since the financial criteria which the Directive adopted
reflected the substantial forms of influence exerted by public authorities
over the commercial decisions of public undertakings.[32]

In Case 118/85 *Re the AMMS* the Court was asked to rule on the scope of **5.66**
Article 2 of the Transparency Directive [1987] ECR 2599. The Italian
Government had failed to furnish information to the Commission in
accordance with the Directive in relation to its state tobacco monopoly. In
its defence to an action brought under Article 169 EEC, the Italian
Government argued that the tobacco monopoly was a public authority and
not an undertaking, so that accordingly there was no relation between an

---

[32] The new "Utilities Directive" (90/531/EEC) on procurement by certain entities adopts a similar
definition of a "public undertaking", see Chap 10.

authority and an undertaking as Article 1 of the Transparency Directive requires for the disclosure requirements to operate.

The Court rejected this argument; the fact that the AMMS lacked a separate legal personality made transparency all the more crucial. On the question of whether there could be financial relations between the state and the tobacco monopoly, the Court concluded:

> "Through the mechanism of budgetary appropriations, the state disposes by definition of the power to influence the economic management of the undertaking, permitting it to grant compensation for economic losses, and to make new funds available to the undertaking, and may therefore permit that undertaking to carry out its activities independently of the rules of normal commercial management, which is precisely the situation which the Directive seeks to make transparent" (at recital 13).

5.67   Article 3 sets out the types of financial relations to which the transparency rules are to apply:

(a) the setting-off of operating losses;

(b) the provision of capital;

(c) non-refundable grants, or loans on privileged terms;

(d) the granting of financial advantages by foregoing profits or the recovery of sums due;

(e) the forgoing of a normal return on public funds used;

(f) compensation for financial burdens imposed by the public authorities.

Article 4 exempts:

5.68   (a) public undertakings as regards services the supply of which is not liable to affect trade between Member States to an appreciable extent; and

(b) public undertakings whose turnover is less than a total of 40 million ECU.

Articles 5 and 6 require Member States to keep available for five years information concerning the financial relations in question and supply such information to the Commission where it so requests.

5.69   The French, Italian and British Governments challenged, unsuccessfully, the Commission's powers to adopt the Directive under Article 90(3) (Cases 188–190/80 [1982] ECR 2545).

While the Commission is prohibited from adopting either rules defining the notion of an aid, or rules applying Articles 92 and 93. This task falls to the Council, on the basis of Article 94. In Cases 188–190/80 the Court of Justice stressed the distinction between a Regulation and surveillance (at grounds 12 and 13).

5.70   The Court justified the requirements of the Transparency Directive on the special nature of the relationship between public authorities and public companies, which was "diverse, often complex and difficult to supervise, even with the assistance of published information." There was therefore "an undeniable need for the Commission to seek additional information on those relations by establishing common criteria for all the Member States and for all the undertakings in question."

(iii) **1984 guidelines on state acquisitions**

In 1984, and as a result of the Court's judgments in *Intermills* and *Leeuwarder*, **5.71** the Commission formulated a set of guidelines, "explaining its general approach to the acquisition of share-holdings by public authorities, and setting out the Member States' obligations in the field" (EC Bulletin, 1984, no 9).

These guidelines concerned the injection of capital into a company by the acquisition of a public holding. This latter concept is widely defined in the Guidelines to include, a direct holding of central, regional or local government, or a direct holding of financial institutions or other national, regional or industrial agencies which are funded from state resources within the meaning of Article 92(1) of the Treaty or over which central, regional or local government can exercise a dominant influence.

The Commission also indicated that holdings by public undertakings would also be covered by the guidelines.[33]

In assessing the compatibility of capital injections, the Commission **5.72** pledged that it would respect the principle of impartiality with regard to the system of property ownership and a principle of equality of treatment between public and private undertakings (section 1 of the guidelines). The main criterion to be applied in categorising state participation as an aid is whether or not that capital "is contributed in circumstances that would not be acceptable to a private investor operating under normal market economy conditions" (section 1, last sentence, section 3.2., first sentence and section 3.3., first sentence).

The guidelines themselves offered some concrete examples of when hold- **5.73** ings would (section 3.3) or would not be classified as a state aid (section 3.2.).

Section 3.4. of the guidelines deals with an intermediate category of acquisitions where "it cannot be decided from the outset whether they do or do not constitute State aids." It specifies the circumstances in which a presumption that there is an aid element will operate.

In Cases 234/84 *Meura* and 40/85 *Boch* the Court confirmed the Commission's approach based on the analogy between the behaviour of private actors on private markets under normal market economy conditions. In order to determine whether a contribution to capital is a state aid, the Court held that it is necessary to see whether the company in question would have obtained the finance on the private capital market. Where the evidence suggests that the beneficiary could not have survived without public funds because it could not have raised the capital required on the open market from a private investor, it is right to conclude that the payment constitutes a state aid.

Further confirmation of the Commission's approach to state partici- **5.74** pation may be discerned in Case C-303/88 *ENI Lanerossi* v *Commission* (judgment of 21 March 1991).[34]

---

[33] The term "public undertakings" is defined in Art 2 of the Transparency Directive.
[34] See also, Case C–305/89 *Italy* v *Commission*, referred to above.

In its Decision 89/43 the Commission had condemned aid amounting to Lire 260.4 billion in the form of capital injections provided by the Italian state-holding company, ENI, via its subsidiary, Lanerossi, to four ailing textile firms between 1983 and 1987, as an illegal state aid, contrary to Article 92(1). The Italian Government appealed against the Commission's decision on the ground, *inter alia,* that it violated the principle of equal treatment of public and private firms on two counts.

It was first argued that there was nothing to prevent private financial holding groups from transferring funds between their member companies to cover losses in one particular sector. Such transfers could be explained by a number of motives, including the safeguarding of the group's overall reputation, or as a result of marketing strategies decided at group level. Hence there could be no objection in Community law where a public holding company embarked on similar strategies.

5.75   Second, it was contended that the criteria adopted by the Commission in determining whether compensation for losses was provided under normal market conditions were too narrow. The motives of the private and public investor should be distinguished, and the latter's should be judged, not by short-term profit motivations, but in the light of social and regional considerations.

Third, the Italian Government protested that the Commission had improperly applied the exemption criteria under Article 92(3)(a) and (c) for aids of a social and regional nature.

5.76   As to the classification of the capital injection as a state aid, the Court had no difficulty in upholding the Commission's decision. It began by recalling its established jurisprudence condemning aids on the basis of their *effect,* not their *form,* so that it was irrelevant whether the aid was provided directly by the state or via a public or private body which had been set up to manage the aid. On the facts of this particular case, the Court reasoned that the capital injections could be attributable to the Italian State. It drew attention to the privileged status of ENI, whose financial activities were guaranteed by the state. It ruled that while it was not necessary to decide whether such a guarantee in itself amounted to a state aid, its very existence distinguished loans provided by ENI from those made available by a private firm.

5.77   As to the violation of the principle of equal treatment, the Court referred back to the Commission's 1984 guidelines. It first endorsed the Commission's general approach therein; that is a direct or indirect capital injection by a state under normal market conditions, could not be qualified as state aid. It then considered whether a private holding company would have provided capital to cover operating losses of a similar nature.

Recalling its approach to the normal market behaviour of a parent company vis-à-vis it subsidiary in Case 234/84 *Meura,* the Court acknowledged that there were situations where the former would be prepared to compensate the operating losses of the latter. This would usually be part a restructuring plan aimed at restoring the subsidiary to profitability. A parent company might also be prepared to shoulder a group company's operating losses for a limited period, not only for direct motivations of profit, but also for related reasons, including the desire to maintain the group's trademark reputation or to re-orient its activities. Where, however, a public investor provided capital injections where there was no likelihood of profit, even in the long term, this would amount to aid in the sense of Article 92 of the Treaty and the compatibility of that aid could only be judged in accordance with the criteria provided in that article.

The Court then went on to find that the Commission had correctly applied the exemption criteria in Articles 92(3)(a) and (c).

(iv) Commission's recent proposals

In July 1991 the Commission announced its decision to introduce an "annual report" procedure for public enterprises in the manufacturing sector[35] which have a turnover of more than 250 million ECUs (*Agence Europe* nos 5541 and 5542, July 1991). In September 1991 it published a Communication on this issue (OJ 1991 C 273/1).   **5.78**

The Commission's action is based on Articles 1 and 5 of the 1980 Transparency Directive. It sets out the principles to be applied on a systematic basis for determining whether an aid is involved. The Communication also makes it clear that the state, in common with any other market economy investor, should expect a normal return obtained by comparable private undertakings on its capital investments, by way of dividends or capital appreciation.

Member States will be required to provide copies of balance sheets and profit and loss accounts for all companies covered by the Decision for the financial years 1989 and 1990 within two months of receipt of the Commission's Communication. In addition to providing each company's annual accounts and for the 1991 financial year and following years, Member States will be required to provide information on the provision of capital, non-refundable grants, loans, guarantees, dividends, retain profits, forgoing of debt repayment. This information is to be provided in so far as it is not contained in the annual accounts, within six months of the end of the previous financial year.   **5.79**

In order to reduce administrative burdens the Commission has indicated that it is prepared to accept consolidated reports for entities which are divided into several legally distinct undertakings. Discussions are already underway with a number of Member States with a view to drawing up agreed lists of companies for which reports will be required.

These reporting requirements will *not* apply for the financial years 1991 and 1992 to the activities of the *Treuhandanstalt,* the body responsible for the privatization of the public sector in the former East Germany.   **5.80**

---

[35] It would appear that in the Commission's view, utilities do not fall within the definition of the "manufacturing" sector. Hence electricity companies have not so far been requested to provide the information set out here.

The Commission's Decision deals only with the identification of aid. Once identified, the aid will be examined in accordance with the normal state aid rules, which also apply to private companies.

CONTENTS OF CHAPTER 6

Chapter 6
Transit and Open Access

1. Introduction

This chapter examines the application of the relevant rules of the EEC **6.1**
Treaty to restrictions on transit. It begins by examining the different senses
in which the term may be used. The terms "common carriage" and "open
access" are then considered. Part I goes on to discuss the application of the
relevant Community law to restrictions on different types of transit which
originate from national regulations and measures. The Commission's latest
proposals on transmission are also discussed.

Part II deals with transit restrictions resulting from the behaviour of the
undertakings involved in electricity supply. The relevant case law is first
examined. The Commission's guidelines on the application of the
competition rules to the telecommunications sector are then analysed, as
these guidelines are clearly relevant to the activities of businesses engaged
in the provision of "network-bound" services, such as electricity.

(i) Types of transit

It is necessary to distinguish several meanings of the term transit. In the **6.2**
first place, the term can be applied to "through transit", that is the transit
of goods originating in one Member State and transported from it across
the territory of another Member State to a third Member State. In the
second place it may refer to cross-frontier transit, that is from the territory
of one Member State directly into that of another. Finally the term may be
applied to internal transit, that is transit within a single Member State.

(ii) "Third party access" and "common carriage"

Third Party Access (TPA) is a system providing for a qualified obligation on **6.3**
companies operating transmission and distribution networks to offer terms
for the use of their systems in particular to individual consumers or
distribution companies.

Common carriage on the other hand involves "a regime providing for a
general obligation on transmission and distribution companies to offer
electricity transport services at any given time, with no distinction between
existing and new clients and by allocating capacity pro rata amongst all
applicants".[1]

---

[1] See the list of definitions adopted by Report of the PCCE on Electricity Transmission and Third
Party Access, Brussels, May 1991.

(iii) **Through transit**

6.4   The right to transit goods from one Member State through or over the territory of another Member State to a third Member State is expressly recognised in Article 36 of the EEC Treaty.

In Case 266/81 *SIOT* [1983] ECR 731 the Court ruled that transit charges imposed for the transport of oil by pipeline from the Italian port of Trieste for onward delivery to Germany and Austria, were permissible only in so far as they reflected the actual costs incurred. The Court held:

> "The Customs Union established by Part Two, Title I, Chapter I of the EEC necessarily implies that the free movement of goods between Member States should be ensured. That freedom could not in itself be complete if it were possible for the Member States to impede or interfere in any way with the movement of goods in transit. It is therefore necessary, as a consequence of the Customs Union and in the mutual interests of the Member States to acknowledge the existence of a general principle of freedom of transit or goods within the Community." (recital 16)
>
> "That freedom of transit means that a Member State may not apply to goods in its territory in transit to or from another Member State transit duties or other charge imposed in respect of transit. However, the imposition of charges or fees which represent the costs of transportation or other services connected with transit is not precluded." (recital 23)

In the same case, however, the Court held that in so far as oil in transit to a non-Member State was concerned, there was no rule in Community law which may be relied upon by individuals in order to challenge the application to goods in transit of the charges at issue.

(iv) **Cross-frontier transit**

6.5   Cross-frontier transit, that is transit in the sense of transmission of electricity from one Member State into the territory of another, is now partly regulated by Directive 90/547/EEC, discussed below.

(v) **Restrictions on internal transit**

6.6   Restrictions on internal transit or transmission may involve restrictions on access to the high voltage network, and related interconnection equipment, or on access to the local distribution network or both. This form of transit is not currently regulated by any secondary Community legislation, so that the legality of any restrictions fall to be assessed in accordance with the general principles of Community law.

Part I

2. **Restrictions imposed by Member States**

(i) **Cross-frontier restrictions and third party access**

Article 1 of Council Directive 90/547/EEC on the transit of electricity   **6.7**
through transmission grids requires Member States to take the measures to
facilitate transit of electricity between high-voltage grids in accordance with
the conditions laid down in the Directive (OJ 1990 L313/30). It does not
require them to oblige or compel transit, although the 10th recital to the
Directive suggests that obstacles to trade can be reduced by making transit
through grids compulsory.

Article 2 of the Directive defines transit to cover transactions for the
transport of electricity where:
(i) transmission is carried out by the entity (entities) responsible for a
high-voltage electricity grid, with the exception of distribution grids;
(ii) the grid of origin or final destination is situated in the Community;
(iii) transport involves the crossing of one intra-Community frontier.

These conditions appear to be cumulative. Thus, for example, electricity
generated in Norway and exported to Germany via Denmark would fulfil
the conditions set out in Article 2; the grid of final destination is situated in
the Community and the transport involves crossing an intra-Community
frontier.

Article 3(1) requires contracts for transit to be negotiated between the   **6.8**
entities responsible for the grids concerned, and where appropriate the
entities responsible for importing and exporting electricity. This terminology does not necessarily endorse the conferral of exclusive rights to
import or export, or to transit electricity through high voltage networks on
particular entities.

Case C-202/88 *"Telecoms"* is authority for the proposition that all exclusive
rights to import or export, as well as any associated rights to market a
particular good, are likely to be in conflict with Article 30 and Article 90(1),
where state measures are involved, and where no justification can be made
out in accordance with the "rule of reason" in Article 30, the public security
exception in Article 36 or in accordance with Article 90(2) (see further
Chap 4).

If there is no state regulation at issue, Article 85(1) prohibits horizontal
agreements between undertakings restricting imports and probably further
transit at least where *non-public* supply is concerned (Commission Dec
91/50 *IJsselcentrale*).

Article 3(2) stipulates that the conditions of transit should be non-   **6.9**
discriminatory and fair for all parties concerned, and should not include
unfair clauses or unjustified restrictions and shall not endanger security of
supply and quality of service, in particular taking full account of the
utilization of reserve production capacity and the most efficient operation
of the existing systems.

This can be interpreted to mean that criteria must be objective and uniformly applied to all parties concerned. Given that these contracts are to be negotiated between entities, then Articles 85 and 86 apply.

Article 3(3) provides that the relevant entities must:

6.10 (a) notify the Commission and the national authorities concerned of any request for transit in connection with contracts for sale of electricity of a minimum of one year's duration;

(b) open negotiations on the conditions of electricity transit requested;

(c) inform the Commission and the national authorities concerned of the conclusion of a transit contract;

(d) inform the Commission and the national authorities concerned of the reasons for the failure of negotiations to result in the conclusion of a contract within 12 months following communication of the request.[2]

In accordance with Article 3(4) each of the entities concerned may request that the conditions of transit should be subject to conciliation by a body set up and chaired by the Commission and on which the entities responsible for the transit grids in the Community are represented. The recitals to the Directive make it clear that this procedure is without binding legal effect.

Notification and conciliation are optional for contracts of less than one year's duration.

(ii) **Transit Directive-assessment**

6.11 The Transit Directive does not invest the Commission with any new substantive powers. Article 4 merely provides that: "If the reasons for the absence of the agreement on a request for transit appear unjustified or insufficient, the Commission acting on a complaint or on its own initiative, shall implement the procedures set out in Community law."

Although the Transit Directive is restricted to transactions between entities responsible for the high voltage electricity grid, and therefore excludes transit by distribution companies or third parties, such as large industrial consumers, the Competition Directorate has indicated that "it takes the view that in certain clearly defined cases and subject to certain conditions, the existing competition rules may require access to networks to be granted to third parties" (Nineteenth Report on Competition Policy, pt 33).

6.12 This view was to a limited extent confirmed in the recent Commission Decision 91/50 *IJsselcentrale* (OJ 1991 L228/32) at least in so far as *non-public* supply is concerned. The Commission has ruled that the application of the competition rules did not obstruct the Dutch company SEP, in its proper performance of the tasks assigned to it. Performance of those tasks does not require absolute control of imports and exports, including imports and exports by private consumers and particularly industrial consumers (at

---

[2] It is unlikely that failure to notify can give rise to a remedy for the benefit of a third party – Case 174/84 *Bulk Oil* v *Sun, loc cit.*

para 44). (This Decision is currently under appeal to the Court of First Instance in Case T-16/91 *Rendo* v *Commission.*)

In this context the Commission observed that SEP's complete refusal to make power lines available to others can be considered an agreement or concerted practice between the generators participating in the SEP which could constitute a separate infringement of Article 85.

(iii) **Internal transit**

This type of transit is not covered by Directive 90/537/EEC. The legality of **6.13** a refusal to transit electricity within a Member State therefore falls to be considered under primary Treaty law.

Again it is necessary to identify the origin of any relevant restriction.

If it arises from a *state measure,* in accordance with Case 8/74 *Dassonville,* Article 30 probably applies: the exclusive right to transit may actually or potentially restrict intra-Community trade, and is a measure having equivalent effect to a quantitative restriction. It will be for the Member State to justify any restriction in the interests of security of supply under Article 36, or of network security as a mandatory requirement under Article 30, or alternatively as falling within the scope of Article 90(2).

It is of course open to argument that interconnection and transit are services, not goods. Following the Court's reasoning in Case C-202/88 *Telecoms,* however, where exclusive rights to provide services intrinsically related to the supply of goods were condemned under Article 30, it is now questionable whether transit rights would be dealt with under Article 59. Even if they were, the Court's jurisprudence on Article 59 essentially mirrors its interpretation of Article 30. Hence "indistinctly applicable measures" restricting the freedom to provide services may also be capable of being caught under Article 59 (Case C-288/89 *STA Gouda* v *Commissariaat voor de Media,* judgment of 25 July 1991, not yet reported).

Once again it would be for the Member State to show that such restrictions are necessary to the attainment of the goals set out in Article 56, as applied to services by virtue of Article 66.

Alternatively, the state measure could be attacked under Articles 90(1) **6.14** and 86(b), at least in cases where the monopoly of transit is also conferred on the production monopoly. This could be seen as an accumulation of monopolies which allows the production company to give preference to its production (Case C-260/89 *ERT*).

It would be for the party attacking the monopoly to establish that this was the case, in the national courts. Alternatively a complaint could be made to the Commission.

The monopoly in turn could seek to defend itself on the basis of Article 90(2) and Article 86(b). Both these tests are difficult to satisfy, however.

If the restrictions on transit result from the autonomous conduct of undertakings, then Article 85 and/or Article 86 may apply. It would therefore be necessary to show that the relevant conduct or agreement was

141

capable of affecting trade between the Member States. This is discussed further in Part II.

(iv) Current proposals on third party access

6.15   In the light of the Court's decision in Case C-202/88 *France* v *Commission*, the Commission considered that Article 90(3) may be used to oblige Member States to dismantle all exclusive rights which directly or indirectly inhibit trade provided that they are not justified by reference to public service obligations. In the gas and electricity sectors this includes the exclusive right to import and export, to build and operate transmission and distribution lines and the right to deny the use of these lines to third parties. At the same time the Commission acknowledged that dismantling exclusive rights would amount to a radical deregulation of the sector, which might put system safety, reliability and integrity at risk. It therefore considered it necessary to introduce harmonised rules for access to the market by new entrants on the basis of Article 100A.

6.16   Initially, the Commission put forward two separate, but interrelated draft proposals designed to introduce TPA in the electricity sector, together with two essentially similar proposals for gas. A draft Directive based on Article 90(3) would have required Member States to remove certain obstacles to trade, whereas the draft Directive to be adopted on the basis of Article 100(a) obliged them to take positive action by adopting measures designed to facilitate, *inter alia*, third party access. Both measures were to enter into effect on the same date.

(a) Proposal for Commission Directive on competition in the electricity sector

6.17   The proposal based on Article 90(3) aimed to specify the obligations of Member States under the Treaty vis-a-vis competition in the electricity market.[3] Its scope, purpose and terminology were closely modelled on the two Commission Directives already adopted for the telecommunications sector (Dir 88/301/EEC, Dir 90/388/EEC). As already explained in Chapter 1 this proposal has now been abandoned. It may remain of some relevance as identifying the types of exclusive rights which the Commission considers as contrary to the Treaty, and which may be the subject of future *decisions* on the basis of Article 90(3) or enforcement proceedings.

(v) Proposed common rules

6.18   As has already been noted in Chapter 1 these rules are to be introduced by a Council Directive, adopted on the basis of Articles 100A 57(2) and 66.

(a) Competition in line construction

6.19   Member States will be required to establish a system of licences to build or operate electricity transmission or distribution lines and associated

---

[3] For the scope of the Commission's powers under Art 90(3) see Case 202/88, *loc cit*.

equipment in accordance with specified criteria (Art 5 (1) and (2)). Licenses can only be refused on the basis of objective criteria which are applied in a transparent fashion.

These criteria shall relate *exclusively to:*
- security and safety of lines and associated equipment;
- environmental protection requirements;
- land use and siting;
- public ground use;
- technical and financial capacity of the applicant undertaking.

Procedures for the expropriation of private property, or the use of public ground must be non-discriminatory. The concept of public interest involved in assessing applications should be broadly interpreted to include the importance of a more open and competitive electricity supply system. **6.20**

Article 5(6) provides that any right to expropriate private property or any right to use public ground shall be granted in a non-discriminatory manner. In so far as the public interest is taken into account when granting a right of expropriation or a right to use public ground, a line shall be deemed of public interest if:

(i)　the line is necessary to meet transmission or distribution requirements which cannot be met by the existing system, or

(ii)　a substantial part of the capacity of the line is either open for use by third parties, or made available to the public at a reasonable and equitable price.

A licence may be refused or deferred if the existing system has sufficient capacity available at a reasonable and equitable price (Art 5(3)).

(b) Direct lines

A direct line is defined in Article 2(8) as a line linking one or more customers with a point of supply without using the interconnected system. In accordance with Article 6 Member States must enact measures which allow electricity producers and suppliers to supply customers in the same or in another Member State, or supply their own premises, subsidiaries or affiliate companies in the same Member State or in another Member State, through a direct line or through use of the interconnected systems. Member States must also ensure that any customer is able to purchase from a producer or supplier of their choice and be supplied through a direct line. **6.21**

(c) Transmission and interconnection

Transmission is defined as transport of electricity on the high voltage interconnected system in view of its delivery to final customers (Art 2(3)). **6.22**

Interconnection is defined as the equipment used to link electricity systems (Art 2(6)).

Interconnected systems are the transmission and distribution systems which are linked together by means of one or more interconnectors (Art 2(7)).

6.23   In accordance with Article 7 the Member States must ensure that electricity producers and suppliers established in their territory are able:

> "1. to supply their own premises, subsidiaries and affiliate companies in the same Member State or in another Member State through the use of the interconnected system, subject to the conclusion of agreements with the relevant transmission and distribution system operators ...
> 2. to supply or to contract to supply customers in the same Member State or another Member State, though the use of the interconnected system, subject to the conclusion of agreements with the relevant transmission and distribution system operators...."

Article 7(2) requires the Member States to ensure that any customer established in their territory is able to purchase or be supplied with electricity from the producer or supplier of their choice, and have it delivered through the distribution system.

6.24   In "stage two" of the Commission's plans to complete the internal market – that is the stage to be achieved by the implementation of the present proposal – Member States will be able to limit the use of the interconnected system to two categories of users. These are:

- companies which consume more than 100Gwh per year at an individual site;
- distribution companies, individually or in association, whose individual or aggregated sales represent at least 3% of the overall consumption in the Member State.

These limits may lowered if the Member States so wish. They will be reconsidered in "stage three".

(d) Transmission system operation

6.25   The Member States will be required to designate or require undertakings which own networks or part of networks to designate a system operator, in a given area or region (Art 8). The designated transmission operator must operate separately from distribution and production activities. It will have a general obligation to connect users to its networks and it must act in accordance with the provisions of Articles 9–15. In accordance with Article 9, the transmission system operator (TSO) is under a duty to "maintain a secure, reliable and efficient electricity system in its area." Thus the TSO must oversee the development of an efficient transmission system and ensure the availability of ancillary services. The TSO will also be prohibited from buying and selling electricity and must not discriminate between users.

The TSO will also be under a duty to ensure the availability of metered operational data and provide interested parties with all information necessary for settlement and payment.

6.26   Article 10 governs the type of information which the TSO must provide to other system users connected to the interconnected system. Article 11 requires the TSO to prepare and publish an annual "ten year forecast" on the evolution of electricity supply and demand.

Within one year of the Directive entering into force, the TSO must develop and publish Technical Rules:

"which shall establish the minimum technical design and operational requirements for the connection to the system of generating installations, final customers' electrical installations, other transmission or distribution systems and direct transmission and distribution lines. These requirements shall be objective and non discriminatory…"(Art 12(1)).

The Technical Rules, which should so far as possible be defined by reference to European standards, must address the following: **6.27**
– voltage and frequency performance requirements
– conditions for connection to the transmission system including tariff metering
– operating procedures and requirements.

The TSO shall be responsible for dispatching the generating installations in its area and for determining the use of interconnectors with other systems. Dispatch and interconnection use must be determined on the basis of criteria which are approved by the Member State concerned. These should in turn reflect the economic precedence of electricity from available generating installations or interconnector transfers, and the technical constraints arising on the system (Art 13(1)-(3)).

Article 13(4) provides that the TSO must give priority:

"to generating installations whose capacity does not exceed 25 Megawatts **6.28** provided that these installations use renewable energy sources or waste or produce combined heat and power and are offered at reasonable prices."

Article 13(5) is of considerable importance. It provides that:

"A Member State may, for reasons of security of supply, direct that priority be given to the dispatch of generating installations using indigenous primary fuel sources, to an extent not exceeding in any calendar year 20% of the overall primary energy necessary to produce the electricity consumed in the Member State concerned. This figure shall be progressively reduced to 15% by 31 December 2000."

Article 14 regulates agreements for use of the transmission system and **6.29** interconnectors. In response to applications for a connection agreement, the TSO must propose an agreement for connection unless "such use would prejudice the transmission of electricity in fulfillment of any statutory obligation or of contractual commitments." The reasons for any refusal must be given to the applicant.

An application should be dealt with within a maximum of three months. **6.30**
The proposal for agreement must include terms relating to an obligation on the part of the TSO:
– to accept into the relevant system at such entry point or points such quantities of electricity as may be specified in the application; and/or
– to enable delivery to be made of such quantities of electricity as are referred to in (i) above (less any transmission losses) at such exit point or

points on the relevant system as may be specified in the application (Art 14(3)).

In addition the TSO must make available to a potential user a "statement of opportunities" which contains sufficient information to enable a potential user to make a reasonable assessment of those opportunities (Art 14(4)).

(e) Transmission charges

6.31 The TSO must also publish the basis upon which the terms for connection and system use are to be set. This must allow the potential user to make a reasonable assessment of the charges likely to be payable (Art 14(5)). These charges must be reasonably related to the long term costs involved in the provision of the relevant service, together with a reasonable rate of return on capital employed in the provision of that service (Art 14(6)).

6.32 In accordance with Article 15 the TSO shall preserve the confidentiality of commercially sensitive information.

(f) Distribution

6.33 Designation of a separate operator for the distribution network connected to the public grid is also to be required (Art 16(2)). Hence vertically integrated undertakings, whether public or private, will be required to "unbundle" their management or operational functions, but not their ownership. The separate divisions will be required to publish separate accounts (Arts 23–24).

The same principles discussed under "Transmission" apply to the distribution operator (Arts 17–22).

(g) Security and safety

6.34 Article 25 provides that in the event of a sudden crisis in the energy market and where physical safety or security of persons, apparatus or installation or system integrity is threatened, a Member State may take the necessary protection measures.

Such measures must cause the least possible disturbance in the functioning of the common market and must not be wider in scope than is strictly necessary to remedy the sudden difficulties which have arisen.

The Member State concerned shall without delay notify these measures to the other Member States and to the Commission, which may decide that the Member State concerned shall amend or abolish such measures, in so far as they distort competition and adversely affect trade to an extent contrary to the common interest.

(vi) Observations

6.35 The Commission's current proposals will result in the elimination of statutory, exclusive rights to transmit electricity through high voltage networks. It is clear that in the Commission's view, in "stage two", the duty to supply electricity on demand can be confined to the distribution companies, or to the distribution arm of a vertically-integrated company. Any remaining statutory restrictions on distribution are to be removed in "stage three".

Part II

3. Transit and agreements between undertakings

It is necessary to consider the legality of restrictions on transit imposed by undertakings from a number of perspectives. In the first place, we must consider the potential application of the competition rules, which are of course addressed to them. In the second place we must consider the position of utilities, public or private, and where relevant, as the beneficiaries of state-imposed exclusive rights or privileges.   **6.36**

(i) Competition rules

Electricity utilities, whether public or private, remain fully subject to Articles 85 and 86, unless of course they can bring themselves with the exemption contained in Article 90(2). This means that where a single undertaking responsible for transmission refuses to transmit electricity on behalf of a third party, or proposes only to do so subject to certain conditions, its behaviour may be deemed abusive under Article 86. Article 86 may also be applied to undertakings considered jointly dominant.   **6.37**

(a) Article 85

Where restrictions result from the terms of an agreement between several undertakings controlling a grid, that agreement may fall within the scope of Article 85(1) (Dec 91/50 *IJsselcentrale*).   **6.38**

Where a number of companies co-operate to acquire a holding in, and operate a transmission line, Articles 85 and 86 may be applicable to the agreements in question.

In 1990 the Commission began a formal investigation in the acquisition by Ruhrgas and its associate company VEB Erdol und Ergas, of 35% and 10% respectively in Verbundnetz Gas, the owner of gas pipelines situated within the territory of the former German Democratic Republic. The Commission was informed that a number of Ruhrgas's competitors who had been interested in partial acquisition or construction of gas pipelines within the territory of the former German Democratic Republic had been refused such possibilities. The Commission commenced investigations, based on the presumption of the creation of a dominant position in the former Federal Republic of Germany. While the investigation was being carried out, the *Treuhandanstalt* as owner of Verbundnetz Gas began negotiations with other interested Community companies; and with non-   **6.39**

Community countries. The objective of the negotiations was to allow other gas producers and transport undertakings to acquire holdings in Verbundnetz Gas and to use its pipelines for the transport of their own gas (See Twentieth Report on Competition Policy, 1991, pt 37).

(b) Article 86 and essential facilities

6.40 A recent Commission Decision and a Court judgment indicate that the refusal to allow access to essential facilities may amount to an abuse of Article 86.

In its Decision in *Sabena* (OJ 1988 L317/47) the Commission imposed a fine on the Belgian airline for having pursued a course of conduct intended to prevent a privately owned air carrier from continuing its flights on the Brussels-Luton route. Sabena had refused this company access to its computerised reservation system called Saphir because it had quoted tariffs at half of the standard IATA tariffs and because it had not assigned the ground handling of its tariffs to Sabena.

6.41 The Commission considered the computerised reservation system to be an *essential facility* needed by air carriers to compete on this particular route. Sabena was dominant on the market for computerised reservation systems, and that a competitor could not survive without access to that system. It is noteworthy that Sabena's conduct was pursued over a period of only two months.

6.42 In Case 311/84 *CBEM* [1985] ECR 3261 the Court condemned as an abuse the refusal of RTL, the Belgian television station, to allow access to its facilities by rival telemarketing advertisers. CLT, which runs RTL refused to sell broadcasting time to advertisers who would continue to use CBEM's telephone number rather than that of its own advertising subsidiary, IPB.

The Court held that CLT's refusal was intended to reserve to the advertising group all telemarketing operations broadcast by the station. It therefore deprived competitors of an essential facility and it did so with the aim of entering the market in which its competitors had hitherto been operating.

(ii) Competition and telecommunications undertakings

6.43 In June 1990 the Commission published its "Guidelines on the application of the EEC competition rules in respect of the telecommunications sector".[4] A second version of these guidelines was published in the *Official Journal* (OJ 1991 C233/2).

These guidelines have no legal effect and have been designed to deal with the specific characteristics of the telecommunications sector, but they are of value in indicating the sort of practices in the electricity sector which, in the Commission's view at least, may or may not conform to the Treaty rules.

6.44 The guidelines essentially concern the direct application of competition rules to undertakings: they do not concern those applicable to states, as

---

[4] July 1990, PR/IB/sh/mvn.

these are considered to have been dealt with in the relevant Commission Directives. While the Commission lays stress on a combined strategy of harmonization of standards, conditions of access etc, and application of the competition rules to achieve its aims in creating a single, unified market, it also stresses that the competition rules continue to apply in the absence of harmonization.

Measures aiming at the compliance of the "essential requirements" as **6.45** specified, for example, in Article 1 of the Services Directive 90/388/EEC, can only be taken by Member States and not by undertakings.

On the scope of Article 90(2), the Commission observes that the benefit of the exemption (see further Chap 4):

> "may still be invoked for an undertakings behaviour when it brings about competition restrictions which its Member State did not impose in application of the 1990 Services Directive. However, the fact should be taken into account that in this case the State whose function is to protect the public and the general economic interest did not deem as necessary to impose the said restrictions. This makes particularly hard the burden of providing that the Article 90(2) exception still applies to an undertaking's behaviour involving these restrictions."

(a) Application of Article 85

The Commission singles out:

(i) agreements restricting "hub competition", that is competition to supply **6.46** large users;

(ii) agreements restricting competition in provision of value-added services from third party undertakings, which are supported by the facilities in question, for example when they impose discriminatory or inequitable trading conditions on certain users.

As to agreements between Telecommunication Operators (TOs) on **6.47** tariffs, where agreements concern only the setting up of common tariff structure or principles, the Commission may consider whether this would not constitute one of the economic benefits under Article 85(3) which outweigh the competition restriction. Indeed, this could provide the necessary transparency on tariff calculations and facilitate users' decisions about traffic flow or the location of headquarters or premises.

Standardization agreements are viewed as favourable, particularly **6.48** because it may offer an alternative to proprietary specifications by undertakings dominant in network provision and related to services. In principle an agreement will be exempted if it brings about more openness and facilitates access to the market. The imposition of standards other than those foreseen by Community law (in the case of the telecoms sector the ONP Directive makes provision for standards) will be viewed with much more suspicion, and will probably be prohibited.

The Commission also notes in the context of standardization agreements, that an important requirement of Article 85(3) is that users must be allowed a fair share of the resulting benefit. This is seen as more likely to happen when they or competing manufacturers are involved in the process of formulating standards.

6.49　　Agreements on the exchange of information may be viewed as necessary for the good functioning of the international telecoms market, but it should not affect the autonomy of each undertaking's commercial policy. Therefore it should not be extended to competition-sensitive information, such as tariff information, customers and commercial strategy.

(b) Agreements between TOs and independents

6.50　　The Commission recognises that this is increasing, but it takes a somewhat agnostic standpoint, partly because such agreements may restrict competition for the provision of telecommunications services:

(i)　between the partners because the TOs may have the required financial capacity, technical and commercial skills to enter the value-added market and could reasonably bear the technical and financial risk of doing so; and

(ii)　from third parties, because there is a strong risk that the participant TO, *i.e.* the monopolist for the network provision, will give more favourable network access to its co-operation partners than to other service providers in competition with the partners.

On the other hand, co-operating may bring economic benefits which outweigh its harmful effect and therefore justify the granting of an exemption under Article 85(3). The economic benefits can consist *inter alia* of the rationalization of production and distribution of telecommunication services, improvement in existing services or the development of new services, or transfer of technology which improves the efficiency and the competitiveness of the European industrial structures.

6.51　　In certain cases, the co-operation could consolidate or extend the dominant position of the TOs concerned to a value-added service market, in violation of Article 86.

The imposition or the proposal of co-operation with the service provider as a condition for the provision of the network may be also deemed abusive if they have no connection with the monopoly service. This could be viewed as a form of tying, contrary to Article 86(d).

(c) Application of Article 86

6.52　　The Commission begins its analysis of the potential application of Article 86 to the telecommunications sector by stipulating that:

> "TOs may hold dominant positions on the market for certain equipment or services, even though they no longer hold any exclusive rights on those markets. After the elimination of these rights, they may have kept very important market shares in this sector, as a result of the inherent advantage of having the monopoly for the network or other related services and a powerful and wide distribution network. When the market share in itself does not suffice to give the TOs a dominant position it could do it in combination with the other factors mentioned above."

Although the maintenance of a monopoly to provide and operate a **6.53** universal network for basic "voice-telephony services" has been recognised in the Green Paper on Telecommunications and subsequent Commission Directives as qualifying for exemption under Article 90(2), the Commission takes the view that where a firm enjoying a monopoly over the "reserved" sector engages in abusive behaviour, such as refusal to supply, discrimination, restrictive tying clauses, unfair prices or other inequitable conditions, then it is not fulfilling its fundamental public obligations. This reasoning would seem to imply that where there is evidence of such practices, the protection of Article 90(2) would be lost.

(d) Example of abusive behaviour

The following example is given of the type of behaviour that may be **6.54** considered abusive:
- taking advantage of a monopoly or at least a dominant position to acquire a foothold or to extend their power in non-reserved neighbouring markets, to the detriment of competitors and customers.

Thus, Article 86 will apply where abusive behaviour results in an appreciable restriction of competition in whatever way.

> "This means that an abuse may occur when the company affected by the behaviour is not a service provider but an end user who could himself be disadvantaged in competition in the course of his own business."

Case 311/84 *CBEM* is cited in support of this wide interpretation of the **6.55** scope of Article 86. Hence where a monopoly extends its activities into other markets by *anticompetitive* means, this would amount to an abuse. The Commission's Decision *British Telecom* is cited to give examples of the types of usage restrictions which run counter to Article 86.[5]

Hence the restrictions which British Telecom imposed on the transmission **6.56** of international messages by third parties were condemned as:
(i) limiting the activity of economic operators to the detriment of technological progress, in contravention of Article 86(b);
(ii) discriminating against these operators, thereby placing them at a competitive disadvantage vis-a-vis TOs not bound by these restrictions, contrary to Article 86(c); and
(iii) making the conclusion of contracts for the supply of telex circuits subject to acceptance by the other parties to supplementary obligations which had no connection with such contracts, in breach of Article 86(d).

Usage restrictions on the provision of reserved services could correspond to the specific examples of abuses listed in Article 86(b),(c) and (d).

Even if a service could be considered to be legally reserved (*i.e.* in conformity with Community law), the fact that a TO actually prohibits the

---

[5] This Decision led to an appeal by another Member State, Italy, on the competence of the Commission to take such a decision, Case 41/83 *Italy* v *Commission* [1985] ECR 873.

usage of the network to some users and not to others could constitute a discrimination under Article 86(c).[6]

6.57　　The Document also enumerates a number of specific types of abuse. These include:

(i)　the imposition of extra charges or other special conditions for certain usages of reserved services.

There is unlikely to be a situation of abuse, however, if it can be shown in each specific case, that the access charges correspond to costs which are entailed directly for the TOs for the access in question. Prices must not, however, reflect the subjective value for a user depending on the profitability of the enhanced service. "This cannot be a criterion on which a dominant undertaking, and above all a public service provider, can base the price of this public service."

(ii)　Discriminatory quality of the service provided.

6.58　　This type of behaviour may include discrimination in maintenance and repair, in effecting interconnection of systems, in providing information about the network, technical standards and all other information about the appropriate usage of the monopoly service. The existence of an abuse implies that systematic discrimination against certain users must be proved, *i.e.* by the user.

(iii)　Tying the provision of the monopoly service to the supply of equipment, in particular through the imposition, pressure, offer of special prices or other trading conditions for the monopoly service linked to the equipment – this may contravene Article 86(d).

(iv)　Tying the provisions of the monopoly service to the agreement of the user to enter into co-operation with the monopoly service provider himself as to the non-reserved service to be carried on the network.

(v)　Reserving to itself for the purposes of non-reserved service provision or to other service providers information concerning users of a reserved service and in particular their needs.

6.59　　In the Commission's view this information could be important for the provision of services under competition to the extent it permits the targeting of customers of those services and the definition of business strategy. The behaviour indicated above could result in discrimination against undertakings to which the use of this information is denied in violation of Article 86(c).

(iii) **Potential application of the competition rules to utilities**

6.60　　Article 90(3) only allows the Commission to address Decisions and Directives to Member States. It does not apply to agreements between undertakings.

As the Court stipulated in Case C-202/88 *France* v *Commission*, the Commission must utilise Articles 85 and 86 and the implementing

---

[6] For a concrete application of Art 86(c) to discriminatory access, see the Commission's position on the Belgian RTT's usage conditions – IP(90) 67 of 29 January 1990.

Regulations to tackle anti-competitive practices on the part of undertakings. It could not use Article 90(3) to require the Member States to adopt measures compelling certain forms of long-term contracts to be withdrawn.

In the event that a Member State failed to comply with its obligations **6.61** under a Directive, or a Decision based on Article 90(3) it is unlikely that an undertaking could rely upon this failure alone as a defence in an action based on either Article 85 or 86.

The past jurisprudence of the Court on Article 85 is consistent on this point. Enterprises not only have to compete (Cases 240–242, 261, 268-269/82 *SSI* [1985] ECR 3831), but they also have a positive duty to compete (Cases 209–215/78 *FEDETAB* [1980] ECR 3125).

The only defences open to the undertakings would have to be based on Article 85(3) if an agreement is involved, or Article 90(2) where either a restrictive agreement or an allegation of abusive conduct is at issue.

Where, however, the enterprise in question is endowed with a statutory monopoly *and* the relevant legislation compels it to, or leaves it no alternative but to abuse that monopoly position, then it is submitted that it is that legislation which is open to attack under the competition rules, and not the behaviour of the enterprise itself.[7]

This was the situation in C-41/90 *Höfner,* where the Court held that a **6.62** Member State will be in breach of its Treaty obligations where the enterprise in question is forced by the simple exercise of its exclusive rights to satisfy the demand for its services, while private competitors were forbidden from entering the market by a legal provision which rendered any contract for such services null and void.

The situation would be different if the utility exceeded the bounds of its statutory tasks (Case 41/83 *British Telecom;* Case 311/82 *CBEM*).

Even if the Member State legislation conferring an exclusive right can be **6.63** exempted under the relevant Treaty rules the enterprise itself must not restrict competition more than is necessary for the performance of its special tasks.

The Commission's current proposal on common rules for competition in the electricity sector anticipates that distribution companies may continue to enjoy a limited monopoly as a quid pro quo for their obligation to supply on demand. If they chose to perform this task, however, by concluding long-term exclusive sales contracts with certain categories of customer, the legality of their autonomous activity would fall to be judged under Article 85(3) and Article 90(2).

---

[7] See, however, Case C–179/90 *Porto di Genova,* where the Court seemed prepared to condemn a range of practices resulting from the autonomous behaviour of the entrusted undertaking, as a consequence of the state measure conferring certain exclusive rights.

CONTENTS OF CHAPTER 7

Chapter 7
Tariffs and Prices

1. Introduction

This chapter focuses primarily on the application of the relevant EEC Treaty **7.1** rules to the prices and tariffs charged to customers of electricity supply customers. There is as yet no case law of the Court of Justice on electricity prices and tariffs, nor have there been any decisions of the Commission applying the competition rules to the sector. There have, however, been a number of decisions on the legality of price controls in general, and this chapter further examines the application of the relevant Treaty rules to tariffs and prices related public service or utility sectors, including the gas industry, and the telecommunications sector. In the penultimate section the Council's Directive on price transparency is analysed, and the final section deals with the relevant rules for prices applicable under the ECSC Treaty.

In discussing the legality of electricity tariffs and prices in Community law it is necessary to maintain a distinction between tariffs which are applied directly or indirectly by the Member State authorities and those which are purely the result of autonomous decisions of the undertaking. It may be stated prima facie that prices and tariffs imposed by Member States are subject to the EEC Treaty articles addressed to them – that is Article 30 and Articles 92 and 93. As a general rule, the pricing practices of private undertakings may be subject to Articles 85 and 86 – the rules addressed to undertakings.

In the electricity sector, however, the application of these two sets of rules **7.2** may often overlap. As discussed in Chapter 5, the definition of a state aid is wide enough to cover the tariffs charged by an independent undertaking, provided that there is some degree of state involvement in the tariff policy process. Hence Articles 92 and 93 may apply, in certain cases, to undertakings as well.

At the same time, the Court of Justice has also held that the competition rules may also be applicable to the Member States. The imposition of certain prices or tariffs on independent undertakings by a Member State may also be caught by Articles 85 and 86 (Case 66/86 *Saeed* [1989] ECR 1091).

According to the Court, Member States infringe their obligations under Article 5 EEC when they not only approve or enforce tariffs which are incompatible with the competition rules, but also when they encourage such practices.

157

7.3   Despite the fact that these various Treaty articles may be applied to similar situations, it is necessary to bear in mind that there are some important differences governing their application and enforcement.

As will become apparent, the Court has been cautious in its application of Article 30 EEC to national price control regimes. It is not enough for the complainant to show that price controls may potentially put imports at a disadvantage; concrete evidence of the discriminatory effects of the regime is necessary.

Where, however, an allegation is made that a firm has benefitted from a state aid, contrary to Article 92, the Court has tended to be less strict in requiring the Commission to demonstrate its restrictive effects on inter-state trade; it is sufficient to show a potential effect on trade (Case 730/79 *Philip Morris;* Case 310/85 *Deufil*).

7.4   A difference in approach is also apparent in the application of Articles 85 and 86, as compared to Article 92. The Court has held in a series of cases on Article 92, that this Article is not subject to a *de minimus* rule, in the same way as Articles 85 and 86.

Finally, the Commission has extensive powers of investigation and access to documentation in proceedings related to Articles 85 and 86, powers which it wholly lacks in connection with Articles 30 and 92.

2. Tariffs deriving from Member States' controls

(i) Tariffs and price controls

7.5   In principle Member States remain free to impose price control as long as their effect is not to put domestic products at an advantage. Tariffs applied by government regulations might be caught by Article 30 if they can be shown to put imported electricity at a disadvantage. Similarly, tariffs which are based on a system of cost calculation which put domestic fuels for use in electricity generation at an advantage over imported fuels may also be contrary to Article 30.

(a) Price regimes which differentiate on the basis of origin

7.6   A price regime which imposed less favourable prices for imported than for domestic products, including electricity or a generating fuel, would constitute a measure having equivalent effect and would be caught by Article 30 (Art 2(3)(b), Dir 70/50/EEC; Case 181/82 *Roussel* [1983] ECR 3849).

It is debatable whether this type of price regime could ever be justified under Article 36. In Case 78/82 *Campus Oil* the Court held that compulsory sales from the state-owned refinery in Ireland to independent oil companies could be justified under the public security exemption in Article 36. It also held that compulsory sales were only justified if the refinery's output could not be freely disposed of at competitive prices. As to the price at which the refined products were to be disposed of, the Court held that if compulsory sales were justified, the price could be fixed by the competent minister on the basis of the costs incurred in the operation of the refinery.

(b) Price regimes which do not distinguish according to origin

A maximum or a minimum selling price applied without distinction to **7.7** domestic and imported products alike will not usually be caught by Article 30, unless it can be shown that the sale of imported products becomes more difficult.

Maximum prices may fall foul of Article 30, however, where imports could only be sold at a loss (Cases 88–90/75 *SADAM* [1976] ECR 323) or where the system of price calculation only includes costs incurred within the territory of the Member States (Case 231/83 *LeClerq*). This would seem to imply that maximum prices should be fixed at a level which would allow the importer to recover his transport costs.

In Case C-347/88 *Commission* v *Greece* [1990] ECR 4747 the Court rejected the Commission's allegations that the Greek regime imposing maximum retail prices on petroleum products put national products at an advantage. The Commission had not provided sufficient evidence to demonstrate conclusively that the various components of the price control regime had been calculated on a basis that disadvantaged importers.

In Case C-249/88 *Commission* v *Belgium* [1991] ECR judgement of 19 **7.8** March 1991, (not yet reported) the Court upheld the legality of a system of maximum price controls which made reference to such factors as "investment and employment", "contribution to exports" etc even although these could be said to benefit national firms directly, and the systematic application of these criteria could put national firms at an advantage. Nevertheless the scheme at issue also contained factors which applied indistinctly to *all* firms, including the cost of production, importation, distribution etc thus taking into account the costs associated with importation.

It is of interest to note that in this case, Advocate-General Tesauro was of the opinion that a Member State could commit a separate breach of Article 30 where it failed to make its decision allocating a particular price to an enterprise sufficiently transparent. Pricing decisions should be adequately reasoned and made available to the applicant. The Court did not follow this approach. It ruled that in accordance with the general principle of Community law that all citizens should benefit from a right of review in their national courts, individuals had a right to obtain a fully reasoned decision, on request. The relevant authorities may issue a summary decision in the first instance, however.

It is apparent from these two recent cases that the Court requires concrete evidence that maximum price control regimes actually put imports at a disadvantage before it is prepared to condemn them.

7.9   A minimum price which is fixed on the basis of purely national components, effectively depriving imported products of any competitive advantage, would be contrary to Article 30 (Case 231/83 *Cullet* v *LeClerc* [1985] ECR 305).

Price freezes imposed on national and imported goods alike may also be condemned under Article 30 if they prevent the increased prices of imported products from being passes on in sale prices, so that traders wishing to import the products in question into the Member State can only do so at a loss (Cases 16–20/78 *Openbaar Ministerie* v *Danis* [1979] ECR 3327).

Maximum gross profit margins fixed at a single amount and applicable both to domestic products and to imports, may be prohibited under Article 30 if the margin does not make any allowance for the costs of importation (Case 116/84 *Roelstraete* [1985] ECR 1705; Case 128/86 *Lefevre* [1987] ECR 2963).

As for minimum profit margins, the Court has held that:

> "the fixing of the minimum profit at a specific amount, and not as a percentage of cost price, applicable without distinction to domestic products and imported products alike is … incapable of producing an adverse effect on imported products which may be cheaper" (Case 82/77 *Van Tiggele* [1978] ECR 25).

(ii) Relationship between Article 30 and Article 92

7.10   In Case 82/77 *Van Tiggele* the Court was not prepared to condemn a minimum profit margin as a state aid contrary to Article 92:

> "the advantage which such an intervention in the formation of price entails for the distributors of the product is not granted, directly or indirectly, through state resources ([1978] ECR 25 at 41).[1]

It has been suggested that there is no a priori reason why a national maximum or minimum price scheme intended to favour a particular sector should not be characterised as a state aid for the purposes of Article 92.[2]

7.11   In December 1990 the Commission approved a German law setting a minimum price for electricity generated from renewable energy sources (windmills, hydroelectric, solar and biomass). The rate of aid varied from 28% to 48% depending on the renewable energy involved. The Commission ruled that the impact of the measure on trade between Member States and on competition would be slight (20th Report on Competition Policy, 1991, pt 291).

The legality of state aids for the promotion of certain types of fuels in electricity generation has been discussed in Chapter 5. In its Decision in March 1990 the Commission approved the enactment of a nuclear fuel levy payable by the newly privatised electricity distributors to the state-owned Nuclear Electric.

---

[1] See, however, the Court's later ruling in Case 290/83 *Commission* v *France* [1985] ECR 439.
[2] Flynn, "The notion of a state aid in the EEC" (1987) 12 EL Rev 124.

(iii) **Application of Articles 85 and 86 to national price regulations**

The Court has been asked in a series of cases to consider the legality of state   **7.12**
price control measures which while not infringing Article 30, might be in
breach of Articles 3(f), 5(2) and Articles 85 and 86.

As explained in Chapter 4, Member States have a duty to abstain from
enacting or enforcing national rules which would deprive the Community
general rules on competition of their effectiveness.

(a) Article 85

In Case 13/77 *INNO* v *ATAB* [1977] ECR 2115 the Court held that a Belgian   **7.13**
fiscal measure compelling manufacturers and importers of tobacco
products to fix a minimum retail price might have the effect of encouraging
an abuse of a dominant position by the undertakings concerned. As the
case was brought on an Article 177 reference, it was for the national courts
to make the necessary findings of fact.

The Court's ruling in *INNO* had obvious far-reaching constitutional
implications, in that it was potentially open for a wide range of national
economic regulations to be condemned as restrictive of competition. In its
subsequent rulings on the application of Articles 85 and 86 to national
price controls, the Court has appeared to draw a distinction as to whether
the final price was fixed by a public authority (as in *Cullet*) or whether it was
delegated to private undertakings (*BNIC* v *Clair*). In the former case, the
measure will only be illegal if it is in breach of Article 30. In the latter case
the combined application of Articles 3, 5 and 85 is conditional upon the
preliminary finding of a cartel prohibited by Article 85.

In Case 267/86 *Van Eycke* [1988] ECR 4769 the Court restated its case law   **7.14**
to mean that a Member State fails to comply with its obligations under
Articles 3 and 5 when:

(a) it requires or encourages undertakings to conclude cartels contrary to
     Article 85 or reinforces the effects thereof; or
(b) when it divests the regulations of their public character by delegating
     to the undertakings the responsibility to take decisions concerning the
     parameters of competition (recital 16).

The Court has applied the first test on a number of occasions:

– in Case 136/86 *BNIC* v *Aubert* [1987] ECR 4789 the Court ruled that
national regulatory measures reinforcing the effects of Article 85 are void.
In this case, cognac producers and retailers had agreed, within the
framework of their interprofessional organization (BNIC) a production
quota system. This arrangement was subsequently extended to the entire
sector by ministerial degree. The Court reasoned that the collusive
arrangement was contrary to Article 85 and that the extension degree
reinforced these effects and deprived Article 85 of its effectiveness;

– in Case 311/85 *VVR*, it was held that a Belgian decree requiring travel   **7.15**
agents to observe price terms previously agreed by trade associations
reinforced the effects of those agreements.

As to the second test – in Case 267/86 *Van Eycke* – the Court indicated that decisions sensitive to competition must be taken by governments, and it would be contrary to Articles 5 and 85 for decisions to be delegated to particular economic operators – in this case banks – and endorsed by subsequent governmental decree.

(b) Article 86

7.16 In Case 30/87 *Bodson* the Court ruled that it would be contrary to Article 90(1) for a local authority to make the exclusive approval of a funeral undertaker in its area conditional upon the charging of prices which amounted to an abuse of Article 86.

In Case 66/86 *Saeed,* the Court suggested that a Member State would be in breach of Articles 5, 85 and 86 where it required or favoured the making of agreements contrary to Article 85 or reinforced their effects.

More recently in Case C-179/90 *Porto di Genova* the Court has held that discriminatory tariffs charged by a harbour enterprise entrusted with a monopoly of the services in question may be contrary to Articles 90(1) and 86(a) and (c).

3. **State aid element in electricity tariffs**

7.17 Preferential tariffs to certain users may be caught by the state aid provisions of the EEC Treaty.

(i) **Application of the state aid rules**

7.18 For Article 92 to apply, it should be recalled that it is necessary:
  (a) that the tariff favours certain undertakings or the production of certain goods competing with the undertakings or production of other Member States; and
  (b) the products in question are traded within the Community;
  (c) the tariff has been imposed by a public authority;
  (d) the tariff results in compensation from the state being paid to the electricity supply, company or in the state receiving less revenue, *i.e.* the tariff is in some way linked to state resources.

Points (a) and (b) have been dealt with at length in Chapter 5.

(ii) **State resources**

7.19 As to points (c) and (d), it will be recalled that in Cases 67, 68 & 76/84 *Gebroeders van der Kooy* v *Commission* [1988] ECR 219, a case involving an allegedly preferential tariff for the benefit of the Dutch horticultural industry, the Court examined the ownership and management of the Dutch gas company, Gasunie. The Dutch state not only held 50% of the shares of the company, but it also was empowered to approve its tariffs.

> "Taken as a whole these factors demonstrated that the contested tariff was the result of action by the State, and thus fell within the meaning of an ''aid' under Article 92 EEC."

It is not clear, therefore, whether the various factors referred to by the Court should be seen as alternative or cumulative. In the absence of a "state aid element", a preferential tariff to a particular user would have to be attacked on the basis of Article 85 or 86.

(iii) **Nature of a preferential tariff**

The Court's rulings in ·*Gebroeders van der Kooy,* and in the recent Case 169/84 **7.20** *Cofaz II* ([1992] CMLR 177), which concerned a special tariff for gas used by ammonia producers, shed some further light on the type of "preferential tariff" that is unlikely to be looked upon favourably by the Court.

In its initial Decision 83/215/EEC (OJ 1983 L97/49), which eventually led to the proceedings in *Gebroeders van der Kooy,* the Commission accepted that a company such as Gasunie may decide to vary its tariffs depending on the use of the goods which it sells, but it considered that such variations;

> "must have sound and comprehensible economic reasons, *e.g.* to ensure the competitiveness of gas on various user markets, and must not discriminate between horticulture and other consumers in a comparable situation."

It was not prepared to endorse Gasunie's argument that the disputed **7.21** preferential tariff was justified largely by the need to guard against the risk that the horticulturalists might convert their heating plants to coal, the price of which was more competitive at that time. It accepted that the price of gas may be fixed on the basis of a fuel other than heavy fuel oil, in particular coal. It doubted, however, whether a tariff whose application is limited to one year will have a significant impact on the decisions of customers whether or not to convert to coal.

In the Commission's view, the gas company should also have taken similar measures to prevent conversion to competing fuels in other industrial sectors. The differences in treatment between the industrial and the horticultural sectors demonstrated, according to the Commission, that the contested tariff was not justified by the desire to resist competition from coal.

The Court held that argument to be irrelevant. It preferred to base its **7.22** conclusion that the tariff was a preferential one on statistical evidence relating to the price differences between coal and gas which would have had to exist before it became economically viable to convert. These statistics did not, however:

> "...explain why Gasunie should decide to align its general horticultural tariff on the equilibrium price for the least efficient type of holding, when 61% of holdings would continue to use gas even at higher prices ... It follows that ... it

was not commercially justifiable for Gasunie to fix its horticultural tariff by reference to such undertakings.

The conclusion must therefore be that Decision 83/215 correctly found that the contested tariff was lower than was necessary in order to take account of the risk of conversion to coal."

7.23   In 1990 the Commission opened Article 93(2) proceedings against Part III of a tariff for natural gas that was to be applied to glasshouse growers in the Netherlands in 1989–94. Part III of the tariff placed a partial ceiling on gas prices when the price of heavy fuel oil, which was used as a basis for calculating the price of natural gas was HFL 415/tonne or more.

The Commission concluded that this mechanism conferred a financial advantage on the Dutch horticultural producers using gas which was equivalent to an operating aid and was therefore incompatible with Article 92(1) (OJ 1990 C103).

In Case 169/84 *Cofaz II* the Commission had challenged a tariff system whereby Gasunie granted special rebates to producers by means of a two–tier tariff, the result of which was to reduce the cost of gas as a raw material. The Commission secured certain changes in the tariff structure to the effect that Gasunie introduced a new tariff, known as Tariff F, for the benefit of large industrial users in the Netherlands.

7.24   In order to qualify for that new tariff users had to consume at least 600 million cubic metres of gas per year and operate 90% of the time or more. They further had to accept total or partial interruptions of supplies at Gasunie's discretion or supplies of natural gas having different calorific values. The new tariff structure formed an integral part of the general tariff structure for users in the Netherlands, and did not discriminate between sectors. Finally, the value of the rebate granted to undertakings eligible for the tariff was even lower than the total value of the savings made by Gasunie on account of the volume of consumption of these large undertakings, and the application of the special conditions just mentioned. The Commission closed the state aid procedure it had initiated against Gasunie.

Cofaz, a French producer, challenged the Commission's decision on the grounds that it was vitiated by manifest errors in the assessment of the essential facts; the errors lay in the conclusion that the Tariff F might be regarded as a general structure of Dutch domestic tariffs, and was not specific to any sector, and was further justified by the savings made on supplies to very large users.[3]

7.25   The Court of Justice found that the new tariff structure as approved by the Commission, still amounted to a preferential tariff system in favour of a certain group of users. It examined in considerable detail Gasunie's economic justification for the difference between the tariffs charged to this group as compared to other large users, and found that the lower tariff for the former was not justified by actual cost savings made to Gasunie. The Commission had greatly miscalculated the extent of these savings, which it

---

[3] A number of French competitors successfully claimed that they had standing to sue under Art 173 EEC to challenge the Commission's decision – Case 169/84 *Cofaz I* [1986] ECR 408.

had found amounted to five cents per cubic metre. The Court asked the opinion of independent experts, who found that maximum savings would be less than one cent per cubic metre. Given this high margin of error, the Court quashed the Commission's decision.

It is submitted that the following general principles can be extracted from this recent line of case law:
– price differentials which are part of an integral tariff system, and can be justified on an objective basis are permitted;
– price reductions will only be tolerated in so far as they are necessary to meet commercial pressures;
– price differentials designed to promote valid environmental objectives or to realise the objectives of the common energy policy – for example, to encourage energy saving and the rational use of energy will be acceptable. The Court will of course apply a proportionality rule here.

(a) Preferential tariffs in long term contracts

The Commission has now considered the compatibility with Article 92 of a **7.26** series of contracts concluded between the French company, EDF, and large industrial users for the supply of nuclear generated electricity at special rates.[4]

One such contract involved payment calculated on the basis of marginal production costs plus a percentage share in the future profits of the customer. The Commission considered that there was potentially an element of state aid in this arrangement and required an annual price increase of 10% over a period of three years.[5] It was understood that the arrangement would only last for the limited period in which EDF had spare nuclear generating capacity.

In 1990 the Commission examined two contracts under which EDF **7.27** proposed to supply electricity to Usinor-Sacilor for a new unit to produce manganese alloys in France, and to Exxon Chemicals for investment in France. In both cases the Commission concluded that the contracts did not include any State aid element and were in line with what a private investor would do under normal market conditions (Twentieth Report on Competition Policy, 1991, pt 186).

4. Commission's proposals on downstream tariffs

Although early drafts of its proposals on common rules for the electricity **7.28** sector seemed to indicate that the Commission was prepared to remove almost all powers to regulate and supervise tariffs at the national level, the most recent version of its draft Directive on common rules for the internal

---

[4] The Commission has reached an informal decision in each case; Aid to Pechiney – *Agence Europe*, no 5110, 13 October 1989 and Nineteenth Report on Competition Policy, pt 168.
[5] *Financial Times*, 12 October 1989.

market in electricity indicates that Member States shall ensure that electricity undertakings are operated on commercial principles (Art 3(1)).

Article 3(3) provides that:

"Without prejudice to Article 16(2) Member States shall not establish, approve, influence or regulate tariffs or prices to customers in respect of the volume for which these customers exercise their right to purchase and to be supplied or to contract to purchase and to be supplied throughout the transmission and distribution system…"

Where, however, a Member State imposes an obligation on distribution companies to supply customers located in a given area, and these customers do not have a right or do not exercise a right to be supplied by other suppliers, in accordance with Articles 6 or 7, then the Member State may regulate tariffs for these "franchise" customers, for instance to ensure equal treatment of the customers concerned (Art 16(2)) (COM (1991) 548, 21 February 1992, final).

In accordance with Article 24(4) of the proposal, electricity distribution undertakings shall be required to distinguish between:
(a)   electricity supply costs from distribution costs and other charges;
(b)   sales of electricity for industrial purposes from sales for other purposes.

5. Competition rules and anti-competitive pricing practices

7.29   Article 85 may apply to agreements and concerted practices between two or more companies to purchase fuels from generators, or alternatively to fix tariffs, or use of system or connection charges, where those agreements:
(i)   have as their object or effect the prevention, restriction or distortion of competition within the common market; and in particular those which;
(ii)   directly or indirectly fix purchase or selling prices; and
(iii) affect trade between Member States.

7.30   Domestic price agreements not extending to imports and exports may not be caught by Article 85(1) (Case 246/86 *Belasco* [1989] ECR 2181).

In its Decision in *Flat Glass* (OJ 1989 L33/44) the Commission decided not to proceed against wholesalers who allegedly came under pressure from a producers' cartel.

(i) Agreements on fuel purchases

7.31   Agreements between parties to buy at maximum or minimum prices, or agreements between parties to bind themselves to published price lists for example, will generally be caught by Article 85(1).

Indeed the Commission and the Court of Justice tend to consider price agreements amount to the most serious infringements of Article 85

(Commission Dec 89/190, OJ 1989 L74/71; Case 123/85 *BNIC* v *Clair;* Case 8/72 *Cementhandelaren* v *Commission;* Dec 91/297 *Solvay,* OJ 1991 L152/1).

In cases of serious overcapacity a "restructuring agreement" might benefit from an exemption.[6]

In its Decision 91/329, *Scottish Nuclear,* (OJ 1991 L178/31) the **7.32** Commission considered the legality under Article 85 EEC of the price arrangements in the Nuclear Agreement between Scottish Nuclear on the one hand, and Scottish Power and Scottish Hydro, on the other. Under the terms of this agreement the two companies are obliged to purchase nuclear-generated electricity at the same price, in accordance with a quota fixed for each company. It found that:

> "The price set in the agreement is independent of the price at which Scottish Power and Hydro-Electric purchase electricity from the other generators, particularly independent generators.
> The formula used for the first four years and taken as a basis for setting prices for the following four years is considered to be an internal calculation formula which does not in any way prejudice the setting of the price at which electricity is purchased from independent generators. The price set in the agreement should not, in particular be used to justify a very low purchase price that would dissuade independent generators and Scottish Nuclear's competitors. This could be deemed to be an abuse of the exemption."

(ii) Agreements on selling prices and tariffs

Price competition is a crucial, if not the principal element of customer **7.33** choice, so that any pricing agreement between utilities would be subject to a rigorous examination by the Commission before any exemption could be granted under Article 85(3).

At the same time it is recognised that the harmonization of tariff structures may be a major element for the provision of Community-wide services in the electricity sector, and for fair competition (this being one of the longer-term aims of Council Dir 90/377/EEC, discussed below).

Agreements which only concern the setting up of common tariff structures or principles may be more favourably received by the Commission, as these may constitute one of the economic benefits under Article 85(3) which outweigh competition restrictions. Such agreements could also contribute to achieving the objectives set out in the Council Recommendation of 1981, *i.e.* more cost-oriented tariffs.

In Case 66/86 *Saeed* the Court gave some indication of the types of tariff **7.34** agreements it would consider to be "fair", albeit with reference to the appropriate Council Directive on scheduled air fares.[7] This Directive provides that air fares are fair:

> "if they are reasonably related to the long-term fully allocated costs of the applicant air carrier, while taking into account other relevant factors. In this

---

[6] See further, Bellamy and Child at 168–169.
[7] Art 3, Dir 87/601/EEC (OJ 1987 L33/74).

connection, they shall consider the needs of consumers, the need for a satisfactory return on capital, the competitive market situation, including the fares of competitors and the need to prevent dumping."

(a) Telecommunications

7.35 The Commission has found that an agreement between the operators of international telecommunications circuits, which recommended, *inter alia* the imposition of a 30% surcharge or an access charge where third party traffic was carried on an international telecommunications leased circuit, or if such a circuit was interconnected, or if such a circuit was connected to the public telecommunications network, substantially restricted competition within the EC (Commission press release IP(90) 188 of 6 March 1990).

(iii) **Abuse of dominant position**

7.36 Article 86 may apply where:
(a) the enterprise is in a dominant position within the common market or a substantial part of it; and it
(b) directly or indirectly imposes unfair purchase or selling prices or other unfair trading conditions.
(c) there is an effect on inter-state trade.

7.37   In Case 66/86 *Saeed* the Court found that agreements fixing tariffs for air fares on one or more routes could infringe Article 85(1) and Article 86:

> "The application of tariffs for scheduled flights on the basis of bilateral or multilateral tariffs may, in certain circumstances, constitute an abuse of a dominant position on the market in question in particular where an undertaking in a dominant position has succeeded in imposing on other carriers the application of excessively high or excessively low tariffs or the exclusive application of only one tariff on a given route."

(a) Abusive selling practices

7.38 The Court has adopted a strict approach to *price discrimination* – substantial price differences between customers is strong evidence of discrimination, in the absence of objective criteria.[8]

Elements of a tariff structure which genuinely reflects the particular costs of providing a service of a general public interest, may be exempted under Article 90(2) (Case 66/86 *Saeed*).

7.39   In its Guidelines for competition in the telecommunications sector (OJ 1991 C233/2) the Commission offers the following examples of discriminatory prices which would amount to an abuse under Article 86:

---

[8] Case 78/70 *Deutsche Grammaphone* [1971] ECR 487 at 501; Case 27/76 *United Brands* [1978] ECR 207, at grounds 204–234.

"…the imposition of access charges to leased circuits when they are connected to the public switched network or other special prices and charges for service provision to third parties. Such access charges may discriminate between users of the same service depending upon the usage and result in imposing unfair trading conditions … Conversely it does not constitute an abuse provided that it is shown, in each specific case, that the access charges correspond to the costs which are entailed directly for the telecommunications operators for the access in question. In this case, access charges can be imposed only on an equal basis to all users including TOs themselves." (p19)

Discrimination in the price or quality of service provided may also **7.40** amount to an abuse under Article 86:

"This behaviour may relate, *inter alia,* to tariffs or to restrictions or delays in connection the public switched network or leased circuits provision, in installation, maintenance and repair, in effecting interconnection of systems or in providing information concerning technical standards and all other information necessary for an appropriate interconnection and interoperation with the reserved service and which may affect the inter-working of competitive services…"

As far as *excessive pricing* is concerned, this may amount to an abuse of **7.41** Article 86, but, unfortunately, the concept is not fully developed and defined in EC law. The Court has ruled that the price level of a product may not, of itself suffice to disclose abuse but could be a determining factor if unjustified by objective criteria.[9]

In Case 27/76 the Court defined an excessive price as one which bears no reasonable relation to the economic value of the product supplied. In determining whether a particular price is excessive, the Commission must look at the supplier's own production costs and its competitors's sales price.

In Joined Cases 110, 241/88 & 242/88 *Lucazeau and Sacem* [1989] ECR **7.42** 2811 the referring court had asked for guidance on the criteria to be applied in establishing whether a service fee was abusive. The Court of Justice ruled that the national court could compare the fee with the level of charges in other Member States. If the charges were significantly higher, the comparison between charge levels being carried out on a homogeneous basis, such differences must be regarded as evidence of a dominant position. It was for the undertaking to justify the difference on the basis of objective criteria.

Article 86 may also be breached if the consumer suffered as the result of such pricing policies, even if no effect on competition could be shown (Case 26/74 *Roquette Frères* v *Commission* [1976] ECR 677).

The criteria involved could include miscalculation of cost components. **7.43** For example, in *British Leyland* the Commission fined British Leyland (BL) for imposing excessive charges for type approvals, which BL had argued were justified on the basis of increased overheads. It is interesting to note

---

[9] Case 40/70 *Sirena* v *Eda* [1975] ECR 1367 at 1378; In Case 27/76 *United Brands* the Court said it would be an abuse to set a price which had no reasonable relation to the economic value of the product.

that although the Commission rejected this argument, it did not attempt to assess accurately the costs involved.[10] As one commentator has remarked "where there is proof in logic, but not in fact of an excessive cost-price difference, a presumption of abuse might lie."[11]

In most cases involving allegations of excessive pricing, however, the Court has required a detailed cost analysis and once this has been established, it will then examine the prices charged by competitors for the same product.[12]

7.44   *Cost escalation clauses* imposed by a dominant party could also fall foul of Article 86(1). An unfair price variation clause may be evidence of abusive behaviour.[13]

Article 86 may also be used to attack *predatory pricing;* a dominant firm may not predate by below-cost pricing on smaller undertakings so as to squeeze them out of the market.

Article 86 does not prescribe any cost-based legal rule to define the precise stage at which price cutting by a dominant firm becomes abusive. The Commission has also been reluctant to utilise a mechanical application of a *per se* test based upon marginal or average variable cost, preferring to focus on the strategic considerations which underlie sustained price cutting.

7.45   In the *ECS/AKZO* decision [1983] CMLR 351 it concentrated on the objectives of the dominant company, AKZO, which were shown to have been to eliminate or damage its rival, ECS. It held that AKZO had been engaged in an aggressive price-cutting over a prolonged period (four years), during which time AKZO never covered its total cost (*i.e.* fixed plus variable cost). AKZO had further offered certain products to its rival, ECS's customers at prices which did not cover its variable costs.

AKZO contended that its prices were not predatory because they covered its average variable costs.

7.46   In Case C–62/86 *AKZO* v *Commission* (judgment of 3 July 1991, not yet reported) the Court upheld the greater part of the Commission's decision. A dominant firm which sells at prices lower than its average variable costs in order to undercut and eliminate a competitor must be considered as abusive (recital 71). Prices which are on average lower than total costs (*i.e.* fixed plus variable) but are higher than variable costs can be considered abusive where:

(i)   they form part of a plan to eliminate a competitor (recital 72);
(ii) they are maintained over a prolonged period of time without objective justification (recital 146).

It may be concluded that a firm which is dominant may not foreclose competition through its pricing policy. This means that rebates or discounts

---

[10] In Case 226/84 *British Leyland plc* v *Commission* [1986] ECR 3263, the Court upheld the Commission's decision.
[11] Green – *Commercial Agreements in Competition Law* 365.
[12] See further, the Commission's Decision in *Sabena*, OJ 1988 L 317/47; *Sterling Airways*, Tenth Report on Competition Policy, paras 136–138.
[13] Case 155/73 *Sacchi* [1974] ECR 409 at 431.

granted with the purpose of strengthening its dominant position are contrary to Article 86. Similarly price differentials which cannot be objectively justified are disallowed.[14]

An interesting feature of the *AKZO* case is the Court's approach to the tactics of a firm which was dominant in one particular market – in this case polymers – to attempt to undercut competition in a related market (in this case, compounds used in flour milling) where it was not dominant. The Court ruled that AKZO's dominance in the former market allowed it to engage in predatory pricing in the latter, related market.

It is submitted that this judgment may be of guidance in assessing whether a dominant electricity producer is engaged in abusive behaviour by trying to undercut local utility prices to potential customers in other Member States.

6. **Downstream tariffs: cross-subsidization and preferential tariffs**

Cross-subsidization may be defined as follows: **7.47**

> "Cross-subsidization means that an undertaking allocates all or part of the costs of its activity in one product or geographic market to its activity in another product or geographic market." (Commission of the EC, Telecoms guidelines, 20)

Whether cross-subsidization between different classes of customers might be prohibited, either as a form of discriminatory pricing, in breach of Article 86 or, as a form of state aid within the meaning of Article 92 EEC, will depend on the circumstances of each case.

The elimination of preferential tariffs helps to avoid distortion of **7.48** competition within the common market. Cross-subsidization between different product or geographic markets is probably not permissible under EC law, except under closely defined circumstances. Although there is no direct authority on this point, certain inferences may be drawn from Commission statements, Council resolutions and most importantly, the jurisprudence of the Court.

In EC law formal and material discrimination is prohibited. This means not only that customers in similar situations should be treated in the same way, but also that customers in different situations should not be subject to the same rigid rules (Case 13/63 *Italy* v *Commission* [1963] ECR 165). It would appear, however, that Article 16(2) of the Commission's proposed Directive on common rules for the electricity market derogates from this principle. Member States may require electricity distribution companies to charge the same tariff or price to a customer, irrespective of the fact the

---

[14] See also the Commission's Decision in *Napier Brown/British Sugar*, OJ 1988 L284/41, and Smith, "The wolf in wolf's clothing" (1989) EL Rev 209.

costs of supplying domestic customers may vary considerably from one geographical area to another within a Member State.

Recital 5 of Council Resolution 81/924 on electricity prices and tariffs provides that "undertakings must ensure equality of treatment of consumers in comparable supply conditions."

Hence in so far as the application of Articles 85 and/or 86 is concerned, substantial differences between the prices charged to different customer classes must be justified by objective criteria.[15]

7.49　　Council Resolution 81/924, for example, requires that tariffs should reflect costs to different categories of consumer. Multiple tariffs designed to transfer demand to off-peak periods or to allow load shedding or interruption of supplies are both acceptable and desirable.

In a sector, such as a public service sector where certain activities may be legitimately reserved to a monopoly, it is nevertheless incompatible with the competition rules to subsidise the costs on a market open to competition by revenues from the monopoly in order to offer certain products at unreasonably low-prices. In this context it should be noted that the Commission has obtained an undertaking from the German PTT that its tariff rates for express postal services must not be lower than the costs of providing the service (IP (85) 10).

(i) Commission's guidelines on telecoms

7.50　　In its recently published guidelines on the application of the competition rules for undertakings in the telecommunications sector, the Commission has offered a useful indication of how it views the application of Article 86 to the activities of undertakings engaged in the provision of a public service.

In so far as telecommunications operators (TO) are concerned, the Commission has drawn a distinction between those activities which are deemed subject to competition (so-called value added network services) and reserved activities (voice telephony) which remain under the monopoly control of the TOs (Commission Dir 90/388/EEC).

Although the Commission has not yet indicated that it is prepared to draw a similar distinction for the electricity sector, reserving certain activities in connection with public supply, for example, to certain operators, the telecommunication guidelines offer useful pointers to its attitude to cross-subsidization in the public service sector.

7.51　　The Commission has declared that

"Under certain circumstances cross-subsidization could distort competition... with offers which are made possible not by efficiency and performance but by artificial means such as subsidies...

Cross-subsidization does not lead to predatory pricing and does not restrict competition when it is the costs of reserved activities which are subsidized by the revenue generated by other reserved activities since there is no competition possible as to these activities. This form of subsidization is even necessary, as it

---

[15] Case 27/76, *loc cit* and Case 78/70, *loc cit*.

172

enables the TOs holders of exclusive rights to perform their obligation to provide a public service universally and on the same conditions to everybody. For instance, telephone provision in unprofitable rural areas is subsidized through revenues from telephone provision in profitable urban areas or long-distance calls. The same could be said of subsidizing the provision of reserved services through revenues generated by activities under competition. The application of the general principle of cost-orientation should be the ultimate goal, in order, *inter alia*, to ensure that prices are not inequitable as between users.

Subsidizing activities under competition, whether concerning services or equipment, by allocating their costs to monopoly activities, however, is likely to distort competition in violation of Article 86. It could amount to an abuse by an undertaking holding a dominant position within the Community. Moreover, users of activities under monopoly have to bear unrelated costs for the provision of these services. Cross-subsidization can also exist between monopoly provision and equipment manufacture and sale. Cross-subsidization can be carried out through:
– funding the operation of activities in question with capital remunerated substantially below the market rate;
– providing for those activities premises, equipment, experts and/or services with a remuneration substantially lower than the market price."(OJ 1991 C233/2 at 20)

7. Relations between electricity companies and independent generators

In relation to prices at which distribution companies purchase electricity, **7.52** for example, from auto-producers and self-generators, the Council has issued Recommendation 88/611 on co-operation between public utilities and auto-producers of electricity (OJ 1988 L335/29). According to this non-binding measure reimbursement for electricity sales to the public supply network should:
– be based primarily on the long-term average costs avoidable by the public utilities in their areas of supply;
– correspond at least to the variable costs avoidable by the public utilities *i.e.* mainly the savings made in fuel costs;
– guarantee the auto-producer additional reimbursement to the extent that he enables the public supply network to make savings in investment costs in the generation or purchase of electricity;
– reimbursement for the purchase of electricity from the public supply network is determined in such a way that auto-producers are treated in the same way as a comparable purchaser who has no means of auto-production;
– the rules regarding this reimbursement are framed so as to be as transparent as possible.

The Commission has been prepared to exempt a German law setting a **7.53** minimum price for electricity generated from renewables on the grounds, *inter alia,* that it was in line with Recommendation 88/611 (Twentieth Report on Competition Policy, pt 291).

(i) Back-up supplies

7.54   The refusal by an electricity production company to make back-up supplies available to an auto-producer at reasonable prices, may be challenged under Article 86. An undertaking in a dominant position may have an obligation to supply all those customers who place orders where no alternative suppliers exist, and refusal by the dominant supplier could put the buyer out of business. Refusal to supply is an abuse if it cannot be objectively justified.[16]

7.55   In its Decision in *Boosey & Hawkes* (OJ 1987 L286/36), the Commission accepted complaints lodged by two former customers of Boosey, a manufacturer of musical instruments, which refused to supply them with essential spare parts, as an abuse of Article 86. The Commission was prepared to recognise however that:

> "there is no obligation placed on a dominant producer to subsidize competition to itself ... where a customer transfers its central activity to the promotion of a competing brand, it may be that even a dominant firm is entitled to review its commercial relations with that customer and on giving adequate notice terminate any special relationship."

In this particular case, the Commission found that Boosey's conduct went beyond that which was reasonably necessary to protect its own interests. Its decision to refuse to supply was abrupt and formed part of a wider campaign against its former customers.

7.56   In its Decision on *British Gypsum* in 1988, the Commission did not find an abuse on the part of the company when it chose to give preferential treatment to loyal customers in times of shortage of supply "in view of the limited direct consequences which this measure had in practice and in the absence of conclusive evidence as to the extent of its likely longer term indirect effects" (para 71).

8. Price transparency

7.57   Council Directive 90/377/EEC introduces a Community procedure to improve the transparency of gas and electricity charged to industrial end-users. It takes Article 213 EEC as its legal basis.[17]

Directive 90/377/EEC does not require the provision of information on

---

[16] *Polaroid, SSI Europe,* Thirteenth Report on Competition Policy, 1983, p95; see also *Sabena, loc cit.*
[17] This is the general power enabling the Community to obtain information. Art 41 ECSC and Art 40 Euratom furnish the Community institutions with specific powers.

fuel and other input costs. In its preamble, however, companies are reminded that the Commission may use its existing powers under the competition rules to require communication of prices and conditions of sale (recital 9).

As the prices charged to domestic users usually take the form of standard tariffs, and are readily available, the main objective of the Directive is to ensure transparency in the prices and terms of sales of gas and electricity to industrial end users, as defined in Annexes I (gas) and II (electricity) of the Directive (for text of Directive see Appendix 3). Recital 4 of the preamble to the Directive recognises, however, that:

> "the price paid by industry in the Community for the energy which it uses is one of the factors which influence its competitiveness and should therefore remain confidential." ·

The Directive attempts to reconcile the goal of transparency with the **7.58** need to protect commercial confidentiality, by requiring only a limited form of data disclosure in relation to prices charged to large consumers. This is evident from the requirements on data compilation and transmission as set out in Annex II to the Directive (discussed below).

Article 1 of the Directive provides that Member States must take the necessary steps to ensure that undertakings which supply gas or electricity to industrial end users communicate certain information to the Statistical Office of the European Community (SOEC).

This information, to be communicated in the form provided for in Article 3, is to include:

> "1. the prices and terms of sale of gas and electricity to industrial end-users;
> 2. the price systems in use;
> 3. the breakdown of consumers and the corresponding volumes by category of consumption to ensure the representativeness of these categories at national level."

In accordance with Article 2 the data referred to in Article 1(1) and (2) **7.59** is to be compiled by the companies on 1 January and 1 July of each year. This must then be sent on to the SOEC and the competent authorities of the Member States within two months.

Information pursuant to Article 1(3) should be sent every two years to the SOEC and the competent authorities in the Member States. This information shall not be published.

Article 3 refers to the form and content of the information to be provided, which must conform to Annex II.

The data on electricity prices charged to "typical reference consumers", **7.60** that is industrial consumers with a maximum net demand of 10MW, need only relate "where possible" to the published tariff applicable to the reference customer. The actual price need not be disclosed. Where there are only quasi-contracts special contracts or freely negotiated prices:

"the most commonly found price (most representative) for the given supply should be reported" (para 6, Annex II).

For customers with a net maximum demand over 10MW a system based on "marker prices" is introduced.

7.61 Marker prices and associated information must be reported for each Member State as described in paragraph 13 of Annex II, that is Germany and the United Kingdom, for three categories of large consumer, *i.e.* those industrial consumers with maximum demands in the region of 25MW, 50MW and 75 MW. Only information on electricity consumption from public utilities is required to be reported, and not that relating to any auto-production.

The marker price for a given MW category (*e.g.* 25MW is the average price payable per kwh for a notional or "marker price" industrial consumer with a normal demand of about 25MW but before any reductions for "special factors" which should be reported separately (para 15, Annex II). These "special factors" include for example, interruptibility clauses. These should be described and the amount of reduction indicated in a representative manner (para 17).

7.62 For Member States where there is more than one utility, each utility shall provide a marker price and related information to an independent statistical body. These bodies shall then pass on the highest and the lowest marker price for the Member State for each MW category, to the national administration and to the SOEC. For the other Member States where only one national utility covers the whole country, the information must be reported directly and simultaneously to the SOEC (para 18, Annex II).

7.63 Information on marker prices need only be reported to the statistical bodies where there at least *three* consumers in the appropriate MW category in the Member State or in the region concerned (para 19).

Article 4 prohibits the SOEC from disclosing data supplied to it which might, by their nature, be subject to commercial confidentiality. Such confidential statistical data is only to be accessible to the SOEC officials and may only be used for statistical purposes.

The SOEC may, however, publish the data in an aggregated form which does not enable individual commercial transactions to be identified.

Article 4 imposes no equivalent confidentiality obligations on Member States, this being a matter of national law.

7.64 Where the SOEC notes discrepancies, anomalies or inconsistencies in the data transmitted to it, it may request the appropriate disaggregated data as well as the methods of calculation or evaluation upon which the aggregated data are based, in order to assess, or even amend any information deemed irregular (Art 5).

The Member States would presumably, in accordance with Article 5 EEC, be under a duty to provide that information, provided that this did not in turn impinge on confidentiality matters.

7.65 The SOEC may also be under an obligation to comply with requests to provide information to national authorities in certain circumstances. In

Case 2/88 *Zwartveld et al* the Court held the Community institutions could, in certain circumstances be obliged, in accordance with the Community principle of mutual, loyal and genuine co-operation between the Member States, as expressed in Article 5 EEC to communicate certain information to national authorities [1990] 3 CMLR 457.

In accordance with Article 8, the Commission must present a summary report on the operation of the Directive to the European Parliament. The Directive came into effect on 1 July 1991.[18]

9. **ECSC Treaty**

The ECSC Treaty's Chapter V deals with prices. It invests the Commission **7.66** (or High Authority) with considerable interventionist powers in pricing matters. In the course of time, some of these rules have proved too rigid to be applied to present conditions, and many of the articles have lost much of their earlier significance (see the Opinion of the Advocate-General in Case 8/83 *Officine Fratelli Nertoli* v *Commission* [1984] ECR 1649 for an overview of the background to, and current application of the pricing rules).

Article 4(b) and Article 60 ECSC contain a prohibition on price discrimination.

Article 4(b) lists among the practices which must be abolished and prohibited:

"– measures or practices which discriminate between producers, between purchasers or between consumers, especially in prices and delivery terms or transport rates and conditions, and measures or practices which interfere with purchaser's free choice of supplier."

Article 60 stipulates:

"1. Pricing practices contrary to Articles 2, 3, 4 shall be prohibited, in particular: **7.67**
– unfair competitive practices, especially purely temporary or purely local price reductions tending towards the acquisition of a monopoly position within the common market;
– discriminatory practices, involving within the common market, the application by a seller of dissimilar conditions to comparable transactions, especially on grounds of the nationality of the buyer.
The High Authority may define the practices covered by this prohibition by decisions taken after consulting the Consultative Committee and the Council.
2. For these purposes,
(a) the price lists and conditions of sale applied by undertakings within the **7.68** common market must be made public to the extent and in the manner prescribed by the High Authority after consulting the Consultative Committee..."

---

[18] In the case of natural gas, the Directive must be implemented in a Member State within five years after the introduction of that form of energy on the market in question.

Article 63 provides that:

"if the High Authority finds that discrimination is being systematically practice by purchasers, in particular under provisions governing contracts entered into by bodies dependent on a public authority it shall make appropriate recommendations to the Governments concerned."

7.69   Article 64 allows it to impose fines upon undertakings which infringe the provisions of the pricing Chapter.

In their complaint against British Coal, NALOO, the independent association of mining operators, alleged that the royalty imposed by BCC on independent producers licensed by it was an infraction of Article 60 because the royalty was excessive and made licensed producers uncompetitive.

The Commission chose to interpret Article 60 narrowly, and held that the provision clearly applies to the pricing practices of *vendors*.

"Article 60 is not applicable to the imposition of a royalty on production." (para 47)

7.70   In Case 1/54 *France* v *High Authority,* however, the Court of Justice construed Article 60 very broadly, as covering "agreements between producers", unfair competitive practices and "discriminatory practices". Further it held that Articles 60 and 65 are not mutually exclusive ([1954–56] ECR 1).

The independent coal miners further alleged that Article 63 had been breached because there had been systematic discrimination by the two generating companies against the licensed producers in offering lower prices and less favourable conditions. As the relevant purchasers were in fact government-owned at the time of the conclusion of the contracts, these contracts were examined under Article 63.

The Commission combined its analysis under this article with Article 86 EEC to find that there had been a breach of these articles by the two generating companies who had systematically offered lower prices and unfair contract terms to the independents (Commission Decision of 25 May 1991, *loc cit,* currently under appeal to the Court of First Instance. The case is registered as Case T-57/91 *NALOO* v *Commission.*).

Chapter 8
Contractual Arrangements

1. Introduction

This chapter covers the application of the relevant EEC and ECSC rules to **8.1** contracts concluded at various stages of the electricity production process, ranging from agreements on research and development and exploitation of electricity plant, agreements on fuel supply for use in electricity generation, agreements on the operation of electricity networks, and finally agreements relating to the sale of electricity. It does not deal directly with those aspects of such agreements which relate to prices or, where relevant, to transit conditions. These issues have been covered in Chapters 6 and 7 respectively.

2. Relevant legal provisions

(i) EEC Treaty

The Commission may assess the legality of contractual agreements between **8.2** electrical engineering and construction companies, *inter se*, between the latter and electricity producers, between electricity producers, *inter se*, and between the latter and its customers, including distribution companies, large users and various categories of commercial and industrial users, under Articles 85 and 86 EEC. In certain cases, and under certain conditions[1], contracts may be exempted under Article 85(3), and where relevant Article 90(2).

It is clear, however, that the Commission cannot rely upon its powers under Article 90(3) (see Chap 4), to require Member States to ensure the adjustment of long-term contractual agreements, unless those agreements were imposed or otherwise encouraged by the Member State itself (Case 202/88 *France* v *Commission, loc cit*).

(ii) ECSC Treaty

The competition rules of the ECSC Treaty – that is Articles 65 and 66 – may **8.3** be of relevance to agreements between coal suppliers and electricity generators in certain circumstances.

---

[1] For a useful example for the energy sector, see the Commission's Decision concerning the IEA agreement disscussed at para 3.33.

The ECSC Treaty applies to undertakings engaged in coal production, and also for the purposes of Articles 65 and 66, to any undertaking or agency regularly engaged in distribution of coal other than sale to domestic consumers (Art 80 ECSC).

In addition Article 63 prohibits systematic discrimination by purchasers in particular under provisions governing contracts entered into by bodies dependent on a public authority.

Article 65 prohibits all agreements between undertakings, decisions and concerted practices tending directly or indirectly to prevent restrict or distort competition within the common market and in particular those tending to fix prices, restrict or control production or share markets, products and customers.

In its recent Decision in *NALOO* the Commission held that Article 65 did not apply to agreements between British Coal and the two major electricity generators.

8.4   It did, however, consider Article 63 ECSC and Article 86 EEC to apply to the relationship between the electricity generators and the independent mining companies. It also went on to set out certain terms and conditions which the generators should comply with in order to discharge their obligations under these two articles (see para 66 of the Commission's Decision of 23 May 1991).

Article 66(1) ECSC which regulates concentrations provides that any transaction which:

> "...has in itself the direct or indirect effect of bringing about... a concentration between undertakings at least one of which is covered by Article 80..."

must have the prior authorization of the Commission.

8.5   Concentrations takes place when one undertaking acquires "control" in another. The concept of control, defined in Decision 24/54/ECSC (JO 1954, 345) is extensive and control may exist if:

> "unusually long contracts with an undertaking concerning an important part of its supplies or outlets make it possible to determine how an undertaking shall operate as regards production, prices, investments, supplies, sales and appropriation of profits."

8.6   In 1990 the Commission approved a joint venture between BHP-UTAH and Meekatharra (NI) Ltd, to set up a joint venture to explore and develop coal reserves in Northern Ireland. The rational exploitation of these reserves is expected to lead to the construction of a large electricity generating station (Twentieth Report on Competition Policy, 1990, pt 126).

Joint distribution ventures and joint production ventures are usually treated as concentrations under Article 66 (*British Fuels Ltd*, OJ 1987 L224/16).

In certain cases agreements and practices may be scrutinised under Article 66 in respect of ECSC products and Article 86 EEC in respect of other products (*Welded Steel Mesh*, OJ 1989 L260/1).

Article 66(7) ECSC provides that:

"If the High Authority finds that public or private undertakings which, in law or in fact, hold or acquire in the market for one of the products within its jurisdiction a dominant position shielding them against effective competition in a substantial part of the common market are using that position for purposes contrary to the objectives of the Treaty, it shall make to them such recommendations as may be appropriate to prevent the position from being so used."

In its Decision in *NALOO,* the Commission held that British Coal had abused its dominant position in breach of Article 66(7), *inter alia,* by levying an unreasonably high royalty on the independent mining companies licensed by it to mine opencast and deep-mined coal. The Commission accepted, however, that a settlement negotiated by the British Government on behalf of BC resulted in a reduction of the royalty level so that:

"the royalty will not prevent efficient companies from making a profit nor impose a significant competitive advantage" (para 74, Decision of 23 May 1991, *loc cit*).

(iii) Euratom Treaty

As already noted in Chapter 3, the rules on competition in the EEC Treaty apply to activities in the field of nuclear energy only to the extent that they do not derogate from the provisions of the Euratom Treaty.

3. Research and development and specialization agreements

(i) General

Regulation (EEC) 417/85 (OJ 1985 L53/1) grants block exemption to certain types of specialization agreements; Regulation (EEC) 418/85 provides block exemption for R & D agreements (OJ 1985 L53/5)[2] and Regulation (EEC) 559/89 grants block exemption for know-how licensing agreements (OJ 1989 L61/1).

In order for an R & D agreement to fall under the block exemption it must meet various conditions, including that the combined market share of the parties does not exceed 20%. If the market share is greater, the agreement may qualify for individual exemption (see for example, the Commission Decision in *KSB-Goulds-Lowara-ITT,* OJ 1990 L19/25).

(ii) Current practice towards mergers and joint ventures

Following the entry into force of the Merger Regulation (Reg (EEC) 4069/89 it is important to establish whether a joint venture is *concentrative*

[2] See further, Korah, *R & D and the EEC Competition Rules,* ESC, 1986.

or *co-operative.* The Regulation itself provides two criteria to be used in establishing whether a joint venture is concentrative: it must be an autonomous economic entity, and it must not result in a co-ordination of its parents other activities.

As a consequence Regulation (EEC) 4064/89 does not deal with operations whose object or effect is the co-ordination of the competitive activities of undertakings that remain independent from each other. Semi-permanent *co-operative* joint ventures will be judged under Article 85(1), and fall to be assessed under the provisions of Regulation 17. The Commission's Notice regarding concentrative and co-operative operations under Regulation (EEC) 4064/89 explains the main considerations which will determine, in the Commission's view, as to when a joint venture is or is not caught by the Regulation (OJ 1989 L395/1).

In general, the Commission has begun to adopt a more lenient approach to co-operative joint ventures providing that the agreement does not have the object or effect of imposing territorial divisions within the EC (see, for example, its recent Decision in *Odin,* OJ 1990 L209/15).

If the creation of a joint venture is judged not to fall within Article 85(1), the Commission will usually go on to examine the specific provisions in all the relevant agreements to determine whether they are merely ancillary restrictions or whether they are restrictions falling under Article 85(1). This will involve an examination of the various clauses to determine, whether in the light of the financial and commercial risks involved, technical difficulties etc, the restrictions are "necessary". The Commission's Notice regarding restrictions ancillary to concentrations offers guidance on this matter (OJ 1990 C203/5).

In its Decision 91/251 *Alcatel/Telettra,* the Commission has also indicated that it may take a favourable attitude to concentration or merger where the arrangements will give the parties access to the other's technology, in this case in transmission products. The proposed merger was declared compatible subject to certain obligations (OJ 1991 L122/48).

(iii) **Electricity sector**

8.11   The Commission has considered a number of joint ventures to promote the development of new technology for electricity generation.

In its Decision 76/248 on the establishment of United Reprocessors Gmbh (URG) (OJ 1976 L51/7) the Commission considered the compatibility of an agreement between three companies, BNFL, KEWA and the French Commissariat à l'Energie Atomique to establish a joint company to market oxide fuels reprocessing services and to provide various associated transport and other ancillary services, under Article 85(1) EEC (see further Chap 3).

8.12   The Commission was prepared to grant an exemption to the agreement under Article 85(3) for a period of 15 years, subject to certain conditions:

"...in view of the position URG will hold on the European reprocessing market during the currency of the authorization, the Commission feels that it must supervise the prices and conditions applied by URG. The parties must therefore be required to communicate to the Commission its prices and conditions, the contracts it concludes which relate to reprocessing or which extend the current scope of its activities, the principles of the marketing policy decided on by its Board, and its annual balance sheets and profit and loss accounts.
This will enable the Commission to follow developments in the load factors of the plans and to ensure that URG allows consumers a fair share of the benefits ... and generally complies with the competition rules of the EEC Treaty. In this connection it should be recalled that URG will remain subject to the provisions of Chapter VI of Title 2 of the Euratom Treaty, and in particular Article 75 as regards reprocessing and Article 52 as regards dealings in source materials and special fissile materials (p13)."

The Commission's related Decisions in GEC/Weir and in Carbon Technologie have been considered in Chapter 3 (see para 3.48).

4. Fuel supply contracts

Contracts between a fuel supplier and an electricity producer raise rather different problems of competition law. In particular these types of contract are often concluded for a relatively long period of time, and for a fixed volume of supply. This could result in exclusivity of either purchase or supply, with the result that competition from potential new market entrants is foreclosed.   **8.13**

A fuel supply agreement which contained prohibitions on resale, and in particular prohibitions on import or export will certainly fall within Article 85(1) and is unlikely to obtain exemption under Article 85(3) (Case 86/62 *Hasselblad* [1984] ECR 883) unless special justification can be made out (see *Industrial Gases,* discussed below).

Where a large investment is involved in fuel production or transmission facilities, these contracts may take the form of "take-or-pay" contracts. These types of contracts have, in the past, been more common to the gas sector than the electricity sector.

(i) Take-or-pay contracts

Take-or-pay (TOP) contracts are a common feature in the natural gas markets in the EC. Existing TOP arrangements were agreed as a risk sharing mechanism between producers and gas companies, whereby gas companies guarantee to pay for a prefixed annual volume at the contract price, regardless of whether that volume is taken. Thus, the volume offtake risk is shifted by these arrangements, on a long term basis, from the producers to the gas companies. The price is normally linked to the oil price and the price risk thus remains with the producers, although the risk operates in both directions as the price may rise or fall.   **8.14**

These TOP contracts were negotiated in order to reduce the risk of producers to a level sufficient to justify investing in the development of high cost gas fields. Further, the European gas market was still developing in the 1970s and 1980s so that there was no established market that guaranteed the offtake.

8.15   The Commission claims that in an interconnected European gas market such a need will exist to a much lesser extent as both the offtake security for the producer and the security of supply for the consumer will be increased (Commission memorandum on "Completion of the internal market in electricity and gas", Brussels, 15 July 1991).

In the Commission's view, in a system with open access for third parties, other ways of sharing risk (*i.e.* between producers and consumers directly) can emerge. Large users, including power stations and feedstock customers, for example, have regular long term offtake needs.

It is therefore anticipated that existing TOP contracts will have to be renegotiated and that any new TOP arrangements will have to take into account the possibility that a customer may wish to buy gas directly.

(ii) Long-term contracts for electricity generating fuels

8.16   The Commission has indicated, if only informally, that it is prepared to allow Member States to protect about 20% of their electricity production by reserving it in various ways to domestic primary energy sources. Long-term exclusive supply agreements which foreclose market opportunities for others will only be tolerated for "specified and defined reasons".

Although the Commission has indicated that this is a temporary policy, until it formulates its own "Community security of supply system", it would seem that in the meantime Member States should be allowed to continue to protect no more than 20% of electricity production on security of supply grounds (see further Chap 1).

8.17   In line with this policy, Member States, and by implication, autonomous electricity undertakings, appear to be permitted to conclude long-term contracts under the terms of which they commit themselves to purchasing a specified proportion of domestically-produced fuels.

In its Notice on the *Jahrhundertvertrag*, for example, the Commission has indicated that it is prepared to consider, despite reservations, a temporary exemption for the system of coal supply arrangements between the German electricity producers and the coalmining industry.

The arrangements leading up to privatization of the electricity industry in Scotland resulted in the notification of a series of agreements between Scottish Power, Scottish Hydro-Electric and Scottish Nuclear. In August 1990 the Commission issued a Notice indicating that it intended to adopt a "favourable position" on each of the agreements notified to it.

This initial assessment appeared to be based on the *de minimis* rule, *i.e.* the geographical location of Scotland "on the fringe of the Community" did not make electricity exchanges very probable, so that inter-state trade was unlikely to be appreciably affected by this series of agreements (Case 5/69 *Volk* v *Vervaecke* [1969] ECR 295).

In its final Decision 91/329 on Scottish Nuclear and the Nuclear Energy **8.18** Agreement, however, the Commission accepted that, given intended developments in network capacity, inter-state trade was likely to be affected by the agreement (para 31) (see Appendix 7).

The Commission was nevertheless prepared to grant exemption under Article 85(3) to the Scottish Nuclear agreement because:

"It ... allows for the long-term planning that is required for reliable production ensuring security of supply and an independent energy market." (para 33)

It was not, however, prepared to agree with the UK Government that the contracts should cover the expected lifetime of the power stations concerned. The period of validity was reduced from 30 years to 15 years.

It should be noted that in this case the relevant plant had been built **8.19** some years before, and that one of the main aims of the contract system was to allow for the eventual elimination of the substantial existing overcapacity in the Scottish nuclear industry.

It may be concluded that the Commission might be prepared to endorse longer-term periods for new projects if that period corresponds to what is required to realise a project of sufficient size to ensure reliable production and to enhance supply security.

Furthermore, the UK Government had put forward the view that it was **8.20** essential for Scottish Power and Hydro-Electric to have access to a balanced mix of different types of generating capacity in order to be financially viable and capable of independent operation (para 11). The Commission did not address this point directly, but merely remarked that for the Scottish market:

"Nuclear-power generation plays and will continue to play an important role, but there are real alternative sources of supply." (para 42)

Diversity of fuel supply has also been a primary goal in the various Community energy statements which might be loosely characterised as "Community energy policy". It would seem illogical, however, if the Commission were to accept this as a justification for long-term contracts when:

(a) the fuel supply market was already diverse; and
(b) the imposition of quotas implicit in these contracts must inevitably put other domestic and imported fuels at a disadvantage.

(iii) Notifications on privatization of electricity industry in England and Wales

A number of notifications concerning the privatization of the electricity **8.21** industry in England and Wales and in Scotland notified to the Commission in early 1990, still await a final decision by the Commission. In several cases justification for the agreement has been sought on the basis of security of supply grounds. The Commission indicated its initial position on these various notifications in a Notice pursuant to Article 19(3) of Regulation 17, published in August 1990 (these Notices are reproduced at Appendix 9).

(a) Coal supply agreements

8.22 The coal supply arrangements between British Coal and National Power and PowerGen, the two major electricity generators in England and Wales, which involve several three-year contracts specifying the quantities and the prices at which coal would be purchased by the two generating companies were notified to the Commission in August 1990.

The British Government contended that these arrangements continued joint commercial negotiations between British Coal and the two electricity generating companies when they were still divisions of the CEGB, and that arrangements which guaranteed raw material price stability for a minimum period were necessary for the orderly transition into the new electricity market.

These contentions have not so far met with Commission approval, although a final decision was expected by late 1991. In the meantime, however, the Commission has indicated that these coal supply agreements foreclose competition, and hence can only be justified in "exceptional circumstances" (para 78 of Commission Decision in NALOO complaint, 25 May 1991, discussed at para 3.85).

(b) Scottish coal

8.23 The agreement on coal-fired generating capacity between Scottish Power and Hydro-Electric, entitles the latter to a specified share of the former's coal-fired capacity. This agreement is to subsist until 31 March 2004 – the expected remaining lifetime of the plants (Case IV/33.479, OJ 1990 C245/10).

(c) Nuclear contract and associated option contracts

8.24 The British Government has put forward the view that the non-fossil fuel obligation and the contracts concluded between Nuclear Electric and the regional distribution companies acting through their joint non-fossil purchasing agency (NFPA) in order to comply with this obligation, are necessary to ensure the security of supply that results from diversity of fuel sources for electricity generation.

A similar set of contracts for renewables was also notified in August 1990, and is likely to be approved.

The NFPA arrangements were also notified separately to the Commission. The NFPA does not have exclusive rights to purchase fuels on behalf of a regional distribution company; it may only act to purchase non-fossil fuel electricity contracted in fulfillment of the NNFO and qualifying for the purposes of the fossil fuel levy.[3]

(d) Hydro

An agreement which entitles Scottish Power to a 200MW share of Hydro-Electric's hydro generating capacity, which is to subsist until 31 March 2039 has also been notified (Case IV/33.476 – Hydro Capacity Agreement). **8.25**

(e) Gas

An agreement relating to the output of the Peterhead Power Station under which Scottish Power is to benefit from the low cost electricity generated from this plant, but which also obliges the company to participate in Hydro-Electric's long-term "take-or-pay" commitment to take gas from the Miller Field, has been notified (Case IV/33.475). It should be noted that in both the Peterhead agreement and the coal-fired generating capacity agreement, one or other of the two Scottish companies may purchase fuels to meet both parties' annual requirements. **8.26**

(f) SEP/Gasunie

The Commission is currently investigating an arrangement between the Dutch electricity company SEP, and the Dutch gas company Gasunie, whereby the SEP agreed with its most important supplier of gas that it would notify it prior to entering into negotiations for gas deliveries from a third party. The Commission's investigation has already given rise to litigation, following SEP's refusal to provide certain information in relation to its supply agreements with the Norwegian company Statoil. The Commission deemed this information necessary to its investigation into the SEP/Gasunie arrangements (Case T-39/90, judgment of 12 December 1991). **8.27**

(iv) **Related Decisions**

(a) Industrial gases

The Commission has negotiated with producers of industrial gases to modify their supply terms. Together these producers accounted for approximately 95% of piped industrial gas in the Community and 75% of bulk supplies. The suppliers agreed to amend their tonnage, on-site and pipeline contracts so that supply and purchasing commitments related to quantities falling within a minimum/maximum range. The Commission accepted that tonnage contracts might continue to be made for 15 years having regard to the high level of investment necessary in the provision of long term supplies (Nineteenth Report on Competition Policy, 1989). **8.28**

---

[3] Purchasing cartels will usually be struck down when they attempt to control the price or rate of supply of essential raw materials. It is, however, possible for exemption to be given under Art 85(3) if the cartel yields the required advantages, *e.g.* improvement of production or distribution and where consumers' share in these benefits. See the Commission's Decision in *National Sulphuric Association* [1980] 3 CMLR 429. An extension for this agreement was granted in 1989 (OJ 1989 L190).

5. Agreements relating to transmission and interconnection

8.29   In general technical agreements having as their sole object the joint use of production facilities and storing and transport equipment are not usually viewed by the Commission as restricting competition because:

> "...they are confined to organizational and technical arrangements for the uses of the facilities. There may be a restraint of competition if the enterprises involved do not bear the cost of utilization of the installation or equipment themselves or if the agreements are concluded or concerted practices applied regarding joint production or the sharing out of production or the establishment or running of a joint enterprise," (Notice on Co-operation Agreements, July 1968, JO 1968 C75/3).

(i) Interconnection agreements which restrict imports and exports

8.30   In its Decision 91/50, *IJsselcentrale,* the Commission concluded that an absolute control over imports and exports via the international interconnectors and high transmission wires owned by the Dutch electricity producers could not be justified under Article 85(3) or Article 90(2) (see para 3.41 and Chaps 4 and 6).

The Commission also indicated that the intended period of validity of the OVS, the agreement at issue, at 25 years probably exceeded the acceptable length necessary for this type of agreement (Commission Decision 91/50, *loc cit* para 47). It did not make any further recommendations on this matter, however.

(ii) Pooling and Settlement Agreement (PSA) between National Grid Company, generators and distributors

8.31   In the view of the Commission, the PSA, which is a key aspect of the new arrangements for the privatised electricity industry in England and Wales, is not considered as an agreement which restricts or distorts competition, and it is not expected to distort or result in disclosure of contract prices agreed between generators and suppliers or generators and final consumers.[4] Further, trade between Member States is not restricted because membership of the pool is open, and indeed the French utility, EDF, is a member.

---

[4] Agreements which restrict access to public markets are closely supervised by DGIV and any restrictive provisions which cause detriment to member or non–member traders or to consumers will be likely to be found in breach of Art 85(1) Case 71/74 *FRUBO* [1975] ECR 563. In its decision in *Sarabex* the Commission was only prepared to grant exemption for an agreement between an association of London foreign exchange dealers when it had secured amendments to the rules of membership which guaranteed that entry would be based on objective criteria [1979] 1 CMLR 262. Negative clearance has also been granted for associations of dealers in a number of commodity markets, but only following deletion of the various provisions on fixed rate commissions and the introduction of revised membership rules based on objective and non-discriminatory criteria (Fifteenth Report on Competition Policy, pp 72–73 and Decision of 13 December 1985, OJ 1985 L369).

(iii) National Grid Company: Grid Code and Connection and use of system agreements

Although the Grid Code is not in itself an agreement, compliance with it is **8.32** required by the Connection and use of system agreements, and indeed these agreements provide for the contractual enforceability of the Grid Code between industry parties.

Finally, the Scottish Interconnector Agreement, which is designed to provide Hydro-Electric with an "import/export" corridor across Scottish Power's high voltage grid to the English and Welsh markets is also to be exempted.

These two sets of agreements were given prima facie approval by the Commission on the ground that they were necessary to facilitate continuity and diversity of supply. The Distribution Code and the Distributors' use of system and connection agreements have received approval on the same basis, as have the Scottish Interconnector Agreement[5] and British Grid Systems Agreement, and the Scottish System Operation Agreement (Case IV/33.478, OJ 1990 C245/12).

Problems of competition law may arise because the generator may **8.33** require that certain ancillary services as specified in the Grid Code must be purchased by the NGC where this is necessary to maintain system stability etc. The costs of these ancillary services are automatically passed on to the suppliers who pay through an uplift to the pool input price. This may potentially raise problems under Article 85(1)(e), or indeed under Article 86 if the ancillary services are considered unjustly "tied".

The three-year agreements between EDF and the National Grid Company for the use of a "substantial part" of the Continental Europe Interconnector which is jointly owned by the NGC/EDF was also notified. In fact if imported electricity is to count towards non-fossil capacity for the purposes of section 32(5)(a) of the Electricity Act 1989 then there must be a collateral contract for the conveyance by means of an interconnector, of the capacity in the purchase contract between the relevant distribution company and EDF.[6] The latter is a member of the pool and all electricity supplied by it is to be sold through the pool.[7]

6. Horizontal co-operation agreements

(i) Agreements between producers

Article 85(1)(b) prohibits agreements which "limit or control...markets" **8.34** and Article 85(1)(c) prohibits agreements which "share markets or sources of supply".

---

[5] Case IV/33.611 – NGC-Scottish Interconnector Agreement and British Grid Systems Agreement, OJ 1990 C245/12.
[6] Electricity (Imported Capacity) Regs 1990, SI 1990/265.
[7] Note however that the electricity supplied by EDF is not subject to the fossil fuel levy.

Article 85(1) will be infringed by an agreement to a territorial division of a market (see for example, Case 246/86 *Belasco* [1989] ECR 2181).

8.35 Agreements to limit or control production in national markets are also prohibited by virtue of Article 85(1)(b). In *Italian Flat Glass* (OJ 1980 L383/19) the Commission condemned the fixing of quotas for cast glass established on the Italian market as this restricted competition at the national level, as well as affecting the ability to export elsewhere in the EC.

The question of whether a state-imposed quota on output, imposed for example, in the context of a national energy plan, may potentially be caught be Article 85(1) in certain circumstances it is difficult to answer.

8.36 In Case 148/85 *Forest* [1986] ECR 3449 the Court dealt with a French system of state-imposed quotas on flour for milling under Articles 30 and 37 EEC, although the potential application of the competition rules to the state regulation imposing the quota had also been raised during the proceedings.

Both the Commission and the Advocate-General rejected this latter line of argument as inapplicable to this particular case. First, there was no question of the regulation in question compelling or encouraging the conclusion of restrictive practices; second, the rule at issue was not capable of having an effect on inter-state trade (see Advocate-General Misho at 3468).

In Case 136/86 *BNIC* v *Aubert* [1987] ECR 4789 at 4815 the Court examined the legality of quota arrangements between French brandy producers under Article 85(1). It held that in this case, where the French State had reinforced the effects of agreements concluded in breach of the Treaty, by enacting a ministerial decree extending the scope of that agreement, and by obliging all economic operators active in the sector to accept it, then the Member State was in breach of its obligations under Articles 3(f), 5 and 85 EEC.

(ii) Collective purchasing agreements

8.37 Collective agreements to purchase raw materials exclusively through agreed arrangements normally infringe Article 85(1).

In its Decision in *National Sulphuric Acid Association* the Commission considered an agreement in which most manufacturers in the United Kingdom agreed to combine and purchase through a "sulphur pool". The agreement was originally set up to counter the market power of the few suppliers on the world market. The Commission exempted the agreement on the condition that the members agreed to buy no more than 25% of their requirements from the pool. The Commission also ruled that the arrangements led to a more flexible and secure system of supply and that the resulting benefits, in the form of lower prices, would be passed on to consumers. The original exemption has recently been extended to 1998 (OJ 1989 L190/22).

In Case 61/80 *Cooperatieve Stremsel* v *Commission* [1981] ECR 851 the Court of Justice upheld the Commission's decision condemning a collective purchasing agreement involving a 100% purchase commitment from a common organization.

(iii) **Information sharing**

Exchange of information agreements may in certain circumstances operate as a substitute for price fixing agreements and will usually infringe Article 85(1). The exchange of information on costs may also amount to an infringement[8], as could the exchange of information on investment (*Zinc Producer Group*, OJ 1984 L220/27). In general the exchange of any confidential business information will be regarded with suspicion.[9]

8.38

(iv) **Eurelectric notification**

In November 1990 the members of Eurelectric (that is the European producers and distributors of electricity) notified to the Commission an agreement concerning the exchange of electricity within the Community via the creation of a type of spot-market.

8.39

The agreement envisages the extension of the existing system of information on short-term surpluses of electricity operated on behalf of its members by UNCPTE.[10] The aim is to create a systematic basis of information exchange between the dispatching services of the members of UNCPTE. On the basis of this information the members may conclude bilateral purchase or sale agreements, on conditions and at prices to be determined on an individual basis. The agreement is silent on the question of transit for or on behalf of parties other than members of the major electricity organizations – UNIPEDE, UCPTE and NORDEL.[11]

The Commission has not yet taken a position on the notification.

7. **Sectoral agreements**

In a number of related sectors, including road, rail and inland waterways, air and sea transport and insurance, the Council has adopted specific rules

8.40

[8] See *TEKO* (OJ 1990 L134/34) joint risk assessment in machinery insurance. The exchange of calculation models will not generally infringe Art 85(1), however, – see, Commission Notice on Co–operation Agreements July 1968, Section II (1), (JO 1968 C75/3).

[9] See *European Wastepaper Information Service,* Eighteenth Report on Competition Policy 1989, pt 63.

[10] The UCPTE, set up in 1951, is responsible for technical co-ordination of the continental European grid network (the UK, Ireland, the Scandinavian countries and the East-European countries are *not* members).

[11] UNIPEDE – Union Internationale des Producteurs et Distributeurs d'Energie Electrique; UCPTE – Union pour la Coordination de la Production et du Transport d'Electricité; NORDEL – the Association of Electrical Companies in North Europe.

to deal with technical co-operation between firms, and in several cases the Commission has adopted block exemptions, defining technical agreements to which Article 85(1) does not apply.

These specialised regimes cannot be dealt with in any detail here, but certain aspects which may be of relevance to the future development of competition policy towards the electricity sector can be briefly considered.

(i) Road, rail and inland waterways

8.41   Council Regulation (EEC) 1017/68 (JO 1968 L175/1) lays down special rules for the application of Articles 85 and 86 to these sectors.

The Commission has published one Decision under this Regulation on the EATE levy (OJ 1985 L219/35) in which it condemned an agreement between French waterway carriers and French forwarding agents imposing a levy of 10% on freight charges for boat charters to destinations outside France. This discriminated against non-French carriers.[12]

In November 1987 the British and French partners in the Euro-tunnel project notified a usage contract concluded between British Rail and the French SNCF (*Eurotunnel II*, OJ 1988 C292/2). The Commission exempted the agreement for a period of three years, and in January 1989 the parties requested an extension of this exemption for the duration of the agreement – 55 years.

In March 1990 the Commission sent a memorandum to various national railway companies on the implementation of the Community competition rules. It drew the companies' attention to two basic principles. The first is that any public or private undertaking in a dominant position for the purchase of goods or services is subject to obligations equivalent to those incumbent on a dominant supplier. The second is that any undertaking in a dominant position either as purchaser or seller is under the obligation not to practise any discrimination between suppliers or between customers in the various Member States of the Community. This means that a rail undertaking may not set out to obtain the supply of goods or services exclusively from undertakings in its country or from its traditional suppliers (Twentieth Report on Competition Policy, pt 115).

(ii) Maritime transport

8.42   Regulation (EEC) 4056/86 (OJ 1986 L 378/14) lays down detailed substantive and procedural rules in respect of the sea transport sector. Articles 3 and 4 provide block exemptions for "liner conference agreements" and agreements between carriers concerning the operation of scheduled services. In June 1990 the Commission proposed to the Council an elaboration of the block exemption procedures in this sector,

---

[12] The Court upheld the Commission on appeal: Case 272/85 *ANTIB* v *Commission* [1987] ECR 2201.

including a proposal for block exemptions for consortia agreements, including those containing provisions for multi-modal transport (OJ 1990 C167/9).

The Commission has generally taken an unfavourable view of agreements which provide for mutual exchange of information and co-operation on tariffs and transport conditions which will restrict price competition in maritime transport (Agreement 1237, OJ 1990 C59/2).

It has indicated that it would exempt similar types of information exchange agreements where membership to the agreement is open and each party retains the right to act independently (*Gulfway Agreement*, OJ 1990 C130/3); *Eurocode*, OJ 1990 C162/13).

(iii) **Air transport**

This controversial area has been the subject of a number of "liberalization **8.43** packages". The first package, adopted in 1987, comprises two Regulations.[13] Regulation (EEC) 3975/87 (OJ 1987 L374/1) lays down procedural rules which correspond to those provided by Regulation 17, except that notification is not obligatory. Regulation (EEC) 3976/87 (OJ 1987 L374/9) empowers the Commission to publish block exemptions. In 1988 the Commission issued three exemptions. Regulation (EEC) 2671/88 deals with joint planning and co-ordination of capacity, sharing of revenue and consultations on tariffs for scheduled air services and slot allocations at airports. Regulation (EEC) 2672/88 deals with computer reservations for air transport services, and Regulation (EEC) 2673/88 on ground handling services.[14]

A second package of measures was adopted in August 1990. Regulations (EEC) 2342, 2343 and 2344/90 and 294/91 provide that the Council shall regulate for such matters as access for air carriers to scheduled intra-Community routes, route licensing, capacity restrictions and cabotage traffic rights.

A third package of measures on access for air carriers and on fares and rate for services was submitted by the Commission to the Council in July 1991 (OJ 1991 C258/10-19).

In general the Commission has been prepared to exempt technical co-operation agreements provided that a number of conditions are satisfied: consultations on tariffs must not lead to the elimination of price competition or the elimination of competition from potential new entrants to the market. The basic principle is that a newcomer should be allowed to compete on equal terms (see Twentieth Report on Competition Policy, pt 73).

---

[13] For a useful summary, see Seventeenth Report on Competition Policy, 1987, pts 43–45.
[14] These Regulations expired in January 1991 and have been extended by new block exemptions adopted in December 1990; Reg (EEC) 82/91, Reg (EEC) 83/91 and Reg (EEC) 89/91 (OJ 1990 L10/7–14).

Where a dominant airline refuses to admit a new competitor on an established route, by refusing to sell it certain services, this may amount to an abuse of a dominant position.[15]

(iv) Insurance

8.44 In May 1991 the Council adopted Regulation (EEC) 1534/91 on the application of Article 85(3) to certain categories of agreements, decisions and concerted practices in the insurance sector. This Regulation empowers the Commission to adopt a Regulation granting block exemption to certain categories of agreements which have as their object co-operation with respect to, *inter alia:*

(a) the establishment of common risk premium tariffs based on collectively ascertained statistics or the number of claims;
(b) the establishment of common standard policy conditions;
(c) the common coverage of certain types of risks;
(d) the settlement of claims.

The Commission Regulation is to define the categories of agreements to which it applies and to further specify the restrictions or clauses which may or may not appear in the agreements and the clauses which must be contained in the agreements or the other practices which must be satisfied.

8. Long-term agreements between electricity suppliers and customers: vertical agreements

(i) Block exemptions on exclusive distribution and exclusive purchasing agreements

8.45 It would appear unlikely that a contractual arrangement between a producer and a distributor would qualify for exemption under either Regulation (EEC) 83/83 (OJ 1983 L173) which provides for block exemption for certain exclusive dealing arrangements, or Regulation (EEC) 84/83 (OJ 1983 L173) which grants block exemption for certain categories of exclusive purchasing agreements.

Article 1 of Regulation (EEC) 83/83 reads:

> "Pursuant to Article 85(93) of the Treaty and subject to the provisions of this Regulation, is hereby declared that Article 85(1) of the Treaty shall not apply to agreements to which only two undertakings are party and whereby one party agrees with the other to supply certain goods for resale within the whole or a defined area of the common market only to that other."

---

[15] See the Commissions's approach to Lufthansa's refusal to "interline" with Air Europe. The relevant Press Notice is discussed in Jones and van der Woude, "Competition Law Checklist", (1990) EL Rev 61.

Article 1 of Regulation 84/83 is expressed in similar terms:

"…Article 85(1)…shall not apply to agreements to which only two undertakings are party and whereby one party the reseller, agrees with the other, the supplier, to purchase certain goods specified in the agreement for resale only from the supplier or from a connected undertaking or from another undertaking which the supplier, to purchase certain goods specified in the agreement for resale only from the supplier…"

(ii) Conditions for benefiting from either exemption

In order to benefit from either exemption, a number of cumulative conditions should be met: **8.46**

(a) Resale

Both Regulations apply only to goods supplied for resale to others. If the dealer acquires the goods for processing and transformation then there is no resale.

The Commission's Notice of 22 June 1983 concerning the application of the two Regulations (OJ 1984 C101/2) explains that:

"the criterion is that the goods distributed are the same as those the other party has supplied to him for that purpose" (para 9).

It would appear doubtful that an electricity distributor which is required to take electricity from a high-voltage network, convert it and re-supply it to customers via a low- or medium-voltage network is involved in a resale transaction.

(b) Bilateral agreements

Only bilateral agreements are covered, that is one supplier and one dealer, although according to paragraph 14 of the explanatory notice the supplier may enter into a series of bilateral exclusive agreements with various dealers and retain the exemption. **8.47**

Further Article 3(c) of Regulation (EEC) 83/83 stipulates that no exemption lies where:

"users can obtain the contract goods in the territory only from the exclusive distributor and have no alternative source of supply outside the contract territory."

In addition, in accordance with Article 3(d), the exemption will not apply if:

"one or both of the parties makes it difficult for intermediaries or users to obtain the contract goods from other dealers inside the common market or, in so far as no alternative source of supply is available there, from outside the common market, in particular where one or both of them … exercises other rights or takes other measures so as to prevent dealers or users from obtaining outside or from selling in, the contract territory contract goods."

As paragraph 33 of the Notice of 22 June 1983 makes clear, the block exemption ceases to apply as from the moment that either of the parties takes measures to impede parallel imports into the contract territory. Agreements in which the supplier undertakes with the exclusive distributor to prevent his other customers from supplying into the contract territory are ineligible for the block exemption from the outset.

(c) Competing manufacturers

The block exemption does not apply if either the parties themselves or undertakings connected with them, are manufacturers, manufacture goods belonging to the same product market and enter into exclusive distribution or purchasing agreements with one another (Arts 3(a) and (b), 4 and 5).

(iii) Exclusive distribution agreements falling outside the block exemption

8.49 The legality of vertical agreements between suppliers and customers may be attacked if the relevant contracts contain exclusionary provisions which have the effect of foreclosing competition on that market. It must of course be demonstrated that the relevant contractual provisions have an effect on inter-state trade (see further Chap 3).

The following factors should be taken into account:

(a) Is the market concentrated?

In *Hoffman-La Roche* the Commission observed:

> "An undertaking which is in a dominant position on a market and ties purchasers (even if it does so at their request) by an obligation or a promise on their part to obtain all or most of their requirements exclusively from the said undertakings abuses its dominant position within the meaning of Article 86 of the Treaty whether the obligation is stipulated without further qualification or whether it is undertaken in consideration of the grant of a rebate." (Case 85/76 [1979] ECR 461 at 539; see also the Commission's Decision in *ICI*, below.)

(b) Do the contracts foreclose the market?

8.50 The existence of a network of exclusive purchasing arrangements may also indicate a tendency to market foreclosure and is viewed with caution by the Commission.

(c) Quantities: fixed volumes or proportions of buyers' requirements

8.51 Whereas the Commission is unlikely to take objection to clauses expressed simply as a fixed volume, it takes a stricter view of requirements contracts concluded for a particular duration. In *BP Kemi* (see below) the Commission observed:

> "When a purchasing obligation of a longer duration is entered into, the relationship of supply is frozen and the role of offer and demand is eliminated to the disadvantage of *inter alia* new competitors who are thereby prevented

from supply this customer and old competitors who in the meantime may have become more competitive than the actual supplier."

Contracts expressed in volume terms, but with equivalent effect to an exclusive purchasing clause may of course be condemned (see *British Industrial Sand Limited*, Sixth Report on Competition Policy, 1976, paras 122-125).

(d) Duration

The longer the duration of the agreement the greater the risk is that the market is foreclosed from competition from potential rival suppliers. The duration of the contract may be justifiable if the supplier has been required to undertake substantial investments, so that the exclusive purchase contract is a means of securing a return on that investment. Alternatively, from the purchaser's point of view, a long-term contract may offer a necessary degree of security of supply.

8.52

In Case 247/86 *Alsatel* v *Novam* [1988] ECR 5987 (see below), a 15 year exclusive rental contract for telecommunications equipment had been challenged as abusive contrary to Article 86. Advocate-General Mancini observed that with regard to the duration of the contract, the national court would have to ascertain to what extent it was necessary for the activities of the supplier, Alsatel, and for the amortization of the capital invested by it. Further, it might be necessary to take into consideration the value of the equipment brought into service, the price paid by the user of the installation and the relationship between the amount of the rent and the cost of maintenance (at 6003).

Article 3(d) of Regulation (EEC) 84/83 provides that no exemption exists for exclusive purchasing agreements if the agreement is concluded for an indefinite duration or for a period of more than five years.

Agreements which specify a fixed term but are automatically renewable unless one of the parties gives notice to terminate are to be considered to have been concluded for an indefinite period.

(iv) **Commission Decisions relating to supply contracts**

In the following section, a number of Commission Decisions which have a bearing on supply contracts in the electricity sector are discussed.

8.53

(a) Producers and distributors

In those Member States where the ESI is not vertically-integrated it is not uncommon for electricity producers and distribution companies to negotiate long-term supply agreements. These may often take the form of *evergreen* contracts, that is fixed quantity requirements contracts which run for an indefinite period, with a fixed term period for notice of termination. Restrictions on further resale are also not uncommon (see for example, the description of the "pyramid" of contractual arrangements in the Dutch electricity sector in Dec 91/50 *IJsselcentrale* – see para 3.41).

In two recent Decisions and in a Notice, the Commission has taken a strict approach to these types of contracts where they have been imposed by a dominant supplier.

(b) Shotton

8.54 In its Notice on *Shotton* (OJ 1990 C106/3) the Commission took objection to a three year purchasing agreement concluded by Shotton, a major British newsprint producer, with two of the largest waste-paper suppliers in the United Kingdom. Shotton is bound to purchase at least 85% of certain specified quantities of waste paper for use as feedstock which the suppliers must deliver.

The new conversion plant envisaged would enable Shotton to almost triple its present output of newspaper. It involved substantial investment in the technology used in treating printed wood-containing paper suitable for de-inking. The purpose of the agreements is to give Shotton security of supply during the plant's start up period. The quantities concerned do not exceed 10% of the UK demand for waste-paper, but imports are negligible.

The agreements have been amended so that the provisions for joint supply of Shotton's total requirements, access by Shotton to the actual prices paid by the supplier's other customers and a right of first refusal for the supply of any additional quantities were removed at the Commission's request.

(c) Industrial Gases

8.55 In *Industrial Gases* the Commission obtained a commitment that requirements contracts for a fixed percentage of customers' needs would be abandoned. The producers also agreed to eliminate restrictions on resale. If on safety grounds, such restrictions were considered essential, the relevant contractual provisions would be notified to the Commission (Nineteenth Report on Competition Policy).[16]

(d) ICI

8.56 In *ICI* (Dec 91/300, OJ 1991 L152/40) the Commission ruled that ICI has abused the dominant position which it holds on the market for soda-ash in the United Kingdom by applying to its major customers a system of loyalty rebates and discounts by reference to marginal tonnage ("top-slice" rebates), contractual arrangements tending to ensure an effective exclusivity of supply for ICI and other devices which have had the object and effect to tying the said customers to ICI for the whole of their requirements and excluding competitors.

Practices designed to block the access of competitors to customers by tying the latter to the dominant supplier are an established form of abusive contract under EEC competition law (Case 40/73 *Suiker Unie* v *Commission;* Case 85/76 *Hoffman-La Roche* v *Commission;* Case 322/81 *Michelin* – see Chap 3).

---

[16] See also *Bayo-n-ox,* OJ 1990 L21/71, for the Commission's attitude to industrial supply agreements which required customers to use the product only to cover their own use requirements.

Until 1979 ICI offered its customers "evergreen contracts" with a two-year notice of termination and which stipulated that the buyer must obtain its total requirements from ICI. This practice was adjusted so that customers were offered a range of contract options which included running contracts on a total requirements basis but terminable on shorter notice (three to six months notice after one year).

The Commission considered that total requirements clauses even for shorter periods were unacceptable in terms of the Community rules. The Commission also objected to the "competition clause" or "English clause", which required the customer to notify ICI of any offer they received from a competitor, "since it would effectively have excluded the possibility that any competitive offer could ever succeed" (para 13).

In addition the Commission took objection to the system of "top-slicing" **8.57** rebates which ICI offered customers, who in addition to the "core" tonnage which they would normally have been expected to take from a major supplier, induced them to buy marginal tonnage (or top-slice) which they might otherwise have purchased from a competitor.

ICI denied that these "top-slice" rebates were motivated by any exclusionary intent and that they were merely related to the large quantities contracted for. The Commission claimed that this assertion was in direct contradiction to the strategy revealed by ICI's own internal documents.

Further, the substantial variations in the "trigger" tonnages at which the rebate was activated, demonstrated that the rebate system and the price advantages which it conferred were not dependent on differences in cost to ICI in relation to the quantities supplied (para 56).

The Commission further ruled that:

> "It is clearly established in law that where a dominant undertaking ties   **8.58** customers – even at their request – by an obligation or promise to obtain the whole or substantially the whole of their requirements exclusively from that undertaking, this will constitute an infringement of Article 86. It is irrelevant whether the obligation in question is stipulated for without further qualification or whether it is undertaken in consideration of the grant of a rebate" (para 57).

The Commission therefore ordered ICI to terminate these practices and to terminate its system of rebates, so that any new system of rebates "would be confined to reflecting in a fair and objective manner the cost savings involved in large tonnage orders." It further imposed a substantial fine of 10 million ECU on ICI. ICI has appealed against this Decision.

(e) Solvay

In the related Decision 91/298 *Solvay* (OJ 1991 L152/16) the Commission   **8.59** imposed fines of ECU 20 million on the Belgian chemical company for abusing its dominant position by foreclosing competition on the market for soda-ash. Solvay was found to have operated a system of fidelity rebates and other inducements to exclusivity which reinforced the links between its customers and their dominant supplier.

Solvay was required to abandon its rebates system and to discontinue its practice of offering "evergreen" contracts with long notice period requirements. Customers should be free to decide for themselves the tonnage they wish to commit to Solvay under "evergreen" contracts, and they should be able to change to anther supplier having given Solvay six months notice. Fixed term supply contracts should not exceed one year.

In conclusion, restrictive clauses may be justified in certain cases, where, for example, they are necessary to ensure investment in a new process, or to ensure security of supply. Special discounts and rebates for large customers must be commercially acceptable and objectively justifiable. Much depends on the market power of the parties to the agreement and on the facts and circumstances of each case. The general rule must always be that, where there is any doubt as to the compatibility of an agreement, it should be notified to the Commission.

9. Option agreements for electricity purchases in England and Wales

8.60   The Commission has indicated that it is prepared to accept that the option contracts concluded between National Power, PowerGen and the 12 regional distribution companies in England and Wales, are a necessary step in the restructuring of the industry and to an orderly transition to full competition (Cases IV/33.466 and 33.467, OJ 1990 C191/11).

The purpose of these contracts is to ensure greater predictability of prices for the supply of electricity by allowing the holder to hedge against fluctuations of the pool price. The option contracts are intended to reproduce the economic effect of longer term electricity supply contracts at predetermined prices. They have a duration of three years.

The initial option contracts were jointly negotiated prior to the restructuring of the British industry in March 1990. They are designed to enable the parties to have a degree of certainty about costs and revenue streams and to take account of various undertakings sought by the UK Government. These included the commitment to stable prices for end users and the guarantee that the regional companies will purchase the necessary volume of electricity in order to guarantee the production by National Power and PowerGen of coal-generated electricity.

10. Distributors and large customers

8.61   Distributors as well as producers, must refrain from market division. In Cases 100-103/80 *MDF* v *Commission* [1983] ECR 1825 the Court upheld the Commission's Decision that the distributors had engaged in concerted practices among themselves to isolate the market in question.[17]

(i) Market sharing agreements

Market sharing agreements which divide the market by sectors or classes of **8.62** customer have also been condemned by the Commission.

In *BP Kemi/DDSF*, BP Kemi, a subsidiary of BPCL, the major EC producer of synthetic ethanol, concluded an agreement with DDSF, the largest supplier of ethanol in Denmark, under the terms of which the latter, having ceased production of the product, agreed to purchase its total requirements from BP Kemi for six years. It was understood that BP Kemi would continue to supply its large customers (taking over 100,000 gallons per year) while DDSF supplied by BP Kemi, would supply small customers. BP Kemi agreed to limit its direct sales to 25% of the combined sales of BP Kemi and DDSF and to pay compensation if that limit was exceeded. The Commission ruled that the sectorial division of the market between the two companies infringed Article 85(1) (OJ 1979 L286/32).

Although the Commission has exempted territorial limitations in the context of R & D, specialization or joint production agreements, as well as in the context of distribution agreements, it will rarely condone absolute territorial protection. As Bellamy and Child have observed, this is almost a *"per se"* rule (at 253).

(ii) Abusive conditions

Exclusive purchasing or exclusive supply contracts between distributors **8.63** and large customers are in principle subject to the same principles of Community law as discussed in section 8 dealing with producers and distributors. A number of factors should be borne in mind however. First, the potential effect of this category of agreements on inter-state trade must be considered. In order for Article 85, or if relevant, Article 86 to apply, it will be necessary to demonstrate that the contractual terms at issue are capable of impeding imports or exports. Second, where the distributor enjoys a regional monopoly as opposed to a national monopoly, it will be necessary to show that the distributor is nevertheless dominant on the relevant product and geographical market if Article 86 is to apply.

(iii) Abusive conditions in regional arrangements

The problems which may arise in connection with the application of the **8.64** EC competition rules to regional monopolies are well illustrated by the Court's judgment in Case 247/86 *Alsatel* v *Novasam* [1988] ECR 5987.

Novasam entered into a series of contracts with Alsatel, a telecom-

---

[17] See also, however, the Commission's Decision in *Flat Glass*, where the behaviour of the wholesalers was not considered to have been the result of autonomous action.

munications rental equipment company. The rental contracts were concluded for a period of 15 years and were renewable by tacit agreement for further five-year terms. Under the terms of the contract, however, the contract was to restart its initial duration, if, as a result of one or more modifications, the initial rental period is increased by an amount equal to or greater than 25%, the basis being the rental specified in the supplements to the contract. In other words the rental was indeterminate. In addition all modifications to the installations could only be made by Alsatel.

Alsatel held approximately one-third of a share of the regional market – a share virtually identical to that held by the state-owned post and telecommunications authorities. In addition, it operated under a standard form of licence granted by these same authorities. The territorial limits of these licence rights were national, and not regional, however.

Novasem terminated the contracts and refused to comply with the penalty clauses. Alsatel brought an action in the *tribunal de grande instance* in Strasbourg, for non payment of the liquidated damages. Novasam invoked a "Euro-Defence", namely that Alsatel had abused its dominant position, contrary to Article 86 EEC. The national court stayed the proceedings and requested the Court of Justice for an interpretation of Article 86.

8.65   In the proceedings before the national court, however, Novasem alleged that the contract clauses at issue were identical to contracts used by other telecommunication installation companies. Furthermore Alsatel belonged to various national associations and was a member of Intertel, a consortium of French companies accounting for over half of the applications lodged for approval with the national telecommunications authorities. The remainder of the market was accounted for by a large number of competitors which were potential competitors, but which, as a result of inter-locking share ownerships with members of the Intertel group, had no real opportunity to compete freely.

Novasem alleged that in these circumstances, there was evidence of parallel behaviour, which potentially fell under the prohibition against concerted practices in Article 85(1). The Commission supported this interpretation of the facts at issue.

8.66   Neither the Court nor the Advocate-General were impressed by the arguments under Article 85(1). There was little concrete evidence before the Court of concerted behaviour, and that which was available appeared contradictory. The Court ruled:

> " If the large share of the regional market held by the plaintiff was the result of an agreement between authorized installers to share out regional markets between them, such an agreement ought to be caught by Article 85 of the Treaty. It is only if such an allocation of markets were carried out by a number of undertakings belonging to the same group that Article 86 could be applicable."[18]

---

[18] For a review of the Court's existing jurisprudence on this point, see the Advocate-General's Opinion at 6002.

The Court declined to examine the allegations of parallel conduct in the absence of suitable evidence.

The Court was also unsympathetic to the arguments advanced under Article 86. It acknowledged that some, but not all of the contested contractual terms might be abusive:

> "Although the obligation imposed on customers to deal exclusively with the installer as regards any modification of the installation may be justified by the fact that the equipment remains the property of the installer, the fact that the price is unilaterally fixed by the installer and the automatic renewal of the contract for a 15-year term ... may constitute unfair trading conditions prohibited as abusive practices by Article 86 of the Treaty..." (para 10).

Nevertheless it remained to be seen whether that abuse amounted to an **8.67** abuse of a dominant position within the meaning of Article 86, and in particular whether it affected trade between Member States. If the contractual clauses referred to had the effect of restricting imports and partitioning the market, the latter condition would obviously be fulfilled.

As to the former condition, the Court recalled the test it had formulated in Case 322/81 *Michelin* [1983] ECR 3461. A dominant position can be inferred where an enterprise enjoys sufficient market strength to hinder the maintenance of effective competition by allowing it to behave to an appreciable extent independently of its competitors and customers. This in turn would depend on the strength of the undertaking on the relevant product and geographical markets.

In this case, it will be remembered, the authorizations to supply **8.68** equipment were valid throughout the whole of the national territory. Hence the Court ruled:

> "It follows that the framework within which the conditions of competition are sufficiently homogenous to enable the economic strength of the undertaking in question to be assessed in the market for telephone installations throughout France" (para 15).

Hence the contractual practices, even although abusive, did not fall within the prohibition of Article 86 as the undertaking did not occupy a dominant position on the relevant market.

(iv) **Bodson**

Alsatel may be contrasted to the Court's ruling in Case 30/87 *Bodson* [1988] **8.69** ECR 2479 where the Court held that Article 86 did apply in a case in which a number of communal concessional monopolies are granted to a single group of undertakings whose market strategy is determined by the parent company, where the monopoly extends over a substantial part of the national territory and affects imports. Article 86 may further apply where such a group of undertakings charges unfair prices even though the level of prices is fixed by the contract specifications which form part of the conditions of the contract for the concession (para 35).

CONTENTS OF CHAPTER 9

Chapter 9
Electricity and the Environment

1. Introduction

In Part I of this chapter the impact of the new Title on Environment, added **9.1** to the EEC Treaty by the Single European Act is examined.* This is followed by a discussion on the application of the general principles of Community law on national measures aimed at protecting the environment. The next section goes on to analyse environmental protection measures, such as taxes, fiscal incentives and subsidies and the relevant EEC Treaty rules. The final section deals with environmental protection measures under the Euratom Treaty. Part II looks at the relevant secondary legislation on electricity and the environment. The Commission's current proposals on energy and environmental matters are outlined in Part III.

Part I
2. EEC Treaty provisions

(i) New environmental title

The Single European Act added a new Title VII on environment to the **9.2** EEC Treaty. Prior to the adoption of the Single European Act, environmental measures were based on either Articles 100 or 235 EEC.

Article 130R(1) sets the following objectives for Community action relating to the environment:

"to preserve, protect and improve the quality of the environment;
to contribute towards protecting human health;
to ensure a prudent and rational utilization of natural resources."

Article 130R(2) sets out the principles on which Community action should be based. These are:
– that preventive action should be taken,
– that environmental damage should be rectified at source, and
– that the polluter should pay.

Finally, "Environmental policy is to be a component of the Community's other policies."

---

* This chapter does not examine the implications of the amendments to Articles 130 R-T in the new Treaty of Union signed on 7 February 1992, which is expected to enter into force on 1 January 1993.

209

9.3   The Council Resolution of 3 March 1975 (OJ 1975 C168/2) had already placed the Community and the Member States under a duty to "take environmental protection requirements into account in all energy policy strategy by taking effective measures."

The Communities' commitment to the pursuance of a balanced policy towards energy and environmental goals has been repeated on a number of occasions. That the commitment is beginning to take concrete form is evident from the latest proposals for draft Directives on competition in electricity markets, discussed in earlier chapters.

9.4   Article 130R(3) states that in preparing its action relating to the environment, the Community shall take account of:
– available scientific and technical data;
– environmental conditions in the various regions of the Community;
– the potential benefits and costs of action or lack of action;
– the economic and social development of the Community as a whole and the balanced development of its regions.

Article 130R(4) sets out the "subsidiarity principle":

"The Community is to act only to the extent to which the objectives referred to in Article 130R(1) can be attained better at Community level than at the level of the individual Member States."

9.5   Article 130R(5) deals with relations with third countries:

"Within their respective spheres of competence the Community and the Member States shall co-operate with third countries and with the relevant international organizations. The arrangements for Community co-operation may be the subject of agreements between the Community and the third parties concerned, which shall be negotiated and concluded in accordance with Article 228.

The previous paragraph shall be without prejudice to Member States' competence to negotiate in international bodies and to conclude international agreements."

(ii) Scope of Community's environmental policy

9.6   The term "environment" is not defined. Further, secondary Community legislation does not provide any explicit definition of the term. Council Directive 85/337/EEC (see below) on the assessment of the effects of certain public and private projects on the environment mentions:

"– human beings, fauna and flora;
– soil, water, air climate and the landscape;
– the interaction between the factors mentioned in the first and second indents;
– material assets and the cultural heritage."

The "working environment" is not covered by Title VII, but by Article 118A. Consequently, measures to protect the working environment must be based on either Article 118A or 100A, depending on their content.

There is no geographical limitation on the "environment" which the **9.7** Community may legislate to protect. Consequently the Community can take measures to protect the environment even outside the territory covered by the Treaty, such as, for example, measures to protect tropical rain forests or to protect the ozone layer. It is also submitted that there can be no distinction between the "Community environment" and a national, regional or local environment. Measures taken by the Community need not be restricted to transfrontier problems.

The Declaration of the Member States on Article 130R(1) states that:

"the Community's activities in the sphere of the environment may not interfere with national policies regarding the exploitation of energy resources."

The scope and legal status of this Declaration is doubtful.[1]

(a) "Polluter pays principle" and state aids

According to this principle, those responsible for pollution must bear the **9.8** cost of compliance with the standards of quality objectives in force.

In accordance with a Council Recommendation of March 1975 (Rec 75/436/Euratom/ECSC/EEC, OJ 1975 L194/1) exceptions to this principle are allowed in two cases:
- where the immediate application of very stringent standards is likely to cause serious economic disruption;
- where, in the framework of other policies, such as regional or agricultural policy, environmental investment is designed to resolve certain structural problems of a regional or sectoral nature, provided that the aid granted complies with the provisions of the Treaty, and in particular Articles 92 and 93.

In addition, the following were not usually regarded as contrary to the **9.9** "polluter pays" principle:
- financial contributions to local authorities to build or manage public environmental protection facilities where the expenditure cannot for the time being be totally covered by the charges levied on the polluter using such facilities;
- funds to offset particularly large burdens imposed on certain polluters to achieve an exceptional level of environmental cleanliness;
- contributions granted to promote research and development in the fields of clean technologies, manufacturing processes and products.

Now that Article 130R(2) has elevated the "polluter pays" principle to a **9.10** Treaty principle, the legal status of this Recommendation is doubtful, especially as the new article does not recognise any exceptions to the principle.

At the same time Article 92(3) allows the Commission some discretion in permitting national subsidies and other forms of aid designed *inter alia* to pursue environmental ends. Following the adoption of Article 130R(2),

---

[1] Toth, "The legal status of the Declaration annexed to the SEA", (1986) CMLRev 803.

however, the Commission initiated a review of the application of the "polluter pays" principle. It subsequently announced that it has decided to extend, until 31 December 1992, the application of its guidelines on state aids for the environment (see below) until the conclusion of the review of Community guidelines.[2]

9.11   In December 1979 the Council adopted a Recommendation regarding the methods for assessing pollution control costs in industry (OJ 1979 L5). This completes the 1975 "polluter pays" Recommendation. The assessment of costs is intended first, to determine the extent of the charge which should be assumed by the economy as a whole or by the different industry sectors, when the authorities take environmental protection measures. Second, the assessment should provide indications as to the means of reducing the pollution to the lowest possible costs.

The polluter pays principle is also affected by the conditions set by Article 130R(3), in particular the requirement to take account of regional differences in environmental conditions.[3]

> It is argued that "environmental" conditions referred to in Article 130R(3) include every indicator of the state of the environment, including water, air and soil pollution levels, the load which can be borne by each part of the environment and the functions of the site .... Economic factors, on the other hand, do not count as environmental conditions."[4]

(iii) Subsidiarity

9.12   The principle of subsidiarity is expressed in Article 130R(4) and implies that the Community shall limit its action relating to the environment to the extent to which objectives can be better attained at Community level than at the level of the individual Member States.

Where does the boundary between Community and national action lie? Some commentators argue that Article 130R(4) should be interpreted to give the Member States primary responsibility for the environment, so that the Community is subsidiary. It is also argued that the article suggests that the Community has to demonstrate case by case that the objectives of its policies can be better achieved at the Community level.

Others have argued that paragraph 4 is not meant to divide competences in any rigid way, but is a guideline or general principle on which the Community must base its political and legal measures (see Kramer, *op cit,* 73).

9.13   The new Fifth Environmental Action Programme, which was due to be published late in 1991, is expected to give a clearer indication of Commission thinking on how the division between Community and national action should be drawn. At the time of completing this book

---

[2] Commission, Sixteenth Report on Competition Policy (1987), 171–172.
[3] See *e.g.* Dir 88/609/EEC, on emissions into the air from large combustion plants, which sets different values for different regions (OJ 1988 L336/1).
[4] Kramer, *EEC Treaty and Environmental Protection* (1990) 68.

(March 1992) a final version of the proposed Programme had not yet been published.

In the meantime, it is evident from a number of proposals emerging **9.14** from the Commission on environmental matters, that the latter interprets the concept of subsidiarity in a pragmatic manner. In the recent Green Paper on the Urban Environment, for example, the competence of local authorities for town planning is seen as primary, but the Commission thinks it is totally appropriate to seek to influence town planning practice in an environmentally sound direction by the production of guidelines, where such guidelines relate town planning to wider environmental issues, such as the greenhouse effect and air pollution.

As to the general problem of the "greenhouse effect" and global climate change, the boundary is particularly difficult to draw, especially when looked at from the perspective of energy policy. From this perspective it is evident that a substantial degree of Community intervention is needed, not only because of the transfrontier effects of pollution, but also to avoid economic distortions. The new CO_2 tax proposals bear this out (see Part III para 9.64 below). The rate of the tax, and the application of the revenue yield would both be decided at Community level. The actual financial management and the techniques of collecting it would be left to Member States.

A more interventionist approach is also to be discerned in the **9.15** Commission's "Strategy on Waste", published in 1989. Waste and its management are characterised by their close links to trade. Article 100A is therefore seen as the most appropriate legal basis. Discretion is to be left to the Member States;

– as to how to limit or recycle waste in so far as their measures do not distort intra-Community trade;
– as to what kind of controls they exercise;
– as to the management of existing waste disposal depositories.

The new proposal on landfill of waste is based on a basic strategy to prevent groundwater and soil pollution, leaving Member States to adapt these basic requirements to their particular requirements.

(iv) External relations

The wording of Article 130R(5) has been criticised as being too unclear to **9.16** provide adequate guidance on the scope of the Community's external powers in the environmental field.

In addition, the Member States appended the following Declaration to the Single European Act:

"The Conference considers that the provisions of Article 130R(5) second subparagraph do not affect the principles resulting from the judgment in the AERT case."

In Case 22/70 *Commission* v *Council* (the *AERT* case) [1971] ECR 263 the Court held that when the Communities adopted their own rules to implement a common policy, the Member States no longer had the right, acting individually or collectively, to undertake obligations vis-à-vis third countries. This judgment is taken to imply that where the Member States have transferred sovereignty to the Community, they are no longer empowered to conclude agreements. This principle is difficult to reconcile with the wording of Article 130R(5).

It has been suggested that, assuming that the Community has already concluded an environmental agreement, it follows from Article 130T that individual Member States may continue to conclude international agreements on the same subject only in order to introduce more stringent measures but not to negotiate alternative ones (Kramer *op cit*, 85).

(v) Procedural aspects

9.17 Article 130S sets out the procedures for adopting environmental legislation.

> "The Council, acting unanimously on a proposal from the Commission and, after consulting the European Parliament and the Economic and Social Committee, shall decide what action is to be taken by the Community.
> The Council shall under the conditions laid down in the preceding subparagraph, define those matters on which decisions are to be taken by a qualified majority."

9.18 It should be noted that no particular form is stipulated for the specific protective measures to be adopted; hence a measure may take the form of a Regulation, a Directive, a Decision, a Resolution or a Recommendation.

It follows from Article 130S(2) that the Council may unanimously define the matters on which further decisions are to be taken by qualified vote. Even if the Council was to adopt a Directive on a specific issue by qualified majority, the co-operation procedure (Art 149) with the European Parliament does not apply. The Parliament need only be consulted.

(a) Article 130T

9.19 "The protective measures adopted in common pursuant to Article 130 shall not prevent any Member State from maintaining or introducing more stringent protective measures compatible with this Treaty."

Only "more stringent" measures are permitted under Article 130T. In other words, although Member States may adopt stricter protective measures, these must be similar in aims and objectives to the Community rules.

Any protective measure must be compatible with the Treaty. In particular they must not constitute a means of arbitrary discrimination or a disguised restriction on trade between Member States in breach of Articles 36 and 100A(4).

It is also generally contended that any protective measures taken by Member States on the basis of Article 130S must be compatible with secondary Community legislation (Kramer, *op cit*, 96).

(vi) Legal basis for environmental legislation

Article 130R now confers upon the Community an express power to enact   **9.20** environmental legislation.

Article 100A, however, allows for the adoption in Council, of secondary legislation for the progressive achievement of the internal market, on the basis of a qualified majority, with the European Parliament acting in co-operation.

In the case of majority decisions a Member State may under certain circumstances pursuant to Article 100A(4) apply national measures to protect the environment which are more stringent than those set down in the Community provisions. It is therefore clear that environmental protection measures can also be based on Article 100A. Further, earlier rulings of the Court prior to the entry into force of the Single European Act clarified that environmental measures could be based on Article 100 (Cases 91 & 92/79 *Commission* v *Italy* [1980] ECR 1099).

Although there are no explicit criteria in the Treaty itself on when one   **9.21** legal basis is to be favoured over another, the rough "rule of thumb" is that "pure" environmental legislation, for example, to protect wild life, should be based on Article 130S but legislation having some degree of "market effect" should take Article 100A as its legal basis.

In practice this line is rather difficult to draw, and the Council has altered the legal basis proposed by the Commission on several occasions. As a result of its decision to change the legal basis of the Directive on titanium dioxide (Dir 89/428/EEC, OJ 1989 L201/56) from Articles 100A to 130S the Commission challenged the legality of the Council's action.

This Directive lays down procedures for harmonising the programmes for the reduction and eventual elimination of pollution from existing industrial establishments and is intended to improve the conditions of competition in the titanium dioxide industry (Art 1). The Commission had selected Article 100A as the Directive was intended to harmonise the conditions of competition in the industry, whereas the Council considered that the primary purpose of the Directive was environmental protection.

In its judgment in Case C–300/89 *Commission* v *Council* (judgment of 11   **9.22** June 1991, not yet reported) the Court ruled that Article 100A was the proper legal basis because the measure was not limited to specific environmental action, but aimed at promoting the integration of the internal market.[5] In particular it would be necessary to consider the effect of the legislation on the production costs of industry. The Directive was therefore annulled.

---

[5] The Court essentially built on its earlier jurisprudence in Case C–62/88 *Greece* v *Council* [1990] ECR 1527.

This ruling has potentially far-reaching consequences. In the first place, the Commission is obliged to re-submit a proposal for the titanium oxide industry, based on Article 100A. In the second place, the Court's ruling calls into question the legal basis of a number of Directives which the Council had adopted on the basis of Article 130S.[6] In the third place, the assumption that all harmonising legislation directed at stationary pollutants, such as power generating plant, should be based on Article 130S, appears no longer tenable. Directive 88/609/EEC on emission standards for large combustion installations, for example, is based on that article.

(a) Differences between the two articles

9.23   The advantages for Member States in using Article 130S are considerable – the unanimity requirement being the most obvious. Also important are:
(a) Article 130R(3) which requires that the Community must take account of different regional environmental conditions. This would seem to indicate a preference for environmental quality objectives, as opposed to uniform standards;
(b) Article 130R measures are minimum standards. A Member State can introduce more stringent national controls so long as these are compatible with the Treaty;
(c) the subsidiarity issue – basically Article 100A provides for essential standards, whereas Article 130S is limited to minimum standards so that there is less scope for diversity at the Member State level where a measure is adopted on the former.

(vii) **Environmental measures and free movement of goods**

9.24   Articles 30 to 36 regulate the question of the relationship of Community law to national law in the absence of Community measures to protect the environment.

It should also be noted that in several cases the Court has now recognised environmental protection as a "mandatory requirement" which may limit the application of Article 30 EEC, as long as the measures in question meet the twin tests of objectivity and proportionality.[7] (See further, the case law discussed in Chap 2.

(viii) **Notification requirements**

9.25   In accordance with Directive 83/189/EEC (OJ 1983 L109/8, as amended by Dir 88/182/EEC, OJ 1988 L81/75) Member States are under a duty to notify the Commission of planned environmental standards relating to

---

[6] Dir 91/156/EEC on waste management (OJ 1991 L78/32) was also amended by the Council and Art 130S used as the legal basis. The Commission and the Parliament have now challenged this decision in the Court of Justice.
[7] Case 240/83 *ADBHU* [1985] ECR 531; and Case 302/86 *Commission* v *Denmark* [1989] *loc cit.*

particular products, or in certain cases, production processes.[8]

Notification gives rise to a standstill period of at least three months during which the compatibility of the planned measure, in particular Article 30, is assessed. The Commission is also required to take into account the objectives set out in Article 130R(2) when conducting its examination.

The standstill period is extended to 12 months if the Commission decides to adopt the national measures in full or in part in the form of a Community measure. After that period, a further standstill period may be implied, on the basis of the principle of co-operation, which derives from Article 5, particularly if the Commission has already proposed a Community solution.

If the Commission proposes to adopt a Community measure based on **9.26** less stringent standards, the options open to a Member State which wishes to maintain its own stricter standard will depend on the legal basis chosen by the Commission and adopted by the Council. If the Council adopts the proposal on the basis of Article 100A, the Member State would have to request a derogation on the basis of Article 100A(4). If, however, the measure is based on Article 130S, the Member State may continue to adopt its own stricter standards, pursuant to Article 130T.

The Community institutions have attempted to avoid recourse to the Article 100A(4) procedures by ensuring a certain amount of flexibility in the deadlines for the introduction of certain standards on emission controls. Council Directive 91/441/EEC on air pollution by emissions from motor vehicles, considered below, offers a good example of this technique (OJ 1991 L242/1).

(ix) Environmental restrictions and Article 85

The Commission has considered on several occasions the environmental **9.27** advantages which certain forms of agreements falling within the scope of Article 85(1) may deliver. In certain circumstances it has been prepared to grant an exemption on the basis of Article 85(3).

In its Decision in *Carbon Gas Technologie* (OJ 1983 L376/17) the Commission approved an R&D agreement between a number of major Community fuel suppliers to collaborate via a subsidiary to produce a coal gasification process. The Commission held that Article 85(1) applied in that at least some parties could have achieved the object of co-operation independently, but granted an exemption under Article 85(3) on the grounds that the agreement would save both time and money in developing a process with important environmental implications.

In the recent Decision 91/38 *KSB-Goulds-Lowara-ITT* (OJ 1990 L19/25), the Commission examined two related agreements between several of the world's largest pump manufacturers concerning R&D co-operation and production specialization. The two agreements were exempted for a limited period on the grounds (a) that they contributed to technical progress and (b) because consumers obtained a share of the benefit:

[8] See Twenty-first General Report (1987), 221.

"the advantages arising from the co-operation benefit consumers at the very least through the improvement in the quality of the water pumps. Moreover, two aspects of the new pumps, *i.e.* energy conservation and the fact that the fluids are not polluted are environmentally beneficial (para 27)."

9.28   In Decision 91/301 *Ansac,* a cartel of soda-ash producers notified an arrangement in respect of selling US produced soda-ash in the EC, the Commission did not accept an environmental justification (OJ 1991 L152/54). Ansac argued *inter alia* that an exemption under Article 85(3) could be justified, because the type of soda-ash concerned, being lower in chloride, was environmentally superior and thus contributed to an improvement in the production of goods and to the promotion of technical progress (see para 15).

The Commission replied that while it did not dispute the environmental arguments in favour of natural rather than synthetic soda-ash:

"Those arguments have no bearing, however, on the marketing of the product, with which alone Ansac's proposals are concerned. Ansac's environmental argument in any case presupposes that it is the only vehicle by which natural soda-ash could reach the Community, *i.e.* that if Ansac were not granted an exemption, no individual US producers or producers would market the product in the EEC. …Further, as Ansac's own documents show, its current marketing plans are limited to supplying only a very small percentage of total demand (around 5%) (para 23)."

3. Environmental protection measures, taxes, fiscal incentives and subsidies

(i) Environmental taxes and Community law

9.29   Member States frequently impose special fiscal charges on particular types of fuel, the use of which they wish to discourage. In addition taxes may be imposed to finance environmental protection measures or as compensation for degradation of the environment.

(ii) EEC Treaty provisions

9.30   Article 95 EEC prohibits any discriminatory taxation of goods imported from another Member State, including all indirect taxes, duties, contributions and all other taxes of whatever kind which are imposed on goods and which do not fall under the prohibition of customs duties and charges having equivalent effect under Articles 9, 12, 13 and 16 EEC (Case 90/79 [1981] ECR 283 at 301).

A tax within the meaning of Article 95 consists of any payment of money imposed by a state which constitutes part of a general internal system of taxation, and which applies to domestic as well as imported goods when those goods cross the border, if these taxes form part of a system covering domestic and imported products alike based on the same characteristics. Article 95 is violated if the imported goods are in practice more heavily taxed than equivalent national goods.

9.31 Some environmental taxes may appear to fall under Article 95 but are in fact to be assessed under Articles 9 and 12. This makes for an important difference, because customs duties and charges of equivalent effect within the meaning of Articles 9 and 12 are *always* prohibited – it is not necessary to show that their effects are discriminatory or protectionist.

Charges falling under Articles 9 and 12 may be defined as a financial burden, however small, imposed only to domestic or foreign goods because they cross the border. Even if these duties are not imposed to benefit the state, and have no discriminatory or protectionist effects, and the affected goods are not in competition with domestic products, they are charges of equivalent effect.

Charges which are levied on domestic as well as imported goods violate Article 12, and not Article 95 when their calculation is based on different features, or when they are designed to balance domestic charges levied at an earlier stage of production or trade.

Parafiscal charges, *i.e.* charges imposed on domestic and imported goods, but exclusively designed to support activities which benefit solely domestic products are also illegal under Article 12 (Case 77/72 *Capalongo* [1973] ECR 611).

9.32 Where such a charge only *partially* offsets the financial burden imposed on domestic goods, then it is discriminatory taxation within the meaning of Article 95 (*Cucchi* v *Avez* [1977] ECR 987). An example in the environmental field might be a charge in the form of fees for inspection of products which is used to determine the environmental compatibility of the product. Article 12 would be violated if the revenues from the fee were attributed to an environmental fund benefitting exclusively domestic undertakings.

In principle Article 95 does not prohibit domestic tax laws from imposing or permitting difference rates of tax for different products, or even on products which may serve similar economic ends. Where a differential tax is levied on similar or competing goods, however, and has the result of taxing imported goods at a higher rate, the taxation system is likely to be in breach of Article 95.

The Court has been asked to consider the compatibility with Community law of a parafiscal charge on petroleum products for the benefit of a French energy conservation agency in Joined Cases C–78–83/90 *Compagnie Commerciale de l'Ouest* v *Receveur Principal des Douanes de la Pallice*. Advocate-General Tesauro, in his Opinion of 11 July 1991, has suggested that Articles 3, 5, 6, 30, 37, and 92 EEC present no obstacle to the levying of the type of parafiscal charge at issue.

9.33   In order to assess the compatibility of a parafiscal charge levied on the same terms on domestic and imported products with the rules relating to charges having equivalent effect and discriminatory taxation, the national court must take account of the destination of the revenue.

If the revenue is intended to finance activities which give a specific benefit to taxed national products so as to compensate fully the burden on those products by reason of the charge, this would amount to a charge having equivalent effect contrary to Articles 9 and 12. If the revenue only partly compensates the burden of the charge, then the parafiscal charge would be a discriminatory tax within the meaning of Article 95.

9.34   In certain cases the Court of Justice has accepted that higher taxation may coincide with a category of products which is largely composed of imported products where there are objective criteria justifying differentiation. This may be due to the nature of the raw materials used or the production processes employed, where the different treatment is itself compatible with the requirements of Community law (Case 132/88 *Commission* v *Greece* [1990] ECR 1567).

Following the oil crisis of 1973-74, national measures which had the effect of limiting oil consumption, and in particular the use of heavy oil fuels, appear to have been assumed to be compatible with Community energy policy.

In Case 277/83 *Commission* v *Italy* [1985] ECR 2049 the Court confirmed its earlier case law, and ruled that the application of Article 95 is not precluded by the provisions on state aids.

(iii) National sovereignty and environmental taxes and charges

9.35   Article 99 EEC provides for harmonization of turnover taxes, indirect taxation, and excise duties, including environmental taxes. As far as the harmonization of these form of taxes are concerned, Article 99 is a *lex specialis* and displaces Article 130S. Hence, once a Community harmonization measure has been adopted, a Member State probably cannot rely upon Article 130S to impose more stringent taxes for environmental purposes.

So long as the Community has not adopted harmonising legislation on the basis of Article 99, Member States may continue to levy new indirect environmental taxes. The proposed Council Directive on the harmonization of excise taxes on mineral oil is based on Article 99 (see below).

The harmonization of other forms of tax, including direct taxes, must be undertaken on the basis of Article 100 or, Article 100A, where the measure is aimed at the realization of the common market. Again Article 130S, as a general norm is displaced.

It should be recalled that whereas measures adopted on the basis of either Article 99 or 100 require unanimity, the Council may adopt measures based on Article 100A on the basis of a qualified vote.

(a) Notification

If a proposed national environmental tax might give rise to a distortion in **9.36**
the conditions of competition in the common market, within the meaning
of Article 101, it follows from Article 102 that the Member State is under a
duty to notify the Commission, and to observe a standstill pending
consultation with the Commission.

(iv) Environmental aids

The Commission has issued three communications on environmental aids **9.37**
to Member States in which it has accorded semi-permanent status to state
aid to the environment provided certain conditions are fulfilled[9]:
– that the aid is limited to 15% in net grant equivalent;
– only undertakings having installations in operation for at least two years
  before the entry into force of the standards in question could qualify for
  assistance;
– the Member States are required to send the Commission an annual
  report on the implementation of programmes for environmental
  protection involving the grant of these aids.
It will be for the Commission to examine the compatibility of these
subsidies with the rules on state aids (see Chap 5).
Planned subsidies which do not fulfil the specific requirements set out
above could still fall under the Article 92(3)(a) and (c) exceptions.[10]

(v) Fiscal incentives and environmental protection measures

In spring 1990 the Commission commenced Article 169 proceedings **9.38**
against the German Government, which has adopted tax reductions for
diesel cars meeting strict pollution norms. The Commission estimated that
although this measure is not a form of state aid, in breach of Article 92 EEC
(because it is an aid to an individual, not to a company so that it does not
discriminate in favour of a particular manufacturer), it may nevertheless be
in breach of Article 30 because it favours the purchase of particular types of
diesel cars.

When the Council adopted its common position on particle emission
standards in Directive 91/441/EEC (see above) the German Government
accepted the Community norm. It then adopted stricter national standards,
however. The final version of Directive 91/441/EEC appears to indicate
that a compromise solution has been found.

Article 3 allows Member States to make provision for tax incentives for
the vehicles covered by the Directive if the incentives meet the provisions
of the Treaty as well as the following conditions:

---

[9] Commission, Tenth Report on Competition Policy (1981) pt 224 *et seq* and extended to 1992,
Sixteenth Report on Competition Policy (1987) pt 259.
[10] See *e.g.* the Commission's recent Decision on aid to Dutch manure reprocessing plant which
amounted to some 35% of the net grant equivalent (not yet reported).

221

- they apply to all domestic production and vehicles imported for marketing and fitted with equipment allowing the European standards to be met in 1992 to be satisfied ahead of time;
- they shall cease upon the deadline set for the compulsory entry into force of the emission values for new vehicles;
- they shall be of a value, for each type of vehicle, substantially lower than the actual cost of the equipment fitted to meet the values set and of its fitting on the vehicle.

In Case 277/83 *Commission* v *Italy* [1985] ECR 2049 the Court followed its decision in Case 73/79 *Commission* v *Italy* [1980] ECR 1533 that the application of Article 95 is not precluded by the provisions on state aids.

4. Coal and nuclear

(i) ECSC Treaty

9.39 The ECSC Treaty makes no express reference to the environment. Hence the EEC provisions apply.

(ii) Euratom Treaty

9.40 Chapter III Euratom on Health and Safety refers primarily to the protection of the health of workers and the general public against the dangers arising from ionising radiations. The Court has interpreted the Commission powers under Articles 30-38 Euratom, to include powers to protect the environment against risks of radioactive contamination.[11]

The Council's decision to adopt Regulation (EEC) 3954/87 (OJ 1987 L371/11) controlling the movement of irradiated foodstuffs in the event of a nuclear accident on the basis of Article 31 of the Euratom Treaty was challenged by the Parliament (Case 70/88 *Parliament* v *Council*).

In its judgment in Case 70/88 the Court rejected the Parliament's narrow interpretation of the scope of Chapter III Euratom, which the latter had argued was restricted to the protection of persons directly connected with the nuclear industry. The Court ruled that the goal of the Chapter is to ensure a coherent and effective protection for the population as whole, whatever the source of radiation and whatever the category of persons at risk. Hence the legal basis chosen by the Council was well founded (judgment of 4 October 1991, not yet reported.)

The Advocate-General has further indicated in his Opinion that although it might be true that the measures anticipated by the Regulation might have an effect on marketing, nevertheless in view of the importance of a coherent and effective policy for protecting health, this alone cannot prevent Article 31 from constituting the correct legal basis of the

---

[11] Case 187/87 *Saarland* v *Minister of Industry* [1988] 1 CMLR. 529, recital 11.

Regulation. Hence he suggested that the Commission's powers under Chapter III of the Euratom Treaty should not be construed narrowly (Opinion of 26 June 1991).

Decisions relating to nuclear plant choice[12], site location, waste disposal, **9.41** and decommissioning are primarily national matters. Article 37 Euratom, however, obliges each Member State to provide the Commission with such general data[13] relating to any plan for the disposal of radioactive waste in whatever form as will make it possible to determine whether the implementation of such a plan is likely to involve radioactive contamination of the water, soil or airspace of another Member State. The Commission must give a non-binding opinion within a period of six months.

In Case 187/87 *Saarland*, the Court ruled that this information should be supplied to the Commission before the competent authorities of the Member States issue the relevant construction authorizations or licenses.

(iii) **Related legislation**

(a) *Notification of nuclear accidents*

Council Directive 89/618/Euratom on informing the general public about **9.42** health protection measures to be applied and steps to be taken in the event of a radiological emergency (OJ 1989 L357/31) is intended to define Community objectives with regard to measures and procedures for informing the general public of health protection in the event of a radiological emergency. Article 2 defines the latter term as a "significant release of radiological material", this term being in turn defined by Article 3.

In accordance with Article 5, certain general information on health protection and emergency action has to be provided to the population likely to be affected in the event of a radiological emergency. That information must at a minimum include the elements set out in Annex I.

Article 6 covers the information to be provided in the event of such an emergency. That information must cover the points contained in Annex II.

(b) *Transport of radioactive waste*

Directive 84/631/EEC (OJ 1984 L326/31) on supervision and control **9.43** within the EC of the transfrontier shipment of hazardous waste expressly excludes nuclear waste. The Commission has now proposed to fill this gap by amending the "basic standards" Directive to cover radioactive waste (Proposal for a Council Directive amending Dir 80/836/ Euratom laying down the basic standards for the health protection of the general public and workers against the dangers of ionizing radiation, OJ 1990 C210/07).

---

[12] Arts 40 and 41 Euratom, however, do oblige Member States to notify proposed investments to the Commission.

[13] As to the data to be submitted, see Council Rec 82/821/ Euratom (OJ 1982 L83/15) as replaced by Commission Rec 91/14/ Euratom (OJ 1991 L6/16). Note that the Recommendation defines waste disposal to include any disposal resulting from the operation of nuclear reactors and the reprocessing of irradiated nuclear fuel.

Part II

5. Community legislation on electricity and the environment

9.44 The reduction of pollution from energy production has been a constant objective, running through the Communities' various Environmental Action Programmes (EAP).[14]

The Fourth EAP (OJ 1987 C328) adopted for the period 1986-92 was noteworthy for the emphasis it placed on environmental management, as opposed to pollution control. Environmental management should address the interactions between sources of pollutants and in general, take a more holistic approach to controlling pollutants at source. In general little has been achieved to further this approach, for example, by way of the adoption of harmonising legislation.

In 1988 the Commission published a Communication on "the greenhouse effect and the Community" (COM (88) 655, 16 November 1988) outlining a series of preventive and adaptive actions to be taken at Community level to reduce CO_2 emissions.

(i) Methods of harmonization

9.45 One problem with the Community's early pollution legislation was the dual reliance on both ambient quality and emission standards. The Directive on the aquatic environment, for example, allows Member States to opt either for effluent control standards, which may be differentiated at national level on an industry or product basis, or water quality standards. The latter strategy offers the advantage that it recognises the divergence in water quality in the Community. The former leads to fewer distortions in competition in intra-Community trade.

Disagreement over the best technology for measuring pollution levels or assessing controls has led to the incorporation of optional control techniques, further widening the potential scope for discretionary enforcement at national level.

The SO_2 limit values the Directive of 1980 (Council Dir 80/779/EEC, OJ 1980 L229/30) (see below) allowed Member States to utilise in lieu of the common ambient air quality standard and associated measurement methods, a fixed alternative standard and associated measurement methods.

This Directive has now been partially amended by Council Directive 89/427/EEC of 14 July 1989 (OJ 1989 L201/53). The recitals note that the dual approach for measuring suspended particulates in the air causes discrimination between Member States. However in order not to call into

---

[14] Council Declaration of 22 November 1973 on a Community Action Programme (OJ 1973 C112/22). For the Second Programme, see OJ 1977 C139; for the third programme, see OJ 1985 C46.

question the completion of the measures already taken by the Member States to observe the limit values, the Commission is undertaking a two-stage review of the Directive.

(ii) Air pollution

The EEC is a party to the Convention on Long-Range Transboundary Air Pollution[15], the Vienna Convention on the Protection of the Ozone Layer (OJ 1988 L297/10) and the Montreal Protocol (OJ 1988 L297/21). Protocols adopted under the Convention on Long-Range Transboundary Pollution commit countries to concrete reductions in air pollution; a protocol on SO_2 reductions was adopted in 1985 and a Protocol on NO_x in 1988.[16]   **9.46**

In furtherance of its obligations under these various Conventions and Protocols[17], the Council has adopted Directive 84/360/EEC (OJ 1984 L188/20) on air pollution from major industrial plants. This is a framework Directive. It requires Member States to bring into force necessary laws, regulations and administrative provisions to comply with the Directive, the purpose of which is to implement measures and procedures designed to reduce and prevent air pollution (defined in Art 2(1)) from industrial plants in the Community.

Member States must take the necessary measures to ensure that the operation of new plants listed in Article 3(1) and Annex I of the Directive require authorization from the competent authorities. The categories of plant covered by Annex I include thermal (but not nuclear) plant of normal heat output of over 50MW. The most important polluting substances are defined in Article 4(2) and listed in Annex II.

Directive 84/360/EEC does not stipulate any maximum values for these polluting substances, although Article 8 provides that the Council may adopt relevant measures.[18] For SO_2 and NO_x the values stipulated in Directives 80/799/EEC[19] and 85/203/EEC[20], respectively apply.   **9.47**

An authorization can only be issued when the competent authorities are satisfied that all appropriate measures against air pollution have been taken, including the application of the best available technology, provided that application does not entail excessive cost (Art 4(1)).

Member States must follow developments as regards the best available technology and the environmental situation, and in the light of such   **9.48**

---

[15] Council Dec 81/462/EEC (OJ 1981 L171/11).

[16] Protocol to the 1979 Convention on Long-Range Transboundary Air Pollution concerning the Control of Emissions of Nitrogen Oxides (1989) 28 ILM 212.

[17] The EC is party to the protocols – Council Dec 86/277/EEC (OJ 1986 L181/1).

[18] It has adopted such measures in the case of new, large combustion plants – Council Dir 88/609/EEC, discussed below, and for the burning of waste – Council Dir 89/369/EEC (OJ 1989 L 163/32) and Council Dir 89/429/EEC (OJ 1989 L203/50).

[19] OJ 1980 L229/30, as amended by Council Dir 81/857/EEC (OJ 1981 L319/18) and Council Dir 89/427/EEC (OJ 1989 L201/53).

[20] Air Quality Standards for Nitrogen Dioxide (OJ 1985 L87/1) as amended by Council Dir 85/580/EEC (OJ 1985 L372/36).

examination, where necessary, impose appropriate conditions on plants authorised in accordance with the Directive on the basis of both these developments and the desirability of avoiding excessive costs for the plants in question, having regard in particular to the economic situation of the plants belonging to the categories concerned (Art 12(2)).

As for *existing* plant Member States are required to implement policies and strategies to bring appropriate measures for the adaption of existing plants of listed categories to the best available technology, but must take account of the plant's technical characteristics, its rate of utilization, and length or remaining life, nature and volume of polluting emissions from it and the desirability of not entailing excessive costs for the plant concerned (Art 15). No time limits are specified for this adaption.

9.49   Directive 88/609/EEC (OJ 1988 L336/1) on the limitation of emissions from certain pollutants into the air from large combustion plants sets emission limit values for SO_2, NO_x and dust for all *new* plants whose thermal output is over 50MW(th), irrespective of the fuel used.[21] These were to be implemented by 1990.

The Directive sets out various emission control standards (Art 4 and Annexes III–VII). It also provides for ceilings and phased reductions for SO_2 and NO_x emissions from existing plants[22] over a period until 2003. The base line for reductions is the 1980 emission level, and each Member State had a different reduction targets set for a particular date.

9.50   Member States are obliged to draw up appropriate programmes for the progressive reduction of total annual emissions from large combustion plants by 1 July 1990. These programmes must set out timetables and the procedures for implementing them.

Abatement measures should be based on the best available technology not entailing excessive costs.

The two media-specific Directives establish global limit values and guide values for, respectively sulphur dioxide and suspended particulates, and for NO_x, that must not be exceeded in the territory of the Member States.

Article 3 of Directive 80/779/EEC as amended provides that Member States shall take "appropriate measures" to ensure that as from 1 April 1983, the concentrations of SO_2 are not greater than the limit values given in Annex I.

9.51   In Cases 361/88 and Case C–59/89 *Commission* v *Germany* (judgment of April 1991, not yet reported) the Court upheld the Commission's contention that a technical circular addressed to certain authorities was not an "appropriate measure" as required under Article 3.

Article 3(2) allows Member States to designate zones in which the limit values imposed under Annex I need not be observed until 1 April 1993.

Article 3(2) of Directive 85/203/EEC on air quality standards for

---

[21] This Directive does not apply to "post combustion plant", that is apparatus designed to purify waste gases from combustion plant where that apparatus is not operated by an independent combustion plant (Arts 1(2) and 2(8)).

[22] Defined as combustion plants authorised before 1 July 1987.

nitrogen dioxide (OJ 1985 L87/1) similarly allows Member States to designate zones in which the limit values set in Annex I of this Directive need not be applied until 1 January 1994.

Article 11 of Directive 80/779/EEC provides that:

"Where Member States fix in border regions values for concentrations of **9.52** sulphur dioxide and suspended particulates in the atmosphere in accordance with Article 4(1) and (2), they shall hold prior consultations." [23]

6. Environmental impact assessment

Council Directive 85/337/EEC (OJ 1985 L175/40) on the assessment of **9.53** effects of certain public and private projects on the environment obliges Member States to implement "environmental impact assessment" (EIA) procedures before decisions to construct certain categories of plant are taken. The aim of the Directive, which entered into force in July 1988, is to introduce common principles of assessment with a view to improving planning procedures governing activities which are likely to have a significant effect on the environment.

Article 3 requires that the EIA must identify, describe and evaluate projects in accordance with Articles 4–11 of the Directive, in the light of their direct and indirect effect on;
– humans, fauna and flora;
– soil, water, air, climate landscape
– the interaction between the factors mentioned in the first and second indent;
– material assets and the cultural heritage.

Directive 85/337/EEC distinguishes between two sorts of project:
– projects of the classes listed in Annex I must be made subject to an EIA (Art 4(1));
– projects of the classes listed in Annex II may be made subject to an EIA "where the Member States consider that their characteristics so require" (Art 4(2)).

Projects subject to Article 4(1) include;
– thermal power stations and other combustion installations with a heat **9.54** output of over 300MW; nuclear power stations, other nuclear reactors and installation solely designed for the permanent storage or final disposal of radioactive waste (see Annex I, paras 2–3).

Projects subject to Article 4(2) include:
(a) industrial installations for the production of electricity (unless included in Annex I);
(b) industrial installations for carrying, gas, steam and hot water; transmission of electrical energy by overhead cables;

---

[23] Art 11 of Directive 85/203 is identical.

(c) installations for the production or enrichment of nuclear fuels;

(d) installations for the reprocessing of radiated nuclear fuels;

(e) installations for the collection and processing of radioactive waste;

(f) installations for hydroelectric production.

9.55   The Member States must nevertheless carry out a preliminary examination of each project in order to determine whether it should be the subject of an EIA. In order to do this they may establish specific criteria or thresholds.

Projects deemed to serve national defence purposes are exempt (Art 1(4)). Likewise the Directive does not apply to projects adopted by a specific act of national legislation (Art 1(5)), nor to specific projects which the Member States exempt in exceptional cases in a whole or in part from the provisions of the Directive (Art 2(3)).

In accordance with Article 5(2) the developer is obliged to provide the following information:

– a description of the project comprising information on the site, design and the size of the project;

– a description of the measures envisaged in order to avoid, reduce and if possible, remedy significant adverse effects;

– the data required to identify and assess the main effects which the project is likely to have on the environment;

– a non-technical summary of the information mention in indents 1-3.

9.56   The Directive does allow some flexibility here: certain information is only required to be made available in so far as it corresponds to the state of progress in the authorization procedure and in so far as the developer can realistically be expected to provide it, bearing in mind the extent of knowledge and of assessment methods. The Directive also authorises public authorities to make certain information available to the public.

The Member States shall then ensure that this information is made available to the public which is to be given an "opportunity to express an opinion before the project is initiated" (Art 6(3)).

9.57   At the same time the information is to be passed to other Member States "likely to be significantly affected" by the project. Article 7 provides that:

> "such information shall serve as the basis for any consultations necessary in the framework of the bilateral relations between two Member States on a reciprocal basis."

The Commission has recently announced that it intends to commence infringement proceedings against the British Government in view of the failure to carry out an EIA in five separate instances (*Financial Times,* 19 October 1991).

The result of the EIA study is just one factor to be taken into account by the competent authorities. Once the decision is taken, the competent authorities must inform the public concerned of the nature of the decision and the conditions attached.

9.58   The Directive only sets certain common principles and it will certainly not ensure full harmonization of environmental impact procedures in each Member State. The Directive recognises this and requires the Commission to draw up a report after five years on its use and effectiveness and to present if necessary, other proposals to ensure a better harmonization of legislation and practices in the Member State.

(i) **Direct effect**

Council Directive 85/337/EEC has been considered to be directly effective, and capable of creating rights for individuals which national courts must uphold, by the Dutch administrative tribunal, the College van Beroep voor het Bedrijfsleven. **9.59**

In January 1991 the President of the Court partially suspended a decision of the Minister of Economic Affairs, approving the Dutch Electricity Plan 1991–2000.

The decision to approve the construction of a coal-fired electricity plant had been contested by Texaco which claimed that its proposed coal-gasification power station would be less detrimental to the environment. It further alleged that the Minister's decision should have been preceded by an environmental impact assessment, as required by Dutch law.

The President of the Court chose to examine the application of Directive 85/337/EEC to the Minister's decision to approve the Electricity Plan. Article 2(1) of the Directive requires that EIAs should be carried out before consent is given to projects likely to have a considerable effect on the environment. The President reasoned that "consent" extended to all decisions necessary to carry out a project, including the approval of the Electricity Plan.[24]

It has been suggested that Council Directive 85/337/EEC could successfully be relied upon before the English courts.[25]

(ii) **Related legislation**

Council Directive 90/313/EEC on freedom of access to information on the environment (OJ 1990 L158/56) aims to ensure freedom of access to, and dissemination of, information on the environment held by public authorities and to set out the basic terms and conditions on which such information should be made available. Article 2(a) defines "information relating to the environment" as: **9.60**

"any available information ... on the state of water, air, soil, fauna, flora, land and natural sites or on activities or measures adversely affecting or likely to so affect these."

Public authorities must make available the information on request, without the person requesting the information having to prove an interest. **9.61**

---

[24] See further Sevenster, (1991) 2 *Utiltities Law Review,* 65–66.
[25] Geddes, "Environmental Directives and direct effect" 1990 6 *Law Society Gazette,* 28; see also *Twyford* [1992] CMLR 101.

Information may only be refused where it affects public security, matters which are *sub judice* and commercial and industrial confidentiality. Where it is possible to separate out this type of information the remaining data should be supplied. A request should be responded to in two months.

Part III

7. Current proposals

(i) Proposal fixing certain rates and target rates for excise duty on mineral oils

9.62　　The proposal fixing certain rates and target rates for excise duty on mineral oils (February 1991) only concerns those mineral oils used as propellants – *i.e.* petrol and diesel. Together these account for 90% of the excise revenue generated from mineral oils within the Community.

This proposal completes and amends the earlier proposal of October 1989 (Com(89) 526) on the approximation of excise duties on mineral oils. It reflects the line adopted by the Dublin European Council of 25 and 26 June 1990 on taking account of environmental concerns in economic and fiscal measures. The proposed legal basis is Article 99 EEC.

The February 1991 proposal builds on the 1989 proposal in which the Commission put forward for *petrol* a system which includes a minimum rate and a target rate;
– the minimum rate must be implemented by each Member State as from 1 January 1993. This was set at 337 ECU per 1,000 litres for leaded and 50 ECUs lower for unleaded petrol;
– a target rate which represents the common level towards which Member States must progressively converge.

9.63　　The 1989 proposal further provided that the level of the different rates should be subject to reexamination every two years, taking into account transport, energy and environment policies. On the basis of the recommendations on the stabilization of CO_2 emissions made in the context of the second World Climate Conference, the target rate for petrol is to be fixed at a level sufficient to raise the consumers' consciousness about CO_2 pollution and its implications for the environment and the greenhouse effect. The proposed long-term target rate of excise duty for leaded petrol shall be 495 ECUs per 1,000 litres. This rate is based on the principle that the excise rate for petrol should include a supplement for CO_2 content. This supplement has been fixed at 45 ECUs per 1,000 litres of petrol which corresponds to a level of 65 ECU per tonne of carbon. To encourage the ongoing process of conversion to unleaded petrol, the target rate for this fuel is being set at 50 ECUs lower than that for leaded petrol – *i.e.* 445 ECU.

These target rates are not obligatory, but every time a Member State adjusts its excise duties, it must do so in the direction of the target rate. The proposed target rates are above all the rates currently applied in the Member States with the exception of Italy.

(ii) Proposed energy/CO_2 tax

In October 1991 the Commission voted in favour of a combined energy CO_2 tax of which the energy and the carbon component would be equally balanced on a 50/50 split. The Energy Ministers' Council of 29 October endorsed the broad aims of the Commission's package, but raised a number of objections to it and referred it back to the Commission for further consideration.   **9.64**

The aim of the Commission's October package was to launch a Community action programme to help security of supply of energy as well as to limit CO_2 emissions by the year 2000 at 1990 levels. As power generation is responsible for 31% of total CO_2 emissions in the EC, the electricity sector is a primary target of the proposed tax.

The proposed package is based on three strategies:
(i)   specific measures such as R&D programmes and voluntary agreements on energy efficiency and sectoral measures in industry;
(ii) complementary national programmes;
(iii) fiscal measures.

In addition, certain specific measures are envisaged for the electricity sector. These include an R & D programme for renewable energy and a proposal on least cost planning. The latter is to create incentives for energy utilities to consider energy saving potentials with its clients on the same basis as the expansion of its production capacity.   **9.65**

Specific measures are also envisaged to encourage users to accelerate low pollution/high performance technologies (combined heat and power generation) and to encourage the use of renewables and biomass products. No concrete proposals have yet been put forward, however.

The proposed fiscal measures are undoubtedly the most controversial of the package. The proposed tax would be levied in equal proportions: 50% as a levy on all energy sources, except renewables, and 50% based on the carbon content of energy. The CO_2 component would fall more heavily on industries with a large share of coal in their fuel mix than those relying on gas or nuclear energy.

The basis for the tax is a $10 surcharge per barrel of oil, to be levied in stages: $3 per barrel as from 1993 and increasing annually by $1 per barrel until the year 2000. Taxation of other energy sources derives from their energy equivalency to one barrel of oil. This means that coal would be taxed at $14 and electricity at $5.   **9.66**

In order to minimise bureaucracy, the Commission document advocates use of existing national fiscal mechanisms to implement the scheme, such as current excise taxes for hydrocarbons. The fiscal framework for coal and electricity has not been fully worked out, however.

It is further proposed that certain industries and even certain Member States would be shielded from the full effects of the tax. Further, the tax would not be applied to energy used as a raw material in industry.

A new programme for the promotion of renewables, ALTENER, is to be presented later this year.

(iii) The new financial instrument (LIFE)

9.67 The new instrument is designed to make for a greater cohesion in the behaviour of Member States with regard to environmental problems. It is to take the form of a Regulation, based on Article 130S. Individual programmes will be implemented on the basis of a Commission Decision addressed to the national or regional authorities concerned or on the basis of contracts or agreements with associations of firms.

LIFE is intended to incorporate existing financial instruments, in particular Council Regulation (EEC) 2242/87 relating to Community actions for the environment (ACE) and the proposed Regulation on Community action for the protection of the environment in the Mediterranean region (MEDSPA).

9.68 Assistance may take the form of part-financing of programmes or projects, interest subsidies, reimbursable subsidies or support for technical assistance. It will have four general objectives:

(i)   to help strengthen and increase the effectiveness of administrative structures or services designed to ensure the implementation of environmental provisions;

(ii)   to help control and reduce the various forms of pollution by means of measures complementing action of a regulatory nature;

(iii) to help protect sensitive areas and maintain biogenetic diversity;

(iv) to provide technical and financial support in third countries for the implementation of international conventions and for the resolution of common or global problems.

(a) Assistance criteria

9.69 Assistance via the new LIFE must contribute to the realization of the general objectives of EC environmental policy and legislation. The level of Community participation will need to take account of the seriousness of the problems to be tackled, especially at the regional level, the particular interest of the operations from a Community point of view, and of the capacity to the beneficiary to contribute.

(b) Implementation

9.70 LIFE is to act as a complement to legislation and to economic and fiscal instruments. Programmes will be adopted by the Commission on the basis of the opinion of a consultative committee for the environment. These will reflect, among other things, the objectives and the priorities of the new Community action programme (the Fifth programme is to be sent to the

Council and the EP in the course of 1992). They will be drawn up by the main bodies concerned (national and regional authorities, economic and social partners, etc).

Two aspects of the proposal should be noted:

(i) It takes the form of a *Regulation* – previously it had been assumed that environmental measures would always take the form of Directives.

(ii) It offers a concrete application of the subsidiarity principle.

(iv) Communication on the European Energy Charter

The Charter is meant to increase the awareness of shared responsibility for supply and environmental problems. The overall objective of the Charter is to define the signatories' energy policy objectives. It proclaims the signatories' will to ensure greater security of supply and to promote the construction of a large European energy market, taking due account of environmental requirements.[26] **9.71**

The optimum use of energy and environmental protection is expressed to imply:

– the development of new and renewable energy sources;

– greater energy savings;

– measures to combat pollution.

(v) Environmental liability

The Commission has now issued a draft Communication on the subject of environmental liability (Brussels, 12 September 1991). **9.72**

Major environmental accidents have placed the issue of civil liability for damage to the environment on the environmental protection agenda in the Community. In order to provide a high level of environmental protection, the Community is considering developing programmes for the restoration of environments already damaged. It anticipates the development of a new mix of legal and economic instruments to allocate responsibilities equitably among all economic sectors. The draft notes that a number of Member States have introduced strict liability systems for various activities posing special risk to the environment, and that if this trend develops and civil liability varies between the Member States, competitive distortions will result. Hence some degree of harmonization at Community level is needed.

The proposed Community measures are to be based on "an integrated, multi-faceted approach combining the strengths of civil liability with the advantages of joint compensation systems." The Commission is therefore considering firstly, the harmonization of the use of civil liability where the damage can be traced to particular parties; and secondly, introducing strict liability for certain types of economic activities or installations which pose particular risks of environmental damage. **9.73**

---

[26] The European Energy Charter was signed in The Hague on 16 December 1991 at an intergovernmental conference comprising representatives from the 50 signatory countries.

CONTENTS OF CHAPTER 10

Chapter 10
Procurement and the Electricity Sector

1. Introduction

This chapter examines the rules applying to procurement of goods and **10.1**
services by electricity undertakings. The Community's rules on procurement for utilities, that is water, energy telecommunications and transport,
form part of the Community's wider regime which aims at creating an
internal procurement market by 1992. Although a Council Directive on
public works was adopted as long ago as 1971 (Dir 71/305/EEC, JO 1971
L185/5) and a further Council Directive on public supplies (Dir 77/62/
EEC, OJ 1977 L13/9) was adopted in 1977, the so-called utilities sectors
were excluded from the scope of these two Directives.

In mid-1980 the Commission undertook a review of the implementation
and impact of the public works and public supplies Directives in the
Member States. It concluded that their effect had been marginal. It
therefore began a "rolling programme" of procurement reform. This
programme has included:
- the substantial modification of Directives 71/305/EEC[1] and
  77/62/EEC[2];
- the adoption of a new Council Directive 89/665/EEC on enforcement
  and remedies for breach of the rules set out in Directives 71/305/EEC
  and 77/62/EEC, as amended[3];
- the adoption of a new Council Directive 90/531/EEC on procurement
  for entities operating in the utilities sectors (water, energy, transport and
  tecommunications) (OJ 1990 L297/1);
- the adoption of a proposal for a separate Directive on enforcement and
  remedies for procurement in the utilities sector;
- the adoption of a proposal for a Council Directive on public services;
  and
- the submission of a separate proposal for a Council Directive on the
  procurement of services in the utilities sector.

While there are a number of common themes running through the so- **10.2**

---

[1] Council Dir 89/440/EEC (OJ 1989 L210/1).
[2] Council Dir 88/295/EEC (OJ 1988 L127/1).
[3] Council Dir 89/665/EEC co–ordinating the laws, regulations and administrative provisions
relating to the application of the review procedures to the award of public supply and public works
contracts (OJ 1989 L395/33).

237

called "general" procurement regime – that is Directive 71/305/EEC as amended, Directive 77/62/EEC as amended, and the new Directive 89/655/EEC on remedies – and the new rules for the utilities sector, the latter set of rules nevertheless constitute a separate regime. This chapter will focus on the rules addressed to public undertakings and firms, or "contracting entities" operating in the utility sector. Reference will be made to the general regime only in so far as this is necessary to clarify or otherwise explain aspects of the utility regime. Similarly, any relevant jurisprudence of the Court of Justice on the general regime shall be discussed.

2. Council Directive 90/531/EEC on procurement by utilities

(i) General aims

10.3 The adoption of this Directive marked an important victory for the Community institutions in their attempt to expose public firms to greater competition. It will come into effect on 1 January 1993 for the majority of the Member States, and on 1 January 1996 for Spain and 1 January 1988 for Greece and Portugal.

Although the Directive does not seek to remove the exclusive rights to provide certain services which these utilities enjoy, it does try to devise procedural rules which will help to eliminate the use of the close relationship between Member States and these utilities as a hidden vehicle for economic and industrial policy measures.

As with the general public works and public supplies Directives, Directive 90/531/EEC aims to contribute to the development of the internal market in public procurement by organising markets in a transparent manner. It also pursues the subsidiary aim, as stated in the Commission's White Book of 1985, of promoting the use of European standards and specifications.

(ii) The common rules

10.4 The Directive follows the logic of the amended Directives 71/305/EEC and 77/62/EEC, in requiring Member States to co-ordinate their national procedures for the award of supply and works contracts above certain thresholds, on the basis of a number of common rules established in the Directive.[4] These are the common rules on technical specifications and standards (Arts 13 and 14) common advertising rules (Arts 15–23) and common criteria for the qualification, selection and award of contracts (Arts 24–29).

---

[4] On the limited aim of the Community rules on public works and public supplies contracts, generally, see Cases 27 to 29/86 *CEI and Bellini* [1987] ECR 3347; Case 31/87 *Beentjes* [1988] *ECR* 4635.

As already noted, the major utilities sectors, had been excluded from the scope of the Public Works Directive 71/305 as amended, and the Public Supplies Directive 77/62, as amended. They are also excluded from Directive 89/665 co-ordinating the laws, regulations and administrative provisions relating to the application of review procedures for public supply and works contracts.

One reason for this exclusion is the diverse public and private legal forms which utilities assume in the Member States.[5] The Community therefore considered it necessary to adopt a special regime for the "excluded sectors". Recital 14 of the preamble to the new Directive states that:

"among the main reasons why entities operating in these sectors do not purchase on the basis of Community-wide competition is the closed nature of the markets in which they operate, due to the existence of special or exclusive rights granted by the national authorities, concerning the supply to, provision or operation of networks for providing the service concerned, the exploitation of a given geographical area for a particular purpose...."

It may not always be easy to decide whether a particular intended **10.5** contractual award falls under the "general regime" or whether it should be subject to the separate rules provided under Directive 90/531/EEC. Article 2(2) of Directive 77/62/EEC, as amended by Article 35(1) of Directive 90/531/EEC, provides that Directive 77/62/EEC shall not apply:

"to contracts awarded in the fields referred to in Articles 2, 7, 8 and 9 of Council Directive 90/531 ... or fulfilling the conditions in Article 6(2) of the said Directive."

Article 35(2) of Directive 90/531/EEC replaces Article 3(4) and (5) of Directive 71/305/EEC so that contracts falling within the scope of the utilities Directive do not fall within the provisions of the works Directive.

In the recent Case 247/89 *Commission* v *Portugal* (judgment of 11 July **10.6** 1991) the Court rejected infringement proceedings instituted against Portugal for its failure to publish in the *Official Journal* a call for tenders for contracts for the construction of a telecommunications exchange at Lisbon Airport, in breach of its obligations under Directive 77/62/EEC. The Portuguese Government disputed the applicability of this Directive. It relied upon its Article 2(2)(a) which excludes from its scope of application "public supply contracts awarded by bodies which administer transport services." Furthermore, it pointed out that the Portuguese airport authority which had awarded the contract was listed in the relevant Annex to Directive 90/531/EEC.

The Commission, however, claimed that the Court should rely upon the wording of Directive 77/62/EEC, as amended by the later Directive 88/295/EEC which has considerably tightened the criteria for exemption. The Court held that it was the unamended version, in force at the time of

---

[5] See recitals 12 and 13 of the preamble to Dir 90/531/EEC (OJ 1990 L297/1).

the disputed call for tenders which was to be applied. Furthermore the Court adopted a broad interpretation of the concept of "related facilities", potentially excluding a variety of works and supplies activities from the scope of the general regime.[6]

(iii) **Scope of the Directive**

10.7   The scope of the definition of the "contracting entities" subject to the Directive reflects the Community's aim of preventing Member States exerting influence on the purchasing practices for supply and works contracts (Art 1(3)) in these closed markets.

(a) Entities covered

10.8   Article 2 defines the entities covered and divides them into two categories:

"1. This Directive shall apply to contracting entities which:
(a) are public authorities and public undertakings, and exercise one of the 'relevant activities' listed in Article 2(2);
(b) or where they are not public authorities or public undertakings, they have as one of their activities any of those referred to in paragraph 2 or any combination thereof and operate on the basis of special or exclusive rights granted by a competent authority of a Member State."

(b) Public authorities

10.9   The definition of a "public authority" includes the state, regional or local authorities, bodies governed by public law, or associations formed by one or more such authorities or bodies governed by public law.

This definition of a "body governed by public law" is essentially equivalent to the definition adopted in the amended works Directive.

A body is considered to be governed by public law when:

(a) it is established for the specific purpose of meeting needs in the general interest, not being of a commercial or industrial nature; and
(b) has legal personality; and
(c) is financed for the most part by the state or regional or local authorities etc or is subject to management supervision by those bodies, or has an administrative, managerial or supervisory board more than half of whose members are appointed by the state, regional or local authorities etc.

(c) Public undertakings

10.10   Article 2(1) introduces the concept of a "public undertaking" which is defined as "any undertaking over which the public authorities may exercise directly or indirectly a dominant influence by virtue of their ownership of it, their financial participation therein, or the rules which govern it."

A dominant influence will be presumed on the part of public authorities

---

[6] See further "Trepte" *Utilities Law Review,* forthcoming.

where they either hold a major part of the undertakings capital, or control the majority of voting shares, or where they may appoint more than half of the members of the undertaking's administrative, managerial or supervisory bodies.

This definition is taken from Commission Directive 80/723/EEC (OJ 1980 L195/1). Although it did not expressly endorse the definition its judgment in Cases 188-190/80 *France, Italy and the United Kingdom* v *Commission* [1982] ECR 2545, the Court held that it did not amount to an abuse of the Commission's powers under Article 90(3).

(d) Private undertakings

Contracting entities which are *private* entities, and   **10.11**

(a) undertake certain relevant activities; and

(b) do so on the basis of special or exclusive rights granted by a competent authority of a Member State are also subject to the Directive.

(e) Relevant activities

Article 2(2) defines the relevant activities as:

(a) the provision or operation of fixed networks intended to provide a   **10.12**
service to the public in connection with the production, transport or distribution of *inter alia* electricity or gas or heat; or

(b) the supply of these fuels to such networks; or

(c) the exploitation of a geographical area for the purpose of *inter alia* exploring for or extracting oil, gas, coal or other solid fuels.

(f) Exclusive rights

Article 2(3) defines special or exclusive rights as rights:

"deriving from authorization granted by a competent authority of the Member   **10.13**
State concerned, by law, regulation or administrative action having as their result the reservation for one or more entities of the exploitation of an activity defined in paragraph 2."

In particular, a contracting entity shall be considered to enjoy such rights where it enjoys:

(a) special privileges in planning law or;

(b) where the entity supplies electricity or gas to a network which is itself operated by an entity which enjoys special or exclusive rights granted by a competent authority....

These definitions are supplemented by lists contained in Annexes 1–X (Art 2(6)).

In order to ensure that the lists are as exhaustive as possible, Member States shall notify the Commission of amendments to them, and the Commission shall revise these annexes in accordance with the procedure in Article 32.[7]

---

[7] *Cf* the provisions of the public works Directive which states that *the Commission* shall ensure that the lists are as exhaustive as possible.

10.14   The concept of "special or exclusive rights" is taken from Article 90(1) of the Treaty, discussed in Chapter 4. It was therefore considered inappropriate to attempt to define it exhaustively.[8] Thus the scope of Article 2(3) is not entirely clear, despite the addition of the qualification that these special rights must result in "the reservation for one or more entities of the exploitation of an activity".[9]

    The existing jurisprudence of the Court of Justice on the concept of "entrusted undertakings", *i.e.* "undertakings to which Member States grant special or exclusive rights" for the purposes of Article 90(1), while relevant, is itself not conclusive. There is no authority, for example, on the manner in which such rights must be conferred for the purposes of Article 90(1).

    It would appear that an undertaking is not "entrusted" for the purposes of Article 90(2) where legislation only authorises it to act, even though there is some element of public supervision.[10]

10.15   In Case 7/82 *GVL v Commission* [1983] ECR 483 the Court held that the relevant German legislation did not confer the management of copyright and related rights on any specific undertaking but defined in a general manner the rules applying to the companies which intended to undertake the collective exploitation of such rights.

    Although the right enjoyed need not be an absolute exclusive right, nor presumably need it extend across the entire territory of a Member State, there must be some degree of reservation or "exclusivity". In other words a right conferred upon those carrying on an economic activity which is open to anyone, who thus form part of an indefinite class is unlikely to be regarded as either exclusive or special (Case 13/77 *INNO v ATAB* [1977] ECR 2115). It may therefore be questioned whether, for example, the holder of a so-called "second tier" licence under the British Electricity Act 1989, to supply electricity to particular consumers, would fall into this category.

10.16   Although the Commission has hitherto used the concepts of special and exclusive rights inter-changeably, it would seem that special rights imply something different than exclusive rights. If the Commission wishes to suppress special rights or attach conditions to their exercise it must clearly define what is meant by a special right. In Case 202/88 *France v Commission* (judgment of 19 March 1991) the Commission annulled those articles of the Directive dealing with special rights for want of proper definition and reasoning.

---

[8] Amended proposal for a Council Directive on the procurement procedures of entities operating in the water, energy, transport and telecommunications sectors, Com (89) 380 final, August 1989.
[9] This is in fact an additional clarification to earlier versions of the draft, which referred only to situations where a prior authorization to engage in the activity was necessary, or where special planning privileges obtained.
[10] See for example, Case 66/86 *Saeed, loc cit.* The Court has on several occasions stated that for such an undertaking to benefit from the exemption provided in Art 90(2), it must be established that its "public service duties" were conferred by way of "act of legislative authority". In the *IJsselcentrale* case, the Commission seemed to indicate that it was sufficient that exclusive rights were implicit in the concession granted to the distribution companies. The grant of a concession is an act of public law (Commission Dec 91/50, paras 40–41, *loc cit*).

(iv) Exemptions

Despite the wide scope of Article 2(2), the Directive exempts certain **10.17** important types of transactions, and certain types of undertakings.

(a) Exempted transactions

The categories of exempted transactions are numerous; the most significant **10.18** include the following.

Article 6 exempts the contracts of contracting entities awarded for purposes other than the pursuit of the relevant activities or for the pursuit of such activities in a non-member country.

Article 6(1) adds the caveat that this must not involve the physical use of a network or a geographical area within the Community. Where a utility is involved in other activities, the Directive does not apply to its contracting practices vis-à-vis those activities. In order to ensure greater transparency in these areas, the Commission is required to publish lists of the activities which it considers to be covered by this exclusion (Art 6(3)).

Article 9(b) excludes contracts which the contracting entities award for **10.19** the supply of energy or of fuels for the production of energy. As both the preamble and Article 9(2) make clear the Council shall re-examine this exemption at a later, if unspecified date.

Article 10 exempts contracts which are declared to be secret by the Member States, where their execution must be accompanied by special security measures or where the protection of the basic security interests of the state so requires.

The Commission has indicated that this provision is to be regarded as an expression of the public security exemption, as provided for in Article 36 EEC, and interpreted by the Court of Justice in *Campus Oil* (Case 72/83 [1984] ECR 2727, in particular at paras 21–36).

Directive 90/531/EEC does not contain any explicit exemption for **10.20** contracts for military goods, but this is already provided for in Article 223(1)(b) of the EEC Treaty.

Contracts below certain thresholds are excluded. Whereas the threshold of 5,000,000 ECU for works contracts is the same as that required under Directive 71/305/EEC, as amended, the thresholds for supply contracts is raised to 400,000 ECU (Art 12).[11]

(b) Exempted undertakings

The Directive provides two exemptions for certain *categories* of undertakings. **10.21**

Firstly, the supply of water, electricity, gas or heat to public networks by contracting entities other than public authorities does not come within the scope of the Directive if that supply is only a marginal part of the entity's overall activities (Art 2(5)(a) deals with electricity).[12]

Thus the supply of electricity will not be covered where its production **10.22** takes place because its consumption is necessary for carrying out an activity

---

[11] For telecommunications contracts the threshold is 600,000 ECU.
[12] Art 2(5)(b) deals with gas and heat.

other than that referred to in Article 2(2) and where such supply depends only on the entity's own consumption and has not exceeded 30% of the entity's total production of energy, having regard to the average for the preceding three years, including the current year.

10.23   Secondly, Article 3 contains a compromise which was accepted by the Council in reaching its common position in March 1990. It is designed to meet the objections raised by the oil and gas exploration industry that their activities were already subject to full competition. At the same time, however, the Community authorities have attempted to secure that the exemption procedure offers a possibility of eliminating a number of discriminatory procedures in national licensing practices.

Article 3 therefore provides for a limited exemption procedure for firms engaged in oil, gas or coal exploration where the Member State responsible for granting exploration or exploitation concessions agrees to respect certain conditions in their procedures for allocating licences or concessions.

(v) Observations

10.24   Despite the considerable scope for the exemption of particular types of transactions as well as for certain categories of undertakings, the concept of a "contracting entity" has a potentially wide application. This is undoubtedly a result of the Commission's declared aim of developing a concept "in terms which transcend the public/private distinction and permit situations which are in substance the same to be treated equally regardless of differences in legal form." [13]

The Commission has attempted to ensure that *the field of application* of the Directive will be sufficiently wide to counteract two types of situations which lead utilities in particular, to pursue procurement policies which privilege national suppliers. The first is market insulation, which may result either from the conferral of special or exclusive privileges or because the utility itself enjoys a natural monopoly. The second situation results from the ability of national authorities to use the award of licences or concessions to influence the procurement patterns of the licensed utility.

10.25   It may be observed, however, that as the definition of a "contracting entity" includes firms which *supply* fixed networks, the Directive may have a broad reach. If one takes the example of a private electricity generator, it will not necessarily enjoy exclusive rights to supply electricity unless this has been conferred by a licence or a concession. [14]

However, in accordance with Article 2(3)(b) it is sufficient that these firms supply a network which is itself operated by a utility enjoying certain

---

[13] Communication from the Commission on a Community regime for procurement in the excluded sectors, Com (88) 376, p91.

[14] Art 2(2) does not make it clear whether the entity need only enjoy special or exclusive rights which reserve an activity to it in a particular area or to supply a particular class of customer. In any event only those in the former category appear to be listed in Annex II of the Directive, detailing the national licensing laws relevant to production, transport or distribution of electricity.

exclusive rights in order for it to be covered by the Directive. It has been suggested that this category of private firm will only be obliged to follow the Directive's procurement rules where there is a prior agreement to supply such networks with energy. Where there is no such agreement and where there is merely an intention to sell the product to the highest bidder, which may or may not be operating a public supply network, the situation is less clear.[15]

3. The common rules

The common rules to be applied to procurement by contracting entities **10.26** are laid down in Titles II (technical specifications and standards); Title III (procedures for advertising of contracts) and Title IV (qualification and selection of candidates and award of contracts).

These rules largely mirror the common rules established under the "general regime" but Directive 90/531/EEC is generally more flexible in a number of important respects.

(i) Title II: the rules on common specifications and standards

Article 13 follows the scheme of the "general regime" by requiring the **10.27** adoption of European specifications wherever they exist. Contracting entities may however establish further complementary specifications, but these should as far as possible indicate performance requirements as opposed to design characteristics.

Although not explicitly stated in Title II, contracting entities remain subject to the general principles of Community law concerning the non-discriminatory use and application of technical specifications (Case 45/87 *Dundalk* [1988] ECR 4929).

Contracting entities may derogate from Article 13(2) in a number of **10.28** situations, for example, where the relevant specification is either inappropriate for the product; or does not take account of recent technical developments; or finally if the product is genuinely innovative in nature.

Where recourse is made to this derogation it must be contained in the notices published pursuant to Article 16(1)(a) or 16(2) (see below).

In the absence of European specifications, the technical specifications **10.29** should be defined as far as possible by reference to other standards having currency within the Community.

(ii) Title III: advertising and publicity rules

Unlike the relevant rules to be found in the "general regime", Title III of **10.30** Council Directive 90/531/EEC does not take as its starting point a general presumption in favour of open tendering.

[15] Trepte,"The application of procurement procedures in the hitherto excluded sectors – war-torn but triumphant", (1990) 1 *Utilities Law Review* 158.

In accordance with Article 15, contracting entities may choose between open, restricted or negotiated procedures (as defined in Art 1(6)), provided a call for competition has been made in accordance with Article 16(2).

A call for competition may be made by a specific notice relating to the particular contract to be awarded (Art 16(1)); by periodic indicative notice (Art 16(1)(b)) or by a notice on the existence of a qualification system (Art 16(1)(c)).

If a periodic indicative notice is so used, it must comply with the provisions of Article 16(2) and Article 17. A periodic notice must now be published at least once a year (Art 17(1)).

10.31   Where the notice is used as a means of calling for competition it must:

(a) refer specifically to the supplies or works which will be the subject of the contract to be awarded;

(b) indicate the type of procedure to be adopted and specify that there will be no further call for competition.

Contracting entities must subsequently invite all candidates to confirm their interest on the basis of detailed information on the contract concerned before beginning the selection of tenderers or participants in negotiations (Art 16(3)).

Article 15(2) allows the use of negotiated procedures *without* a call for competition in a variety of circumstances (see Art 15(2(a)-(i) for a full list). These include, for example;

(a) where there is an absence of tenders in response to a prior call for competition, provided that the original contract conditions have not been substantially changed; or

(b) where the contract is a pure research contract and does not involve any profit or cost recover element; and

(c) for contracts awarded on the basis of a framework agreement, provided that the condition referred to in Article 5(2) is fulfilled.

(a) Framework agreements

10.32   Article 5 of the Directive also makes special provisions for "framework agreements" (as defined in Art 1(4)). Where contracting entities intend to award a framework agreement, they must do so in accordance with the procedures set out in the Directive, but they may avail themselves of Article 15(2)(i) when awarding contracts based upon it.

(b) Post-contractual notices

10.33   Article 18 requires contracting entities to communicate the award of a contract to the Commission within two months. The contents of the notice are specified in Annex XV, which divides the information to be provided in two parts.

Section 1 of Annex XV covers information for publication in the *Official Journal*. The awarding body must provide certain minimum details as to the nature of the contract (*i.e.* supply or works); a summary indication of the nature of the products, works or services provided; the form of call for competition that was used, or if no call was made, the relevant justification as provided under Article 15(2); the nature of the award procedure (*i.e.* open, restricted or negotiated); the number of tenders received, the name and address of the successful supplier, and information on sub-contracting.

Section 2 of Annex XV specifies the information which has to be provided **10.34** for the Commission's own internal use. This includes *inter alia* the value of the contract, the country of origin of the product or service; whether recourse was made to the exceptions to the use of European specifications; the award criteria used (*i.e.* lowest price or most economically advantageous – see below).

(c) Time-limits

Article 20 sets out the time-limits for the receipt of tenders.

Article 20(2)(b) allows for time-limits to be fixed by mutual agreement **10.35** between the contracting entity and the selected candidates "provided that all tenders are given equal time to prepare and submit tenders."

Article 22 provides that relevant contract documents must be sent within six days of the final date for tender submission. If the documentation is too voluminous, arrangements must be made for on-the-spot inspection, and the time-limits should be adjusted accordingly.

(d) Employment obligations

As a consequence of the Court's decision in Case 113/89 *Rush Portugesa* v **10.36** *Office National d'Immigration* [1990] 1417 a contracting entity which supplies information relating to the employment protection provisions and the working conditions which are in force in the relevant area or region of the Member State where *works* are to be carried out, *shall* request tenders or candidates to indicate that they have taken these obligations into account when drawing up their bid. This is stated to be without prejudice to the provisions of Article 27(5) (see below).

(iii) Title IV: qualification and selection of candidates

This Title sets out the common rules on competition. It contains separate **10.37** provisions on the criteria for the selection of candidates and for the subsequent award of contracts.

In Case 31/87 *Beentjes* [1988] ECR 4635, the Court ruled that:

> "Even though the [Works] Directive ... does not rule out the possibility that examination of the tenderer's suitability and the award of the contract may take place simultaneously, the two procedures are governed by different rules" (recital 16).

Where a contracting entity establishes a qualification or selective list **10.38** system, that is a pre-established list of suitable candidates, this must be operated in accordance with Article 24. Article 24 sets out the basic principle that these lists must be drawn up on the basis of objective criteria and the rules and criteria for qualification must be available on request. A candidate may only be refused inclusion on the list, or subsequently excluded from it, on the basis of objective criteria.

The qualification system must be the subject of a notice drawn up in the form to be found in Annex III, and published in the *Official Journal.* If the intended duration of the system is longer than three years, the notice must be renewed annually (Art 24(9)).

(a) Selection for restricted or negotiated procedures

10.39   Article 25 lays down rules for the initial selection of candidates to participate in restricted or negotiated procedures. It states that:

> "Contracting entities which select candidates to tender in restricted procedures or to participate in negotiated procedures shall do so according to objective criteria and rules which they lay down and which they shall make available to interested suppliers or contractors" (Art 25(1)).
>
> "The criteria may be based on the objective need of the contracting entities to reduce the number of candidates to a level which is justified by the need to balance the particular characteristics of the contract award procedure and the resources required to complete it" (Art 25(3)).

10.40   In Cases 27-29/86 *CEI and Bellini* [1987] ECR 3347 the Court ruled that the purpose of the equivalent articles in the public works Directive was:

> "not to delimit the power of the Member States to fix the level of financial and economic standing and technical knowledge required in order to take part in procedures for the award of public works contracts, but to determine the references or evidence which may be furnished in order to establish the contractors' financial and economic standing and technical knowledge or ability."

In Case 31/87 *Beentjes,* the Court added:

> "Nevertheless, it is clear from these provisions that the authorities awarding contracts can check the suitability of the contractors only on the basis of criteria relating to their economic and financial standing and their technical knowledge and ability" (recital 17).

10.41   The Court thus held that the criterion of specific experience for the work to be carried out is a legitimate criterion of technical ability and knowledge for the purposes of ascertaining the suitability of contractors.

It is also clear that the criteria for selection and their method of application must comply with the basic principles of Community law, in particular with the principles of freedom to provide services and the freedom of establishment.

Thus the Court has found that a requirement under Italian law that only undertakings in which there was a majority holding by an Italian company would be eligible to supply software services to the State was contrary to Articles 52 and 59.

In Cases 27–29/86 *CIE and Bellini* the plaintiff had its tender excluded on the ground that it did not satisfy the criteria laid down by the Belgian legislation for recognition in an official list of recognised contractors, as required by the contract documents. The plaintiff had however obtained such recognition in Italy.

On the basis of an analysis of the overall scheme of the Directive, and of **10.42** the "function" of a contractor's inclusion in an official list of recognised contractors in a Member State, the Court held that the Directive does not preclude an awarding authority from requiring a contractor recognised in another Member State to furnish certain information even when that contractor was recognised in his Member State of origin "in an equivalent class". Acceptance of classifications established by authorities of one Member State is required only in so far as they were "based on equivalent criteria in regard to the capacities required" (recital 27).

Article 25(3) requires that the number of candidates selected must take account of the need to secure adequate competition. There is no minimum limit on the number to be selected, as for example in Article 22(3) of Directive 71/305/EEC which requires that the number of candidates should be no less than three.

(b) Contract award

Article 27 deals with contract award. As with the two earlier Directives it **10.43** provides that the only criteria on which the contracting entities shall base their awards shall be:
(a) the most economically advantageous tender; or
(b) the lowest price only.

Where (a) is the criterion, contracting entities shall state in the contract documents or in the tender notices all the criteria they intend to apply to the award (Art 27(2)).

In Case 31/87 *Beentjes,* the Court clarified the scope of the awarding **10.44** authorities' discretion under the first alternative:

"Although [the most economically advantageous criterion] leaves it open to the authorities awarding contracts to choose the criteria on which they propose to base their award of the contract, their choice is limited to criteria aimed at identifying the offer which is economically the most advantageous...
Furthermore, the [public works] Directive does not lay down a uniform and exhaustive body of Community rules; within the framework of the common rules which it contains, the Member States remain free to maintain or adopt substantive and procedural rules in regard to public works contracts on condition that they comply with all the relevant provisions of Community law, in particular the prohibitions flowing from the principles laid down in the Treaty in regard to the right of establishment and the freedom to provide services." [16]

---

[16] See also Cases 27–29/86.

The "lowest price"

10.45   Article 27(5) allows contracting entities to reject, under certain conditions, tenders which appear "abnormally low" in relation to the services required.

The Court has interpreted the scope of the awarding authority to reject such tenderers rather narrowly: Case 76/81 *Transroute* v *Ministère de Travaux Publics* [1982] ECR 417 and Case 103/88 *Fratelli Costanzo* v *Commune di Milano* [1989] ECR 1839.

Article 27(5) allows Member States to require that tenders be examined when those tenders appear to be abnormally low, and not only when they are obviously abnormally low.

In Case C–295/89 *Impresa Dona Alfonso di Dona Alfosna & Figli snc* v *Consorzio per lo Sviluppo Industriale del Commune de Monfalcone* (judgment of 18 June 1991) the Court held that Article 29(5) of the public works Directive 71/305/EEC prohibits Member States from introducing provisions which require the automatic exclusion from procedures for the award of contracts of certain tenders determined according to a mathematical criterion, instead of obliging the awarding authority to apply the examination procedure laid down in the Directive, giving the tenderer an opportunity to furnish explanations. When implementing the public works Directive Member States may not depart to any material extent from the provisions of Article 29(5).

State aids

10.46   If the contracting entity believes that a contract is abnormally low because the recipient is in receipt of a state aid, the onus is on the tenderer, following consultation with the contracting entity to show that the aid has been notified. If the Article 93(3) EEC procedure has not been complied with, the contracting entity may reject the bid and must notify the Commission accordingly.

(c) Additional criteria

10.47   Article 28(1) provides that contract awards may be based on other criteria designed to give preference to certain tenderers provided those rules are compatible with the Treaty. It follows from the Court's jurisprudence on the "general regime" and particularly its judgment in Case 31/87 *Beentjes*, that any additional criteria must not be discriminatory, and that in any event they must be mentioned in the relevant contract notices.

10.48   Article 28(2) allows regional preference schemes to be operated, under certain conditions until 31 December 1992. As a result of the Court's judgment in Case C-21/88 *Du Pont de Nemours* ([1990] ECR 889) and in Case 351/88 *Laboratori Bruneau* v *Unita Sanitaria Locale de Monterondo* (judgment of 11 July 1991) the legality of regional preference schemes is not free from doubt.[17]

---

[17] See further Commission Communication on public procurement ... regional and social aspects (OJ 1989 C311/7) where the Commission examines the problems that regional preference schemes pose from the point of view of their compatibility with the fundamental aims of Community procurement policy, and indeed the Treaty itself.

Following its judgment in Case 31/87 *Beentjes,* Member States appear in principle free to pursue certain social and regional policy objectives in contract award procedures, however, providing that these are not incompatible with the basic Treaty rules and are not discriminatory, and provided that these criteria are applied in conformity with all the procedural rules laid down in the Directive. A general reference, for example to a provision of national legislation specifying certain social policy goals, cannot satisfy the publicity requirement.

4. The Community preference rule

Directive 90/531/EEC, unlike the works or the supplies Directives, provides **10.49** a third ground for legitimate rejection which is of considerable importance to non-Community based suppliers. Article 29 contains the so-called Community preference rule. It provides that any:

> "tender for the award of a supply contract may be rejected where the proportion of the products *originating in third countries* determined in accordance with Council Regulation 802/68 ... on the common definition of the concept of the origin of goods in the total value of the products constituting the tender exceeds 50%" (JO 1968 L148/1).

Where two or more tenders satisfy the Article 27 award criteria, **10.50** preference should be given to the Community bid, if the price difference does not exceed 3%, unless the acceptance of that tender would oblige the contracting entity to acquire material having technical characteristics different from those of existing material, or would lead to technical difficulties of operation, or disproportionate costs.

In accordance with Article 29 the question of whether the offer is made by an EC subsidiary of a non-EC company or by a non-EC company itself is irrelevant. Indeed even if the tender is submitted by an EC company this will be of no assistance if more than 50% of the products are of non-EEC origin.

Article 5 of Regulation (EEC) 802/68 supplies the basic test that where **10.51** two or more countries are involved in the production of a product, origin is conferred on the country in which the last substantial process operation that is economically justified was performed, having been carried out in an undertaking equipped for the purpose and resulting in the manufacture of a new product, or representing an important stage of manufacture.

This definition has stimulated academic and judicial debate as to whether the test is a technical one, related to the nature of the work carried out, or an economic test, requiring a minimum economic added value for the operations before they can be capable of conferring origin, or alternatively that the appropriate test is a mixture of both.[18]

---

[18] Trepte, "War-torn but triumphant", *op cit* at n15.

10.52   In its recent ruling on the meaning of "last substantial process or operation" for the purposes of Article 5 in Case C-26/88 *Brother International GmbH* v *Hauptzollamt Giessen*[19] the Court seemed to favour the use of the technical test, with could be supplemented by an economic test where the technical test is inadequate.

The Court has also confirmed that Article 5 of Regulation (EEC) 802/68 provides that the process conferring origin is the last substantial process in the manufacturing chain and not necessarily the *most* substantial process.[20] Unfortunately, however, the Court has not given clear indications of the circumstances in which the technical test alone would be insufficient to make an origin determination, in which case the auxiliary value-added test could be used.

10.53   Article 29 also stipulates more clearly that the Community can, by way of Council Decision, extend the benefits of the Directive by bilateral or multilateral agreement to third countries. The Commission is now also under an obligation to submit an annual report on progress on such negotiations, and the Council, acting by qualified majority may amend Article 29 in the light of developments.

5. Proposal on services procurement by utilities

10.54 In 1991 the Commission put forward a proposal for a public services Directive to complement the public supplies and public works Directive (Com (91) 322, 30 August 1991). It has now issued a Working Document for services procurement in the utilities sector. The Commission's intention is to extend the procedural provisions of Directive 90/531/EEC, by amendment, to cover services. Hence the proposed Article 1(4) incorporates the definition of services into that for the other types of contracts. In accordance with the proposal's aim, service contracts are defined in such a way as to cover all services purchased in the sectors in question which do not fall within the definition of supply and works already covered by Directive 90/531/EEC.

10.55   The Commission is of the view that certain provisions can be applied to all three types of contract (that is works, supplies and services). Hence, if and when the latest proposal is adopted, the following provisions will apply automatically to services:

– Article 2 – scope;
– Article 4(2) and (4) – non-discrimination;
– Article 5 – framework contracts;
– Article 10 – contracts declared to be secret;
– Article 13 – technical specifications;
– Articles 19-22 – procedural obligations;

---

[19] [1989] ECR 4253.
[20] Case 34/78 *Yoshida Nederland BV* v *Kamer van Koophandel* [1979] ECR 115 and Case 114/78 *Yoshida GmbH* v *Industrie- und Handelskammer Kassel* [1979] ECR 151.

– Article 24 – qualification system;
– Article 25 – selection criteria;
– Article 27(2) to (5) – award criteria;
– Article 34 – statistical reporting.

The proposal also covers design contests (as defined by Article 1(6)), the **10.56**
purpose of which is to weigh up competing ideas. Specific procedural rules
are laid down in Article 17A to ensure that such contests are held on a
transparent and non-discriminatory basis. This article provides that:

> "Design contests shall be subject to the rules set out below. When design
> contests are held as a separate procedure (*i.e.* separate from the normal
> procedures for awarding supply, services or works contracts) these rules are
> only applicable when the total amount of prizes and payments to participants
> is not less than ECU 200,000.
> The admission of participants to design contests shall not be limited by
> reference to the territory or part of the territory of a Member State.
> In the case of design contests with a limited number of participants, contracting
> entities shall apply the rules of Article 25."

(i) Exemptions

The Commission aims only to cover services which are acquired under **10.57**
"arms' length" contracts; services provided in house within a contracting
entity that constitutes a single legal person are not regarded as service
contracts. Similarly, intra-group transactions are to be excluded. The
proposed new Article 11A provides the Directive shall not apply to contracts
for services which:
(a) a contracting entity awards to affiliated undertakings;
(b) are awarded by a joint venture formed by a number of contracting
    entities for the purposes of carrying out a relevant activity in the sense
    of Article 2(2) (see above at para 10.7).

The intention is to exempt those service contracts which are awarded to
an affiliate whose essential purpose is to act as a central service provider to
the group to which it belongs, rather than to sell its services commercially
in the open market. The proposed Article 1(3) defines "affiliated
undertakings" somewhat restrictively.

Furthermore Article 10A provides that the Directive shall not apply to **10.58**
the award of service contracts which contracting entities have to award to
an entity which itself is a contracting entity in the sense of Article 1(b) of
the proposed Directive on public services (Com (90) 372) pursuant to an
exclusive right established by a published law, regulation or administrative
provision which is compatible with the Treaty.

The proposal makes a distinction between service categories – that is
between priority and non-priority services and provides for a system of
"two-tier application".

Priority services are services to which the Community rules are to be
applied to immediately. These are listed in Annex XVIA and are to be

subject to rules similar to those laid down in Directive 90/531/EEC in accordance with the provisions of Titles II, III and IV.

10.59   Annex XIVA includes land and air transport services, financial services, R & D services, architectural and engineering services etc while Annex XVIB covers legal services, placement services, educational and vocational services, investigation and security services etc.

Non-priority services are listed in Annex XVIB and are only to be subject to transparency requirements (Art 12B). Hence such contracts must be awarded in accordance with Articles 13 and 18 of Directive 90/531/EEC.

Article 12C provides that contracts which have as their object services listed in both Annexes XV1A and XV1B shall be awarded in accordance with the provisions of Titles II, III and IV where the value of the services listed in Annex XVIA is greater than the value of the services listed in Annex XV1B.

(ii) Community preference and services

10.60   As there are no international rules governing trade in services, there is no guarantee that third countries would grant Community firms access to their markets. At the same time there are no Community rules defining the origin of services. Hence it is not possible to extend the provisions of Article 29 of Directive 90/531/EEC to service contracts.

Article 29A therefore introduces arrangements applicable solely to the services covered by the proposed Directive which enable the Commission to attempt to solve by negotiation any problems of access to third-country markets which may arise. Article 29A(4) also allows the Commission to take measures to limit access by third country firms where it is established that the countries in question prevent Community firms from entering their markets. The Council may, by qualified majority, decide to amend these measures.

6. Enforcement

(i) Commission monitoring

10.61   In order to monitor the enforcement of Directive 90/531/EEC, Article 33 allows the Commission to request certain information from contracting entities relating to contract award procedures from contracting entities which shall be sufficient to permit them to justify their decisions on:

(a) the qualification and selection of contractors or suppliers and award of contracts;

(b) recourse to derogations from the use of European specifications;

(c) use of procedures without a prior call for competition;

(d) non-application of Titles II and IV in accordance with the derogations provided for in Title I.

This information must be kept for a minimum of four years, and must be available to the Commission on request.

Article 33 also requires Member States to prepare annual reports which should include for each category of activity referred to in Annexes I–X, a breakdown between supply and works contracts; the breakdown between the means of call for competition provided for in Article 16, as well as those awarded without a prior call for competition; the breakdown between supply and works contracts; and the breakdown between contracts awarded to suppliers inside and outside the Community and from each of the Member States.   **10.62**

This information must be kept for a minimum period of four years, and must be available to the Commission on request.

Article 34 also provides that Member States must compile a statistical report for the Commission.

Contracting entities are also obliged to communicate certain information to the Commission within two months of awarding a contract.   **10.63**

Action has also been taken to monitor contracts financed by the Community itself, via the structural funds and loans from the European Investment Bank. The availability of Community finance is made expressly conditional on respect for the procurement obligations. Where entities fail to comply, the finance can be withheld or reclaimed (see Notice C(88) 2510, OJ 1989 C22/3).

(ii) Commission enforcement

The Commission's enforcement powers under the EEC Treaty are primarily those conferred upon it by Articles 186 and 169 of the Treaty. It has also indicated that it may use its powers under Article 90(3) to ensure compliance with the procurement Directives (see Chap 4 for a discussion of Article 90(3)).   **10.64**

Article 169 EEC empowers the Commission to institute proceedings in the Court of Justice against a Member State which has failed to fulfil its obligations under the Treaty.[21]

Actions are brought under Article 169 against Member States. The Court has been prepared to adopt an extensive definition of the "Member State" for the purposes of this article.

In Case 16/69 *Commission* v *Belgium* [1970] ECR 237 it ruled:

"the liability of a Member State under Article 169 arises whatever the agency of the State whose action or inaction is the cause of the failure to fulfil its obligations, even in the case of a constitutionally independent institution" (at 243).

Hence Member States may be liable for infringements by autonomous provincial or regional authorities (Case 169/82 *Commission* v *Italy* [1984] ECR 1603).

---

[21] Similar powers are to be found in Art 88 ECSC and Art 141 Euratom.

10.65   The responsibility of Member States may also be engaged through a private body whose activities are subject to direct or indirect governmental control. In Case 249/81 *Commission* v *Ireland* [1982] ECR 4005 the Court held Ireland responsible for infringing Article 30 in respect of the activities of the Irish Goods Council. The Irish Government had appointed the chairman and the members of the Council, given directions as to its aims and objectives and provides most of the funds for achieving them.

(a) Interim measures

10.66   If Article 169 proceedings are to be effectively used against infringements of the procurement rules, the Commission will usually be required to apply for interim measures on the basis of Article 186 EEC to prevent the contract in question from being awarded. For an order for interim measures to be granted by the Court of Justice several conditions must be satisfied.

First, an application for interim measures can only be made by a party to, and in respect of, a case pending before the European Court. In other words the Court can only intervene when the "judicial phase" of the Article 169 proceedings has been reached.[22] This means that the Member State in question must have been given the opportunity to respond to a "reasoned opinion" issued by the Commission as the culmination of the first, "administrative" stage of the Article 169 proceedings.

10.67   This "reasoned opinion" usually stipulates a time-limit sufficient to enable the Member State to regularise its position. This is usually two months, but the Court has recognised that in cases of emergency much shorter periods of as little as six days may be justified (Case 293/85 *Commission* v *Belgium* [1988] ECR 305).

Second, for an order for interim measures to be granted by the Court, an application must state the circumstances giving rise to urgency and the factual and legal grounds establishing a prima facie case for the interim measures applied for (Art 83(2) of the Rules of Procedure of the Court of Justice).

Third, the Court shall have to be convinced that the balance of interests "tilts in the Commission's favour".

10.68   In a recent case concerning a failure on the part of the Italian authorities to advertise a public works contract, the Commission applied for an interim injunction to prohibit any award of a contract until the invitation to tender had been properly advertised in the *Official Journal* (Case 194/88R *Commission* v *Italy* [1988] ECR 4547). The Italian Government countered that the completion of the project was urgently required for environmental reasons, so that the procedural requirements of the Directive could be dispensed with.

The Court, on a review of the facts, found for the Commission and moreover, accepted its argument that a failure to comply with the public works Directive 71/305/EEC constitutes a serious breach of Community law:

---

[22] European Court Rules of Procedure, Art 83.

"particularly since a declaration of illegality by the Court obtained under Article 169 cannot make good the damage suffered by the undertakings ... which were excluded from the tendering procedures ...." (recital 17).

In the future the Commission should also be able to invoke the "corrective **10.69** mechanism" procedures available under the proposed remedies Directive where it considers that a clear and manifest infringement of Community provisions in the field of public procurement has been committed during a contract award procedure (Art 9 of the 1991 draft, discussed below).

The Court has, however, refused to grant interim measures where a Member State has claimed the urgency of a project on environmental grounds – Case 45/87R *Commission* v *Ireland* [1987] ECR 1369.

(iii) Private enforcement

(a) New enforcement Directive for the utilities sector

Given that the procurement rules for this sector extend to the activities of **10.70** private as well as public firms, the Commission has been required to address a number of complex legal problems in its draft Council Directive co-ordinating the laws, regulations and administrative provisions relating to the application of Community rules on the procurement procedures of entities operating in the water, energy, transport and telecommunications sector (hereafter, the "enforcement Directive"). As utilities have in many cases not been subject to *any* regulation of their procurement procedures, national systems of remedies simply do not exist.

At the same time, however, the new proposal, which was initially **10.71** submitted to the Council and the Parliament in autumn 1990 (Com (90) 297, final) and resubmitted in amended form in June 1991[23], endeavours to ensure that the remedies provided are as close as possible to those already adopted for the general system of public procurement review system.

Nevertheless, "account must be taken of the specific nature of certain legal orders by authorising the Member States to choose between the introduction of different powers for the review bodies which have equivalent effects."[24] The proposed Directive is to come into effect on the same dates as those contained in Directive 90/531/EEC (Art 13).

(b) The proposal

The Council reached a common position on the Commission's amended **10.72** proposal on 16 October 1991. In its current form, the draft Directive shall apply to:

(a) contract award procedures falling within the scope of Directive 90/531/EEC; and

---

[23] Amended proposal for a Council Directive co-ordinating the laws, regulations and administrative provisions relating to the application of Community rules on the procurement procedures of entities operating in the water, energy, transport and telecommunications sector (OJ 1991 C179/18).

[24] Preamble to amended proposal, *ibid.*

(b) contracting entities falling within the scope of Article 3(2)(a) of that Directive (Art 1).

Member States are obliged to ensure that contract awards by such entities can be reviewed effectively and rapidly where it is alleged that such decisions have infringed Community law or national implementing laws. Further, Member States are obliged to ensure that the decisions taken by review bodies can be effectively enforced (Art 2(8)).

(c) Review procedures

10.73 In accordance with Article 2, Member States may choose between different forms of review procedures, which need not in themselves have suspensive effect. In other words the Member States have a choice between direct intervention in utilities' decisions (suspension of procedures, setting aside of decisions) and indirect measures (damages). Member States can choose between the alternatives in accordance with their legal or political priorities. The procedures shall include the powers, either:

(a) to take interim measures with the aim of correcting the alleged infringement or preventing further damages, including measures to suspend or to ensure the suspension of the procedure for the award of a contract or the implementation of any decision taken by the contracting entity;

(b) to set aside or ensure the setting aside of unlawful decisions;
or

10.74 (c) to take other measures with the aim of correcting the infringement or preventing further damage, in particular the power to award penalty damages of a particular sum, in cases where the infringement has not been corrected or prevented.

Article 2(5) provides that this sum must be set at a level high enough to dissuade the contracting entity from committing or persisting in an infringement. The payment of the sum may be made dependent on a final decision that the infringement has actually taken place.

The Member States may exercise this choice either for all contracting entities or for categories of contracting entities which are defined by objective criteria.

10.75 (d) and, to award damages to persons injured by the infringement.

Furthermore the Member States may provide that where damages are claimed on the grounds that the decision was taken unlawfully, the contested decision must be first set aside or declared illegal. Member States can only require the setting aside of a decision if their national law already contains such a requirement (Art 2(1)).

The effects of the exercise of the powers listed in Article 2(1) on a contract concluded subsequent to its award are to be determined by national law. The individual Member States may also limit the available remedies after the conclusion of the contract to damages (Art 2(6)).

10.76 Where a claim is made for damages representing the costs of preparing a bid or of participating in an award procedure, the person making the claim is required to prove that Community law (or the implementing national rules) has been infringed, and that he would have had a real chance of winning the contract, and that as a result of the infringement, that chance was adversely affected. He is not required to prove that, in the absence of the infringement, he would have been awarded the contract.

The bodies responsible for review need not be judicial in character, but they must follow certain procedural rules and their decisions must be subject to judicial review by another body which is a court or tribunal within the meaning of Article 177 EEC.

(d) Attestation

Article 3 introduces the new "attestation procedure". This is envisaged as an alternative form of control to the remedies outlined in Article 2. Member States shall give contracting entities whose contract award procedures fall within the scope of Directive 90/531/EEC[25] the possibility of having recourse to an attestation procedure in accordance with Articles 4-7 of the draft Directive. The aim of this periodic procedure is to obtain an attestation or *ex post facto* review that the entity's procedures and practices are in conformity with Community law.   **10.77**

It follows that Member States are not obliged to set up an attestation system; they need only offer that possibility. If contracting entities are willing to use an attestation system existing in another Member State, the contracting entity *must* be allowed to do so.

Article 5 sets out the procedures for preparing the attestation report.   **10.78**

Article 6 governs the qualifications of attestors. The attestors must be independent of the contracting entities. The Member States may identify persons, professions and institutions whose staff satisfy the requirements of Article 6(1). The Member State need not formally approve the choice of a particular attestor, however.

Article 7 states that the provisions of Articles 4, 5 and 6 shall be considered as essential requirements for the development of European standards on attestation. It would appear that the Commission intends to develop relevant standards to be available when the Directive comes into force. Article 12 provides that four years after the application of the Directive, the Commission shall review, *inter alia,* the use of European standards.

(e) The corrective mechanism

Article 8 confers certain powers on the Commission to invoke certain notification procedures when, prior to a contract being concluded, it considers that a clear and manifest infringement of Community procurement rules has been committed.   **10.79**

The Commission must notify the Member State and the contracting entity concerned, giving its reasons. The Member States has then 30 days to notify the Commission that the infringement has been corrected, or that

---

[25] But presumably not those subject to Art 3(2)(a).

the contract has been suspended, or alternatively it may provide a "reasoned submission as to why no correction was made" (Art 8(3)).

(f) Conciliation

10.80   As an alternative to litigation Articles 9 and 10 of the draft propose a *voluntary* conciliation procedure at Community level. This may be invoked by written notification to Commission or to the appropriate national authorities, listed in the Annex to the draft. The conciliation procedure is conducted via a working group appointed by the chairman of the Advisory Committee on Public Contracts. The contracting entity, the tenderer or any other candidate may make written or oral representations to the working group. Where an interested party other than the person invoking the conciliation procedure is already pursuing judicial or other review proceedings, the contracting entity must inform the working group. The chairman may then invite the party to such procedures to participate in the conciliation procedure. If he refuses, the working group may decide to halt the conciliation procedure if it considers the participation of that party is necessary to resolve the dispute.

The conciliation procedure is stated to be without prejudice to any action that the Commission or any Member State may take pursuant to Articles 169 or 170 of the Treaty, or pursuant to Article 8 (the corrective mechanism) or to the rights of the persons invoking the conciliation procedure, those of the contracting entity or any other person (Art 11).

7. **Remedies for non-implementation of Directives**

10.81   What is the position of private parties when a Member State has either failed to implement a Directive within the time limits laid down in it, or has implemented it incorrectly?

(i) **Direct effect**

10.82   In Case 31/87 *Beentjes* the Court restated its established jurisprudence to the effect that when applying national law specifically introduced in order to implement a Directive, a national court is required to interpret its national law in the light of the wording and the purpose of the directive in order to achieve the result referred to in Article 189(3).

Directives which have not been implemented within the prescribed period, or which have been incorrectly implemented, may be relied upon by individuals on condition that the subject matter is unconditional and sufficiently precise.

10.83   In *Beentjes* the Court ruled that the rules in the public works Directive on the economic and technical suitability of candidates, on the criteria to be used for the award, and on the publication of theses criteria (Arts 20, 26 and 29) were sufficiently precise and unconditional to be relied upon before the national courts (see also Case 76/81 *Transporoute* v *Ministère de Travaux Publics* [1982] ECR 417 where Art 29 of the public works Directive was held to be directly effective).

Where a Directive requires a Member State to adopt specific implementing measures, for example, to set up the review tribunal referred to in the proposed Directive on enforcement in the utilities sector, then the relevant provisions of the Directive will probably not be directly effective. Nevertheless the Court's recent case law requiring national courts to ensure that Community rights are made fully effective by providing the requisite remedies to realise these rights, is of considerable importance here (Case 340/89 *Vlassopolou* judgment of 7 May 1991; Case C-213/89 *Factortame* [1990] ECR 2433).

(ii) Horizontal direct effect

Beentjes, Transporoute and *Fratelli Costanzo* all concerned allegations that the   **10.84** Member State (including a local authority in the *Fratelli Costanzo* case) had not complied with the provisions of the public works Directive. In other words, these cases were confined to issues involving *vertical direct effect.*

A significant issue raised by Council Directive 90/531/EEC is whether its provisions may be invoked by individuals against the contracting entities which fall within the scope of its Article 2, including public undertakings and "private entities" which perform one of the functions listed in Article 2(2), and do so on the basis of special or exclusive rights.

The Court of Justice has confined its jurisprudence on the direct effect of a Directive, to situations where the Directive's provisions are invoked against the "state" or "public authorities" (Case 152/84 *Marshall* v *Southampton and South-West Hampshire Area Health Authority* [1987] ECR 723). The doctrine of "horizontal direct effect" while applicable to certain Treaty articles has not been extended to Directives.

At the same time, however, the Court has tended to interpret the concept   **10.85** of a "public authority" or an "emanation of the state" rather widely.

In Case C-188/89 *Foster* v *British Gas* [1990] ECR not yet reported) the Court concluded on the basis of its past decisions that:

> "It follows ... that a body, whatever its legal form, which has been made responsible, pursuant to a measures adopted by the State for providing a public service under the control of the State and has for that purpose special powers beyond those which result from the normal rules applicable in relations between individuals is included in any event among the bodies against which the provisions of a directive capable of having direct effect may be relied upon" (recital 20).

It would appear from the jurisprudence cited in *Foster* that the element   **10.86** of control is not the decisive criterion in defining the concept of "public authority". There is an additional *functional* test that the relevant body – whatever its legal form – must be responsible for the exercise of certain duties, such as for example "the provision of a public service in the public

261

interest which would not be expected of a private individual or commercial undertaking."

10.87 In *Beentjes* the Court was prepared to recognise that for the purposes of Directive 71/305/EEC, the term state must be interpreted in functional terms if the aims of the objective were to be realised (recital 11).

In *Foster* the Court observed that in addition to the potential influence which the Secretary of State could exercise over the then statutory corporation – British Gas – the BGC was also responsible for developing and maintaining a system of gas supply and had a monopoly over that supply.

(iii) Indirect effect

10.88 It may be the case that the Court will gradually abandon the complexities involved in the application of a restrictive doctrine of direct effect to a wide category of "public undertakings", given the inevitable inconsistencies which will arise in the application of Community law in the different Member States.

In the recent Case 108/89 *Marleasing SA* v *La Commercial Internacional de Alimentacion* (judgment of 13 November 1990 [1990] ECR 1599) the Court appears to have circumvented if not altogether abandoned the entire notion of "direct effect" of Directives. In Case 106/89 the Court was asked whether a provision of a Company law Directive was directly effective as between two private companies. In accordance with the doctrine of "horizontal direct effect" this would not have been the case. Nevertheless the Court concluded that all national legislation, irrespective of whether it pre- or post-dated the Community Directive, must be reconciled with the provisions of that Directive.

10.89 In other words, the national court was obliged, so far as possible to "interpret" existing national law as if it had been amended by the Community Directive. The application of this so-called doctrine of "indirect effect" is not restricted by the vertical/horizontal dichotomy discussed above.

The first obligation of the national court is to try to reconcile national and Community law. If that fails then the court should consider whether the rights laid down in the Directive can apply to the parties through the doctrine of direct effect.

(iv) Damages for non-implementation

10.90 In Cases C-6/90 and C-9/90 *Francovich and Bonifaci* Advocate-General Misho proposed that Member States should be liable in damages to individuals or businesses for losses suffered when their governments fail to implement Community law. The Court of Justice has now ruled that individuals can sue for damages against governments which have caused direct harm to them by failing to implement Community law properly (judgment of 19

November 1991). The Court did, however, set a number of conditions which had to be met before a citizen could sue a government. The Directive in question has to grant rights to private individuals; the extent of those rights has to be identifiable from the text; and the harm suffered by the individuals has to be caused by the government's breach of its obligations. Damages claims resulting from breaches of Community law must be settled in national courts according to national civil liability law.

8. Conclusion

The Community's efforts to open up public procurement in the utilities **10.91** sector in general raises a number of novel issues in Community law, particularly in the area of legal remedies. The scope or "field of application" of Council Directive 90/531/EEC has been drawn very widely, so that not only state-owned but also privately owned utilities which benefit from special or exclusive rights are subject to the Community procurement rules. This chapter has contended that the definition supplied by Article 2 may be difficult to operationalise in practice. It might be noted in this context that, should the Commission persuade the Council to adopt its present proposals on the completion of the internal electricity market, the Member States will be required to remove or adjust many of the special and exclusive rights presently enjoyed by national electricity utilities. In particular, exclusive rights to generate, to transmit and otherwise supply electricity will have to be removed. This could mean that a large number of *privately owned* utilities might fall completely outside the scope of Directive 90/531/EEC. If this is the case, the Commission may have to reconsider the current definitions applied in that Directive.

APPENDICES

Text of key source material relating to Electricity

COUNCIL RECOMMENDATION 81/924/EEC

of 27 October 1981

on electricity tariff structures in the Community [1]

THE COUNCIL OF THE EUROPEAN COMMUNITIES,

Having regard to the Treaty establishing the European Economic Community, and in particular Article 235 thereof,

Having regard to the draft recommendation from the Commission,

Having regard to the opinion of the European Parliament,

Whereas in its resolution of 13 February 1975 the Council emphasised the need to make it possible for prices to cover, gradually and to the fullest extent feasible, the costs of making energy available and the amortization of necessary investments;

Whereas consistency in energy pricing structures is a fundamental element of economic and energy policy;

Whereas rational tariff structures make for better utilization of resources;

Whereas tariff structures founded on common principles lead to more homogeneous conditions of supply and enable electricity prices to be fixed more consistently throughout the Community;

Whereas the distribution of electricity is a public service, irrespective of the legal status of the undertakings involved; whereas for that reason undertakings must ensure equality of treatment of consumers in comparable supply conditions;

Whereas electricity supply undertakings should, in accordance with the principles of sound management, cover their costs on the basis of the most objective allocation possible of such costs among the various categories of users;

Whereas promotional tariff structures preventing the rational use of energy should be avoided;

Whereas the principles underlying electricity tariff structures vary between countries in the Community, although certain of these structures already reflect a common approach; whereas efforts to bring about simplification and unification must be pursued,

HEREBY RECOMMENDS TO THE MEMBER STATES:

That they take appropriate steps, if they have not already done so, to ensure that electricity tariff structures are based on the following common principles:

(1) Electricity tariff structures should be drawn up and adopted so as to allow the application of a rational price policy and to reflect the costs incurred in supplying the various categories of consumer; tariff structures should be designed with the rational use of energy in mind, should avoid encouraging unjustifiable consumption and should be as clear and simple as possible.

(2) The two-part tariff system which, of the various tariff options available, best reflects the cost structure of providing electricity, should be generally used. (The term "two-part tariff" covers tariff structures consisting of a fixed component and a component which varies with the amount of electricity used.)

(3) Promotional tariff structures which encourage unnecessary consumption and in which the price of electricity is artificially lowered as increasing amounts of electricity are used should be discontinued.

(4) Tariffs based on the use to which electricity is put should be eliminated, unless such tariffs conform with the general requirements of Point 1 above and contribute to the achievement of long-term energy policy objectives.

[1] OJ 1981 L337/12

267

(5) With the aim of transferring demand to off-peak periods or to allow load-shedding, provision should be made for multiple tariffs with differential rates and/or for the possibility of interruptible supplies.

(6) Tariffs should not be kept artificially low, for example on social grounds or for anti-inflationary policy reasons; in such cases, separate action, where warranted, should be taken.

(7) Tariffs should be formulated in such a way that it is possible to up-date prices at regular intervals;

That research be pursued and developed, in close co-operation at Community level, into the characteristics of electricity demand for different categories of consumers and their evolution in the long term, with the objective of further improving tariff structures;

That electricity prices on the market be characterised by the greatest possible degree of transparency, and that these prices and the cost to the consumer be made known to the public as far as possible.

COUNCIL RECOMMENDATION 88/611/EEC

of 8 November 1988

to promote co-operation between public utilities and auto-producers of electricity [1]

THE COUNCIL OF THE EUROPEAN COMMUNITIES,

Having regard to the Treaty establishing the European Economic Community, and in particular Article 235 thereof,

Having regard to the proposal from the Commission,

Having regard to the opinion of the European Parliament,

Having regard to the opinion of the Economic and Social Committee,

Whereas, in its resolution of 16 September 1986 concerning new Community energy policy objectives for 1995 and the convergence of the policies of the Member States, the Council adopted as sectoral objectives improved energy efficiency in all sectors and a greater contribution from new and renewable sources of energy;

Whereas, in accordance with the resolution of 26 November 1986 on a Community orientation to develop new and renewable energy sources, the Council adopted, on 9 June 1988, Recommendation 88/349/EEC on developing the exploitation of renewable energy sources in the Community (OJ 1988 L160/46);

Whereas on 25 October 1977 the Council adopted Recommendation 77/714/EEC on the creation in the Member States of advisory bodies or committees to promote combined heat and power production and the exploitation of residual heat (OJ 1977 L295/5);

Whereas combined heat and power generation (CHP) and waste energy (combustion of waste and use of residual heat in industry), with their potential for oil substitution and savings of

exhaustible primary energy sources, could make an important contribution to the achievement of the Community's 1995 energy policy objectives;

Whereas the generation of electricity is a common field of application not only for renewable sources of energy but also for waste energy and for CHP (in total hereafter called RWC) and is therefore of crucial importance to the development of this energy supply potential;

Whereas these power generation processes are mainly suited, because of inherent factors, to auto-production outside the public supply system;

Whereas the profitability of RWC auto-production will also depend on the conditions of co-operation with the public utilities[2] as regards sales of surplus electricity, purchases of additional electricity, and the provision of reserve capacity;

Whereas certain existing laws and administrative provisions can constitute an obstacle to the development of RWC auto-production;

Whereas the price for the auto-producer's electricity sales to the public network should be geared as closely as possible to the costs that can be avoided in the public supply system in order to guarantee appropriate revenues for the auto-producer;

Whereas a framework of appropriate measures should govern co-operation on electricity between auto-producers and public utilities by establishing common principles and hence creating better

[1] OJ 1988 L335/29.

[2] For the purposes of this Recommendation, "public utility" shall mean an undertaking whose principal objective is the generation, transmission and/or distribution of electricity for supply to third parties. Public utilities may have different corporate structures.

conditions for the further development of RWC auto-production of electricity in the Community,

HEREBY RECOMMENDS TO THE MEMBER STATES:

(1) that, in order to promote auto-production of electricity, based on renewable energy sources, waste energy and combined heat and power (RWC), they should provide a framework for co-operation between public utilities and all RWC auto-producers, under which the conditions concerning the quantity and price of electricity exchanges are agreed in accordance with common principles;

(2) that they should facilitate the creation of this framework by the introduction of standard contract criteria:

- either by voluntary arrangements between the parties concerned, or

- if necessary, through specific legal or administrative provisions,

and that existing legal or administrative provisions at variance with such criteria should be adapted accordingly. The need for defining specific procedures for resolving disputes about contract conditions should also be examined;

(3) that they should ensure within such arrangements or provisions:

(a) that the public utilities should be obliged to offer to purchase those quantities of electricity which arise out of RWC auto-production, always provided that the smooth economic operation of existing public generating plants is not thereby jeopardised;

(b) that, with regard to quantities, RWC auto-production of electricity is authorised in principle as long as a public interest is not thereby infringed, and that it is impeded neither by legal and adminis-trative provisions nor by conditions imposed by the public utilities;

(c) that with regard to prices

- reimbursement for electricity sales to the public supply network from RWC auto-production should:

  - be based primarily on the long-term average costs avoidable by the public utilities in their area of supply,

  - correspond at least to the variable costs avoidable by the public utilities, *i.e.* mainly the savings made in fuel costs,

  - guarantee the auto-producer additional reimbursement to the extent that he enables the public supply network to make savings in investment costs in the generation or purchase of electricity. The size of this reimbursement should depend on how regularly the auto-producer's electricity production capacity is available, especially at peak periods,

- reimbursement for the purchase of electricity from the public supply network is determined in such a way that auto-producers are treated in the same way as comparable purchasers who have no means of auto-production,

- the rules regarding this reimbursement are framed so as to be as transparent as possible;

(4) that they report to the Commission after three years on the progress on co-operation between public utilities and auto-producers of electricity.

COUNCIL DIRECTIVE 90/377/EEC

of 29 June 1990

concerning a Community procedure to improve the transparency of gas and electricity prices charged to industrial end-users [1]

THE COUNCIL OF THE EUROPEAN COMMUNITIES,

Having regard to the Treaty establishing the European Economic Community, and in particular Article 213 thereof,

Having regard to the Commission's proposal,

Having regard to the opinion of the European Parliament,

Having regard to the opinion of the Economic and Social Committee,

Whereas energy price transparency, to the extent that it reinforces the conditions ensuring that competition is not distorted in the common market, is essential to the achievement and smooth functioning of the internal energy market;

Whereas transparency can help to obviate discrimination against users by increasing their freedom to choose between different energy sources and different suppliers;

Whereas, at present, the degree of transparency varies from one energy source and one Community country or region to another, thus calling into question the achievement of an internal energy market;

Whereas, however, the price paid by industry in the Community for the energy which it uses is one of the factors which influence its competitiveness and should therefore remain confidential;

Whereas the system of standard consumers used by the Statistical Office of the European Communities (SOEC) in its price publications and the system of market prices due to be introduced for major industrial electricity users will ensure that transparency is not an obstacle to confidentiality;

Whereas it is necessary to extend the consumer categories used by the SOEC up to the limits at which the consumers remain representative;

Whereas in this way end-users price transparency would be achieved without endangering the necessary confidentiality of contracts; whereas in order to respect confidentiality there must be at least three consumers in a given consumption category for a price to be published;

Whereas this information which concerns gas and electricity consumed by industry for energy end-users, will also enable comparisons to be drawn with other energy sources (oil, coal, fossil and renewable energy sources) and other consumers;

Whereas undertakings which supply gas and electricity as well as industrial gas and electricity consumers remain, independently of the application of this Directive, subject to the Treaty's competition rules and whereas consequently the Commission can require communication of prices and conditions of sale;

Whereas knowledge of the price systems in force forms part of price transparency;

Whereas knowledge of the breakdown of consumers by category and their respective market shares also forms part of price transparency;

Whereas the communication to the SOEC of prices and conditions of sale to consumers and price systems in operation as well as the breakdown of consumers by consumption category should inform the Commission sufficiently for it to decide, as necessary, on appropriate action or proposals in the

---

[1] OJ 1990 L185/16.

light of the situation of the internal energy market;

Whereas the data supplied to the SOEC will be more reliable if the undertakings themselves compile these data;

Whereas familiarity with the taxation and parafiscal charges existing in each Member State is important to ensure price transparency;

Whereas it must be possible to check the reliability of the data supplied to the SOEC;

Whereas the achievement of transparency presupposes the publication and circulation of prices and price systems as widely as possible among consumers;

Whereas to implement energy price transparency the system should be based on the proven expertise and methods developed and applied by the SOEC regarding the processing, checking and publication of data;

Whereas, with the prospect of the achievement of the internal market in energy, the system of price transparency should be rendered operational as soon as possible;

Whereas the uniform implementation of this Directive can only take place in all the Member States when the natural gas market, in particular with regard to infrastructure, has reached a sufficient level of development,

HAS ADOPTED THIS DIRECTIVE:

Article 1

Member States shall take the steps necessary to ensure that undertakings which supply gas or electricity to industrial end-users, as defined in Annexes I and II, communicate to the SOEC in the form provided for in Article 3:

(1) the prices and terms of sale of gas and electricity to industrial end-users;

(2) the price systems in use;

(3) the breakdown of consumers and the corresponding volumes by category

of consumption to ensure the representativeness of these categories at national level.

Article 2

1. The undertakings referred to in Article 1 shall assemble the data provided for in Article 1 (1) and (2), on 1 January and 1 July of each year. These data, drawn up in conformity with the provisions referred to in Article 3, shall be sent to the SOEC and the competent authorities of the Member States within two months.

2. On the basis of the data referred to in paragraph 1, the SOEC shall publish each May and each November, in an appropriate form, the prices of gas and electricity for industrial users in the Member States and the pricing systems used to that end.

3. The information provided for in Article 1 (3) shall be sent every two years to the SOEC and to the Member States' competent authorities. The first communication shall concern the situation as at 1 January 1991. This information shall not be published.

Article 3

The implementing provisions concerning the form, content and all other features of the information provided for in Article 1 are set out in Annexes 1 and II.

Article 4

The SOEC shall not disclose data supplied to it pursuant to Article 1 which might, by their nature, be subject to commercial confidentiality. Such confidential statistical data transmitted to the SOEC shall be accessible only to officials of the SOEC and may be used only for statistical purposes.

This provision shall not, however, prevent the publication of such data in an aggregated form which does not enable individual commercial transactions to be identified.

Article 5

Where the SOEC notes statistically significant anomalies or inconsistencies in data transmitted under this Directive, it may ask the national bodies to allow it to inspect the appropriate disaggregated data as well as the methods of calculation or evaluation upon which the aggregated data are based, in order to assess, or even amend, any information deemed irregular.

Article 6

Where appropriate, the Commission shall make the necessary changes to the Annexes to this Directive in the light of specific problems identified. Such changes may, however, cover only the technical features of the Annexes and may not be of a nature such as to alter the general structure of the system.

Article 7

In the case of any changes to the Annexes, as referred to in Article 6, the Commission shall be assisted by a committee of an advisory nature composed of the representatives of the Member States and chaired by the representative of the Commission.

The representative of the Commission shall submit to the committee a draft of the measures to be taken. The committee shall deliver its opinion on the draft within a time-limit which the chairman may lay down according to the urgency of the matter, if necessary by taking a vote.

The opinion shall be recorded in the minutes; in addition each Member State shall have the right to ask to have its position recorded in the minutes.

The Commission shall take the utmost account of the opinion delivered by the committee. It shall inform the committee of the manner in which its opinion has been taken into account.

Article 8

Once a year the Commission shall present a summary report on the operation of this Directive to the European Parliament, the Council and the Economic and Social Committee.

Article 9

Member States shall adopt the laws, regulations and administrative provisions needed to comply with this Directive no later than 1 July 1991. They shall forthwith inform the Commission thereof.

In the case of natural gas, the Directive will not be implemented in a Member State until five years after the introduction of that form of energy on the market in question. The date of introduction of that energy source on a national market is to be explicitly reported to the Commission by the Member State concerned without delay.

Article 10

This Directive is addressed to the Member States.

COUNCIL DIRECTIVE 90/531/EEC

of 17 September 1990

on the procurement procedures of entities operating in the water, energy, transport and telecommunications sectors [1]

THE COUNCIL OF THE EUROPEAN COMMUNITIES,

Having regard to the Treaty establishing in the European Economic Community and in particular the last sentence of Article 57 (2), Article 66, Article 100a and Article 113 thereof,

Having regard to the proposal from the Commission,

In co-operation with the European Parliament,

Having regard to the opinion of the Economic and Social Committee,

Whereas the measures aimed at progressively establishing the internal market, during the period up to 31 December 1992, need to be taken; whereas the internal market consists of an area without internal frontiers in which free movement of goods, persons, services and capital is guaranteed;

Whereas the European Council has drawn conclusions concerning the need to bring about a single internal market;

Whereas restrictions on the free movement of goods and on the freedom to provide services in respect of supply contracts awarded in the water, energy, transport and telecommunications sectors are prohibited by the terms of Articles 30 and 59 of the Treaty;

Whereas Article 97 of the Euratom Treaty prohibits any restrictions based on nationality as regards companies under the jurisdiction of a Member State where they desire to participate in the construction of nuclear installations of a scientific or industrial nature in the Community;

Whereas these objectives also require the co-ordination of the procurement procedures applied by the entities operating in these sectors;

Whereas the White Paper on the completion of the internal market contains an action programme and a timetable for opening up public procurement markets in sectors which are currently excluded from Council Directive 71/305/EEC of 26 July 1971 concerning the co-ordination of procedures for the award of public works contracts (JO 1971 L185/5), as last amended by Council Directive 89/440/EEC (OJ 1989 L210/1), and Council Directive 77/62/EEC of 21 December 1976 co-ordinating procedures for the award of public supply contracts (OJ 1977 L13/1), as last amended by Directive 88/295/EEC (OJ 1988 L127/1);

Whereas among such excluded sectors are those concerning the provision of water, energy and transport services and, as far as Directive 77/62/EEC is concerned, the telecommunications sector;

Whereas the main reason for their exclusion was that entities providing such services are in some cases governed by public law, in others by private law;

Whereas the need to ensure a real opening-up of the market and a fair balance in the application of procurement rules in these sectors requires that the entities to be covered must be identified on a different basis than by reference to their legal status;

Whereas, in the four sectors concerned, the procurement problems to be solved are of a similar nature, so permitting them to be addressed in one instrument;

Whereas, among the main reasons why entities operating in these sectors do not purchase on the basis of Community-wide competition is the closed nature of the markets in which they operate, due to the existence of special or exclusive rights granted by the national authorities, concerning the supply to, provision or operation of, networks for providing the service concerned, the exploitation of a given geographical area for a particular purpose, the provision or operation of public telecommunications networks or the provision of public telecommunications services;

Whereas the other main reason for the absence of Community-wide competition in these areas results from various ways in which national authorities can influence the behaviour of these entities, including participations in their capital and representation in the entities' administrative, managerial or supervisory bodies;

Whereas this Directive should not extend to activities of those entities which either fall outside the sectors of water, energy and transport services or outside the telecommunications sector, or which fall within those sectors but nevertheless are directly exposed to competitive forces in markets to which entry is unrestricted;

Whereas it is appropriate that these entities apply common procurement procedures in respect of their activities relating to water; whereas certain entities have been covered up to now by the Directives 71/305/EEC and 77/62/EEC in respect of their activities in the field of hydraulic engineering projects, irrigation, land drainage or the disposal and treatment of sewage;

Whereas, however, procurement rules of the type proposed for supplies of goods are inappropriate for purchases of water, given the need to procure water from sources near the area it will be used;

Whereas, when specific conditions are fulfilled, exploitation of a geographical area with the aim of exploring for or extracting oil, gas, coal or other solid fuels may be made subject to alternative arrangements which will enable the same objective of opening up contracts to be achieved; whereas the Commission must ensure that these conditions are complied with by the Member States who implement these alternative arrangements;

Whereas the Commission has announced that it will propose measures to remove obstacles to cross-frontier exchanges of electricity by 1992; whereas procurement rules of the type proposed for supplies of goods would not make it possible to overcome existing obstacles to the purchases of energy and fuels in the energy sector; whereas, as a result, it is not appropriate to include such purchases in the scope of this Directive, although it should be borne in mind that this exemption will be re-examined by the Council on the basis of a Commission report and Commission proposals;

Whereas Regulations (EEC) 3975/87 (OJ 1987 L374) and (EEC) 3976/87 (OJ 1987 L374/9), Directive 87/601/ EEC (OJ 1987 L374/12) and Decision 87/602/EEC (OJ 1987 L374/19) are designed to introduce more competition between the entities offering air transport services to the public and it is therefore not appropriate for the time being to include such entities in the scope of this Directive although the situation ought to be reviewed at a later stage in the light of progress made as regards competition;

Whereas, in view of the competitive position of Community shipping, it would be inappropriate for the greater part of the contracts in this sector to be subject to detailed procedures; whereas the situation of shippers operating sea-going ferries should be kept under review; whereas certain inshore and river ferry services operated by public authorities should no longer be excluded from the scope of Directives 71/305/EEC and 77/62/ EEC;

Whereas it is appropriate to facilitate compliance with provisions relating to activities not covered by this Directive;

Whereas this Directive should not apply to procurement contracts which are declared secret or may affect basic State security interests or are concluded according to other rules set up by existing international agreements or international organizations;

Whereas the Community's or the Member States' existing international obligations must not be affected by the rules of this Directive;

Whereas products, works or services must be described by reference to European specifications; whereas, in order to ensure that a product, work or service fulfils the use for which it is intended by the contracting entity, such reference may be complemented by specifications which do not change the nature of the technical solution or solutions set out in the European specification;

Whereas the principles of equivalence and of mutual recognition of national standards, technical specifications and manufacturing methods are applicable in the field of application of this Directive;

Whereas, when the contracting entities define by common accord with tenderers the deadlines for receiving tenders, they shall comply with the principal of non-discrimination, and whereas, if there is no such agreement, it is necessary to lay down suitable provisions;

Whereas it could prove useful to provide for greater transparency as to the requirements regarding the protection and conditions of employment applicable in the Member State in which the works are to be carried out;

Whereas it is appropriate that national provisions for regional development requirements to be taken into consideration in the award of public works contracts should be made to conform to the objectives of the Community and be in keeping with the principles of the Treaty;

Whereas contracting entities must not be able to reject abnormally low tenders before having requested in writing explanations as to the constituent elements of the tender;

Whereas, within certain limits, preference should be given to an offer of Community origin where there are equivalent offers of third country origin;

Whereas this Directive should not prejudice the position of the Community in any current or future international negotiations;

Whereas, based on the results of such international negotiations, this Directive should be extendable to offers of third country origin, pursuant to a Council Decision;

Whereas the rules to be applied by the entities concerned should establish a framework for sound commercial practice and should leave a maximum of flexibility;

Whereas, as a counterpart for such flexibility and in the interest of mutual confidence, a minimum level of transparency must be ensured and appropriate methods adopted for monitoring the application of this Directive;

Whereas it is necessary to adapt Directives 71/305/EEC and 77/62/EEC to establish well-defined fields of application; whereas the scope of Directive 71/305/EEC should not be reduced, except as regards contracts in the water and telecommunications sectors; whereas the scope of Directive 77/62/EEC should not be reduced, except as regards certain contracts in the water sector; whereas the scope of Directives 71/305/EEC and 77/62/EEC should not, however, be extended to contracts awarded by carriers by land, air, sea, inshore or inland waterway which, although carrying out economic activities of an industrial or commercial nature, belong to the State administration; whereas, nevertheless, certain contracts awarded by carriers by land, air, sea, inshore or inland waterway which belong to the State administration and are carried out only for reasons of public service should be covered by those Directives;

Whereas this Directive should be re-examined in the light of experience;

Whereas the opening up of contracts, on 1 January 1993, in the sectors covered by this Directive might have an adverse effect upon the economy of the

Kingdom of Spain; whereas the economies of the Hellenic Republic and the Portuguese Republic will have to sustain even greater efforts; whereas it is appropriate that these Member States be granted adequate additional periods to implement this Directive,

HAS ADOPTED THIS DIRECTIVE:

Title 1
General provisions

Article 1

For the purposes of this Directive:

1. "public authorities" shall mean the State, regional or local authorities, bodies governed by public law, or associations formed by one or more of such authorities or bodies governed by public law.

A body is considered to be governed by public law where it:

– is established for the specific purpose of meeting needs in the general interest, not being of a commercial or industrial nature, and

– has legal personality, and

– is financed for the most part by the State, or regional or local authorities, or other bodies governed by public law, or is subject to management supervision by those bodies, or has an administrative, managerial or supervisory board more than half of whose members are appointed by the State, regional or local authorities, or other bodies governed by public law;

2. "public undertaking" shall mean any undertaking over which the public authorities may exercise directly or indirectly a dominant influence by virtue of their ownership of it, their financial participation therein, or the rules which govern it. A dominant influence on the part of the public authorities shall be presumed when these authorities, directly or indirectly, in relation to an undertaking:

– hold the major of the undertaking's subscribed capital, or

– control the majority of the votes attaching to shares issued by the undertaking, or

– can appoint more than half of the members of the undertaking's administrative, managerial or supervisory body;

3. "supply and works contracts" shall mean contracts for pecuniary interest concluded in writing between one of the contracting entities referred to in Article 2 and a supplier or contractor and which have as their object:

(a) in the case of supply contracts, the purchase, lease, rental or hire-purchase, with or without options to buy, of products or of software services. These contracts may in addition cover siting and installation operations.

Software services shall be covered by this definition where they are procured by a contracting entity exercising an activity defined in Article 2 (2) (d) and are for use in the operation of a public telecommunications network or are intended to be used in a public telecommunications service as such;

(b) in the case of works contracts, either the execution, or both the execution and design or the realization, by whatever means, of building or civil engineering activities referred to in Annex XI. These contracts may, in addition, cover supplies and services necessary for their execution.

Contracts which include the provision of services other than those referred to in (a) and (b) shall be regarded as supply contracts if the total value of supplies, including siting and installation operations necessary for the execution of the contract and of software services within the meaning of subparagraph (a), is greater than the value of the other services covered by the contract;

4. "framework agreement" shall mean an agreement between one of the contracting entities defined in Article 2 and one or more suppliers or contractors, the purpose of which is to establish the terms, in particular with regard to the prices and, where appropriate, the quantity envisaged, governing the contracts to be awarded during a given period;

5. "tenderer" shall mean a supplier or contractor who submits a tender and

"candidate" shall mean a person who has sought an invitation to take part in a restricted or negotiated procedure;

6. "open, restricted and negotiated procedures" shall mean the award procedures applied by contracting entities whereby:

(a) in the case of open procedures, all interested suppliers or contractors may submit tenders;

(b) in the case of the restricted procedures, only candidates invited by the contracting entity may submit tenders;

(c) in the case of negotiated procedures, the contracting entity consults suppliers or contractors of its choice and negotiates the terms of the contract with one or more of them;

7. "technical specifications" shall mean the technical requirements contained in particular in the tender documents, defining the characteristics of a set of works, material, product or supply, and enabling a piece of work, a material, a product or a supply to be objectively described in a manner such that it fulfils the use for which it is intended by the contracting entity. These technical prescriptions may include quality, performance, safety or dimensions, as well as requirements applicable to the material, product, or supply as regards quality assurance, terminology, symbols, testing and test methods, packaging, marking or labelling. In the case of works contracts, they may also include rules for the design and costing, the test, inspection and acceptance conditions for works and methods or techniques of construction and all other technical conditions which the contracting entity is in a position to prescribe under general or specific regulations, in relation to the finished works and to the materials or parts which they involve;

8. "standard" shall mean a technical specification approved by a recognised standardizing body for repeated and continuous application, compliance with which is in principle not compulsory;

9. "European standard" shall mean a standard approved by the European Committee for Standardization (CEN) or by the European Committee for Electrotechnical Standardization (CENELEC) as a "European Standard (EN)" or "Harmonization Document (HD)", according to the common rules of those organizations, or by the European Telecommunications Standards Institute (ETSI) according to its own rules as a "European Telecommunications Standard (ETS)",

10. "common technical specification" shall mean a technical specification drawn up in accordance with a procedure recognised by the Member States with a view to uniform application in all Member States and published in the Official Journal of the European Communities;

11. "European technical approval" shall mean a favourable technical assessment of the fitness for use of a product for a particular purpose, based on fulfilment of the essential requirements for building works, by means of the inherent characteristics of the product and the defined conditions of application and use, as provided for in Council Directive 89/106/EEC of 21 December 1988 on the approximation of laws, regulations and administrative provisions of the Member States relating to construction products (OJ 1989 L40/12). European technical approval shall be issued by an approval body designated for this purpose by the Member State;

12. "European specification" shall mean a common technical specification, a European technical approval or a national standard implementing a European standard;

13. "public telecommunications network" shall mean the public telecommunications infrastructure which enables to be conveyed between defined network termination points by wire, by microwave, by optical means or by other electromagnetic means.

"Network termination point" shall mean all physical connections and their technical access specifications which form part of the public telecommunications network and are necessary for access to, and efficient communication through, that public network;

14. "public telecommunications services" shall mean telecommunications services

the provision of which the Member States have specifically assigned notably to one or more telecommunications entities.

"Telecommunications services" shall mean services the provision of which consists wholly or partly in the transmission and routing of signals on the public telecommunications network by means of telecommunications processes, with the exception of radio-broadcasting and television.

Article 2

1. This Directive shall apply to contracting entities which:
(a) are public authorities or public undertakings and exercise one of the activities referred to in paragraph 2;
(b) or, when they are not public authorities or public undertakings, have as one of their activities any of those referred to in paragraph 2 or any combination thereof and operate on the basis of special or exclusive rights granted by a competent authority of a Member State.

2. Relevant activities for the purposes of this Directive shall be:
(a) the provision or operation of fixed networks intended to provide a service to the public in connection with the production, transport or distribution of:
    (i)   drinking water, or
    (ii) electricity, or
    (iii) gas or heat,
    or the supply of drinking water, electricity, gas or heat to such networks;
(b) the exploitation of a geographical area for the purpose of:
    (i)   exploring for or extracting oil, gas, coal or other solid fuels, or
    (ii) the provision of airport, maritime or inland port or other terminal facilities to carriers by air, sea or inland waterway;
(c) the operation of networks providing a service to the public in the field of transport by railway, automated systems, tramway, trolley bus, bus or cable.
    As regards transport services, a network shall be considered to exist where the service is provided under operating conditions laid down by a competent authority of a Member State, such as conditions on the routes to be served, the capacity to be made available or the frequency of the service;
(d) the provision or operation of public telecommunications networks or the provision of one or more public telecommunications services.

3. For the purpose of applying paragraph 1 (b), special or exclusive rights shall mean rights deriving from authorizations granted by a competent authority of the Member State concerned, by law, regulation or administrative action, having as their result the reservation for one or more entities of the exploitation of an activity defined in paragraph 2.

A contracting entity shall be considered to enjoy special or exclusive rights in particular where:
(a) for the purpose of constructing the networks or facilities referred to in paragraph 2, it may take advantage of a procedure for the expropriation or use of property or may place network equipment on, under or over the public highway;
(b) in the case of paragraph 2(a), the entity supplies with drinking water, electricity, gas or heat a network which is itself operated by an entity enjoying special or exclusive rights granted by a competent authority of the Member State concerned.

4. The provision of bus transport services to the public shall not be considered to be a relevant activity within the meaning of paragraph 2(c) where other entities are free to provide those services, either in general or in a particular geographical area, under the same conditions as the contracting entities.

5. The supply of drinking water, electricity, gas or heat to networks which provide a service to the public by a contracting entity other than public authority shall not be considered as a relevant activity within the meaning of paragraph 2(a) where:
(a) in the case of drinking water or electricity:

- the production of drinking water or electricity by the entity concerned takes place because its consumption is necessary for carrying out an activity other than that referred to in paragraph 2, and
- supply to the public network depends only on the entity's own consumption and has not exceeded 30% of the entity's total production of drinking water or energy, having regard to the average for the preceding three years, including the current year;

(b) in the case of gas or heat:

- the production of gas or heat by the entity concerned is the unavoidable consequence of carrying on an activity other than that referred to in paragraph 2, and
- supply to the public network is aimed only at the economic exploitation of such production and amounts to not more than 20% of the entity's turnover having regard to the average for the preceding three years, including the current year.

6. The contracting entities listed in Annexes I to X shall fulfil the criteria set out above. In order to ensure that the lists are as exhaustive as possible, Member States shall notify the Commission of amendments to their lists. The Commission shall revise Annexes I to X in accordance with the procedure in Article 32.

Article 3

1. Member States may request the Commission to provide that exploitation of geographical areas for the purpose of exploring for, or extracting, oil, gas, coal or other solid fuels shall not be considered to be an activity defined in Article 2 (2) (b) (i) and that entities shall not be considered as operating under special or exclusive rights within the meaning of Article 2 (3) (b) by virtue of carrying on one or more of these activities, provided that all the following conditions are satisfied with respect to the relevant national provisions concerning such activities:

(a) at the time when authorization to exploit such a geographical area is requested, other entities shall be free to seek authorization for that purpose under the same conditions as the contracting entities;

(b) the technical and financial capacity of entities to engage in particular activities shall be established prior to any evaluation of the merits of competing applications for authorization;

(c) authorization to engage in those activities shall be granted on the basis of objective criteria concerning the way in which it is intended to carry out the exploitation for extraction, which shall be established and published prior to the requests and applied in a non-discriminatory manner;

(d) all conditions and requirements concerning the carrying out or termination of the activity, including provisions on operating obligations, royalties, and participation in the capital or revenue of the entities, shall be established and made available prior to the requests for authorization being made and then applied in a non-discriminatory manner; every change concerning these conditions and requirements shall be applied to all the entities concerned, or else amendments must be made in a non-discriminatory manner; however, operating obligations need not be established until immediately before the authorization is granted; and

(e) contracting entities shall not be required by any law, regulation, administrative requirement, agreement or understanding to provide information on a contracting entity's intended or actual sources of procurement, except at the request of national authorities and exclusively with a view to the objectives mentioned in Article 36 of the Treaty.

2. Member States which apply the provisions of paragraph 1 shall ensure, through the conditions of the authorization or other appropriate measures, that any entity:

281

(a) observes the principles of non-discrimination and competitive procurement in respect of the award of supplies and works contracts, in particular as regards the information that the entity makes available to undertakings concerning its procurement intentions;

(b) communicates to the Commission, under conditions to be defined by the latter in accordance with Article 32, information relating to the award of contracts.

3. As regards individual concessions or authorizations granted before the date on which Member States apply this Directive in accordance with Article 37, paragraphs 1 (a), (b) and (c) shall not apply, provided that at that date other entities are free to seek authorization for the exploitation of geographical areas for the purpose of exploring for or extracting oil, gas, coal or other solid fuels, on a non-discriminatory basis and in the light of objective criteria. Paragraph 1 (d) shall not apply as regards conditions or requirements established, applied or amended before the date referred to above.

4. A Member State which wishes to apply paragraph 1 shall inform the Commission accordingly. In doing so, it shall inform the Commission of any law, regulation or administrative provision, agreement or understanding relating to compliance with the conditions referred to in paragraphs 1 and 2.

The Commission shall take a decision in accordance with the procedure laid down in Article 32 (4) to (7). It shall publish its decision, giving its reasons, in the *Official Journal of the European Communities*.

It shall forward to the Council each year a report on the implementation of the article and review its application in the framework of the report provided for in Article 36.

...

Article 9

1. This Directive shall not apply to:
(a) contracts which the contracting entities listed in Annex I award for the purchase of water;
(b) contracts which the contracting entities specified in Annexes II, III, IV and V award for the supply of energy or of fuels for the production of energy.

2. The Council shall re-examine the provisions of paragraph 1 when it has before it a report from the Commission together with appropriate proposals.

...

Article 25

1. Contracting entities which select candidates to tender in restricted procedures or to participate in negotiated procedures shall do so according to objective criteria and rules which they lay down and which they shall make available to interested suppliers or contractors.

2. The criteria used may include the criteria for exclusion specified in Article 23 of Directive 71/305/EEC and in Article 20 of Directive 77/62/EEC.

3. The criteria may be based on the objective need of the contracting entity to reduce the number of candidates to a level which is justified by the need to balance the particular characteristics of the contract award procedure and the resources required to complete it. The number of candidates selected must, however, take account of the need to ensure adequate competition.

...

Annex II
Production, Transport or Distribution of Electricity

BELGIUM

Entities producing, transporting or distributing electricity pursuant to *article 5: Des régies communales et intercommunales* of the *loi du 10 mars 1925 sur les distributions d'énergie électrique*.

Entities transporting or distributing electricity pursuant to the *loi relative aux intercommunales du 22 décembre 1986*.

EBES, *Intercom, Unerg* and other entities producing, transporting or distributing electricity and granted a concession for distribution pursuant to *article 8 – les concessions communales et intercommunales* of the *loi du 10 mars 1952 sur les distributions d'énergie électrique*.

The *Société publique de production d'électricité (SPÉ)*.

DENMARK

Entities producing or transporting electricity on the basis of a licence pursuant to § *3, stk. 1,* of the *lov nr. 54 af 25. februar 1976 om elforsyning, jf. bekendtgørelse nr. 607 af 17. december 1976 om elforsyningslovens anvendelsesområde*.

Entities distributing electricity as defined in § *3, stk. 2,* of the *lov nr. 54 af 25. februar 1976 om elforsyning, jf. bekendtgørelse nr. 607 af 17. december 1976 om elforsyningslovens anvendelsesområde* and on the basis of authorizations for expropriation pursuant to Articles 10 to 15 of the *lov om elektriske stærkstrømsanlæg, jf lovbekendtgørelse nr. 669 af 28. december 1977*.

GERMANY

Entities producing, transporting or distributing electricity as defined in § *2 Absatz 2* of the *Gesetz zur Förderung der Energiewirtschaft (Energiewirtschaftsgesetz) of 13 December 1935*. Last modified by the *Gesetz of 19 December 1977*, and auto-production of electricity so far as this is covered by the field of application of the Directive pursuant to Article 2, paragraph 5.

GREECE

Δημόσια Επιχείρηση Ηλεκτρισμού (Public Power Corporation) set up pursuant to the law 1468 of 2 August 1950 Περί ιδρύσεως Δημοσίας Επιχειρήσεως Ηλεκτρισμού, and operating pursuant to the law 57/85: Δομή, ρόλος και τρόπος διοίκησης και λειτονργίας της κοινωνικοποιημένης Δημόσιας Επιχείρησης Ηλεκτρισμού.

SPAIN

Entities producing, transporting or distributing electricity pursuant to Article 1 of the *Decreto de 12 de marzo de 1954*, approving the *Reglamento de verificaciones eléctricas y reglaridad en el suministro de energía* and pursuant to *Decreto 2617/1966, de 20 de octubre, sobre autorización administrativa en materia le instalaciones eléctricas*.

Red Eléctrica de España SA, set up pursuant to *Real Decreto 91/1985 de 23 de enero*.

FRANCE

Électricité de France, set up and operating pursuant to the *loi 46/6288 de 8 avril 1946 sur la nationalisation de l'électricité et du gaz.*

Entities *(sociétés d'économie mixte* or *régies)* distributing electricity and referred to in article 23 of the *loi 48/1260 du 12 août 1948 portant modification des lois 46/6288 du 8 avril 1946 et 46/2298 du 21 octobre 1946 sur la nationalisation de l'électricité et, du gaz.*

Compagnie nationale du Rhône.

IRELAND

The Electricity Supply Board (ESB) set up and operating pursuant to the *Electricity Supply Act 1927.*

ITALY

Ente Nazionale per l'energia elettrica set up pursuant to *legge n. 1643, 6 dicembre 1962 approvato con Decreto n. 1720, 21 dicembre 1965.*

Entities operating on the basis of a concession pursuant to article 4, n. 5 or 8 of *legge 6 dicembre 1962, n. 1643 – Istituzione dell'Ente nazionale per la energia elettrica e trasferimento ad esso delle imprese esercenti le industrie elettriche.*

Entities operating on the basis of concession pursuant to article 20 of *Decreto del Presidente delle Repubblica 18 marzo 1965, n. 342 norme integrative della legge 6 dicembre 1962, n. 1643 e norme relative al coordinamento e all'esercizio delle attività elettriche esercitate da enti ed imprese diverse dell'Ente nazionale per l'énergia elettrica.*

LUXEMBOURG

Compagnie grand-ducale d'électricité de Luxembourg, producing or distributing electricity pursuant to the *convention du 11 novembre 1927 concernant l'établissement et l'exploitation des réseaux de distribution d'énergie électrique dans le grand-duché du Luxembourg approuvée par la loi du 4 janvier 1928.*

Société électrique de l'Our (SEO).

Syndicat de Communes SIDOR.

NETHERLANDS

Elektriciteitsproduktie Oost-Nederland.

Elektriciteitsbedrijf Utrecht–Noord-Holland–Amsterdam (UNA).

Elektriciteitsbedrijf Zuid-Holland (EZH).

Elektriciteitsproduktiemaatschappij Zuid-Nederland (EPZ).

Provinciale Zeeuwse Energie Maatschappij (PZEM).

Samenwerkende Elektriciteitsbedrijven (SEP).

Entities distributing electricity on the basis of a licence *(vergunning)* granted by the provincial authorities pursuant to the *Provinciewet.*

PORTUGAL

Electricidade de Portugal (EDP), set up pursuant to the *Decreto-Lei nº 02/76 de 30 Junho de 1976.*

Entities distributing electricity pursuant to *artigo 1º do Decreto-lei nº 344-B/82 de 1 de Setembro de 1982,* amended by *Decreto-Lei nº 297/86 de 19 de Setembro de 1986.* Entities producing electricity pursuant *to Decreto Lei nº 189/88 de 27 de Maio de 1988.*

Independant producers of electricity pursuant to *Decreto Lei nº 189/88 de 27 de Maio de 1988.*

Empresa de Electricidade dos Açores – EDA, EP, created pursuant to the *Decreto Regional nº 16/80 de 21 de Agosto de 1980.*

Empresa de Electricidade da Madeira, EP, created pursuant to the *Decreto-Lei nº.12/74 de 17 de Janeiro de 1974* and regionalised pursuant to the *Decreto-Lei nº 31/79 de 24 de Fevereiro de 1979, Decreto-Lei nº 91/79 de 19 de Abril de 1979.*

UNITED KINGDOM

Central Electricity Generating (CEGB), and the Areas Electricity Boards producing, transporting or distributing electricity pursuant to the *Electricity Act 1947* and the *Electricity Act 1957.*

The North of Scotland Hydro-Electricity Board (NSHB), producing, transporting and distributing electricity pursuant to the *Electricity (Scotland) Act 1979.*

The South of Scotland Electricity Board (SSEB) producing, transporting and distributing electricity pursuant to the *Electricity (Scotland) Act 1979.*

The Northern Ireland Electricity Service (NIES), set up pursuant to the *Electricity Supply (Northern Ireland) Order 1972.*

COUNCIL DIRECTIVE 90/547/EEC

of 29 October 1990

on the transit of electricity through transmission grids[1]

THE COUNCIL OF THE EUROPEAN COMMUNITIES,

Having regard to the Treaty establishing the European Economic Community, and in particular Article 100a thereof,

Having regard to the proposal from the Commission,

In co-operation with the European Parliament,

Having regard to the opinion of the Economic and Social Committee,

Whereas it is necessary to adopt measures with the aim of progressively establishing the internal market over a period expiring on 31 December 1992; whereas the European Council has recognised, at its successive meetings, in particular in Rhodes, the need for a single internal market in energy and whereas the achievement of the internal market more specifically in the electricity sector will help the further development of the Community's energy objectives;

Whereas there must be greater integration of the European energy market if the single internal market is to be achieved; whereas electricity is an essential component of the Community's energy balance;

Whereas the achievement of the internal market for energy, more particularly in the electricity sector, must take into account the objective of economic and social cohesion, that is to say, in concrete terms, guarantee an optimum supply of electricity to all the citizens of all the Community regions, with a view to improving and harmonising the living conditions and development bases in particular in the least-favoured regions;

Whereas energy polices, more than any other measure contributing to the achievement of the internal market, must not be implemented with the sole aim of reducing costs and maintaining competition, but must also take account of the need to ensure the security of supplies and the compatibility of energy production methods with the environment;

Whereas to attain that objective, account should be taken of the specific characteristics of the electricity sector;

Whereas there is increasing trade in electricity each year between high-voltage electricity grids in Europe; whereas the European Community's security of electricity supply would be improved and costs reduced by co-ordinating the building and operation of the interconnections required for such trade;

Whereas the exchange of electricity between electricity grids which is based on contracts with a minimum duration of one year is so great that requests for transactions and their consequences should be systematically known to the Commission;

Whereas it is possible and desirable to increase electricity transfers between grids and also take account of the imperatives of security and quality of electricity supply; whereas studies show that such greater electricity transfers between grids can minimise the cost of investment and fuels involved in electricity generation and transmission and ensure optimum use of the means of production and infrastructure;

Whereas there are still obstacles to such trade; whereas, provided that they are not due to the nature of technology used or the nature of the grids themselves, such obstacles can be reduced by making the transit of electricity through grids compulsory and introducing an appropriate system for monitoring compliance with this obligation;

[1] OJ 1990 L313/30.

287

Whereas this obligation and monitoring system concern the transit of electricity involved in trade which is in the Community interest, *i.e.* transit through high-voltage grids;

Whereas the contract conditions concerning the transit of electricity between grids must be negotiated between the responsible entities; whereas the conditions of transit should be fair and should not bring about, directly or indirectly, conditions contrary to Community competition rules;

Whereas, in order to facilitate the conclusion of transit contracts, the Commission is providing for the creation of a conciliation procedure under which submission must be made at the request of one of the parties, without the result of that procedure having legally binding effect;

Whereas it is necessary to approximate the provisions taken by the Member States which affect the transit of electricity;

Whereas the establishment of an internal electricity market will stimulate the dynamic process of better integration of national electricity grids, and whereas in this context special infrastructure measures and programmes should therefore be implemented to accelerate the efficient and socially advantageous linking-up of outlying areas and islands in the Community to the interconnected grid;

Whereas the interconnection of major European grids over which trade must be co-ordinated extends over a geographical territory which does not coincide with the Community's frontiers; whereas there is an obvious advantage in seeking co-operation with third countries involved in the interconnected European network.

HAS ADOPTED THIS DIRECTIVE:

Article 1

Member States shall take the measures necessary to facilitate transit of electricity between high-voltage grids in accordance with the conditions laid down in this Directive.

Article 2

1. Every transaction for the transport of electricity under the following conditions shall constitute transit of electricity between grids, within the meaning of this Directive, without prejudice to any special arrangements concluded between the Community and third countries;

(a) transmission is carried out by the entity or entities responsible in each Member State for a high-voltage electricity grid, with the exception of distribution grids, in a Member State's territory which contributes to the efficient operation of European high-voltage interconnections;

(b) the grid of origin or final destination is situated in the Community;

(c) the transport involves the crossing of one intra-Community frontier at least.

2. The high-voltage electricity transmission grids and the entities responsible for them in the Member States, which are listed in the Annex, shall be covered by the provisions of this Directive. This list shall be updated after consultation with the Member State concerned whenever necessary by decision of the Commission, within the context of the objectives of this Directive and in particular taking into account paragraph 1 (a).

Article 3

1. Contracts involving transit of electricity between transmission grids shall be negotiated between the entities responsible for the grids concerned and for the quality of service provided and, where appropriate, with the entities responsible in the Member States for importing and exporting electricity.

2. The conditions of transit shall, pursuant to the rules of the Treaty, be non-discriminatory and fair for all the parties concerned, shall not include unfair clauses or unjustified restrictions and shall not endanger security of supply and quality of service, in particular taking full account of the utilization of reserve production capacity and the most efficient operation of existing systems.

3. Member States shall take the measures necessary to ensure that the entities under their jurisdiction referred to in the Annex act without delay to:
- notify the Commission and the national authorities concerned of any request for transit in connection with contracts for the sale of electricity of a minimum of one year's duration,
- open negotiations on the conditions of the electricity transit requested,
- inform the Commission and the national authorities concerned of the conclusion of a transit contract,
- inform the Commission and the national authorities concerned of the reasons for the failure of the negotiations to result in the conclusion of a contract within 12 months following communication of the request.

4. Each of the entities concerned may request that the conditions of transit be subject to conciliation by a body set up and chaired by the Commission and on which the entities responsible for transmission grids in the Community are represented.

Article 4

If the reason for the absence of agreement on a request for transit appear unjustified or insufficient, the Commission, acting on a complaint from the requesting body or on its own initiative, shall implement the procedures provided for by Community law.

Article 5

Member States shall bring into force the laws, regulations and administrative provisions necessary to comply with this Directive not later than 1 July 1991. They shall forthwith inform the Commission thereof.

Article 6

This Directive is addressed to the Member States.

Annex
List of entities and grids in the Community covered by the Directive

Member State	*Entity*	*Grid*
Germany	Badenwerk AG	
	Bayernwerk AG	
	Berliner Kraft und Licht AG (Bewag)	
	Energie-Versorgung Schwaben AG (EVS)	
	Hamburgische Elektrizitätswerke (HEW)	Interconnection grids
	Preussen-Elektra AG	
	RWE Energie AG	
	Vereinigte Elektrizitätswerke Westfalen AG (VEW)	
Belgium	CPTE – Société pour la coordination de la production et du transport de l'électricité	Coordinating body for public supply grid
Denmark	ELSAM ELKRAFT	Public supply grid (Jutland) Public supply grid (Seeland)
Spain	Red Eléctrica de España S.A.	Public supply grid
France	Électricité de France	Public supply grid
Greece	Δημόσια Επιχείρηση Ηλεκτρισμού (ΔΕΗ)	Public supply grid
Ireland	Electricity Supply Board	Public supply grid
Italy	ENEL	Public supply grid
Luxembourg	CEGEDEL	Public supply grid
Netherlands	SEP	Public supply grid
Portugal	EDP	Public supply grid
United Kingdom	National Grid Company Scottish Power Scottish Hydro-Electric Northern Ireland Electricity	High voltage transmission grids

COMMISSION DECISION 91/50/EEC

of 16 January 1991

relating to a proceeding under Article 85 of the EEC Treaty
(IV/32.732 – IJsselcentrale and others)[1]

THE COMMISSION OF THE EUROPEAN COMMUNITIES,

Having regard to the Treaty establishing the European Economic Community,

Having regard to Council Regulation 17 of 6 February 1962, first Regulation implementing Articles 85 and 86 of the Treaty (JO 1962, 204), as last amended by the Act of Accession of Spain and Portugal, and in particular Article 3 thereof,

Having regard to the application made to the Commission on 26 May 1988 under Article 3 of Regulation 17 by NV IGMO, of Meppel, Centraal Overijsselse Nutsbedrijven NV, of Almelo, NV Regionaal Energiebedrijf Salland, of Deventer, and the Municipality of Hoogeveen, requesting it to find that NV Samenwerkende Elektriciteitsproduktiebedrijven (SEP) and the electricity generation companies in the Netherlands have infringed Article 85,

Having given SEP and the electricity generators the opportunity of being heard on the matters to which the Commission has taken objection, in accordance with Article 19 (1) of Regulation 17 in conjunction with Commission Regulation 99/63/EEC of 25 July 1963 on the hearings provided for in Articles 19 (1) and (2) of Regulation 17 (JO 1963, 2268),

Having consulted the Advisory Committee on Restrictive Practices and Dominant Positions,

Whereas:

I. The Facts

1. The complaint

(1) On 26 May 1988 an application was made under Article 3 of Regulation 17

---
[1] OJ 1991 L28/32.

by NV IGMO (Intercommunaal Gasbedrijf Meppel en Omstreken) of Meppel; the Hoogeveen municipal distribution undertaking (the two of these have since been merged into Rendo NV); NV Regionaal Energiebedrijf Salland, of Deventer, and Centraal Overijsselse Nutsbedrijven NV of Almelo.

The complaint is against IJsselcentrale; it was made in the course of civil proceedings concerning the imposition by IJsselcentrale of an import and export ban coupled with an exclusive purchasing obligation, and the imposition of an extra cost equalization charge.

The complaint relates to three matters:

1. The import ban explicitly laid down both in the 1971 General SEP Agreement (Article 2) and in the 1986 Co-operation Agreement (Article 21).
2. The exclusive purchasing obligation deriving from the agreements between the complainants and IJsselcentrale, and particularly from Article 2 (2) of the General Terms and Conditions applying. According to the complainants this obligation to purchase, which in effect also prevents imports, is in its turn a consequence of the relevant provisions of the Co-operation Agreement.
3. IJsselcentrale's power to determine prices unilaterally, and the equalization charge which in fact was unilaterally imposed on the complainants by IJsselcentrale under a decision of its Board (*Raad van Commissarissen*) taken on 26 October 1984.

This equalization charge was imposed by IJsselcentrale in order to eliminate differences between the costs of distribution to small and large consumers by, on the one hand, IJsselcentrale, and on the other hand municipal or regional distributors and is based on the fact that IJsselcentrale primarily supplies country regions and that the municipal or regional distributors primarily supply city regions.

For the time being the operation of the extra cost equalization charge is outside the scope of this proceeding; but according to the complainants the import ban makes the imposition of the extra charge possible.

The complainants are local distributors which in their turn are supplied by a regional distributor namely IJsselcentrale.

2. The electricity undertakings

(2) There are at present four electricity generating companies in the Netherlands: NV Elektriciteitsbedrijf Zuid-Holland ("EZH"), of Voorburg; NV Energieproduktiebedrijf UNA, of Utrecht; NV Elektriciteits-Produktie-maatschappij Zuid-Nederland ("EPZ"), of Eindhoven; and NV Elektriciteits-Produktiemaatschappij Oost- en Noord-Nederland ("EPON"), Zwolle; there are at the moment 38 distribution undertakings.

The generators are companies whose share capital is owned by local authorities, both provinces and municipalities, either directly, as in the case of EZH and UNA, or indirectly, through the large distributors which cover the relevant area, in the case of EPZ and EPON.

The shares in the distribution undertakings are likewise held directly or indirectly by the provinces and municipalities, where the distributor is not actually a department of public administration.

(3) On 3 June 1949 these companies, or in some cases their predecessors, set up NV Samenwerkende Elektriciteits-produktiebedrijven ("SEP").

SEP is a public limited company intended to serve as a vehicle for co-operation between the electricity generators. Initially its object was to administer mutual assistance in the event of breakdowns, by making the best possible use of national and international interconnections.

At present there are a total of four high voltage interconnections between the Netherlands and Germany and three between the Netherlands and Belgium. Except for the Musselkanaal-Lathen interconnection, which is the property of the Elektriciteitsbedrijf voor Groningen en Drenthe ("EGD"), all of these are the property of SEP. SEP also have the use of the one interconnection which is not its own property.

SEP's statutes provide that its shareholders must be public-law bodies, or private-law bodies with legal personality, which in the Netherlands either operate a public electricity generation undertaking or administer a co-operative arrangement between a group of operators of public electricity generation undertakings.

SEP's objects are laid down in its statutes as follows:
– to draw up a joint Electricity Plan;
– to operate (principally in the capacity of an owner) the 380/220 kV grid;
– to conclude agreements with foreign electricity undertakings concerning imports and exports and the use of international interconnections;
– to arrange the joint purchase of fuels for the purpose of generation;
– to pool energy and generation costs;
– to make the best possible use of domestic electricity generation.

These tasks were given a general basis in legislation with the entry into force of the Electricity Law 1989.[2]

3. The agreements

(4) The Co-operation Agreement which was concluded on 22 May 1986 between the predecessors of the present four generators on the one hand and SEP on the other replaced the General SEP Agreement on 1 February 1971, and was concluded for a duration of 25 years.

[2] Full title: Law of 16 November 1989 laying down rules on the generation, import, transmission and sale of electricity (Electricity Law 1989); published *Staatsblad* 535, 7 December 1989.

Article 2 (1) of the Co-operation Agreement lays down among other things that parties to the Agreement are to be shareholders in the Company (*i.e.* SEP). Parties are also to hold a valid authorization from the Minister with responsibility for electricity supply to build or to operate, or both, one or more generation plants with a view to the public supply of electricity.

(5) Article 21 of the Co-operation Agreement deals more specifically with imports and exports, as follows:

"1. Electric capacity may be provided and electric power supplied to or by electricity undertakings established outside the Netherlands only through the Company.

2. In supply agreements with undertakings which distribute electric power the parties shall stipulate that those undertakings shall not obtain or supply electric power, with or without any associate electric capacity, from or to electricity undertakings established outside the Netherlands.

3. Paragraphs 1 and 2 of this article shall not apply to supply operations, up to a ceiling to be determined by implementing rules laid down in accordance with Article 32 of this Agreement, carried out solely for reasons connected with the local distribution of electric power."

(The implementing rules referred to in paragraph 3, which are intended to cover the supply of power to firms located near the border, exempt from this prohibition supply operations with a capacity of not more than 5,000 kW and a tension of 15kV.)

Moreover, Article 10 (4) of the OVS States:

"Participants are obliged – and are responsible for the proper implementation of this obligation – to stipulate in supply agreements with distributors of electric power that all electricity of a nominal capacity, generated by their installations, will be delivered to the company through the intermediary of the Participant in whose territory the relevant installation is located. This capacity equals or exceeds the threshold referred to in Article 12 (3)."

The old General SEP Agreement of 1 February 1971, which was replaced by the Co-operation Agreement, also included provisions similar to those to be found in the Co-operation Agreement covering such matters as the electricity plan, interconnections, supply and settlement, and implicitly imports and exports.

(6) The general terms and conditions for the supply of power to municipalities with their own distributors in the territory of IJsselcentrale's concession, which have been in force since 1 April 1965, include an Article 2 (2) under which the municipality undertakes "to obtain electric power for supply in its territory exclusively from IJsselcentrale, and to use that power only for its own consumption or for supply to third parties for consumption in the territory of the Municipality." This clause imposes an exclusive purchasing obligation on the municipality, and a ban on supplying third parties outside its territory. In Article 13 (1) IJsselcentrale undertakes not to supply electric power to third parties in the territory of the municipality without the municiality's consent, with a few stated exceptions.

The complainants in this proceeding, in their capacity as distributors and purchasers from IJsselcentrale, which supplies only as a main distributor, also impose an exclusive purchasing obligation. Thus the Municipality of Deventer, for example, in its Large Consumer's Contract for the supply of electricity, includes the following clause in Article 1: "The consumer undertakes to obtain the electric power needed for his business in Deventer from the Municipality."

Under the model General Terms and Conditions for the supply of electricity to large consumers (1984), drawn up and published by the Vereniging van Exploitanten van Elektriciteitsbedrijven in Nederland (Association of Operators of Electricity Undertakings in the Netherlands – "VEEN"), the distributors apply a provision in Article 19 (2) which reads as follows:

"The consumer may not without the written consent of the distributor:

(a) obtain electric power from third parties;

(b) operate or procure the operation of autogenerating plant alongside the public grid;

(c) use the power supplied otherwise than on his own premises."

Thus consumers too are bound by an exclusive purchasing obligation and a ban on supplying power to third parties.

(7) Before the entry into force of the Electricity Law 1989, electricity undertakings frequently operated under concessions granted by the authorities. Production and distribution were then frequently in the same hands. This was the case with IJsselcentrale, which was granted a concession by the Royal Order of 13 June 1918, No 54. Such concessions, including IJsselcentrale's, were for the construction and operation of plant and of works for the production, transmission, transformation, distribution and supply of electricity, with the exception of electricity for telegraph and telephone purposes; at least in IJsselcentrale's case they did not confer any exclusive rights in the territory of the concession. The concession contains a supply obligation. If this obligation is not properly performed, the concession may be revoked.

(8) On 5 June 1975, during the currency of the General SEP Agreement of 1 February 1971, an agreement was concluded between the State of the Netherlands, SEP, and the eleven electricity generators of the time, which, like SEP itself, were all parties to the General SEP Agreement. This new agreement is commonly known as "the Compact (*Covenant*) of 1975." The main objective of the Compact was to require SEP to submit the Electricity Plan it drew up for approval by the Minister for Economic Affairs. This Compact entered into force on 3 July 1975 and was to apply for the duration of the Co-operation Agreement.

4. The legislation

(9) Until very recently the legislation governing the electricity market in the Netherlands was very restricted in scope. Only a part of the Electricity Law of 22 October 1938 (published *Staatsblad* 1938, 523) had actually entered into force. The concessions granted by the authorities to electricity undertakings were not based on that legislation. The Law, which applied until 8 December 1989, did not prevent parties other than electricity undertakings from importing electricity themselves. Under the Law of 10 December 1936, however (*Staatsblad* 524), authorization was required for any such imports. In principle such authorization could be obtained by anyone.

Under the old legislation there was an agreement between the distributors and the national authorities which made the prices charged to final consumers (maximum prices) subject to approval by the Minister for Economic Affairs. The prices charged to large consumers were the subject of negotiations between organizations representing large consumers and electricity undertakings.

Two developments can be observed on the Dutch market: on the one hand there is a movement towards concentration on the generation side with the result that only four generators remain; and on the other hand there is a movement towards a more formal type of regulation of the market by means of legislation. On 8 December 1989 the new Electricity Law 1989 entered into force with the exception of certain provisions for which there is a transitional period. It represents an important step to a more open electricity market in the Netherlands.

Broadly speaking, the scheme laid down in the Co-operation Agreement has been given a basis in legislation. In some respects, however, the Law allows greater freedom than the Co-operation Agreement.

The main features of the new Law are as follows:

– As regards the national electricity supply, Article 2 provides that licensees *i.e.* the electricity generators which operate electric power stations and produce for the public electricity supply and the Designated Company[3]

---

[3] *i.e.* the SEP. Designation was made by Ministerial Order of 20 March 1990 (*Staatscourant* 58, 22. 3. 1990).

are jointly to ensure the reliable and efficient operation of the national public electricity supply at costs which are as low as possible and in a socially responsible fashion, subject to the provisions of the Law and any rules made under it.

- The designated company is every two years to draw up an Electricity Plan covering developments in the supply of electricity in the Netherlands (Article 15 (1)).

- Any person who operates one or more electric power stations for the public electricity supply may supply any electricity available when the generating capacity of that plant exceeds a stated threshold using those power stations or otherwise, only to the designated company, and may supply the electricity supplied to him by that company only to distributors (Article 11 (1)).

- Notwithstanding any provision to the contrary, the owner of a distribution undertaking is entitled to have electricity supplied and electric capacity provided to him by the licensee (Article 12 (1)). Generators thus have an obligation to supply to distributors. Article 12 (3) provides that notwithstanding any provision to the contrary any person is entitled to have electricity supplied and electric capacity provided to him by any person who operates the public supply of electricity to consumers in the territory in which he requests such supply of electricity or provision of capacity.

  Thus distributors also have an obligation to supply to final consumers.

- SEP, as the "Designated Company", is to have the sole right to import electric power with a view to public supply (Article 34) with the exception of electricity with a voltage below 500 volts. Distributors are therefore prohibited from importing electricity with a view to public supply. Certain final consumers however may import electric power for their own consumption (this follows

from Article 34).[4]

- Large private consumers are no longer to be bound by an exclusive purchasing obligation to their local or regional distributor (Article 13 (2)).[4]

- Distributors and large-scale consumers who find their own generator or distributor too dear may transfer to another supplier within the Netherlands (who will normally be operating outside their territory); this is known as "cross-shopping" (*horizontal winkelen*).[5]

- Consumers may themselves generate current and may feed any surpluses of autogenerated current to distributors (Article 41).

- Anyone who with a view to public supply operates lines for the transmission of electric power, with the associated transformers, sub-stations and other accessory plant is upon written application obliged to make an offer concerning the transmission for the applicant of electricity for public supply, of electricity for large private consumers, or of imported electricity (Article 47 (1)).[5]

- Any owner of a distribution under-taking is obliged to accept an offer for the supply of electricity made by:

(a) a natural or legal person who generates that electricity in the terri-tory in which electricity is supplied to consumers by that distribution undertaking or by a distribu-tion undertaking to which that

---

[4] As one of a number of stimuli to competition introduced by the Law, according to a summary of the Law drawn up by the Ministry of Economic Affairs.

[5] On the obligation to transmit, the explanatory memorandum has the following to say: "Where an application for transmission is made, the line operator must, if necessary, show that he is unable to satisfy the application for lack of transmission capacity. SEP, as the operator of the interconnections with foreign countries, may here refer to multiannual contracts it has already concluded regarding imports for purposes of public supply." Reference: Lower House, 1987/88 session; 19591 (hereinafter referred to as "*Kamerstukken* No 19591"), No 3, p 56

distribution undertaking supplies electricity;
(b) a distribution undertaking to which the relevant distribution undertaking supplies electricity.
This obligation does not apply where the electricity:
(a) is generated by a power station;
(b) is generated by a natural or legal person to which imported electricity is also available for use in the relevant establishment (Article 41).
–   The designated company may not, without the approval of the Minister, conclude any agreement under which electric capacity outside the Netherlands is to be provided to that company. The Minister may withhold approval from an agreement only where this is necessary in the interests of proper electricity supply (Article 35).
–   The Law broadens the scope for local electricity generation by distributors: they may always operate their own autogenerating plant up to a maximum capacity of 25 MW, and approval for the construction or operation of autogenerating plant with a higher capacity may be withheld only if certain requirements are not met (Article 40).
–   As the Law does not regulate exports, it is to be assumed that anyone, private consumers as well as distributors, is free to export. The Law does not, however, impose any obligation to transmit electricity for export similar to the obligation to transmit imported electricity.
The Electricity Law 1989 entered into force on 8 December 1989. It itself provides, in Article 61, that certain of its Articles are to enter into force only on 1 July 1990, of which Articles 11 and 34 concern us here; and in Articles 58 and 59 that Articles 2 to 11 of the Electricity Law 1938 (*Staatsblad* 1938, 523) are repealed and that the Law of 10 December 1936 (*Staatsblad* 524) is repealed (Articles 58 and 59).

5. Consumption, importation and exportation of electricity and autogenerated electricity in the Netherlands

(10) The electricity consumed in the Netherlands may be generated by the electricity undertakings responsible for public supply, or imported or generated by the users themselves.

The turnover in money terms represented by consumption in the Netherlands in 1988 was approximately Fl 8,300 million on the basis of final consumer prices.[6]

Like imports, the figures for autogenerated energy are considerable; they have been growing in recent years, and in 1988 accounted for about 15,6% of total power generated.[7]

Autogenerators also feed a substantial quantity back into the public grid; in 1988 this accounted for about 3% of consumption in the Netherlands, and 18% of autogenerated electrical energy.

As regards the external trade balance, in the years 1984 to 1988 the Netherlands was a net importer. Until 1985 import/export trade took place via four international interconnections; at present there are seven such interconnections. Further details are given in the table.

(11) The organization of international connecting networks between the Netherlands and other countries is regulated through the Union for the Coordination of the Production and Transport of Electric Power (UCPTE), in which along with the Netherlands,

[5] *Continued.* The memorandum in response to the Final Report reads: "This obligation applies in the case of cross-shopping by both distributors and especially large consumers. It also applies in the case of purchase of current abroad by final consumers, and, in particular, by especially large consumers. The obligation applies to imports only in so far as it can reasonably be said that capacity is sufficient. The owner or owners of the grid may not avoid their obligation to transmit by asking an unreasonably high price. The Bill therefore provides that transmission must be provided against payment of the costs reasonably attributable to such transmission itself, in proportion to consumption. To avoid any misunderstanding it should be pointed out that in practice of course, this will almost be fictitious transmission." *Kamerstukken* No 19591, No 9, p 8.

	1984	1985	1986	1987	1988
Consumption in the Netherlands, GWH	54,970	56,370	57,320	60,400	62,410
Net generation in SEP framework, TWh	53	52,8	56,4	56,8	56,6
Autogeneration	7,486	8,190	8,555	9,967	10,800
(% of generation)	(12%)	(13%)	(12,7%)	(14,6%)	(15,6%)
Fed to public grid	888	1,072	1,320	1,680	1,940
(% of Netherlands consumption)	(1,6%)	(2%)	(2,3%)	(2,8%)	(3,1%)
(% of autogeneration)	(11,9%)	(13%)	(15,5%)	(16,8%)	(18%)
Imports	not available	5,240	2,370	3,645	5,840
(% of consumption)		(9,5%)	(4,2%)	(6,4%)	(9%)
Including ESD's imports (see recital 14)	not available	294	222	46	0

Sources: – Information supplied by SEP to the Commission

– *Elektriciteit in Nederland 1988*, publication commissioned by SEP and VEEN.

– Information supplied by VEEN.

NB: the figures in the brochure *Elektriciteit in Nederland* differ somewhat from those in SEP annual reports. The effect on the percentage figures is only slight.

Belgium, France, Germany, Austria and Switzerland are also represented. For more than 30 years trade has been managed by this private-law co-operative association of the national electricity organizations, which themselves conclude commercial agreements for the exchange of electric power, based on three forms of co-operation:
– exchange hour-to-hour, on the basis of costs,
– contracts for net transfers, mainly short-term,
– more long-term agreements, for example where a power station in a neighbouring country is jointly owned.

About 8% of total consumption in these countries is exchanged via these interconnections.[8]

This arrangement is thus based on voluntary co-operation between the national monopolies and has no binding character.

6. Imports of electric power into the Netherlands in the future

(12) The Dutch electric power grid is connected with grids in other Member States by lines which are the property of SEP or which are controlled and administered by SEP. Depending on the year considered, imports and exports leave the Netherlands a net importer of power by between 4% and 9% of Dutch consumption.

SEP regularly draws up an electricity plan, which also covers foreseeable imports and exports of electric power and an estimate of the autogeneration by the industry. The Co-operation Agreement lays down specific rules here. (13) In the 1989-98 electricity plan SEP discusses the imports to be expected in future. On page 8 the plan has this to say:
"Agreement has been reached with foreign electricity undertakings for import contracts guaranteeing a capacity of 1,050 MW. There would be 300 MW provided in the period running from 1996 to 2006, and 750 MW in the period from 1997 to 2008. ...Together with the guaranteed imports already agreed with VEW, this will make full use of the scope for importation."

And on page 39 of the same plan we read the following

---

[6] Source: *Elektriciteit in Nederland 1988*
[7] Source: *Elektriciteit in Nederland 1988*

[8] Source: UCPTE brochure *Elektrisch Europa*, 1987.

"Electricity imports
A useful way to meet part of the new capacity requirement has been found in the conclusion of import contracts for a determined period with a guaranteed capacity available. A guaranteed supply has already been agreed with VEW for the period from 1990 to 2000, through for separate reasons. This is for a capacity of 800 MW in the period after 1993.

After completion of the circular 380 kV grid, which is already underway, and after the Meeden-Diele interconnnection with the North German electricity grid has been connected to the 380 kV grid, as decided in this plan, it will, in principle, be possible to meet a capacity requirement of about 2,000 MW by means of imports convered by a capacity guarantee. The interconnections with foreign grids would also continue to be used for mutual assistance and exchanges on a spot market-basis."

7. Purchases of foreign electricity by Elektro-Schmelzwerk Delfzijl BV

(14) Elektro-Schmelzwerk Delfzijl BV ("ESD"), based in Delfzijl, is a subsidiary of the Wacker-Chemie group, which has its head office in Munich. Between 1982 and 1987 ESD purchased power in Germany via the Musselkanaal-Lathen international interconnection. The power was imported at ESD's request, but SEP in fact acted as importer. In the middle of 1987 this operation ran into difficulties, which according to SEP were of a technical nature. ESD expressed the wish to import power itself, and no longer through SEP. When it became clear that under the Law of 1936 this was not possible without authorization, ESD sought authorization from the Minister of Economic Affairs, and obtained it on 23 January 1987. In a letter to the Lower House of Parliament dated 23 January 1987 the Minister told the House that SEP did not wish to continue importing for ESD during 1987, although this would have been technically possible (for example using the Meeden-Diele interconnection). In the same letter the Minister said that ESD was dependent for

further imports on the willingness of SEP, but that SEP had "major reservations" on the point.

(15) A letter from SEP to the Ministry of Economic Affairs dated 17 February 1987 makes it clear that SEP was very unhappy at the granting of the authorization, and that SEP itself had agreed only to temporary import 'for' ESD. SEP took it that these imports would be "specifically earmarked" for a particular purchaser.

It was still being assumed, therefore, that power would be imported for, and not by, the purchaser. In the same letter SEP observed that it would be possible to introduce "special rates" for large private consumers, so that imports would no longer be an alternative.[9]

(16) In a letter of 5 March 1987 the Ministry stated that imports by individual purchasers had been repeatedly discussed but that SEP had each time expressly rejected the possibility, and it again urged SEP to import for ESD. The letter also mentioned the practice of "specific earmarking" and stated that the use of this terminlogy struck at the heart of SEP's policy, noting that only SEP imports and that SEP as a monopolist decides whether or not an individual consumer is allotted a share of the imported electricity. In its reply of 17 March 1987 SEP said among other things that application of Article 27 of the Co-operation Agreement (separate rates for a large private consumer) would make "imports by third parties" unnecessary, once the category of large private consumers became interested, as SEP anticipated.

By letter of 13 October 1987 SEP made an offer to ESD under which SEP would import for use by ESD power generated

---

[9] On the question of rates for large consumers, SEP's annual report for 1987 says the following , on page 9: "Every purchaser in this category is free to choose between a contract on the basis of the LBT (Landelijk Basis Tarief, *i.e.* the national basic tariff), importation, autogeneration, or the new tariff for large consumers; where the new tariff is chosen it must cover the total electricity requirement, and the choice may not be changed during the currency of the contract."

by the German electricity undertaking PREAG via the Meeden-Diele line. SEP would import and supply to EPON, and the power imported would be for the use of ESD only. SEP would charge transmission and other costs.

SEP also said that after 1 January 1988 it would be able to apply special rates for large consumers, and consequently advised ESD to agree any imports only up to that date.

By letter of 14 October 1987 ESD told SEP that in view of the pressure of time it would accept this offer, for the period up to 1 April 1988, with an option until 1 January 1989. Thus ESD did not make use of its authorization to import directly, but continued to buy through SEP.

This is also clear from a letter from ESD to SEP dated 30 December 1987, in which ESD agreed to purchase from the distributor EGD (Electriciteitsbedrijf voor Groningen en Drenthe) for the first quarter of 1988. The letter said that ESD continued to be interested in importing, and as a directly interested party would be glad to attend the negotiations on imports if these resumed.

The above described practice of SEP is in line with its view of its "planning" function as set out in its letter of 22 September 1988 to the Commission and is connected with its supply obligation towards its final consumers. The import monopoly according to SEP is the logical consequence and imports and exports must therefore be integrated into the capacity planning function which is necessary because of its supply obligation.

8. "Import gains"

(17) At least from 1984 onward SEP's annual accounts show that SEP had built up a financial reserve out of what were termed "import gains" (*importvoordelen*). This reserve is clearly accounted for by the difference between the costs of the power imported by SEP and the cost of power generated within the Netherlands.

This means that the lower price paid by SEP for imported power was not passed on to consumers, or at any rate not directly passed on in full.

Furthermore, it means that private consumers can obtain benefits from imports.

On page 37 of the Annual Report for 1985 it was stated that this arrangement was intended as far as possible to avoid sudden changes in rates in future. In 1985 about FI 73 million was added to the reserve out of import gains.

In 1985 the reserve amounted to about FI 277 million, and the Annual Report stated that a sum of FI 193 million would be put to a use to be determined by the Minister for Economic Affairs.

In the year covered by the report imports came mainly from France (EdF) and West Germany (RWE) and to a lesser extent from Belgium and Switzerland.

The Annual Report for 1986 stated that out of the tariff equalization reserve, which then amounted to ± FI 341 million, a sum of about FI 235 million would in the future be allocated for a purpose to be determined by the Minister for Economic Affairs. The gains from electricity imports were falling rapidly, the report said, and would ultimately disappear, because prices in the Netherlands and abroad had arrived at the same level.

(18) The Annual Reports for 1987 and 1988 no longer make express reference to import gains as the source of the tariff equalization reserve. In 1988 the reserve amounted to about FI 381 million, of which about FI 350 million was once again to be allocated by the Minister for Economic Affairs.

On page 30 of the Annual Report for 1988 we find the following:

"The increase in consumption is covered almost entirely by an increase in imports. Imports of power totalled 5,840 GWh, which amounts to about 9% of national consumption. Never before has the import balance reached such a high level."

(19) The Commission has no knowledge of cases in which exports of electricity by others than SEP has been obstructed by the latter. On the contrary there is a case of effective export by the distributor Provinciale Limburgse Elektriciteits-Maatschappij, which since recently

supplies VEGLA (Vereinigte Glaswerke GmbH) at Aachen, West Germany. According to SEP there are no objections against this because VEGLA is supplied via their own powerline located on Dutch territory. From this it may be concluded that SEP does not consider supplies to be exports as long as the "plug" of the consumer is located on Dutch territory.

9. The Co-operation Agreement in conjunction with the entry into force of the Electricity Law 1989

(20) Although the Electricity Law 1989 entered into force on 8 December 1989, the provisions dealing with imports in Article 34 entered into force on 1 July 1990.

By letter of 15 December 1989 SEP informed the Commission that in the meantime Article 21 of the Co-operation Agreement would continue to apply. According to SEP that Article would not be adjusted to take account of the new Law even after 1 July 1990. As far as is known to the Commission this Article has not yet been adapted. The same is true for the General Terms and Conditions for the supply of electricity to large-scale consumers of "VEEN". This Decision consequently relates both to the period before the Electricity Law 1989 entered into force and to the period thereafter.

The immediate subject matter of this Decision is Article 21 of the Co-operation Agreement in so far as it relates to imports by private consumers, or is applied by SEP to such imports, and combined with SEP's control of the interconnections has the effect of restricting imports and exports by those consumers, and exports by distributors.

II. Legal Assessment

A. Article 85 (1) of the Treaty

1. *Agreements between undertakings*
(21) The Co-operation Agreement is an agreement between undertakings within the meaning of Article 85 (1). It must be considered in the light of the fact that the four electricity generation companies are shareholders in SEP, a joint

subsidiary which acts as a vehicle for co-operation between them.

The Agreement is a matter of private law only. Despite the influence which the Dutch authorities exercise over planning and generation of electricity for public supply, there is no evidence that the Agreement was concluded under pressure from the authorities. Nor does the Compact between the State and the electricity generators which has already been referred to form any bar to the generators' own responsibility. The General SEP Agreement, the predecessor of the Co-operation Agreement, in any event predates the Compact.

(22) SEP has argued that the participating electricity generators together form an economic unit, because they are components in "one indivisible public electricity supply system." The real function of Article 21 of the Co-operation Agreement, according to SEP, is to secure an allocation of tasks between the generators, with certain tasks being centralised and allocated to SEP. SEP here invokes the Court of Justice's Judgement in *Hydrotherm* v *Compact* (Case 170/83 [1984] ECR 2999). SEP contends that there can therefore be no question of competition between the parties, so that Article 85 does not apply.

(23) This reasoning cannot be accepted. It is true that Article 85 is not concerned with agreements between undertakings belonging to the same group of companies, and having the status of parent company and subsidiary, if the undertakings form an economic unit within which the subsidiary has no real freedom to determine its course of action on the market, and if the agreements are concerned merely with the internal allocation of tasks as between the undertakings (Court of Justice, Case 30/87 *Bodson* [1988] ECR 2479); but that is not the situation here.

(24) To begin with, the four participants do not belong to a single group of companies. They are separate legal persons, and are not controlled by a single person, natural or legal. Each generating company determines its own conduct independently. It is hard to see

how else there could be differences between the prices different generators charge for power making it worthwhile for a consumer to buy in another distribution zone (the so-called "cross-shopping"). This observation certainly applies after the introduction of the Electricity Law 1989, which expressly permits cross-shopping.

The fact that the generators all form part of one indivisible system of public supply changes nothing here. The distributors likewise form part of the same system, but there is no reason to suppose that they form an economic unit with the generators on that ground alone.

Finally, it cannot be said that SEP itself forms an economic unit with one or more of the generating companies. SEP is a joint venture controlled by its parent companies together.

2. Restriction of competition

(25) Article 21 of the Co-operation Agreement, the subject of this Decision, prohibits the importation and exportation of electricity by undertakings other than SEP; it does so:

- horizontally, by prohibiting generators from exporting or importing (paragraph 1);
- vertically, by requiring generators to impose the same ban on distributors in their supply agreements (paragraph 2).

These prohibitions restrict competition.

(26) The parties to the Agreement also undertake, in Article 10 (4) of the Agreement, to include a clause in their supply agreements requiring all power autogenerated by distributors (with a minimum capacity per establishment of 5 MW or more) to be supplied to SEP via the party in whose supply territory the relevant plant is located. Distributors are therefore prevented from exporting locally generated power, or supplying it direct to purchasers. This means that local generation is not an alternative to the imports prohibited by Article 21.

Article 10 (4) of the Co-operation Agreement thus reinforces the restrictive effect of Article 21.

(27) In the course of the administrative proceedings SEP emphasised that Article 21 does not prevent anyone who is not a distributor from importing or exporting. After investigation, however, the Commission has reached the conclusion that within the structure of electricity supply in the Netherlands the way in which SEP applies Article 21 in practice enables it to exercise total control of imports and exports.

(28) In this connection it must be pointed out first of all that in their general terms and conditions distributors impose an exclusive purchasing obligation on their customers (usually local energy undertakings), and that those customers do the same to their own customers (large customers); imports are thus made impossible. The distributors who impose this exclusive purchasing obligation are themselves bound by an exclusive purchasing obligation towards the generators grouped in SEP. Thus the purchasing obligation which the generators impose works its way down the distribution chain, with the result that large consumers who purchase from the public grid cannot also import. This is also clear from the inclusion of the same purchasing obligations in the 1984 General Terms and Conditions for the Supply of Electricity to Large Consumers, which were drawn up by VEEN and are generally applied by the distributors. The succession of exclusive purchasing obligations forms a coherent system in conjunction with Article 21 of the Co-operation Agreement as it is applied by SEP and the generators, so that these provisions of the General Terms and Conditions together with Article 21 form a whole, operating both among generators and ultimately between them and their industrial consumers.

(29) Secondly, SEP operates and/or owns the international interconnections through which all imports and exports must be channelled, whether for public or private supply. Lines privately owned by consumers are not a real alternative.

SEP itself imports substantial quantities of electricity, from other

Member States and elsewhere (see recitals 10 *et seq.*). In principle it is technically possible to make power lines available to private importers at reasonable prices, provided SEP has sufficient capacity available, as is now provided in the Electricity Law 1989. But SEP has not been prepared to do this. The ESD case (see recitals 14 to 16 above) is an illustration: it was not ESD but SEP which ultimately imported from Germany. From the correspondence between SEP and the Ministry of Economic Affairs already referred to it is clear that SEP was opposed to direct imports by ESD, and indeed regarded importation for ESD by SEP itself as a temporary measure. From ESD's letter to SEP dated 30 December 1987 it is clear that SEP was keeping ESD from having contact with the German supplier. In any event it is plain that SEP wished to reserve importation, even as a temporary arrangement, to itself, and wishes to continue doing so in future too. As a last resort SEP was prepared to apply a special tariff which was so attractive that ESD decided not to import, and agreed to be supplied by EGD.

SEP has thus been applying Article 21 of the Co-operation Agreement in such a way that it in practice prevents private industrial consumers from themselves importing electricity. SEP is claiming what in fact amounts to an import monopoly. It may be mentioned, too, that SEP's complete refusal to make power lines available to others can be considered an agreement or concerted practice between the generators participating in SEP, which could constitute a separate infringement of Article 85.

(30) In the third place, SEP itself has argued that power imported for the importers' own use cannot be considered separately from power intended for public supply. In its planning function SEP must take account of imports. In practice, in any case, a final consumer who proposes to import himself will have to announce his intention in good time beforehand to the supplier with whom he has a supply contract. SEP will be informed, because

its co-operation is indispensable for transmission over the international interconnections and the high-tension grid. Consumers cannot feed surpluses of imported power back into the public grid.

(31) The Commission concludes that Article 21 of the Co-operation Agreement enables SEP to control the import and export of power in the interest of its shareholders. The consumers' theoretical entitlement to import themselves is thereby rendered inoperative in practice, and they are consequently deprived of access to other sources of supply.

3. *Effect on trade between Member States*
(32) The import and export ban in Article 21 is liable appreciably to affect trade between Member States. This is the more so as the Co-operation Agreement is to apply for a period of 25 years, and covers the entire territory of the Netherlands. In addition, as has already been pointed out, imports by industrial consumers are rendered difficult in a way which conflicts with the achievement of a single market in energy.

B. The operation of the Co-operation Agreement under the Electricity Law 1989
(33) According to SEP Article 21 of the Co-operation Agreement continues to apply even after the entry into force of the Electricity Law 1989, and particularly Article 34 of this Law. SEP evidently considers that the new Law changes nothing in Article 21 of the Co-operation Agreement. The Commission would make the following observations in this respect.

1. *Imports*
(34) Article 34 of the Electricity Law 1989 prohibits anyone other than SEP from importing power with a view to public supply. On the other hand, imports for purposes other than public supply are no longer subject to prior authorization. Imports by final consumers, and essentially industrial consumers, are therefore unrestricted, provided they are

302

intended for the importer's own consumption: imported power cannot be supplied to third parties (Article 37 (1) of the new Law), nor can it be fed into the public supply (Article 41 (2) (b)).

Under Article 47 (1) (c) SEP now has an obligation to transmit any power imported SEP must allow the importer access to its connections on reasonable terms, provided there is sufficient capacity available.

Under the new rules, therefore, an industrial consumer is indeed entitled to import, but for the technical facilities needed he remains dependent on SEP, which with its control of the high-tension grid is still in a position to place difficulties in the way of imports. This may occur particularly where the connections are full loaded as a result of power imports by SEP itself.

(35) Contrary to SEP's claims, therefore, Article 21 has not simply been incorporated into the Law. If that had been done Article 21 would now no longer serve any purpose. The fact that SEP wishes to continue to apply Article 21 is an indication that the article continues to have significance alongside the Law. All this confirms the Commission's view that Article 21 is being applied in a way which goes beyond the terms of the Law.

2. *Exports*

(36) The Electricity Law 1989 makes no rules regarding the export of power, except for the obligation of generators to supply electricity only to SEP (Article 11). In response to a questionnaire the Dutch Government informed the Commission that the export of power from the Netherlands is completely unrestricted. According to the Dutch Government not only SEP but also distributors and private consumers are free to export. This applies whether the power involved is taken from the public grid or autogenerated.

(37) Like importers, however, exporters continue to be dependent on SEP for transmission. The new Law does not impose an obligation to transmit power for export. A potential exporter must

therefore reach agreement with SEP and with the owners of foreign grids. SEP thus retains a key role. The way in which it plays that role depends on the way in which it applies Article 21 of the Co-operation Agreement.

3. *Conclusion*

(38) It must be concluded that the application of Article 21 of the Co-operation Agreement continues to infringe Article 85 of the Treaty under the rules introduced by the new Law.

C. Article 90 (2) of the Treaty: non-public supply

(39) Article 90 (2) of the Treaty states that undertakings entrusted with the operations of services of general economic interest are to be subject to the rules contained in the Treaty, in particular to the rules on competition, in so far as the application of such rules does not obstruct the performance, in law or in fact, of the particular tasks assigned to them. The development of trade must not be affected to such an extent as would be contrary to the interests of the Community.

SEP invokes the exception laid down in Article 90 (2). It argues that the electricity industry possesses special features: on the one hand, it is under an obligation to guarantee supply, and on the other, as a necessary consequence of that obligation, it must be able to exercise control of generation, imports and exports.

1. *The undertakings are entrusted with the operation of services of general economic interest*

(40) SEP's main task is to ensure the reliable and efficient operation of the national public electricity supply at costs which are as low as possible and in a socially responsible fashion (Article 2 of the Electricity Law 1989). This definition of SEP's tasks is complemented by the generators' obligation to supply to distributors (Article 12 (1) of the Law). The arrangement is clearly based on the terms of the concessions formerly granted by the Minister for Economic

Affairs. The generators' obligation to supply was a central feature there too (*cf,* IJsselcentrale's concession, recital 7).

In these circumstances it can be accepted that both SEP and the participating generators are engaged in "the operation of services of general economic interest."

(41) The operation of these services now has a basis in legislation, which it did not have before the entry into force of the new Law. But even before the new Law these tasks had been assigned to the generators by an act of public law, namely the grant of concessions by the Minister of Economic Affairs. It must be concluded that both before and after the entry into force of the Electricity Law 1989 SEP and the generators were "entrusted" with the operation of these services.

(42) The first test of Article 90 (2) is therefore satisfied.

2. *The application of the competition rules does not obstruct the performance of the tasks assigned.*

(43) In the Commission's view the application of the competition rules does not obstruct SEP in the proper performance of the tasks assigned to it, because the performance of those tasks does not require absolute control of imports and exports, including imports and exports by private consumers and particularly industrial consumers, which as we have seen is the consequence of Article 21 of the Co-operation Agreement.

(44) As far as imports are concerned this can be seen from the following considerations.

(a) In 1988 15,6% of total power generated in the Netherlands was accounted for by what are known as autogenerators (see recital 10 above). These autogenerators feed their surpluses into the public grid. Autogeneration evidently does not interfere with the performance of SEP's tasks. There is no reason to suppose that importation should be any different.

SEP has argued in this respect that importation is a one-off operation, whereas autogeneration has a structured

and therefore more long-term character. But the distinction SEP is suggesting does not, in fact, exist. Imports too have to be planned. Part of SEP's function is to adapt its own generation activities to the scale of imports and local generation. Imports too have to be notified to SEP in advance (see recital 30). Imports too are allowed for in the Electricity Plan. Thus there is no difference here between importation and autogeneration.

Furthermore, in the case of autogeneration as in the case of importation the distributors are released from their obligation to supply; a consumer who announces his intention of meeting his power requirements wholly or partly by means of importation or autogeneration cannot in an emergency simply fall back on the public supply. He may conclude a back-up contract with the distributor, under which a stated capacity is "set aside" for him against payment. There is no obligation to conclude such a contract under the new Law.

(b) The Dutch authorities do not believe that absolute control of imports by SEP is necessary to the performance of the tasks assigned to it. It would be difficult to explain otherwise why the new Law expressly leaves imports for the importer's own consumption unrestricted. In the course of the Parliamentary debate on the new Law the Minister for Economic Affairs referred to the similarities between autogeneration and importation which have just been discussed (*Kammerstukken,* Verslag van een schriftelijk overleg, No 15, pp 8, 17 and 18). In both cases the "absolute obligation to supply" does not apply. There is consequently no need for "absolute control of generation and importation" either.

Thus the absolute control of imports given to SEP by Article 21 of the Co-operation Agreement is not considered by the Dutch authorities themselves to be indispensable to the performance of these tasks of general interest.

(c) Lastly, SEP's rights of ownership over the international interconnections do not justify total control over imports. Even before SEP's obligation to transmit was laid down in legislation (Article 47

(1) (c) of the new Law), the power lines could be made available on reasonable terms to other parties for the transmission of power they were importing themselves. The other requirements that SEP might lay down for transmission operations could be that nothing must be done to endanger the reliability of the grid; that the transaction must be an economically justifiable one with some measure of regularity (no spot transactions); that the operations must have a measure of continuity over a reasonable period; and that the prices must be reasonable and non-discriminatory. As a general rule these requirements will be met only by private consumers with significant power requirements, such as large consumers or groups of several industrial consumers. Thus there was and is no reason for absolute control as a consequence of SEP's operation of the power lines.

(45) With regard to exports of power by private industrial consumers there are in principle the same reasons for holding that control by SEP cannot be justified for the purposes of Article 90 (2) of the Treaty.

(a) As SEP has itself argued, when power is obtained from the public grid the Dutch electricity undertakings do not "look behind the meter": they supply current to a customer, and are not concerned with what the customer does with it, whether he consumes it himself, exports it, or supplies it in his turn to someone else. There is no reason why autogenerated current should not be exported in the same way. It does not after all affect the public supply, indeed that is why the new Law leaves it unrestricted.

(b) Here again the new Dutch legislation leaves industrial consumers, including autogenerators, free to export.

(c) Rights of ownership over the interconnections cannot justify absolute control of exports either.

(46) It must be concluded that the second test of Article 90 (2) is not satisfied.

3. *The development of trade*
(47) In view of the foregoing there is no need to consider the last sentence of Article 90 (2). It is clear, however, that obstruction of imports and exports such as that deriving from Article 21 of the Co-operation Agreement does affect trade to an extent contrary to the interests of the Community. In the light of the Community's efforts to achieve a single internal market in energy such obstruction of imports and exports, which moreover is intended to continue for a period of 25 years, cannot be accepted.

(48) Thus the provision of Article 90 (2) is in any event not satisfied either.

D. Article 90 (2) of the Treaty: public supply

(49) To the extent that Article 21 is applied to imports with a view to public supply, and to exports by generators and distributors, the following observations are in order.

1. *Imports*
(50) The ban on imports by generators and distributors otherwise than through SEP in the context of public supply, is now laid down in Article 34 of the Electricity Law 1989. The present proceeding is a proceeding under Regulation 17, and the Commission will not pass judgement here on the question whether such restriction of imports is justified for the purposes of Article 90 (2) of the Treaty. To do so would be to anticipate the question whether the new Law is itself compatible with the Treaty, and that is outside the scope of this proceeding.

2. *Exports*
(51) An export ban imposed on generators in the field of public supply can be deduced from the supply obligation imposed by Article 11 of the Electricity Law 1989 which obliges the generators to supply their electricity only to SEP and to supply exclusively to distributors the electricity supplied to them by SEP. Again, no judgement will be made on this export ban under the present proceedings.

The ban on exports, including those made outside the field of public supply, by distributors imposed by Article 21 of the Co-operation Agreement, conflicts with the scheme of the new Law in which these exports are left unrestricted. It appears doubtful to the Commission whether the parties to the Co-operation Agreement are entitled to impose an export ban that runs counter to the Law in this way, but to judge by what is said in SEP's letter to the Commission of 15 December 1989 SEP evidently considers that the possibility does exist.

Accepting therefore that the ban on exports by distributors laid down in Article 21 continues to apply, the Commission takes the view that it cannot be justified by Article 90 (2). There is no apparent reason why exports by these distributors should endanger the public supply. As long as distributors are in a position to meet their supply obligations domestically, there is no reason to prevent them from exploiting any surpluses by exporting them.

(52) It must be concluded that the ban on exports which continues to be imposed by Article 21 of the Co-operation Agreement on distributors even after the entry into force of Article 34 of the Electricity Law 1989 cannot be justified by reference to Article 90 (2).

E. Article 85 (3) of the Treaty

(53) The Co-operation Agreement was not notified to the Commission in accordance with Article 4 of Regulation 17. Neither were earlier agreements between the participants in SEP ever so notified. Even if the Co-operation Agreement were to be notified, it would not qualify for exemption under Article 85 (3). It follows from the foregoing that the absolute effect which SEP has given to the import and export ban in Article 21 is not indispensible to the attainment of the objectives of the Co-operation Agreement. The third test of Article 85 (3) is thus in any event not satisfied.

F. Conclusion

(54) The Commission concludes that Article 21 of the Co-operation Agreement between SEP and the Dutch electricity generators, as applied in conjunction with the control and influence in fact exercised over inter-

national supplies of power, constitutes an infringement of Article 85 (1) of the Treaty in so far as it has as its object or effect:

(a) the restriction of imports by private industrial consumers, and

(b) the restriction of exports by distributors and industrial consumers, including autogenerators,

and that is does not satisfy the conditions for application of Article 90 (2) of the Treaty.

G. Article 3 of Regulation 17

(55) Article 3 of Regulation 17 allows the Commission to adopt a decision finding that an infringement has been committed in the past, in order to clarify the legal position, and to require the undertakings concerned to bring such infringement to an end, to the extent that it still continues.

SEP has stated that it will continue to apply Article 21 of the Co-operation Agreement, so that it cannot be said that SEP and the electricity generators participating in it have put an end to the infringement. They must therefore be required to do so. One way in which the infringement could be ended would be for SEP to inform the parties to the Co-operation Agreement, and purchasers, that the Agreement is to be interpreted and applied as meaning that exports of quantities of electric power not intended for public supply, and direct imports by private industrial consumers, are unrestricted, and will not, without good reason, be obstructed by virtue of the ownership or operation of the power grid by SEP and the parties to the Agreement; and that the Agreement will be applied accordingly.

The Commission will allow the parties three months from the date of notification of this Decision to make proposals for the ending of the infringement.

HAS ADOPTED THIS DECISION:

Article 1

Article 21 of the Co-operation Agreement concluded on 22 May 1986 by the predecessors of the present four electricity generating companies on the one hand and by NV Samenwerkende Elektriciteitsproduktiebedrijven on the other, as applied in conjunction with the control and influence in fact exercised over the international supply of electricity, constitutes an infringement of Article 85 (1) of the Treaty in so far as it has as its object or effect the restriction of imports by private industrial consumers and of exports of production outside the field of public supply, by distributors and private industrial consumers, including autogenerators.

Article 2

The companies referred to in Article 3 shall take all necessary steps to bring the infringement referred to in Article 1 to an end. Within three months of reception of this Decision they shall submit to the Commission proposals for the ending of the infringement.

Article 3

This Decision is addressed to:

- NV Samenwerkende Elektriciteitspro-duktiebedrijven, Utrechtseweg 310, 6812 AR NL-Arnhem;
- NV Electriciteitsbedrijf Zuid-Holland, Von Geusaustraat 193, 2274 RJ NL-Voorburg;
- NV Energieproduktiebedrijf UNA, Keulsekade 189, 3534 AC NL-Utrecht;
- NV Elektriciteits-Produktiemaat-schappij Zuid-Nederland EPZ, Begijnenhof 1, 5611 EK NL-Eindhoven;
- NV Elektriciteits-Produktiemaat-schappij Oost- en Noord-Nederland, Dr Stolteweg 92, 8025 AZ NL-Zwolle.

COMMISSION DECISION 91/329

of 30 April 1991

relating to a proceeding under Article 85 of the EEC Treaty
(IV/33.473 – Scottish Nuclear, Nuclear Energy Agreement)[1]

THE COMMISSION OF THE EUROPEAN COMMUNITIES,

Having regard to the Treaty establishing the European Economic Community,

Having regard to Council Regulation 17 of 6 February 1962, First Regulation implementing Articles 85 and 86 of the Treaty , as last amended by the Act of Accession of Spain and Portugal, and in particular Articles 6 and 8 thereof,

Having regard to the notification dated 27 February 1990 by Scottish Nuclear Limited, concerning the Nuclear Energy Agreement drawn up in the context of the reorganization of the electricity industry in Scotland,

Having regard to the summary of the notification published pursuant to Article 19 (3) of Regulation 17,

After consulting the Advisory Committee on Restrictive Practices and Dominant Positions,

Whereas:

I. Facts

A. The notification

(1) On 27 February 1990, Scottish Nuclear Limited notified to the Commission, pursuant to Article 4 of Regulation 17, an agreement between itself and Scottish Power plc and Scottish Hydro-Electric plc.

(2) Scottish Nuclear Limited has applied for negative clearance or, failing that, exemption pursuant to Article 85 (3) of the EEC Treaty.

B. General framework

(3) Until 31 March 1990 Scotland's electricity requirements were met by two publicly-owned corporations, North of Scotland Hydro-Electric Board and

South of Scotland Electricity Board, which generated, transmitted and distributed electricity in their assigned geographical areas, covering the north and south of Scotland respectively.

(4) In reorganising the industry in advance privatization, the United Kingdom Government decided to maintain vertical integration in the Scottish electricity industry, since it is better suited for the supply of electricity to sparsely-populated areas which are characteristic of many areas of Scotland.

(5) The United Kingdom Government has therefore decided to create two separate, independent and competing vertically-integrated electricity utility companies from the two Boards. Scottish Power plc ("Scottish Power") has taken over the non-nuclear business of the South of Scotland Electricity Board and Scottish Hydro-Electric plc ("Hydro-Electric") the business of the North of Scotland Hydro-Electric Board. Both companies will be privatised. The Scottish nuclear stations at Hunterston and Torness which previously were owned by the South of Scotland Electricity Board are now owned and operated by a separately established generating company, Scottish Nuclear Ltd ("Scottish Nuclear") which will remain in public ownership. Scottish Nuclear does not supply direct to customers, selling all its output under contract to Scottish Power and Hydro-Electric.

(6) The Electricity Act 1989 and subordinate legislation made thereunder set out the framework for the new regulatory system for the electricity industry in Scotland. Under this Act any undertaking generating, transmitting or supplying electricity in Scotland needs a licence issued by the Secretary of State for Scotland or the Director-General for Electricity Supply, unless exempted by

[1] OJ 1991 L178/31.

order under the Act. Scottish Power and Hydro-Electric are each by licence obliged and entitled to transmit and supply electricity to customers within their authorised areas. These areas are essentially the same as those of the former Boards. Both utilities are entitled to generate electricity themselves. There is no restriction on the proportion of its electricity requirements which either utility can meet from its own generation resources.

(7) The right of the two companies to supply customers within their authorised areas is however not exclusive; premises having a demand above 1 MW are free to choose their supplier; after four years this threshold will be reduced to 0,1 MW and after eight years totally phased out.

(8) It is possible for Scottish Power and Hydro-Electric, on receipt of the appropriate "second-tier licences" to supply to those customers in each other's authorised area or their supplier (as described above). The opportunity to apply for such "second-tier licences" is available to any person in the United Kingdom or the rest of the Community wishing to supply electricity to customers in Scotland. It should be noted that Scottish Nuclear has been granted a generation licence only.

(9) The licences place obligations on Scottish Power and Hydro-Electric not to discriminate between comparable customers, to avoid cross-subsidies and to allow all other users access to their transmission and distribution systems on a transparent and non-discriminatory basis.

(10) Furthermore the licences oblige the licence holders to comply with certain codes and agreements which have been approved by the Director-General of Electricity Supply, including codes governing the operation of the transmission and distribution systems and the trading of electricity.

(11) In the view of the United Kingdom Government it is essential for Scottish Power and Hydro-Electric to have access to a balanced mix of different types of generating capacity in order to be financially viable and capable of independent operation. Therefore the

non-nuclear generating assets of the two former Boards, which had been built to meet Scotland's requirements in their entirety, had to be redistributed between the new companies. This could not be achieved by simply allocating the different power stations to one or the other utility, since the nature and location of the generating assets rendered this impractical. The United Kingdom Government therefore decided that the necessary restructuring should be achieved by means of contractual arrangements which create rights and obligations between the two utilities in relation to certain of the generating assets and transmission systems of each, effectively replacing ownership of these assets with long-term contractual entitlements the duration of which corresponds to the currently expected lifetime of the power stations concerned. These contractual arrangements replace the former loose non-commercial agreements between the two Boards on cost-sharing and operational matters. The principal contracts between Scottish Power and Hydro-Electric concern the sharing of coal-fired plant capacity, hydro capacity and gas/oil-fired capacity. Furthermore, Scottish Power and Hydro-Electric divide between them the total output of Scottish Nuclear at present.

(12) The new structure of the electricity industry in Scotland is designed to introduce competition progressively both at the level of electricity generation and at the level of electricity supply. At present the electricity sector in Scotland has substantial overcapacity in electricity generation, which on present estimates is likely to continue at least for the next ten years, and a high concentration of nuclear generation capable of meeting over 50% of current Scottish electricity demand. Trading with England and Wales is possible through the interconnector which links the transmission grids in Scotland and England.

C. The product and the market

(13) The relevant product market is that of the production, supply and

distribution of electricity.

(14) Total electricity generation in the United Kingdom reached 312 Twh (1 Tw = 10^3 Gw = 10^6 Mw (output capacity)) in 1989, total net production 292 Twh and total imports 12.9 million Kwh (0.013 Twh). Exports reached 0.8 million Kwh.

(15) The energy sources are conventional thermal production (71.6%), nuclear production (21.7%) and hydroelectrical production (2.2%).

(16) Generating capacity in England and Wales reached 56,679 GW (1 Twh = 10^3 Gwh = 10^6 Mwh (electricity output)) on 31 March 1990. Coal is the most important fuel source (62.8%), followed by oil (17.7%) and then nuclear (14.7%).

(17) Generating capacity in Scotland reached 11,640 GW on 1 April 1989 and the electricity sent out in the year up to 31 March 1989 reached 29.3 Twh. Nuclear power stations are the most significant source of electricity in Scotland (13 Twh, 44%), followed by coal fired stations (30%), hydro (14%) and then gas oil (10%).

(18) The turnover relative to the production and supply of electricity for the financial year ended 31 March 1989 was £ 11,284 million, 90 % of sales being in England and Wales and 10% in Scotland.

D. The Agreement

(19) Under the terms of the Nuclear Energy Agreement, Scottish Power and Hydro-Electric are obliged to purchase all the electricity generated by Scottish Nuclear from its Hunterston and Torness plant on a take or pay basis. Scottish Nuclear is obliged to try to produce maximum output from these two nuclear power stations which have together a capacity of 2,400 MW. Scottish Power will have to take 74.9% of Scottish Nuclear's output and Hydro-Electric 25.1%. Scottish Nuclear is not permitted to supply electricity to any other party without the consent of both Scottish Power and Hydro-Electric. Scottish Nuclear Ltd cannot supply power except for Scottish Power and Hydro-Electric unless the contract has been terminated.

(20) Because of the existing overcapacity in electricity production in Scotland and in particular nuclear electricity there is no present intention for there to be a non-fossil fuel obligation in Scotland nor a corresponding fossil fuel levy. This non-fossil fuel obligation was imposed in England and Wales by the British Government in order to favour nuclear electricity and renewable electricity.

(21) The agreement contains provisions for the calculation of the prices to be paid to Scottish Nuclear by Scottish Power and Hydro-Electric. From 1991 to 1994 the price is fixed on the basis of a two-tier structure; a base price per kilowatt hour for the first tranche of 5,000 Gwh and a lower set price for units in excess of 5,000 Gwh, this lower price being similar to the cost of replacement energy to the purchasers (This point has already been examined within the framework of the decision on state aid to the electricity sector in Scotland (30 March 1990). The Commission decided not to raise any objections against the proposed aid for the reorganization of the production of nuclear electricity).

(22) The companies are obliged to pay against availability even if they do not take energy, but Scottish Power and Hydro-Electric can request Scottish Nuclear to reduce their individual share of generation.

(23) Scottish Nuclear is required to declare availability one day in advance. If it fails to achieve the declared level, it pays compensation in addition to the loss of revenue resulting from lower availability.

(24) The actual two-tier price arrangement in the Nuclear Energy Agreement was set in 1990, and combines an energy charge of 1.5p/kWh with a payment recognising the value of Scottish Nuclear's baseload capacity, of 4.5p/kWh spread over the first 5,000 units of Scottish Nuclear's output per annum. The basis and level of the prices which Scottish Power and Hydro-Electric have been paying to independent producers of electricity pre-date by several years the reorganization of the electricity industry in Scotland, and have not been affected by it. According to the affirmation of the notifying parties, there is no link at all

311

between the respective methodologies.

(25) The Nuclear Energy Agreement will remain in force until 31 March 2005 although it may be terminated earlier if, for example, Scottish Nuclear consistently fails to meet production requirements.

E. The arguments of the parties to the agreement

(26) The Nuclear Energy Agreement promotes economic progress as it is part of the United Kingdom Government's proposals for the privatization of the electricity industry in Scotland which aims at promoting competition and efficiency within the energy supply market within the United Kingdom.

(27) There will remain competition between Scottish Power and Hydro-Electric and with other types of fuel. Accordingly the parties do not consider that their arrangements eliminate competition in respect of substantial part of the goods in question. The price at which Scottish Power and Hydro-Electric can resell the electricity purchased from Scottish Nuclear is not fixed in terms of the Nuclear Energy Agreement.

II. Legal Assessment

A. Article 85 (1)

1. Agreement between undertakings

(28) The Nuclear Energy Agreement is an agreement between undertakings within the meaning of Article 85 (1) of the EEC Treaty.

2. Restrictions of competition

(29) The agreement restricts competition in three ways:

– the requirement that nuclear electricity be sold exclusively to Scottish Power and Hydro-Electric limits Scottish Nuclear's market. Scottish Nuclear is not permitted to supply electricity to any other parties unless the contract has been terminated. If the contract has been terminated, Scottish Nuclear can sell electricity only to other parties not situated in the same geographical area as the purchaser in respect of

which the contract is still in force,

– the requirement that Scottish Power and Hydro-Electric purchase, on the basis of quotas arranged between them, all the nuclear electricity generated restricts the two companies' sources of supply, with Scottish Power having to purchase 74.9% of Scottish Nuclear's output and Hydro-Electric 25.1%. Since they may not deviate from the quotas, they are unable to gain any competitive advantage one over the other,

– the price at which nuclear electricity is purchased is fixed under the agreement and is identical for the two companies. The fact that, from 1995 to 1998, the price will be based on the terms of the agreement and on alignment with the market price in England and Wales and that, after 1998, it will be entirely aligned on the market price indicates that the present price derives from a restrictive agreement.

3. Restriction of trade between Member States

(30) Intra-Community trade is confined to that between the United Kingdom and France via the interconnector linking the French grid to the grid in England and Wales. Its capacity is 2 GW, equivalent to 4% of the electricity output of England and Wales. During the last three years, the net flow of trade was from France to England and Wales, amounting to 12.9 Twh in 1988 and 13.6 Twh in 1989.

(31) However, the reorganization of electricity generation in Scotland and the prospect of a medium-term increase in the transmission capacity of the interconnector (net capacity of 850 MW in 1991, planned increase to 1,600 MW in three to four years) will help to reduce the relative isolation of the Scottish market, to create greater interdependence between the markets and to increase trade between Member States. Because of the interdependence of the networks, on the one hand between Scotland and England and on the other hand between England and France, and also because of the proposed development of these interconnections, the

agreement is therefore likely to affect trade between Member States.

B. Article 85 (3)

(32) The Nuclear Energy Agreement, covering a 15-year period from 27 February 1990 to 31 March 2005, meets the necessary conditions for exemption under Article 85 (3) of the Treaty.

1. *Improving the production or distribution of goods*

(33) The Nuclear Energy Agreement forms an integral part of the electricity privatization scheme in Scotland, the aim of which is to improve the generation and distribution of electricity. It gives Scottish Nuclear a guaranteed market by requiring Scottish Power and Hydro-Electric to purchase all the nuclear-generated electricity on a take or pay basis. It thus allows the long-term planning that is required for reliable production ensuring security of supply and an independent energy supply market.

Furthermore in order to ensure the profitability of the nuclear power stations and to offset the investment costs which are particularly high, it is necessary to have the stations functioning at their full capacity.

(34) Because their marginal cost is much lower than the marginal cost per KW generated by a thermal power station (between 0.55 and 0.75 p per unit in the case of nuclear generation and 0.97 p in the case of gas, 1.7 p in the case of coal and 1.55 p in the case of oil), it is economical to have the nuclear power stations operating at maximum capacity. Consequently, the agreement allows considerable economies of scale to be achieved by increasing nuclear generation and thus makes it possible to rely less on generators whose generation and transmission costs are higher.

(35) So as to induce Scottish Nuclear to maximize its output, the price at which electricity is sold to Scottish Power and Hydro-Electric has been fixed, under the agreement, for the initial four years, in such a way that the first-tier price for the first tranche of 5,000 Gwh allows a satisfactory rate of return on the capital

invested. The second-tier price is set in terms of the full costs resulting from the operation of a coal-fired power station, which is equivalent to the marginal cost of the electricity generated by the Scottish system.

(36) The improvement in the generation and distribution of electricity in Scotland which the agreement will help to achieve will allow overcapacity to be gradually eliminated. Measures to organise generation and the market, limited in time, are necessary in order to allow transition from the structure which has applied hitherto to a market-based electricity industry.

2. *Fair share of the resulting benefit for consumers*

(37) The Nuclear Energy Agreement forms part of the reorganization of a system which has hitherto been monopolistic. The benefit to consumers, both industrial and private, derives from the gradual introduction of competition into the system. It is notable that premises whose demand exceeds 1MW are already free to choose their supplier; after four years this threshold will be reduced to 0.1 MW and after eight years totally phased out.

3. *Need for the restrictions*

(38) Competition between Scottish Power and Hydro-Electric under the privatization of electricity in Scotland is not restricted by the agreement beyond what is necessary. Although the two companies are obliged to purchase nuclear-generated electricity at the same price, the agreement will gradually allow them to compete in their relations with their customers.

(39) The quotas which have been fixed between Scottish Power and Hydro-Electric for the purchase of nuclear electricity output do not reflect the market share of both companies as each company is free to determine individually their output and meet their demand.

(40) The agreement, which was originally to apply for a period equivalent to the remaining lifetime of the nuclear power stations, *i.e.* 30 years, has at the

Commission's request, been limited to 15 years. This period of validity provides the stability and guarantee necessary for long-term planning and allows the necessary adjustments to be made to the new situation after a reasonable start-up period. However, this period seems necessary to allow Scottish Nuclear to attain profitability and become competitive.

(41) The price set in the agreement is independent of the price at which Scottish Power and Hydro-Electric purchase electricity from the other generators, particularly the independent generators.

The formula used for the first four years and taken as a basis for setting prices for the following four years is considered to be an internal calculation formula which does not in any way prejudice the setting of the price at which electricity is purchased from independent generators. The price set in the agreement should not, in particular, be improperly used to justify a very low purchase price that would dissuade independent generators and Scottish Nuclear's competitors. This could be deemed to be an abuse of the exemption.

4. *No elimination of competition*

(42) The agreement introduces a system of gradual competitiveness into the electricity industry and creates scope for competition between Scottish Power and Hydro-Electric. In addition, the market in the generation of electricity, except nuclear-generated electricity, remains sufficiently open for the agreement not to create any barriers to entry. Nuclear-powered generation plays and will continue to play an important role, but there are real alternative sources of supply.

C. Articles 6 and 8 of Regulation 17

(43) Pursuant to Article 6 (1) of Regulation 17, this Decision will take effect as from the date of the notification, *i.e.*, 27 February 1990. Exemption is granted, pursuant to Article 8 (1) of Regulation 17, for the period of the validity of the agreement, reduced at the Commission's request from 30 to 15 years, *i.e.*, from 27 February 1990 to 31 March 2005, the expiry date for the present agreement,

HAS ADOPTED THIS DECISION:

Article 1

Pursuant to Article 85 (3) of the EEC Treaty, the provisions of Article 85 (1) are hereby declared inapplicable, for the period between 27 February 1990 and 31 March 2005, to the Nuclear Energy Agreement concluded between Scottish Nuclear Ltd and Scottish Power plc and Scottish Hydro-Electric plc.

Article 2

This Decision is addressed to:
– Scottish Nuclear Limited,
   Incorporated in Scotland No SC1-17121, Cathcart House, Spean Street,
   UK – Glasgow G44 4BE
– Scottish Power plc,
   Incorporated in Scotland No SC1-17120, Cathcart House, Spean Street,
   UK – Glasgow G44 4BE
– Scottish Hydro-Electric plc,
   Incorporated in Scotland No 117119,
   16 Rothesay Terrace,
   UK – Edinburgh EH3 7SE.

NOTICE

Pursuant to Article 19 (3) of Council Regulation 17/62
(IV/33.151 – "Jahrhundertvertrag")[1]

1. On 1 June 1989, the Gesamtverband des deutschen Steinkohlenbergbaus (General Association of the German Coalmining Industry – GVSt), whose registered office is in Essen, Federal Republic of Germany, notified to the Commission the "Supplementary agreement on the sale of German coal up to 1995", concluded on 23 April 1980 with the Vereinigung Deutscher Elektrizitäts-werke eV (Association of the German Public Electricity Supply Industry – VDEW), whose registered office is in Frankfurt, Federal Republic of Germany, as a follow-up to the "Agreement on the sale of German coal to the public electricity supply industry in the years 1978 to 1987" concluded on 10 May 1977.

2. Under the supplementary agreement of 23 April 1980 in conjunction with the agreement of 24 March 1980, coal procurement by the electricity-generating public electricity supply companies was extended to 31 December 1995 and a total amount was agreed for the period from 1 January 1981 to 31 December 1995. The individual coal supply agreements are entered into between the individual mining companies (six in total) and the individual electricity supply companies (44 in total) that are parties to the "Jahrhundertvertrag" agreement.

3. The "Jahrhundertvertrag" consists of the agreement concluded between the VDEW and the GVSt, an agreement between the Vereinigung Industrielle Kraftwirtschaft eV (Association of the industrial producers of electricity – VIK) and the GVSt and an agreement between the Federal German Railways and the GVSt. However, the notification relates only to the agreement between the VDEW and the GVSt.

4. The notification was carried out in response to a letter sent by the Directorate-General for Competition on 12 April 1989 suggesting that the parties to the agreement might consider notifying it formally. The GVSt takes the view that the supplementary agreement between the VDEW and the GVSt of 23 April 1980 does not require authorization under Article 85 of the EEC Treaty and therefore emphasised that the notification was purely precautionary in nature. At the same time, the GVSt applied for negative clearance or alternatively for exemption under Article 85 (3) of the EEC Treaty.

5. The total amount which the electricity supply companies, each according to its quota, are required to purchase under the agreement principles of 24 March 1980 during the 15-year period from 1 January 1981 to 31 December 1995 is 511.5 million tonnes of coal units. The partial amounts specified for the period 1991 to 1995 (third five-year period) amount to an average of 37.5 million tonnes of coal units per year. The partial amounts stipulated for the period 1986 to 1990 (second five-year period) amount to an average of 34.6 million tonnes of coal units per year.

In actual fact, the electricity supply companies did not purchase in full the quantities stipulated for the period 1986 to 1990 under the agreement. As a result of negotiations between the Federal Government and the parties to the agreement, it has been agreed in 1989 that during the third five-year period the electricity supply companies will only be obliged to purchase 34.4 million tonnes of coal units per year.

6. The additional costs incurred by the electricity supply companies from converting German coal into electricity are to a large extent offset by grants from the Ausgleichsfonds zur Sicherung des Steinkohleneinsatzes (equalization fund for safeguarding the use of coal);

[1] OJ 1990 C159/7.

however, in respect of a certain proportion of the domestic coal amounts purchased, the electricity supply companies receive instead of the grants annual entitlement certificates for the procurement of non-Community coal. (In the Federal Republic of Germany, imports of coal from non-Community countries are restricted by law).

7. The notified agreement between the mining industry and the public electricity supply industry was encouraged and recommended by the Federal Government, but not imposed on the parties, so that it cannot be considered to be part of the Law on the conversion of coal into electricity or any other Law or as a "State measure". The Commission views the agreement as an agreement between undertakings designed to share markets and sources of supply and falling under the provisions of Article 85 (1).

8. Trade between Member States is affected, since, to the extent that the electricity supply companies are obliged to use German coal for the generation of electricity, the use of other primary sources of energy such as heavy fuel oil, natural gas or nuclear energy is excluded; however, the use of coal from other Member States does not in principal seem to be excluded, witness the fact that some quantities of coal from Houillières du Bassin de Lorraine are used for electricity generating. It should be noted in this context that intra-Community trade in coal is of little or no significance. Trade between Member States is also affected since, to the extent that the electricity supply companies are obliged to use German coal for electricity generating, the import of electricity from other Member States is excluded.

9. However, the agreement between the VDEW and the GVSt seems to justify exemption under Article 85 (3) subject to certain conditions. The above-mentioned measures benefit electricity consumers and the general public since they serve to safeguard electricity supplies and hence contribute to improving the generating and distribution of electricity. On the other hand, it is not evident that the amounts of German coal specified for generation of electricity under the agreement notified are actually indispensable to the attainment of these objectives and justify elimination of competition to this extent.

10. The Commission therefore intends, also with a view to the creation of a genuine internal market for energy within the Community, to limit authorization of the agreement notified to the period up to 31 March 1991, subject to the condition that the requirement imposed on the electricity supply companies to purchase German coal does not in the period 1 January 1990 to 31 March 1991 exceed a total of 42 millions tonnes of coal units; this is in line with the present position regarding the amounts of German coal actually supplied to the electricity supply companies.

11. However, before the Commission takes a decision under Article 85 (3) on the abovementioned agreement, it invites all interested third parties to send their comments on this case within one month of the date of publication of this notice, quoting the reference "IV/33.151 – Jahrhundertvertrag", to:

Commission of the European Communities,
Directorate-General for Competition, Directorate C,
rue de la Loi 200, B-1049 Brussels.

NOTICE

Pursuant to Article 19 (3) of Council Regulation 17/62 (1) (IV/33.151 – "Jahrhundertvertrag")[1]

1. On 1 June 1989, the Gesamtverband des deutschen Steinkohlenbergbaus (General Association of the German Coalmining Industry – GVSt), whose registered office is in Essen, Federal Republic of Germany, notified to the Commission the "Supplementary agreement on the sale of German coal up to 1995", concluded on 23 April 1980 with the Vereinigung Deutscher Elektrizitäts-werke eV (Association of the German Public Electricity Supply Industry – VDEW), whose registered office is in Frankfurt, Federal Republic of Germany, as a follow-up to the "Agreement on the sale of German coal to the public electricity supply industry in the years 1978 to 1987" concluded on 10 May 1977.

2. The content of the notified agreement and the Commission's legal analysis have already been published in a previous Notice under Article 19 (3) of Council Regulation 17. The Commission now however intends to grant an exemption which extends the period mentioned in the previous Notice and which, taking account of the need to secure a basic electricity supply, requires that coal purchasing obligations shall be reduced by an adequate amount.

3. However, before the Commission takes a decision under Article 85 (3) on the abovementioned agreement, it invites all interested third parties to send their comments on this case within one month of the date of publication of this notice, quoting the reference "IV/33.151 – Jahrhundertvertrag", to:

Commission of the European Communities,
Directorate-General for Competition,
Directorate C,
rue de la Loi 200,
B-1049 Brussels.

---

[1] OJ 1991 C116/6.

NOTICE

Pursuant to Article 19 (3) of Council Regulation 17/62 concerning the reorganization of the electricity industry in England and Wales [1]

I

Since 31 March 1990 the electricity industry in England and Wales has a completely new structure. The Central Electricity Generating Board (CEGB) which until that date was responsible for the generation of electricity in bulk and the transmission of this electricity through the high voltage transmission system (super grid) to the 12 Area Electricity Boards has been split into four companies, two fossil-fuel generating companies, National Power plc (National Power) and Power Gen plc (Power Gen), one nuclear generating company, Nuclear Electric plc (Nuclear Electric) and the National Grid Company plc (NGC), which owns and operates the super grid. National Power and Power Gen will be privatised, Nuclear Electric will remain in public ownership. NGC is in the ownership of a holding company jointly owned by the 12 Regional Electricity Companies (RECs), which have replaced the former Area Electricity Boards and distribute electricity to customers in their assigned geographical areas. Each REC owns the relevant local low voltage electricity distribution network which is connected to the super grid.

The Electricity Act 1989 sets out the legislative framework under which the new electricity industry operates. Under this Act, any person generating, transmitting or supplying electricity in England and Wales needs a licence issued by the Secretary of State for Energy or the Director General of Electricity Supply, unless exempted by order under the Electricity Act. The licences contain provisions reflecting the transitional arrangements agreed by the industry with the Secretary of State to ensure an orderly and progressive transition to a

fully competitive market. In fact, for the first four years, only premises having a demand above 1 MW (roughly 30% of the market) will be free to choose their supplier. For the same period the two generators, National Power and Power Gen, are limited by the licence condition to supplying direct only a proportion of the demand in any one REC's area. After four years premises having a demand above 0.1 MW will also be free to choose their supplier (roughly 50% of the market). The two generators will continue to be limited in supplying in the area of any one REC, though to a lesser extent than previously. After eight years all these restrictions are expected to disappear and the RECs will no longer have a monopoly situation. Furthermore the licences oblige the licence holders to comply with certain codes or agreements which have been approved by the Secretary of State or the Director General of Electricity Supply. There are provisions contained in the licences that those who own the transmission or distribution systems, and generators owning electric lines, are obliged to offer use of their systems on a "common carriage" basis.

In the framework of this reorganization numerous contractual agreements, which are closely interrelated with each other and with legislation, licences and codes, have been entered into by the various parties of the electricity industry in England and Wales. The Commission was formally notified of the most important of these agreements in February 1990. They are the subject of this notice (A reorganization of the electricity industry in Scotland has also been carried out. The most important contractual agreements which have been entered into in this context were also formally notified to the Commission and are intended to be the subject of a separate publication.)

[1] OJ 1990 C191/9.

II

Case No IV/33.458 – British Coal

Coal supply arrangements for electricity generation in England and Wales.

National Power and Power Gen have concluded with the British Coal Corporation (British Coal) contracts on the purchase of minimum quantities of coal for use in electricity generation. The contracts are for a period of three years from 1 April 1990. They involve an aggregated supply of 70 million tonnes (at a specified average calorific value) for each of the first two years, decreasing to 65 million tonnes in the third year. (The average annual purchases of coal from British Coal by CEGB during the last three years were about 75 million tonnes). Of the 70 million tonnes fixed for the first and second year, National Power will be obliged to take 43,552 million tonnes and Power Gen 26,448 million tonnes. Of the 65 million tonnes fixed for the third year, National Power will be obliged to take 40,441 million tonnes and Power Gen 24,559 million tonnes.

The initial average price is broadly the average price which was recently paid by CEGB to British Coal. Under the terms of the contracts this price will decrease in real terms over the period of the contracts, but is still likely to be higher than the price for coal on the world market. There are provisions for price revision either upwards or downwards in the event of significant movements in the US $/£ exchange rate.

These contracts follow joint commercial negotiations between British Coal and the two electricity generating companies when they were still divisions of CEGB. The UK Government considers them as a necessary transition to full competition in fuel supply and in electricity generation and supply.

In the view of the UK Government during this transitional stage some degree of certainty as to raw material prices, which represent the largest element of electricity prices, is considered as crucial for ensuring the orderly transition into the new electricity market without undue disruption in prices and terms of electricity supply and for ensuring the successful privatization of the industry, which in the long-term is expected to benefit consumers. Furthermore, these arrangements which are degressive and limited in time will provide a transitional period of three years for British Coal to further restructure and rationalise its production capacity in an orderly manner.

The UK Government and British Coal have given assurances to the Commission that any coal supply arrangements between British Coal and National Power and Power Gen which will succeed the present notified contracts will be the subject of entirely separate negotiations between each of the generating companies and British Coal and will be on a fully commercial basis.

The Commission is currently investigating complaints made against these contracts. The Commission has not yet decided whether to adopt a favourable decision in respect of these contracts and the details have been published here to enable third parties to comment.

The Commission invites interested third parties to sent their comments within 30 days of the date of publication of this corrigendum to the following address;

Commission of the European Communities,
Directorate-General for Competition,
Directorate C,
200 rue de la Loi,
B-1049 Brussels.

Case No IV/33.471 – Pooling and Settlement Agreement

Under the new structure of the sector, all significant physical trades of electricity within England and Wales have to occur through a single pool for electricity. The pool is operated and administered by the National Grid Company. Under the terms of the Pooling and Settlement Agreement NGC is responsible for the scheduling and dispatch of power plants in merit order.

NGC also operates a system for financial settlement.

Every day generating companies bid their available generating capacity for the following day into the pool. For the power scheduled to be supplied they receive the "pool input price". This is composed of two factors, (a) the system marginal price which is derived every half hour from those bids, that is to say, the offer price of the highest priced station scheduled by NGC to be in operation during that time, and (b) a capacity related element. All persons buying out of the pool pay the "pool output price" which includes an additional element to the pool input price to cover the cost of reserve generation scheduled to be available to the system and the costs of services to provide system stability and to take account of transmission constraints and scheduling inefficiencies. In addition, generators and purchasers have to pay appropriate charges for use of the transmission and distributions systems, under the connection and use of system agreements referred to below.

NGC uses the offer prices as the basis of the merit order, scheduling and dispatching the lowest price plant first, so as to meet demand at least cost. A single pool purchase price is determined in each half hour of trading by the balance of energy supply and demand.

The transfer of money from the pool purchasers to the generators which follows the trading through the pool is also carried out by NGC in its capacity as administrator of the settlement system. NGC receives all meter readings and identifies those generators that supplied power and the quantities supplied by them and those persons who took power and the quantities taken by them. Purchasers are charged for the energy they have taken from the pool at the pool output price. Generators are reimbursed for the energy they have generated at the pool input price. Out of the difference between the pool output and pool input prices, the settlement system compensates generators also for the provision of reserve which has been scheduled by NGC and for the lost profit from not being able to generate or the costs of having to generate because of the effects of transmission constraints.

Membership of the pool is compulsory for all significant producers of electricity, for the 12 RECs and for all other persons (second-tier licensees) buying for onward supply to customers. The terms of all licences to such persons issued by the Secretary of State or the Director-General of Electricity Supply require the licence holders to be party to the Pooling and Settlement Agreement. Membership of the pool is open, based on objective criteria, to final consumers of a certain importance, so that for example large industrial consumers have the possibility of purchasing electricity from the pool instead of purchasing from an REC or direct from a generator.

Generators from other Member States wishing to export electricity to England and Wales are like the UK generators obliged to sell through the pool.

However, all members of the pool as well as other market participants are free to enter into contractual arrangements (option contracts or "contracts for differences" to reduce the impact of the volatility of the pool price. These contracts are essentially financial instruments and are not directly related to the physical delivery of electricity. They are explained in separate notifications below.

In the view of the UK Government the Pooling and Settlement Agreement lies at the core of the new industry structure. The market for electricity could not operate satisfactorily without this system. Special arrangements are in fact necessary because all power-stations are connected through the transmission and distribution systems to each other. It is therefore impossible to distinguish electricity generated by one station from that produced at another. The main characteristic of the pool is that it is based on merit order dispatch, which will finally benefit consumers.

Adherence to the Pooling and Settlement Agreement is imposed on all licence holders by the licences, in order to ensure the proper operation of the market. In the view of the Commission the Pooling and Settlement Agreement is not be considered as an agreement between undertakings aiming at preventing, restricting or distorting competition. The pool is not expected to distort or result in disclosure of contract prices agreed between generators and suppliers or generators and final consumers. As a measure of safeguard it will be closely monitored by the Director-General of Electricity Supply in order to ensure that there is no anti-competitive behaviour.

Trade between Member States does not appear to be negatively affected by the pool system, as membership is open to generators and purchasers from other Member States on the basis of essentially the same objective criteria applied to applicants from the United Kingdom. In fact EdF has already become a member of the pool.

At present there exists only a single interconnector between England and France. The Pooling and Settlement Agreement does not affect the use of this interconnector and does not preclude opportunities offered for trading across this interconnector.

The Commission intends, on the basis of the information presently available, to adopt a favourable position.

Case No IV/33.466 – Option contracts – National Power

and

Case No IV/33.467 – Option contracts – Power Gen

As described above, the pool price is a potentially volatile spot price. Generators on the one hand and suppliers (particularly RECs) as well as large end consumers on the other hand may wish for greater predictability of prices for the supply of electricity. This can be achieved by entry into option contracts (or "contracts for differences"). The option

contract is a bilateral contract in a form able to be entered into by a generator and supplier or a generator and any other third party. However, option contracts or variations therein, can be negotiated and entered into between any persons interested. In its basic form the option contract permits one or other party to call for a payment representing the difference between the price specified in the bilateral contract and the actual pool price in respect of a given number of kWh. Thus the option contract, which is a purely financial instrument and does not entitle the option holder to the physical delivery of electricity, permits hedging against the fluctuations of the pool price. The option contracts are intended to reproduce the economic effect of longer term electricity supply contracts at predetermined prices.

The initial range of option contracts entered into by the two fossil generators, National Power and Power Gen, with Nuclear electric and with the 12 RECs, were jointly negotiated before the restructuring of the industry on 30 March 1990 as a part of the initial transitional arrangements. They are designed to enable the parties to have a degree of certainty about costs and revenue streams during the initial period of three years and to take account of undertakings sought by the UK Government to ensure on the one hand that there is no undue disruption in prices to end consumers during this initial period and to ensure on the other hand that the RECs will purchase the necessary volume of electricity in order to guarantee the sale of electricity which is expected to be produced by National Power and Power Gen over the next three years by burning coal contracted with British Coal.

However, none of these option contracts has a duration of longer than three years and a number (including nuclear option contracts which are subject of a separate nofication below) will expire within one to two years.

The RECs are only able to recover the costs resulting from entering into these initial option contracts because they continue for eight years to benefit from transitional arrangements assuring them a considerable part of their present market.

The initial option contracts are expected to enable the RECs to limit to around the level of general inflation their price increases to franchise customers during the initial three year period (in line with licence requirements) and to non-franchise customers, that is to say, those over 1 MW, for the period of one year, as requested by the UK Government.

In the view of the UK Government, the initial option contracts, which are the product of joint negotiations within the electricity industry, are indispensable for the demerger of the sector and an orderly transition to a fully competitive market. These transitional trading arrangements were prepared on the basis of detailed guidelines established by the UK Government, notably concerning prices and duration.

The Commission intends, on the basis of the information presently available, to adopt a favourable position.

Case No IV/33.474 – Nuclear contract and associated option contracts

This notification concerns the contractual arrangements between Nuclear Electric and the Regional Electricity Companies.

The UK Government has imposed on the RECs an obligation (non-fossil fuel obligation – NFFO) to contract for specified amounts of non-fossil generation (including both nuclear and renewables generation). Thus the RECs are required to contract for an average 8 GW of non-fossil fuel capacity from nuclear sources over the eight-year period 1990 to 1998. The principal party with whom the RECs have contracted is Nuclear Electric. A fossil-fuel levy has been introduced in order to compensate the RECs for the additional costs of non-fossil electricity purchased in compliance with the NFFO as compared to alternative purchases of fossil electricity. In order to obtain the benefit of the levy the non-fossil electricity must be contracted under "qualifying arrangements"; these are defined as arrangements for the joint purchase of non-fossil electricity under the NFFO. The 12 RECs will therefore purchase collectively through their jointly owned non-fossil purchasing agency (NFPA), which is the subject of a separate notification below.

Nuclear generated electricity accounts at present for 17.3% of total electricity generation in England and Wales. The essential feature of the Nuclear Contract is that a specified capacity must be made available by Nuclear Electric to each REC over specified periods of the eight-year term of the contract.

Under the terms of the principal contract, NFPA buys on behalf of the 12 RECs the total output of Nuclear Electric which is delivered through the pool in accordance with the Pooling and Settlement Agreement. Nuclear Electric will thereby recover for all its nuclear generation the pool price. However, for the number of kilowatt hours supplied in order to fulfil the non-fossil fuel obligation a pre-determined supplementary payment will be added to the pool price (adjusted premium) to cover additional costs associated with nuclear generation compared to fossil generation (The State aid element inherent in these contracts was approved by the Commission on 28 March 1990). Nuclear Electric will not receive this premium price for any electricity delivered above the level necessary to fulfil the NFFO.

In addition to the principal contract, Nuclear Electric may enter into option contracts with RECs and other third parties to hedge against the risks of selling and purchasing electricity at a potentially volatile pool price. An initial range of option contracts for a term not exceeding two years has been jointly negotiated and entered into by Nuclear Electric with the 12 RECs, as part of the initial transitional arrangements. After this transitional period the option contracts will be negotiated and concluded individually with each REC.

323

In the view of the UK Government, the non-fossil fuel obligation and the contracts concluded between Nuclear Electric and the RECs acting through their agent, the non-fossil purchasing agency, in order to comply with this obligation are necessary to ensure security of supply that results from diversity of fuel sources for electricity generation. Under this aspect they will also benefit consumers. Furthermore these arrangements are limited in time, eight years, and will be degressive over this period in terms of percentage of total electricity output.

The Commission intends to adopt a favourable position for the envisaged period of eight years.

Case No IV/33.472 – Non-fossil purchasing agency arrangements

The NFPA arrangements have been designed in order to satisfy the statutory obligation imposed on the RECs under the Electricity Act to make available to them sufficient quantities of non-fossil generated electricity. The Electricity Act also provides that these arrangements must be made jointly to be able to qualify for the benefit of the levy. For administrative convenience all the 12 RECs have constituted a jointly owned company, NFPA Ltd.

The principal object of NFPA is to act as agent for the RECs in purchasing non-fossil electricity contracted in fulfilment of the non-fossil fuel obligation and thus qualifying for the purposes of the fossil fuel levy. The NFPA has no power to enter into contracts for the purchase of electricity which is not in fulfilment of the NFFO. There is no provision in the Articles of Association to prevent the RECs from purchasing electricity which is not a qualifying arrangement for the purposes of the NFFO, individually and without passing through the NFPA.

The Commission intends, on the basis of the information presently available, to adopt a favourable position.

Case No IV/33.470 – Renewable contracts

As described above, the non-fossil fuel obligation also covers renewables generation (hydro, tidal, wind, solar, etc). There will be increases in the quantities of renewables generation as required under the NFFO over the period of eight years. The initial obligation will be rather small; new schemes are under consideration and it is expected that the obligation will be set at approximately 800 MW by the year 1998, which would then represent less than 1% of total electricity generation in England and Wales.

The obligation will be imposed on the 12 RECs on an equitable basis. NFPA will act as an agent for the RECs to enter into contracts for the supply of renewables generated electricity in fulfilment of the NFFO. The renewables generators with whom the RECs through the NFPA will contract will be chosen from among the number of actual and potential renewables generators whose proposals are presently being evaluated.

Since declared capacity from renewable generating plants is usually low, a number of contracts will need to be entered into to satisfy the obligation and thereby obtain the benefit of the levy. Any purchases of electricity from renewables sources which are not made pursuant to qualifying arrangements for the purposes of the non-fossil fuel obligation will not be purchased through NFPA and not benefit from the levy.

The structure of the proposed contracts provides for the purchase of the entire output of the generating units which have been retained at a negotiated price which, during the period to 1998 and in respect of up to a specified number of kilowatt hours per year, include a premium payment over the pool price (The State aid element inherent in these contracts was approved by the Commission on 28 March 1990). However, in view of the fact that most renewable generating plants are too small to be subject to central dispatch through the pool, the electricity generated from these plants will be delivered direct to the local REC in the area where the renewable generating plant is located.

The Commission intends, on the basis of the information presently available, to adopt a favourable position.

Case IV/33.468 – National Grid Company: Grid code and Connection and use of system agreements

Under the terms of the transmission licence, NGC is required to draw up and implement a Grid code. This Grid code essentially covers all general technical conditions regarding connection to the high voltage transmission system (super grid) which is owned by NGC. The Grid code is also designed to permit the development, maintenance and efficient operation of the super grid and to ensure security and efficiency of the electricity system in England and Wales as a whole.

The NGC transmission system conveys electricity from generating stations to the supply points at which it is transformed down for delivery to the lower voltage distribution systems, or in certain cases, delivered direct to large industrial consumers. NGC also operates the interconnectors with Scotland and France.

The Grid code specifies the technical standards and procedures which NGC and users of the super grid, namely each REC, the electricity generating companies and other suppliers of electricity are required to comply with as a condition of their respective licences.

NGC's duty is to facilitate competition in electricity generation and supply. NGC is obliged by the licence to offer use of the super grid on a "common carriage" basis. The licence further provides that all charges made by NGC for the connection to and the use of the transmission system must be transparent and on a non-discriminatory basis.

The terms of the Grid code have been approved by the Director General of Electricity Supply and it may be altered only with his consent.

The Grid code is not in itself an agreement, but compliance with it is required by the Connection and use of system agreements.

The Connection and use of system agreements have the object of establishing a contractual framework between NGC and all users of the super grid (generators, RECs, other suppliers and directly connected customers). All parties agree with each other party to be bound by and to comply in all relevant respects with the provisions of the Grid code and with the provisions of the Distribution code of the relevant REC. A principal purpose of these agreements is to provide for contractual enforceability of the Grid code as between industry parties, in recognition of the important consequences for the whole system resulting from non-observance of the rules by any industry participant.

The agreements entered into in this contractual framework with any generator may require that certain ancillary services as specified in the Grid code be provided by the generator to NGC. Under the transmission licence NGC is obliged to purchase such ancillary services which are necessary to maintain system stability and frequency control on the transmission system from the most economic source available. Suppliers will pay for these ancillary services through an uplift to the pool input price.

The Connection and use of system agreements are designed to facilitate the continuous supply and diversity of supply of electricity within the NGC transmission system and together with the Grid code to cover technical and safety aspects necessary to facilitate competition in England and Wales in the generation and supply of electricity. This is expected to be achieved in particular by allowing independent generators and electricity supply companies or RECs access to the NGC transmission system on a non-discriminatory basis.

The Commission intends, on the basis of the information presently available, to adopt a favourable position.

Case No IV/33.469 – Distribution code and Distributors' use of system and connection agreements.

The 12 RECs are each obliged by licence to prepare, implement and comply with a Distribution code relating to the lower voltage networks.

The model Distribution code is a document setting out the technical standards and requirements with which compliance is necessary to permit the proper functioning of the relevant REC's system for the distribution of electricity. It covers all technical aspects relating to connection to and the operation and use of these distribution systems, and so far as is necessary for this purpose, the operation of electrical lines and electrical plant connected to an REC's distribution system.

The model Distribution code is very similar to the NGC Grid code described above. Each REC is however free when establishing its own Distribution code to adopt modifications to the model code in order to take into account the characteristics of its own local distribution network.

The Distribution code of each REC must be approved by the Director General of Electricity Supply, who may also require changes to be made.

Similar to the NGC Grid code, it is a condition of all licences that the licence holder has to comply so far as applicable with the Distribution codes of each REC.

Under the terms of the licence, each REC is obliged to offer third parties connection to and use of its distribution system on a transparent and non-discriminatory basis. Model forms of connection and use of system agreements have been prepared, which constitute in effect standard terms and conditions which may be used by RECs in contracting with third parties, and which cover various different situations. The appropriate form of agreement will depend in the concrete case on the nature of the other contracting party; for example, if this is a generator, a contract customer of the REC or another supplier of electricity taking advantage of its right as third party to obtain use of the REC's distribution system for the transport of electricity to its customers.

The Distributors' use of system and connection agreements are designed to facilitate competition in England and Wales in the generation and supply of electricity. This is why the RECs are required to make provisions for the connection to and use of their distribution systems by third parties.

The Commission intends, on the basis of the information presently available, to adopt a favourable position.

Case No IV/33.620 – Arrangements with Electricité de France – Contracts for the use of the interconnector with France

The Continental Europe Interconnector (interconnector) is a link between the French grid operated by Electricité de France (EdF), and the super grid transmission system of England and Wales. This interconnector is the only existing link between the United Kingdom and the European continent. It has a capacity of 2 GW, representing about 4% of England and Wales' generating capacity. It can provide supplies of electricity in one direction or the other.

The assets of this interconnector which were formerly owned by EdF and CEGB are now owned by EdF and NGC.

In principle the interconnector is available for two-way trading and for mutual support in times of system stress. However over the last three years the net flow of trade has been from France to England and Wales.

NGC has entered into a three-year agreement with EdF for use of a substantial part of the interconnector capacity, which will enable imports of electricity from France to England and Wales to continue, as well as enabling EdF to import from the United Kingdom where it wishes to do so, thereby maximizing the benefits of the interconnector in permitting mutual system support in the two countries.

As already mentioned in this notice, EdF is a member of the England and Wales pool and all the electricity supplied by it to England and Wales will be sold through the pool. At the same time, EdF has entered into a series of three-year option contracts with RECs. The electricity supplied by EdF is not subject to the fossil fuel levy in England and Wales.

The Commission intends, on the basis of the information presently available, to adopt a favourable position.

III

Before adopting a favourable attitude to the above described applications the Commission invites interested third parties to send their comments within 30 days from the date of publication of this notice to the following address; quoting the reference of the relevant case:

Commission of the European Communities,
Directorate-General for Competition (DG IV), Directorate C,
200 rue de la Loi,
B-1049 Brussels.

NOTICE

Pursuant to Article 19 (3) of Council Regulation 17/62 concerning the reorganization of the electricity industry in Scotland[1]

I

Until 31 March 1990 Scotland's electricity requirements were met by two publicly owned corporations, North of Scotland Hydro-Electric Board and South of Scotland Electricity Board, which generated, transmitted and distributed electricity in their assigned geographical areas, covering the north and south of Scotland respectively. The whole generating and transmission system in Scotland was planned and operated on a joint basis by these two publicly owned utilities so that electricity was always generated from the cheapest station first, in order to meet demand at the least cost. All costs of the system were pooled and met in proportion to the number of units of electricity sold. Total Scottish electricity demand was met by the two utilities roughly in the proportion of 1:3, North:South.

In reorganising the industry in advance of privatization, the United Kingdom Government decided to maintain vertical integration in the Scottish electricity industry, since it is better suited for the supply of electricity to sparsely populated areas which are characteristic of many areas of Scotland. The relatively small total size of the Scottish electricity market – demand being approximately one-tenth of that in Great Britain as a whole – and the fact that domestic and other small users account for a high proportion in the customer mix, were further reasons for the United Kingdom Government to conclude that a disaggregated structure like that which has been introduced since 31 March 1990 in England and Wales was not suitable for Scotland.

The United Kingdom Government has therefore decided to create two separate, independent and competing vertically integrated electricity utility companies from the two Boards. Scottish Power plc ("Scottish Power") has taken over the non-nuclear business of the South of Scotland Electricity Board and Scottish Hydro-Electric plc ("Hydro-Electric") the business of the North of Scotland Hydro-Electric Board. Both companies will be privatised. The Scottish nuclear stations at Hunterston and Torness which previously were owned by the South of Scotland Electricity Board are now owned and operated by a separately established generating company, Scottish Nuclear Ltd ("Scottish Nuclear") which will remain in public ownership. Scottish Nuclear does not supply direct to customers, selling all its output under contract to Scottish Power and Hydro-Electric.

The Electricity Act 1989 and subordinate legislation made thereunder set out the framework for the new regulatory system for the electricity industry in Scotland. Under this Act any undertaking generating, transmitting or supplying electricity in Scotland needs a licence issued by the Secretary of State for Scotland or the Director-General of Electricity Supply, unless exempted by order under the Act. Scottish Power and Hydro-Electric are each by licence obliged to and have the right to transmit and supply electricity to customers within their authorised areas. These areas are essentially the same as those of the former Boards. Both utilities are entitled to generate electricity themselves. There is no restriction on the proportion of its electricity requirements which either utility can meet from its own generation resources.

The right of the two companies to supply customers within their authorised areas is however not exclusive; premises having a demand above 1 MW are free to choose their supplier, after four years this

[1] OJ 1990 L245/8.

329

threshold will be reduced to 0.1 MW and after eight years totally phased out.

It is possible for Scottish Power and Hydro-Electric, on receipt for the appropriate "second-tier licences" to supply to those customers in each other's authorised area or indeed in England and Wales who are free to choose their supplier (as described above). The opportunity to apply for such "second-tier licences" is available to any person in the United Kingdom or the rest of the Community wishing to supply electricity to customers in Scotland. It should be noted that Scottish Nuclear has been granted a generation licence only.

The licences place obligations on Scottish Power and Hydro-Electric not to discriminate between comparable customers, to avoid cross-subsidies and to allow all other users access to their transmission and distribution systems on a transparent and non-discriminatory basis.

Furthermore the licences oblige the licence holders to comply with certain codes and agreements which have been approved by the Director-General of Electricity Supply, including codes governing the operation of the transmission and distribution systems and the trading of electricity.

In the view of the United Kingdom Government it is essential for Scottish Power and Hydro-Electric to have access to a balanced mix of different types of generating capacity in order to be financially viable and capable of independent operation. Therefore the non-nuclear generating assets of the two former Boards, which had been built to meet Scotland's requirements in their entirety, had to be redistributed between the new companies. This could not be achieved by simply allocating the different power stations to one or the other utility, since the nature and location of the generating assets rendered this impractical. The United Kingdom Government therefore decided that the necessary restructuring should be achieved by means of contractual arrangements which create

rights and obligations between the two utilities in relation to certain of the generating assets and transmission systems of each, effectively replacing ownership of these assets with long-term contractual entitlements the duration of which corresponds to the currently expected lifetime of the power stations concerned. These contractual arrangements replace the former loose non-commercial agreements between the two Boards on cost-sharing and operational matters. The principal contracts between Scottish Power and Hydro-Electric concern the sharing of coal-fired plant capacity, hydro capacity and gas/oil fired capacity. Furthermore, Scottish Power and Hydro-Electric divide between them the total output of Scottish Nuclear.

The new structure of the electricity industry in Scotland is designed to progressively introduce competition both at the level of electricity generation and at the level of electricity supply. At present the electricity sector in Scotland is characterised by substantial over-capacity in electricity generation, which on present estimates is likely to continue at least for the next ten years and by a high concentration of nuclear generation capable of meeting over 50% of current Scottish electricity demand. Trading with England and Wales is possible through the interconnector which links the transmission grids in Scotland and England.

The geographical location of Scotland on the fringe of the Community and the resultant physical constraints of the system does not make electricity exchanges with other Member States very likely. Unavoidable power losses may make it uneconomic to transmit electricity over such long distances. Accordingly there is not much prospect of Scottish generated electricity displacing electricity supplies from other Member States, in particular electricity supplied from the Continent to the South of England, nor of Scottish generated electricity being supplied to other Member States.

Within the framework of the reoganization of the electricity industry in Scotland described above, the various parties in the industry in Scotland and in England and Wales have entered into numerous contractual agreements, which are closely interrelated with each other and with the legislation, licences and codes governing the supply of electricity in the United Kingdom. The Commission has been formally notified of the most important of these agreements for the electricity industry in Scotland. They are the subject of this notice.

II

Case No IV/33.479 – Agreement on coal-fired generating capacity

Scottish Power owns two large coal-fired power stations at Cockenzie and Longannet which together account for an output capacity of 3,456 MW. The agreement entitles Hydro-Electric which does not own any coal-fired station to a 576 MW share (approximately one-sixth) of the present capacity. Hydro-Electric thus has the right to require the supply of electricity output from that share of capacity, or if the declared available overall capacity on certain days is less, the equivalent proportion.

Hydro-Electric has the option of purchasing its own coal for use in the two power stations or to purchase with Scottish Power. At present a procedure is set down for the purchase of coal by Scottish Power to meet both parties' annual requirements until 1 April 1995. After that date these purchasing arrangements will no longer apply and Hydro-Electric will purchase its own coal for delivery to the stations.

Hydro-Electric is also entitled to participate in any conversion of the two power stations to a fuel other than coal and to share in the resulting capacity.

The agreement will subsist until 31 March 2004. This is the expected remaining lifetime of the two power stations. However, the duration of the agreement may be extended by mutual consent of the parties.

The Commission intends, on the basis of the information presently available, to adopt a favourable position.

Case No IV/33.476 – Hydro Capacity Agreement

This agreement entitles Scottish Power to a 200 MW share of Hydro-Electric's hydro generating capacity of approximately 1,050 MW. In those periods of the year when rainfall is expected to be low and during periods with unusually low rainfall, Scottish Power's entitlement will be reduced.

The agreement will subsist until 31 March 2039. Its duration can be extended by mutual consent of the parties after the first 15 years.

The Commission intends, on the basis of the information presently available, to adopt a favourable position.

Case No IV/33.475 – Peterhead Agreement

The dual-fired Peterhead Power Station has the possibility of burning heavy fuel oil or natural gas or natural gas liquids or a mixture of these fuels. It has an output capacity of 1,284 MW which will be increased in the future by up to 230 MW with the installation of two gas turbines, destined to burn gas from the North Sea Miller Field which is expected to be onstream in 1992.

Hydro-Electric has a long-term contract for the supply of gas from the Miller Field to the Peterhead Station. The contract between Scottish Power and Hydro-Electric allows Scottish Power to participate in the low cost electricity which will be generated with this gas supply, but also obliges Scottish Power to participate in the risks of Hydro-Electric's long-term "take or pay" commitment.

Therefore the Peterhead Agreement which normally entitles Scottish Power to a 50% share of the oil/gas generating capacity of the Peterhead power station obliges Scottish Power to take 70 % of the electricity generated when natural gas from the Miller Field is flowing at peak levels (approximately 1992 to 1997). Thereafter the 50 % share of Scottish Power will again apply.

Hydro-Electric has also existing contracts for the supply of heavy fuel oil to be burnt at the Peterhead power station. At present, Scottish Power has the right to purchase its own supplies, but Hydro-Electric may purchase heavy fuel oil to meet both parties' annual requirements, an arrangement analogous to the coal purchase previously described, which may last until 1 April 1995. After the date these purchasing arrangements will no longer apply and Scottish Power will purchase its own heavy fuel oil for delivery to the station.

The agreement will subsist until 31 March 2012. This is the expected remaining lifetime of this power station. However the duration of the agreement may be extended by mutual consent of the parties.

The Commission intends, on the basis of the information presently available, to adopt a favourable position.

Case No IV/33.473 – Nuclear Energy Agreement

Under the terms of the Nuclear Energy Agreement Scottish Power and Hydro-Electric are obliged to purchase all the electricity generated by Scottish Nuclear from its Hunsterston and Torness plant on a take or pay basis. Scottish Nuclear is obliged to try to produce maximum output from these two nuclear power stations which have together a capacity of 2,400 MW. Scottish Power will have to take 74.9% of Scottish Nuclear's output and Hydro-Electric 25.1%. Scottish Nuclear is not permitted to supply electricity to any other party without the consent of both Scottish Power and Hydro-Electric.

There is no present intention for there to be a non-fossil fuel obligation in Scotland nor a corresponding fossil fuel levy.

The agreement also contains provisions for the calculation of the prices to be paid to Scottish Nuclear by Scottish

Power and Hydro-Electric. From 1991 to 1994 the price is fixed on the basis of a two-tier structure: a base price per kilowatt hour for the first tranche of 5,000 GWh and a lower base price for all subsequent kilowatt hours. From 1995 to 1998 the price will be based on a combination of the pricing formula used previously and a formula based on the "market price" in England and Wales. After 1998 the price will be based on the wholesale market price in England and Wales.

The Nuclear Energy Agreement will remain in force until 31 March 2005 although it may be terminated earlier if, for example, Scottish Nuclear consistently fails to meet production requirements.

The Commission intends to adopt a favourable position for the envisaged period of 15 years.

Case No IV/33.632 – The Dounreay Agreement

Under the terms of the Dounreay Agreement Scottish Power and Hydro-Electric have to share the available output of the Dounreay nuclear power station which is operated by the United Kingdom Atomic Energy Authority.

By virtue of an agreement entered into by its predecessor, North of Scotland Hydro-Electric Board, Hydro-Electric is obliged to purchase all of Dounreay's available output. The maximum capacity of the station is approximately 240 MW. The notified agreement provides for Scottish Power to take 74.9% of this output and Hydro-Electric 25.1%. The price payable by Scottish Power to Hydro-Electric will be 74.9% of the charge payable by Hydro-Electric to the United Kingdom Atomic Energy Authority.

The agreement will expire on 1 April 1994 or earlier if the Dounreay station ceases to operate beforehand.

The Commission intends to adopt a favourable position for the envisaged period of five years.

Case No IV/33.611 – NGC – Scottish Interconnector Agreement and British Grid Systems Agreement

The Scottish Interconnector is a link between the high voltage electricity grid of the South of Scotland operated by Scottish Power and the high voltage super grid of England and Wales operated by the National Grid Company ("NGC"). The interconnector, which has a nominal capacity of approximately 850 MW, is the only link between Scotland and England and is available for two-way trading and for mutual support in times of system stress. However, the net flow of trade in the foreseeable future is expected to be from Scotland to England and Wales.

NGC has entered into an agreement with Hydro-Electric (which operates the high voltage electricity grid of the North of Scotland) and Scottish Power, allowing them the use of the entirety of the interconnector capacity, with the obligation that they will respectively make available any part of the inter-connector capacity which they do not themselves require, to any user of the NGC grid or of the Scottish Power or the Hydro-Electric grids respectively. The agreement will continue indefinitely but is terminable on five years notice served by any party on the others, or by the Director-General of Electricity Supply by giving five years notice to the parties.

Access by each user to the inter-connector will be facilitated by means of a sub-contract agreement between Hydro-Electric or Scottish Power as the case may be and the user, and a separate user agreement between NGC and each such user. The Director-General of Electricity Supply must approve the conditions of access by the user to the interconnector under the sub-contract agreements and the terms of the user agreements are to be settled by him in default of agreement between the parties.

NGC, Scottish Power and Hydro-Electric have also entered into the *British Grid Systems Agreement* ("BGSA"), an agreement governing the interconnection of the super grid of England and Wales with the South of Scotland grid and also the interconnection of the North of Scotland grid with the South of Scotland grid. It incorporates a series of codes, similar in concept to the grid codes required by each party's transmission or combined electricity licence respectively. These codes form the basis of liaison on a technical level between the parties for the purpose of ensuring the operation of the interconnector circuits between the three grids. The parties to the BGSA have also entered into ancillary services agreements for the purchase by NGC from Scottish Power or Hydro-Electric and by Scottish Power or Hydro-Electric from NGC of ancillary services, for purposes of system stability, pursuant to the BGSA and, where appropriate, the NGC grid code.

The Commission intends, on the basis of the information presently available, to adopt a favourable position.

Case No IV/33.477 – Scottish Power – Hydro-Electric – Scottish Interconnector Agreement

The purpose of this agreement is to enable Hydro-Electric to have access to a proportion of the daily capacity of the Scottish end of the interconnector owned by Scottish Power and linking the high voltage electricity grid of Scottish Power with that of NGC as described above. The agreement provides Hydro-Electric with a 46 % share of the existing nominal capacity of 850 MW; thereby granting Hydro-Electric an "export/import" corridor across Scottish Power's high voltage grid to the English and Welsh markets. Hydro-Electric will be entitled to participate in any future increase of the capacity of the interconnector. Under their licences Scottish Power and Hydro-Electric are obliged to give third parties access to their respective shares of the interconnector.

This agreement will continue indefinitely until terminated by mutual consent of both parties or the loss of either party's transmission licence.

333

The Commission intends, on the basis of the information presently available, to adopt a favourable position.

Case No IV/33.478 – System Operation Agreement

Hydro-Electric and Scottish Power each own and operate systems for the generation, transmission, distribution and supply for electricity in Scotland. These systems are interconnected and have in the past been co-ordinated by North of Scotland Hydro-Electric Board and South of Scotland Electricity Board and operated as an interconnected system in the interests of safety, efficiency and economic running of the systems.

The notified agreement co-ordinates the operation of the transmission systems of Scottish Power and Hydro-Electric and in many ways replicates the principles and procedures set down in the British Grid Systems Agreement ("BGSA") referred to above. The System Operation Agreement seeks to ensure that the transmission systems of Scottish Power

and Hydro-Electric operate in a secure, safe and efficient manner and assists in the implementation of the generation agreements referred to above.

This agreement will continue indefinitely until terminated by mutual consent of both parties or the loss of either party's transmission licence.

The Commission intends, on the basis of the information presently available, to adopt a favourable position.

III

Before adopting a favourable attitude to the above described applications the Commission invites interested third parties to send their comments within 30 days from the date of publication of this Notice to the following address, quoting the reference of the relevant case:

Commission of the European Communities,
Directorate-General for Competition (DG IV), Directorate C,
200 rue de la Loi,
B-1049 Brussels.

(a) National Association of Licensed Opencast Operators, 3 The Bigg Market, UK – Newcastle upon Tyne NE1 1UN

(b) Federation of Small Mines of Great Britain, 13a King Street, UK – Newcastle upon Lyme ST5 1ER

(c) South Wales Small Mines Association, Ffynonau-Duon Farm, Pentwyn, Fochriw, Near Bargoed, UK – Mid Glamorgan CF8 9NR

Dear Sirs,

Subject: Complaints concerning the Supply of Electricity Generating Coal

This letter which sets out a Commission decision deals with certain aspects of the complaints made by the National Association of Licensed Opencast Operators, the Federation of Small Mines of Great Britain and the South Wales Small Mines Association. It deals with the position in England and Wales, in the light of the new situation arising from the entry into operation of the coal supply contracts between British Coal Corporation, National Power and Power Gen on 1 April 1990. Other issues particularly those regarding the situation in Scotland, the situation before 1 April 1990, the market for industrial coal and matters relating to British Coal Corporation's licensing powers are not dealt with.

The complaints were made under Articles 60, 63, 65 and 66 of the Treaty establishing the European Coal and Steel Community and under Articles 85 and 86 of the Treaty establishing the European Economic Community.

A. The Facts

I. *Introduction*

1. Complaints have been made by the National Association of Licensed Opencast Operators (NALOO) and the Federation of Small Mines of Great Britain (FSMGB), on 28 March 1990, and

by the South Wales Small Mines Association (SWSMA), on 5 June 1990, concerning the supply of coal to the electricity generating industry in the United Kingdom.

2. On 1 April 1990 new contracts for the supply of steam coal to power stations in England and Wales (hereafter referred to as "the coal supply contracts" came into operation between the British Coal Corporation (BCC) and National Power (NP) and Power Gen (PG). These contracts provide, *inter alia,* for BCC to sell and NP and PG to buy, 70 million tonnes of coal in each of the first two years and 65 million tonnes in the third year. The contracts expire on 31 March 1993.

3. The members of the complaint associations are engaged in the production of coal under licence from BCC. A substantial part of their output has always been sold to the electricity generating companies.

II. *The parties*

4. NALOO is a trade association of 34 companies engaged in the production of coal in the United Kingdom, primarily from opencast mines. Some of these companies also have underground mining operations.

5. FSMGB is a trade association representing nine regional associations of companies engaged in underground mining. There are about 160 member companies in total. One of the constituent associations, SWSMA, has

made a separate complaint. SWSMA has about 93 member companies.

6. British Coal Corporation (BCC) is a state-owned corporation which, with minor exceptions, is the beneficial owner of all the United Kingdom coal reserves. It is the successor to the National Coal Board which was set up to manage and exploit British coal when the coal industry was nationalised in 1946. BCC is by far the largest coal producer in the UK and is also the largest in the Community.

7. BCC has the power to licence private production of coal and it is authorised by UK legislation to charge royalties on this production.

8. NP and PG are public limited companies all of whose shares were held by the United Kingdom authorities until they were partially (60%) privatised in March 1991. Between them they operate all the coal and oil-fired electricity generating stations in England and Wales.

III. *Coal supply in the United Kingdom*

9. Total coal production in the United Kingdom was about 96 million tonnes in 1989/90.

10. BCC produced approximately 93 million tonnes of coal in 1989/90. Of this approximately 17 million tonnes were extracted from opencast sites by contractors (including some of the members of the complainant associations) on BCC's behalf, 1.4 million tonnes were reclaimed from spoil heaps and the remainder was deep-mined.

11. In addition BCC bought in about 1 million tonnes from licensed mines, some 734,000 tonnes on "delivered" opencast licences, and the rest by spot purchases almost exclusively from licensed underground mines.

12. BCC has in the past granted two types of licences: a "royalty licence" under which the licensee pays a royalty to BCC on each tonne extracted and is responsible for the eventual sales of the coal, and a "delivered licence" under which the licensee in return for an agreed price delivers the coal to BCC and pays

no royalty. Most royalty licences are for a standard royalty. BCC will in some circumstances, where the licensee would suffer severe financial hardship, impose lower rates. BCC has announced its intention to phase out delivered licences.

13. In 1989/90 the licensed mines paid royalties of £13 million on some 2.1 million tonnes of coal. Total production of licensed coal, including the coal produced under delivered licences, was approximately 3 million tonnes.

14. In addition there is non-vested coal production, which comes from two sources. First, there are small coal reserves which for various reasons were not vested in the National Coal Board when the industry was nationalised in 1946. Second, coal is also obtained by the reworking of spoil heaps. There are no reliable statistics on the production of such non-vested coal. It is estimated that non-vested coal production as a whole amounted to 1-3 million tonnes in 1989/90.

15. The private sector of the coal industry is made up of a large number (around 200) of small and medium sized companies. The size of individual private mines is restricted by statute. Until the passage of the Coal Industry Act 1990 the limits were a maximum of 30 employees for an underground mine and reserves of 25,000 tonnes for an opencast mine. (The average number of employees at a BCC deep mine is currently about 900 and the average size of BCC's opencast sites is about 2 million tonnes). The 1990 Act increased the limits for licensed mines to 150 employees and 250,000 tonnes. The larger private mining companies operate more than one mine.

16. In 1989/90 licensed production totalled 2.827 million tonnes made up of 1,026,100 tonnes of deep-mined coal, 1,066,700 of opencast coal on royalty licences and 733,700 tonnes of opencast coal on delivered licences.

17. BCC mined, itself or through contractors, 93 million tonnes out of the 96 million tonnes mined in the United Kingdom in 1989/90, it was therefore

responsible for some 97% of the total output.

18. In recent years total imports of coal into the United Kingdom have been around 12 million tonnes a year, of which approximately 8 million tonnes have been coking coal for the steel industry. The bulk of the remainder has been sold on the domestic and industrial markets. Imports have not been an important source of coal for UK power stations. However, both NP and PG have said that they intend to increase their imports significantly.

19. The overall supply situation for 1989/90 in the United Kingdom can be summarised, in millions of tonnes, as follows:

British Coal	90
Licensed mines	3
Imports	12
Non-vested coal (estimates)	1-3
Total Supply	106-108

Exports from the UK were 3 million tonnes, almost exclusively from BCC.

IV. *Demand for coal in the United Kingdom*

20. In the United Kingdom BCC in 1989/90 sold 90 million tonnes of coal (including approximately 1 million tonnes of coal supplied by the licensed mines under delivered licences and coal bought in from the licensed mines at market rates), some 84% of total UK demand.

21. In the same year BCC supplied 75.8 million tonnes of steam generating coal to power stations, 94% of their require-ments. This can be broken down as follows: England and Wales 72.5 million tonnes, Scotland 2.4 million tonnes and Northern Ireland 0.9 million tonnes.

22. The electricity generating companies in England and Wales bought approxi-mately 2.7 million tonnes of coal from suppliers other than BCC in 1989/90. This figure includes licensed coal, imported coal used in blends and non-vested coal.

V. *The electricity generating industry's energy requirements*

23. Electricity generation in the UK consumes the equivalent of about 123 million tonnes of coal a year. Three sources of very low marginal cost production, hydro generation, nuclear generation and electricity imports from France account for 29.4 million tonnes of coal equivalent, leaving 93.3 million tonnes of coal equivalent for oil and coal. In 1989/90 BCC supplied 81% of this requirement.

24. Coal can be replaced as a fuel for power stations by oil to the extent that there is oil-fired capacity that is not fully utilised at present. However, the price of heavy fuel oil is extremely volatile.

25. Existing port facilities could perhaps handle an additional 10-15 million tonnes of imports of steam coal (*i.e.* coal suitable for use in electricity generating stations or for industrial steam raising) a year. Higher levels of imports would require substantial investment in ports and infrastructure and could not be achieved within the time period of the coal supply contracts.

26. Any significant increase in purchases of steam coal on the international market would be likely to increase the price as the world trade in steam coal is only about 200 million tonnes a year.

27. In the short to medium term BCC will remain the most important supplier of fuel to the generating companies in England and Wales. Part of the fuel requirements of the electricity supply industry in England and Wales cannot be met from sources other than BCC.

VI. *Changes in the electricity supply industry*

28. Until 1 April 1990, coal-fired and oil-fired power stations in Great Britain were operated by the Central Electricity Generating Board in England and Wales and the South of Scotland Electricity Board in Scotland, both of which were state-owned. In preparation for the privatisation of the electricity industry the generation of electricity in conventional

thermal power stations was vested in National Power (NP) and Power Gen (PG) in England and Wales, and Scottish Power (SP) in Scotland.

29. Nuclear generation will be kept under state control in Nuclear Electric and Scottish Nuclear.

30. Both NP and PG have a limited amount of hydro-electric generating capacity. Scottish Hydro and SP operate hydro-electric capacity in Scotland.

31. BCC on the one hand and NP and PG on the other in 1989/90 negotiated coal supply contracts. The main features of these contracts are:

– they cover the period from 1 April 1990 to 31 March 1993;

– they guarantee BCC sales of 70 million tonnes a year in the first two years and 65 million tonnes in the third year;

– the basis price was fixed at 170p/GJ gross, 177.9p/GJ net;

– there are formulae for the escalation (and de-escalation) of the basis price to take account of movements in the retail price index and the £/$ exchange rate.

VII *The situation of the licensed mines*

32. When the coal supply contracts came into effect on 1 April 1990, NP and PG offered prices of between 122p/GJ and 139p/GJ at the mine for coal from the independent sector, including the licensed production.

33. In general, apart from coal produced under delivered licences, licensed mines had no secure outlet for their production, the purchase arrangements most commonly used being spot purchases, purchase under tender for an undefined period or tonnage and one-off contracts.

34. The royalties paid to BCC were £11.00 a tonne for opencast coal and £0.67 a tonne for deep-mined coal.

VIII. *The complaints*

35. NALOO, FSMGB and SWSMA complain that BCC has abused its position as the dominant supplier of electricity generating coal to secure favourable terms for itself, particularly in terms of volume and price, which had a detrimental effect on its competitors, the small licensed mines, contrary to Article 66 (7) of the ECSC Treaty.

36. It is further alleged by all the complainants that the generating companies are jointly dominant, in that they are the only purchasers of electricity generating coal, and that the generating companies are abusing their dominant position contrary to Article 86 of the EEC Treaty by discriminating against the members of the complainant associations in comparison with BCC, by refusing to purchase coal in sufficient quantity and by offering prices that were unjustifiably lower than those paid to BCC.

37. NALOO and FSMGB also complain that there have been infractions of the following Articles of the ECSC and EEC Treaties:

– Article 60 ECSC: it is alleged that the royalty imposed by BCC on the licensed producers is an infraction of Article 60 because the royalty is excessive and makes licensed producers uncompetitive;

– Article 63 ECSC: it is alleged that the generating companies are systematically discriminating against the licensed producers in offering lower prices and less favourable conditions;

– Article 65 ECSC: the coal supply contracts are claimed to foreclose a preponderant part of the market for electricity generating coal to suppliers of coal other than BCC. It is alleged that as a result licensed mines receive only marginal terms and conditions;

– Article 85 EEC: the complainants allege that to the extent that Article 65 ECSC is not applicable then Article 85 EEC applies.

38. On 28 August 1990 the Directorate-General for Competition wrote to the UK authorities outlining its concern about various aspects of the situation. These concerns have since been fully explained

in meetings and correspondence.

IX. *The Department of Energy offer*

39. The UK authorities, on behalf of BCC, NP and PG, made a series of offers to the complainants culminating in final offers dated 24 October 1990.

40. The terms of the offer to NALOO and FSMGB included:

- prices on a net calorific value basis for licensed coal supplied under contract which, taking into account transport costs of up to 10p/GJ, net back to some 157p/GJ at the final point of dispatch;

- transport costs of up to 10p/GJ where the increased costs can be fully justified;

- the price at the final point of dispatch to be escalated on the same basis as BCC's;

- guarantees that NP and PG will "increase their purchases from the private licensed sector in 1990/91 compared with 1989/90";

- a commitment from NP to increase its purchases of licensed coal in 1991/92, and the expectation of maintaining this higher level in 1992/93;

- the expectation that PG would maintain purchases in 1991/92 and 1992/93 at at least the level of 1990/91;

- a committment to pay additional transport costs if supplies were diverted from one named power station to another;

- a commitment not to impose any further sulphur penalties on production from existing sources until after 31 March 1993;

- a reduction of the royalty for opencast licensed production to a new flat rate figure inclusive of administrative charge, of

  - £5.50 a tonne for the first 50,000 tonnes produced at each site; and

  - £6.00 a tonne thereafter;

- an undertaking from BCC to use reasonable efforts to maintain its purchases from the licensed mines at current levels, about 1 million tonnes a year for coal bought on delivered licenses and other purchases;

- a reduction of the royalty for deep-mined licensed production to a new flat rate, inclusive of administrative charge, of 40p.

41. A similar offer was made to SWSMA. The principal differences between this offer and the offer made to NALOO and FSMGB are that it:

- guaranteed that supplies from licensed mines to blenders would receive at least 147p/GJ net; and

- guaranteed purchases of 5,000 tonnes a week from the existing three blenders for the period from 1 April 1990 to 31 March 1993;

- promised to take 1,000 tonnes a week from a fourth blender, should such an operation be set up by one or more licensed mines.

42. The offers were conditional upon being accepted by all complainants and on all complaints being withdrawn unconditionally.

43. The offers were rejected by NALOO, FSMGB and SWSMA. However the terms relating to prices and volumes, including a retrospective element to 1 April 1990, are now being incorporated in contracts being negotiated or renegotiated between the licensed mines and NP and PG. BCC reduced its royalties to the levels outlined in the offers with effect from 1 April 1990.

44. NALOO, FSMGB and SWSMA were informed of the intention to give these terms in letters from the Department of Energy dated 22 November 1990.

B Legal Assessment

X *Article 60 ECSC*

45. NALOO and FSMGB claim that the royalty charged by BCC is excessive and likely to make the private producers,

particularly opencast producers, uncompetitive. The royalty is therefore, according to the complainants, an unfair competitive practice infringing Article 60 ECSC.

46. Article 60 ECSC states "Pricing practices contrary to Articles 2, 3 and 4 shall be prohibited..." and continues by identifying certain practices as unfair or discrimantory.

47. This provision clearly applies to the pricing practices of vendors. Article 60 ECSC is not applicable to the imposition of a royalty on production.

XI. *Article 63 ECSC, Article 66 (7) ECSC and Article 86 EEC Discrimination*

48. Article 63 ECSC requires the Commission to make an appropriate recommendation if it finds that there is systematic discrimination by purchasers of coal or steel products, in particular under provisions governing contracts entered into by bodies dependent upon public authorities.

49. BCC, NP and PG were wholly owned by the government of the United Kingdom at the time that the coal supply contracts were signed. The nature of these contracts fails to be examined, *inter alia*, under Article 63 ECSC.

50. Article 66 (7) ECSC requires the Commission to make appropriate recommendations if it "finds that public or private undertakings which, in law or in fact, hold or acquire in the market for one of the products within its jurisdiction a dominant position shielding them against effective competition in a substantial part of the common market are using that position for purposes contrary to the objectives of this Treaty...."

51. In 1989/90 BCC was responsible for 97% of the coal mined in the United Kingdom and 84% of the total UK supply. In the same year BCC supplied over 90% of the requirements for electricity generating coal in England and Wales and over 60% of the total energy requirements for power stations in England and Wales.

52. In England and Wales and in the United Kingdom as a whole BCC is the dominant producer of coal. BCC is also the dominant supplier of fuel to the electricity generating industry in England and Wales. The United Kingdom produces over 40% of Community coal an is therefore a substantial part of the common market.

53. The terms of the coal supply contracts BCC has negotiated with NP and PG in 1990 are not in themselves unfair, as they provide for:

– lower prices than BCC previously enjoyed. Also they offer only partial protection against inflation so that real prices will fall over the duration of the contracts;

– a relatively short period, three years; fuel supply contracts for power stations are typically for over 10 years and often for over 20;

– a reducing tonnage, 70 million tonnes in each of the first two years and 65 tonnes in the third.

54. Article 86 states that "any abuse by one or more undertakings of a dominant position within the common market or a substantial part of it shall be prohibited as incompatible with the common market in so far as it may affect trade between Member States."

55. In England and Wales, with insignificant exceptions NP and PG are the only purchasers of coal for electricity generation; they are therefore jointly dominant as buyers of this coal in England and Wales.

56. At the time of the entry into operation of the coal supply contracts, the licensed mines had little or no contractual security and were paid the equivalent of between 122p/GJ and 139p/GJ at the mine by the electricity generating companies. Lower prices were paid for blends and recovered coal. There was therefore discrimination against the licensed mines after 1 April 1990.

57. The price now offered by NP and PG to the licensed mines with effect from 1 April 1990, is equivalent to 157p/GJ net

at the mine, compared with 177.9p/GJ paid to BCC.

58. In South Wales, where some of the small mines sell their output to blenders who mix coal from different sources, the small mines are guaranteed a price of 147p/GJ by the blenders who are themselves now guaranteed the price of 157p/GJ. NP has undertaken to buy coal at 157p/GJ from a new blending operation to be set up and operated by the small mines themselves. The complainants have accepted that there is a case for a certain price differential between BCC and the licensed producers.

59. The Commission considers that the new differential reflects the inability of the members of the complainant associations to supply the same volume as BCC and the additional costs involved in dealing with a large number of small transactions, in particular those relating to administration, handling, sampling, blending, etc.

60. The price paid to the complainants will be subject to the same retail adjustment as BCC's. The small mines, however, will not be exposed, as BCC is, to variations in the £/$ exchange rate. The contracts between BCC and NP and PG provide for the purchase price to be modified when the £/$ exchange rate moves outside certain limits.

61. Not all of the elements to be taken into account when considering the difference in price can be precisely quantified. However the actual differential of 20.9p/GJ or 12% between BCC coal and licensed coal delivered directly to NP and PG is not so large as to constitute discrimination justifying further intervention by the Commission. Nor have the complainants put forward convincing arguments for a lower figure.

62. NP and PG have negotiated or are now negotiating individual contracts with licensed mines. These contracts incorporate or will incorporate the terms of the final offers made on behalf of the generating companies by the UK authorities dated 24 October 1990. These contracts cover periods agreed between the parties up to 31 March 1993.

63. The contractual commitments to purchase licensed coal that have already been agreed are as follows (in thousands of tonnes):

	1990/91	1991/92	1992/93
National Power	1,520	1,370	993
PowerGen	373	465	285
BCC – delivered	749	501	210
– other	300	—	—
Total	2,942	2,336	1,448

The table shows that for 1990/91 contractual commitments have already been made which exceed the total production of the licensed mines in 1989/90. The commitments for the future are lower primarily because the existing licensed opencast mines (*i.e.* those licensed before the increase in the maximum size to 250,000 tonnes) are small and have a short life, 6 to 18 months in general. These mines cannot make long-term commitments and BCC is phasing out delivered licenses and has yet to replace them by a system to buy in coal in the market. This will be necessary if BCC is to maintain its purchases at approximately 1 million tonnes a year.

64. In 1989/90 BCC produced approximately 93 million tonnes. The coal supply contracts gave it a guaranteed outlet for 70 million tonnes in each of the first two years and 65 million tonnes in the third year, *i.e* 75% and 70% of its 1989/90 production respectively. Total production by the licensed mines in 1989/90 was 2.827 million tonnes including that delivered to BCC under delivered licenses. For the licensed mines' position to be no less favourable than BCC's, they would they require guaranteed outlets for 2.12 million tonnes in 1990/91 and 1991/92 and 1.98 million tonnes in 1992/93. The commitments could be made either by the generating companies or by BCC.

65. The commitments for purchases from the licensed mines for 1990/91 and 1991/92, 3.05 million tonnes and 2.33

341

million tonnes respectively, are substantially above the 2.12 million tonnes that would secure them, in the present circumstances, equivalent treatment to BCC.

66. In their dealings with mining companies National Power and PowerGen shall comply with their obligations under Articles 63 ECSC and 86 EEC. Since certain questions have been raised about what this means in practice, it should be made clear that they may refuse to contract in certain circumstances, for example:

– if the cost of transporting that mine's coal to the power station, although less than 10p/GJ, is above the cost of transporting coal from another small mine, providing that this does not cause the generating company's total purchases to fall below the overall quantity which it has undertaken to buy;

– for quality reasons, as far as new contracts are concerned if objective, technically justified, non-discriminatory quality standards are applied to all suppliers including BCC. The generating companies will also be expected to fulfil their obligations under existing contracts.

67. The Commission understands that NP and PG are making contracts with the licensed mines (or the blenders in South Wales) on the basis of the principles set out above. The present decision is based on the assumption that these contracts will result in the elimination of discrimination between BCC and the licensed mines. The Commission reserves the right to reopen the case if this assumption should turn out to have been unfounded.

XII. *Article 65 ECSC*

68. The complainants claim that the coal supply contracts between BCC and NP and PG are contrary to Article 65 ECSC.

69. Article 65 ECSC only applies to agreements between at least two undertakings within the meaning of the ECSC Treaty. Article 80 ECSC defines an ECSC undertaking, for the purpose of Article

65, as engaged in the production or distribution of coal and steel. BCC is an ECSC undertaking, NP and PG are not. Consequently, the coal supply contracts do not fall within the scope of Article 65 of the ECSC Treaty.

XIII. *Article 66 (7) ECSC royalty and licensing*

70. The complainants allege that BCC has used its dominant position as a supplier of electricity generating coal to levy a royalty, and that it has abused its power to license competitors. In addition they allege that BCC's licensing power is in itself an abuse of its dominant position.

71. Under the Coal Industry Nationalisation Act 1946 almost all coal in the UK was vested in BCC (then the National Coal Board). BCC thus has a property right in the coal. There is therefore no objection under EC law to charging the licensed mines a royalty on each tonne of coal they extract.

72. The level of royalty cannot be considered in isolation. The relationship between the price received for the coal and the costs, including the royalty, of producing that coal must be such as to enable efficient companies to make a profit and must not impose a significant competitive disadvantage on them.

The royalty, including the administrative charge for deep mined coal is now £0.40 a tonne (previously £0.675 + £0.3365 administration charge). This is scarcely more than the previous administrative charge and cannot be regarded as unreasonable or anti-competitive.

73. In so far as the opencast mines are concerned the royalty has been reduced from £11.00 a tonne before 1 April 1990 to £5.50 a tonne (£6.00 a tonne after the first 50,000 tonnes) while the price the small mines receive has increased by over 23%.

74. The price now available for licensed coal, 157p/GJ, or approximately £40.00 a tonne is over 20% or £8.00 a tonne higher then the price that was given to the small mines when the coal supply contracts came into operation. This coupled with a

reduction in royalty of at least £5.00 a tonne will result in a large improvement in the gross profit margins of the licensed opencast mines. In 1989/90 the average sales revenue achieved by BCC on its opencast operations was £41.50 a tonne or about 160p/GJ, that is to say approximately the same level as the price now available to the licensed mines. BCC made a profit of £ 12.68 a tonne on this production. Although there are differences, notably of scale, between the opencast operations of BCC and those of NALOO members, this would appear to confirm that the current royalty for opencast coal is not sufficiently high as to be unlawful. Thus the royalty will not prevent efficient companies from making a profit nor impose a significant competitive disadvantage.

75. This letter does not deal with BCC's licensing powers or with any alleged abuses of those powers.

XIV *Article 85 EEC*

76. Article 85 EEC prohibits as incompatible with the common market "all agreements between undertaking, decisions of associations of undertakings and concerted practices which may affect trade between Member States and which have as their object or effect the prevention, restriction or distortion of competition within the common market...."

77. NALOO and FSMGB allege that the coal supply contracts between BCC, NP and PG largely foreclosed the market to suppliers other than BCC and meant that the licensed mines could only obtain marginal terms.

78. An agreement by which a dominant supplier obtains the right to provide some 94% of the requirements of the two largest customers, forecloses the market and can be justified only in the most exceptional circumstances. This letter does not deal with the general question of the compatibility of the supply agreements with the competition rules of the EEC Treaty. This matter is being delate with separately under the normal procedures. However as the licensed mines

should now obtain contracts giving them access to markets on terms comparable to those given to BCC there are no longer grounds for complaint under Article 85 EEC.

XV *Conclusions*

79. This decision deals with the situation in England and Wales arising from the entry into operation of the coal supply contracts on 1 April 1990 between BCC on one hand and NP and PG on the other.

80. Articles 60 and 65 ECSC are not applicable. Those parts of the complaint made by NALOO and FSMGB based on these articles are hereby rejected.

81. The Commission considers that the complaints made under Articles 63, 66 (7) ECSC and 85 and 86 EEC were justified, in so far as they concerned the situation after 1 April 1990 when the coal supply contracts entered into operation.

82. If the terms of the UK authorities' offers dated 24 October 1990 are incorporated into contracts on the basis set out in this decision, the licensed mines will no longer be discriminated against in comparison with BCC. On this basis those parts of the complaints under Article 63 ECSC, Article 66 (7) ECSC in so far as it concerns purchase conditions, Article 85 EEC and Article 86 EEC are no longer valid and in so far as they relate to the present situation are rejected.

83. With regard to the part of the complaints under Article 66 (7) ECSC concerning the royalty levled by BCC, the new royalty levels set out in the UK authorities' letter dated 24 October 1990 and subsequently implemented by BCC with effect from 1 April 1990, are not unreasonably high. That part of the complaints concerning royalty payments under Article 66 (7) ECSC is therefore no longer valid and in so far as it relates to the present situation is rejected.

Yours faithfully

For the Commission

Sir Leon Brittan

Vice-President

Index

ABUSE OF DOMINANT POSITION
abuse, concept of, 3.64-3.70
Article 86,
  buyers and sellers, applying to, 3.12
  enterprises, addressed to, 4.45
  inter-state element, 3.6-3.14
  national court, application by, 3.103
  text of, 3.52
  wider concept of, 3.64
coal production undertakings, by, 8.7
consequences of, 3.11
dominant position,
  determining, 3.54
  downstream demand and supply, 3.56
  geographical market, in, 3.59-3.61
  relevant product market, in, 3.55
  upstream demand and supply, 3.57-3.58
electricity prices and tariffs, in relation to,
  7.36-7.46
electricity sector, in, 4.63-4.64
exclusive right, creation through grant of,
  4.46-4.48
exploitative conduct, extension to, 3.64
joint dominance, 3.71-3.72
list of, non-exhaustive, 3.53
market power, 3.62
mergers and acquisitions, notification of,
  3.73-3.76
positive duties, 3.65-3.66
prohibition of, 3.2, 4.47
relevant product market, 3.68
sub-market, extension into, 3.67
substantial part of market,
  meaning, 3.13
  test, 3.63
telecommunications operators, by, 6.54-6.59
AIR TRANSPORT
sectoral agreements, 8.43

BLOCK EXEMPTIONS. *See* COMPETITION
RULES

COAL
British Coal and National Power, supply
  arrangements between, 8.22
electricity generating, complaints
  concerning supply of, 4.20, App 11
monopoly purchasers of, 3.12
production undertakings,
  ECSC competition rules, application of,
  8.3-8.7
Scottish, 8.23

use in electricity generation, state aids,
Commission, examination by, 5.12
indirect aid, 5.13-5.14
objectives, 5.10
scope of, 5.11
COMPETITION RULES
abuse of dominant position. *See* ABUSE OF
  DOMINANT POSITION
agreements restricting competition,
  application to, 3.22-3.23
Article 85,
  concerted practice, concept of, 3.20
  concession or licensing agreements, not
    applying to, 3.23
  co-operation, permissible,
    Article 85(3), requirements in, 3.29-3.33
    negative clearance, 3.33
    Notices on, 3.28
  electricity prices and tariffs, application to,
    7.12-7.15, 7.29-7.35
  electricity sector, application to, 3.34-3.51.
    See also ELECTRICITY SECTOR
  environmental restrictions, and, 9.27-9.28
  horizontal, 3.24
  inter-state element, 3.6-3.14
    prohibited agreements, examples of,
    3.25-3.26
  restrictive practices and agreements,
    prohibiting, 3.2
    independent undertakings, between, 3.18
  telecommunications undertakings,
    application to, 6.46-6.69
  third country, application where
    undertaking in, 3.21
  transit agreements between undertakings,
    application to, 6.38-6.39
  vertical, 3.24
Article 86,
  abuse of dominant position, prohibiting,
    3.2, 4.47. *See also* ABUSE OF DOMINANT
    POSITION
  buyers and sellers, applying to, 3.12
  electricity prices and tariffs, application to,
    7.16
  enterprises, addressed to, 4.45
  inter-state element, 3.6-3.14
  monopolies cases, application in, 4.39-4.49
  national court, application by, 3.103
  text of, 3.52
  transit agreements between undertakings,
    application to, 6.38-6.39
  wider concept of, 3.64

345